Family Spending

A report on the 2013 Living Costs and Food Survey

Edition No.: **2014**

Editor: Giles Horsfield

Office for National Statistics

2014

The data displayed in this document was correct at the time of printing 22/12/14

Contents:	Page Number:

List of Tables:

Appendices:

Contents (cont): Page Number:

02 December 2014

Office for National Statistics

About this edition

Abstract

This report presents the latest information from the Living Costs and Food Survey for the 2013 calendar year (January to December). The Expenditure and Food Survey (EFS) was renamed as the Living Costs and Food Survey (LCF) in 2008 when it became a module of the Integrated Household Survey (IHS).

Acknowledgements

1. A large scale survey is a collaborative effort and the authors wish to thank the interviewers and other ONS staff who contributed to the study. The survey would not be possible without the co-operation of the respondents who gave up their time to be interviewed and keep a diary of their spending. Their help is gratefully acknowledged.

List of contributors

Editor: Giles Horsfield

Authors:

Joanna Bulman

Laura Dimond

Rachael Ryan

Rhian Jones

Living Costs and Food Survey team:

Jana Kubascikova-Mullen

Linda Williams

Michelle Cooper

Paul Bloomfield

Sarah Whiting

Tracy Lane

Field Team and Interviewers

Coders and Editors

Review and additional commentary:

Chris Daffin

David Matthewson

Richard Tonkin

Yanitsa Petkova

Introduction

This report presents the latest information from the Living Costs and Food Survey for the 2013 calendar year (January to December). The Expenditure and Food Survey (EFS) was renamed as the Living Costs and Food Survey (LCF) in 2008 when it became a module of the Integrated Household Survey (IHS).

The current LCF is the result of the amalgamation of the Family Expenditure and National Food Surveys (FES and NFS). Both surveys were well established and important sources of information for government and the wider community, charting changes and patterns in Britain's spending and food consumption since the 1950s. The Office for National Statistics (ONS) has overall project management and financial responsibility for the LCF while the Department for Environment, Food and Rural Affairs (DEFRA) sponsors the specialist food data.

The survey continues to be used primarily to provide information for the Consumer Prices Index and the Retail Prices Index; National Accounts estimates of household expenditure; the analysis of the effect of taxes and benefits; and trends in nutrition. However, the results are multi purpose, providing an invaluable supply of economic and social data.

The 2013 survey

In 2013 4,993 households in Great Britain took part in the LCF survey. The response rate was 48% in Great Britain and 61% in Northern Ireland. The fieldwork was undertaken by the Office for National Statistics and the Northern Ireland Statistics and Research Agency (NISRA). Further details about the conduct of the survey are given in Appendix B.

This year's report includes an overview chapter outlining key findings, and detailed chapters focusing upon expenditure on housing, patterns of spending by equivalised income and trends in household expenditure over time.

Data quality and definitions

The results shown in this report are of the data collected by the LCF, following a process of validation and adjustment for non-response using weights that control for a number of factors. These issues are discussed in the section on reliability in Appendix B.

Figures in the report are subject to sampling variability. Standard errors for detailed expenditure items are presented in relative terms in table A1 (153.5 Kb Excel sheet) and are described in Appendix B. Figures shown for particular groups of households (for example income groups or household composition groups), regions or other sub-sets of the sample are subject to larger sampling variability, and are more sensitive to possible extreme values than are figures for the sample as a whole.

The definitions used in the report are set out in Appendix B, and changes made since 1991 are described in the Technical Report. Note particularly that housing benefit and council tax rebate (rates rebate in Northern Ireland), unlike other social security benefits, are not included in income but are shown as a reduction in housing costs.

Income and expenditure balancing

The LCF is designed primarily as a survey of household expenditure on goods and services. It also gathers information about the income of household members, and is an important and detailed source of income data. However, the survey is not designed to produce a balance sheet of income and expenditure either for individual households or groups of households. For further information on the balancing of income and expenditure figures, see 'Response to the survey', Appendix B.

Related data sources

Details of household consumption expenditure within the context of the UK National Accounts are produced as part of Consumer Trends. This publication includes all expenditure by members of UK resident households. National Accounts figures draw on a number of sources including the LCF: figures shown in this report are therefore not directly comparable to National Accounts data. National Accounts data may be more appropriate for deriving long term trends on expenditure.

More detailed income information is available from the Family Resources Survey (FRS), conducted for the Department for Work and Pensions. Further information about food consumption, and in particular details of food quantities, is available from the Department for Environment, Food and Rural Affairs, who produce their own report of the survey.

Additional tabulations

This report gives a broad overview of the results of the survey, and provides more detailed information about some aspects of expenditure. However, many users of LCF data have very specific data requirements that may not appear in the desired form in this report. ONS can provide more detailed analysis of the tables in this report, and can also provide additional tabulations to meet specific requests. A charge will be made to cover the cost of providing additional information.

The tables in Family Spending 2014 are available as Excel spreadsheets.

Anonymised microdata from the Living Costs and Food Survey (LCF), the Expenditure and Food Survey (EFS) and the Family Expenditure Survey (FES) are available from the United Kingdom Data Service. Details on access arrangements and associated costs can be found at http://ukdataservice.ac.uk/ or by telephoning 01206 872143.

Background notes

1. **Symbols and conventions used in Family Spending 2014 edition**

   [ ] Figures should be used with extra caution because they are based on fewer than 20 reporting households.

   .. The data is suppressed if the unweighted sample counts are less than 10 reporting households.

   \- No figures are available because there are no reporting households.

   Rounding: Individual figures have been rounded independently. The sum of component items does not therefore necessarily add to the totals shown.

   Averages: These are averages (means) for all households included in the column or row, and unless specified, are not restricted to those households reporting expenditure on a particular item or income of a particular type.

   Period covered: Calendar year 2013 (1 January 2013 to 31 December 2013).

2. **Contacts**

   For information about the content of this publication, contact ONS Social Surveys Data Advice and Relations Team.

   Tel +44 (0)1633 455678

   Email: socialsurveys@ons.gsi.gov.uk

   Other customer enquiries

   ONS Customer Contact Centre

   Tel: 0845 601 3034

   International: +44 (0) 1633 817521

   Minicom: +44 (0)1633 815044

   Email: info@ons.gsi.gov.uk

   Fax: +44 (0)1633 652747

   Post: Room D265, Government Buildings,

Cardiff Road, Newport, South Wales NP10 8XG

www.ons.gov.uk

Media enquiries
Tel: +44 (0)845 604 1858

Email: press.office@ons.gsi.gov.uk

Editor

Giles Horsfield

giles.horsfield@ons.gsi.gov.uk

3. A National Statistics publication

National Statistics are produced to high professional standards set out in the Code of Practice for Official Statistics. They are produced free from political influence.

4. About us

The Office for National Statistics

The Office for National Statistics (ONS) is the executive office of the UK Statistics Authority, a non-ministerial department which reports directly to Parliament. ONS is the UK government's single largest statistical producer. It compiles information about the UK's society and economy, and provides the evidence-base for policy and decision-making, the allocation of resources, and public accountability. The Director-General of ONS reports directly to the National Statistician who is the Authority's Chief Executive and the Head of the Government Statistical Service.

The Government Statistical Service

The Government Statistical Service (GSS) is a network of professional statisticians and their staff operating both within the Office for National Statistics and across more than 30 other government departments and agencies.

5. Copyright and reproduction

For further information, contact the Office of Public Sector Information, Crown Copyright Licensing and Public Sector Information, Kew, Richmond, Surrey, TW9 4DU.

Tel: +44 (0)20 8876 3444

Email: psi@nationalarchives.gsi.gov.uk

ISSN 2040-1647

6. Details of the policy governing the release of new data are available by visiting www.statisticsauthority.gov.uk/assessment/code-of-practice/index.html or from the Media Relations Office email: media.relations@ons.gsi.gov.uk

   These National Statistics are produced to high professional standards and released according to the arrangements approved by the UK Statistics Authority.

Copyright

This document is also available on our website at www.ons.gov.uk.

Office for National Statistics

Chapter 1: Overview

Abstract

This chapter presents the key findings of the 2013 Living Costs and Food Survey (LCF). The overview covers: expenditure in 2013; trends in spending over time; expenditure in different areas of the UK; expenditure by income group; ownership of home computers and access to the internet at home. Some of these topics are explored in more depth in the publication. Links are provided to the sections of Family Spending that contain the detailed coverage.

Key points

- Total average weekly household expenditure was £517.30 in 2013.
- Housing (net), fuel and power had the highest average spending in 2013, at £74.40 per week, accounting for 14% for household spending, on average. This category excludes mortgage payments.
- Transport was the second highest-spending category, at £70.40 per week, on average.
- Average spending decreased between 2006 and 2013, once the figures have been adjusted to allow for changes in prices (inflation).
- Households in the South East and London spend the most, while those in the North East spend the least.
- Expenditure in rural areas was higher than in urban areas

Spending is presented using Classification Of Individual COnsumption by Purpose (COICOP)[1] categories, unless stated otherwise. COICOP is an internationally-recognised classification system, consistent with that used by UK National Accounts. It does not include all types of payments, and some types of housing-related expenses, such as mortgage payments, are excluded. However, due to the high interest in the topic, chapter 2 provides a detailed analysis of housing-related expenditure, including the items not included under COICOP.

Notes

1. From 2001, the Classification Of Individual COnsumption by Purpose (COICOP) was introduced as a new coding frame for expenditure items. COICOP is the internationally agreed classification

system for reporting household consumption expenditure. Total expenditure is made up from the total of the COICOP expenditure groups (1 to 12) plus 'Other expenditure items (13)'. Other expenditure items are those items excluded from the COICOP categories, such as mortgage interest payments, council tax, domestic rates, holiday spending, cash gifts and charitable donations.

Household expenditure in 2013

Table 1.1 shows average weekly household expenditure in the United Kingdom (UK) by the 12 COICOP categories. In 2013, average weekly household expenditure in the UK was £517.30.

Table 1.1: Average household expenditure by COICOP category and total, 2013

COICOP category	£ per week	% of total expenditure
Housing (net)[1], fuel and power	74.40	14
Transport	70.40	14
Recreation and culture	63.90	12
Food and non-alcoholic drinks	58.80	11
Restaurants and hotels	40.40	8
Miscellaneous goods and services	39.10	8
Household goods and services	33.10	6
Clothing and footwear	22.60	4
Communication	14.50	3
Alcoholic drinks, tobacco and narcotics	12.00	2
Education	8.80	2
Health	6.20	1
Total COICOP expenditure	444.30	86
Other expenditure items	73.00	14
Total expenditure	517.30	100

Table source: Office for National Statistics

Table notes:

1. Excluding mortgage interest payments, council tax for GB households and domestic rates for Northern Ireland households.

   Totals may not add up due to the independent rounding of component categories.

Download table

XLS XLS format
(26.5 Kb)

As seen in table 1.1 housing (net), fuel and power (excluding mortgages) was the highest expenditure COICOP category, at £74.40 per week; this represents 14% of total expenditure. The next two highest categories were transport (£70.40) and recreation and culture (£63.90). Average weekly expenditure on food and non-alcoholic drinks in 2013 was £58.80. A full breakdown of spending by detailed category can be found in table A1 (153.5 Kb Excel sheet).

Average weekly household expenditure in the housing (net), fuel and power category in 2013 was made up of:

- net rent: £32.00
- fuel and electricity: £26.50
- maintenance and repairs: £7.10
- water supply and miscellaneous charges (such as refuse collection): £8.70.

Household expenditure on housing, including types of spending not included in the COICOP category such as mortgage payments, averaged £147.90 per week in 2013. This is double the spending recorded under the COICOP definition.

Unless otherwise stated, figures in this report are averaged across all households. This means, for example, that average weekly expenditure on buying vehicles is averaged across all households, whether or not they bought a vehicle. The exception, where stated, is for spending on rent and mortgages, where spending is also presented only for households that pay mortgages, or rent, respectively. Considering only households that pay mortgages, average weekly expenditure on mortgages was £145.40. Spending on net rent, for households that rented their accommodation, averaged £92.10 per week. These are the only spending figures in family spending that are not averaged across all households. 'Net rent' refers to the rent paid by the householders themselves, so any rebates and allowances (including housing benefit) are excluded from the total.

Figure 1.1: Transport expenditure by selected items, 2013

United Kingdom

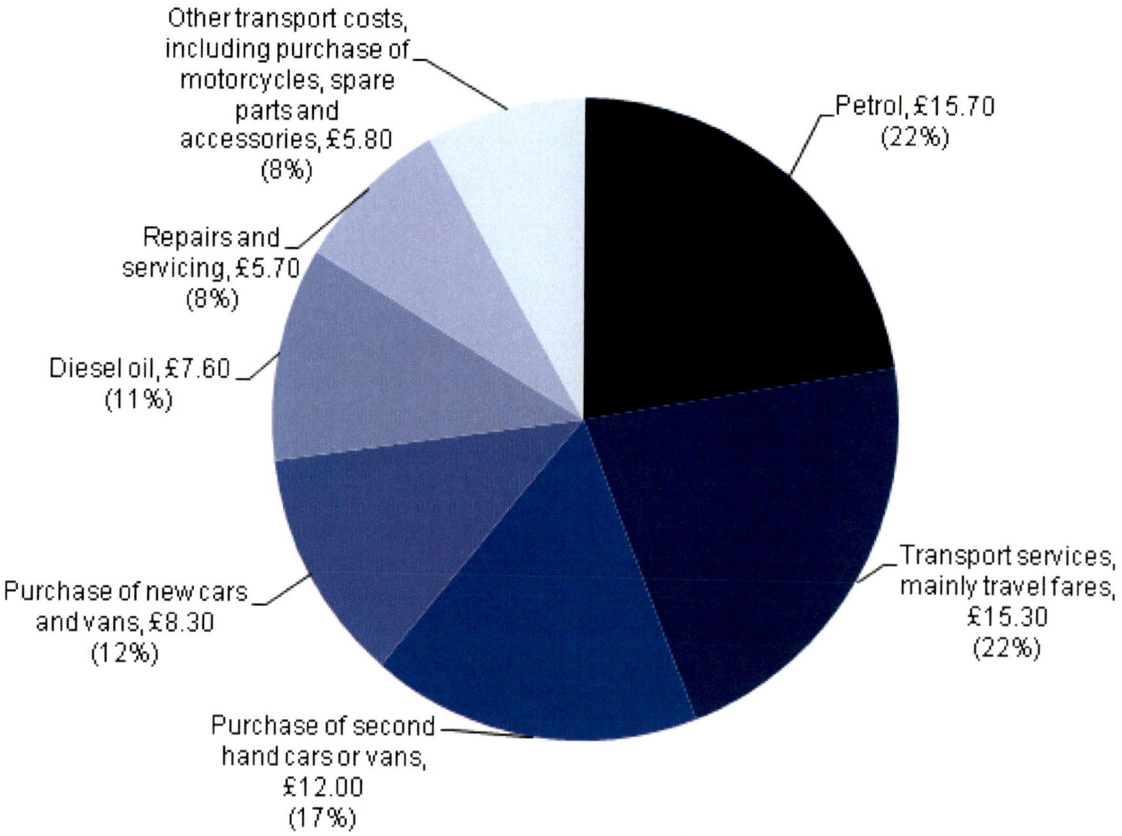

Source: Living Costs and Food Survey - Office for National Statistics

Download chart

XLS XLS format
(57 Kb)

Different households have different transport requirements, with some relying on public transport and others more on cars. Not all households buy a vehicle in any given year, but it is a major expense for those that do. The transport expenditure figures are presented averaged across all households, whether they spent on a particular item or not.

On average, one third of household expenditure on transport was spent on motor fuels, at £23.50 per week. This included £15.70 per week on petrol and £7.60 on diesel, as shown on figure 1.1.

The average amount spent weekly on buying vehicles was very similar to the amount spent on motor fuels. Households spent £21.10 per week on buying vehicles. More was spent on second hand cars and vans (£12.00) than new (£8.30).

Households spent an average of £15.30 per week on transport services, such as rail fares and air fares. This was substantially lower than on either buying or fuelling vehicles. Spending on air fares

(£5.40 per week) was about the same as the combined spend on rail and tube fares (£3.90 per week) and bus fares (£1.60 per week).

Figure 1.2: Recreation and culture expenditure by selected items, 2013

United Kingdom

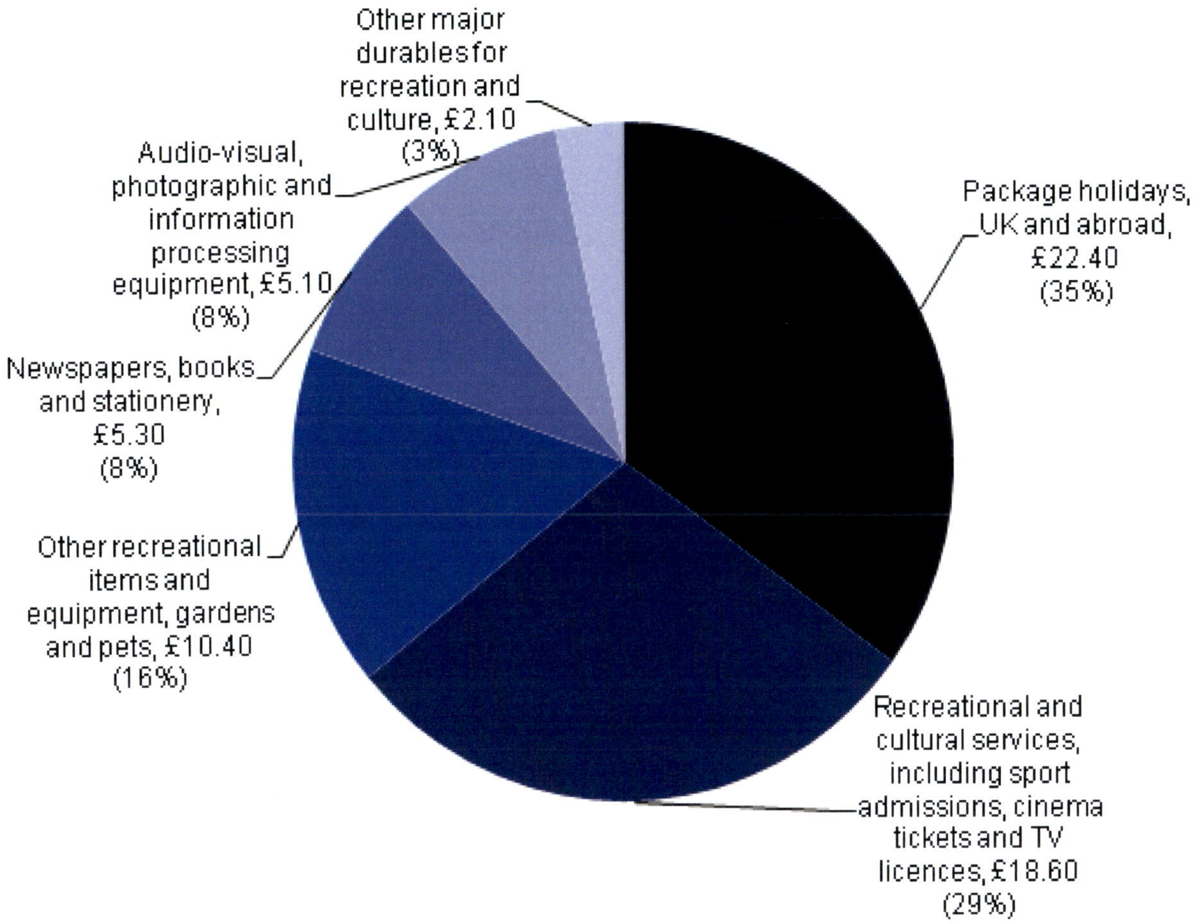

Source: Living Costs and Food Survey - Office for National Statistics

Download chart

XLS XLS format
(52 Kb)

Expenditure within the recreation and culture category represents a broad range of goods and services. An important part of the spending in this area is the sub-category recreational and cultural services, which accounted for £18.60 per week. There is a wide range of choice available in this area, including:

- sports admissions, subscriptions, leisure class fees and equipment hire (£5.50)
- cinema, theatre and museums etc (£2.30)
- TV subscriptions and licences (£6.70).

Expenditure on package holidays averaged £22.40 per week; this includes both domestic and foreign holidays.

Also within recreation and culture, an average of £4.30 per week was spent on pets and pet food, and £2.30 on games, toys and hobbies.

The fourth highest category of household spending was food and non-alcoholic drinks, averaging £58.80 per week. A similar amount was spent on bread, rice and cereals (£5.60 per week) and non-alcoholic drinks (£4.90 per week); this compares with £4.30 per week on fresh vegetables and £3.30 on fresh fruit.

Trends in spending over time

In chapter 4 spending figures over time are adjusted to take account of inflation. This enables a comparison of expenditure to be made between survey years that allows for changing prices.

Household average weekly expenditure has decreased since 2006, once inflation has been taken into account. Average weekly household spending was £539.80 in 2006, and started declining, just before the economic downturn, in 2007 (when £531.70 per week was recorded). Average spending decreased further to £501.00 in 2012, and then increased to £517.30 in 2013[1]. Between 2001/2 and 2006, average expenditure was at a higher level than that seen since 2006.

The trends observed in total household spending after 2008 are broadly consistent with the wider economic context. This is explored in more detail in chapter 4.

Not all types of household spending have decreased in recent years. Spending on housing (net), fuel and power increased from £61.70 in 2001/2, to £74.40 in 2013, after adjusting for inflation. Rent payments make up the largest proportion of expenditure in this category. The number of households renting accommodation has increased over recent years, as shown in table A50 (50 Kb Excel sheet) for 2013, and the corresponding table for 2006. These tables show the proportion of households renting increased, from 29% in 2006, to 35% in 2013. Therefore, the increased proportion of households renting has contributed to higher spending on housing (net), fuel and power.

Average household spending on transport decreased between 2001/2 (adjusted to 2013 prices) and 2013. However, it increased to £70.40 in 2013, from £64.80 per week in 2012. Households allocated an average of 14% of total expenditure to transport in 2013.

Higher average household expenditure on transport between 2012 and 2013 can partly be attributed to an increase of new car purchases. Vehicle purchases were recorded as being at a six-year high with 1,074,622 new private cars registered. Purchasing new cars is an area where households could moderate or defer expenditure, which may lead to demand building up over time. This is sometimes referred to as “pent up demand”. This may have fuelled the increase in sales of new cars seen in 2013, with consumers replacing vehicles they kept hold of through the recent downturn.

Recent years have seen the price of petrol and diesel increase substantially, with costs rising above the overall rate of inflation in 2012. However, between 2012 and 2013 prices decreased slightly, so the increase in transport expenditure in 2013 cannot be attributed to spending on fuel.

Figure 1.3: Expenditure on selected categories based on COICOP classification, 2001-02 to 2013, at 2013 prices

United Kingdom

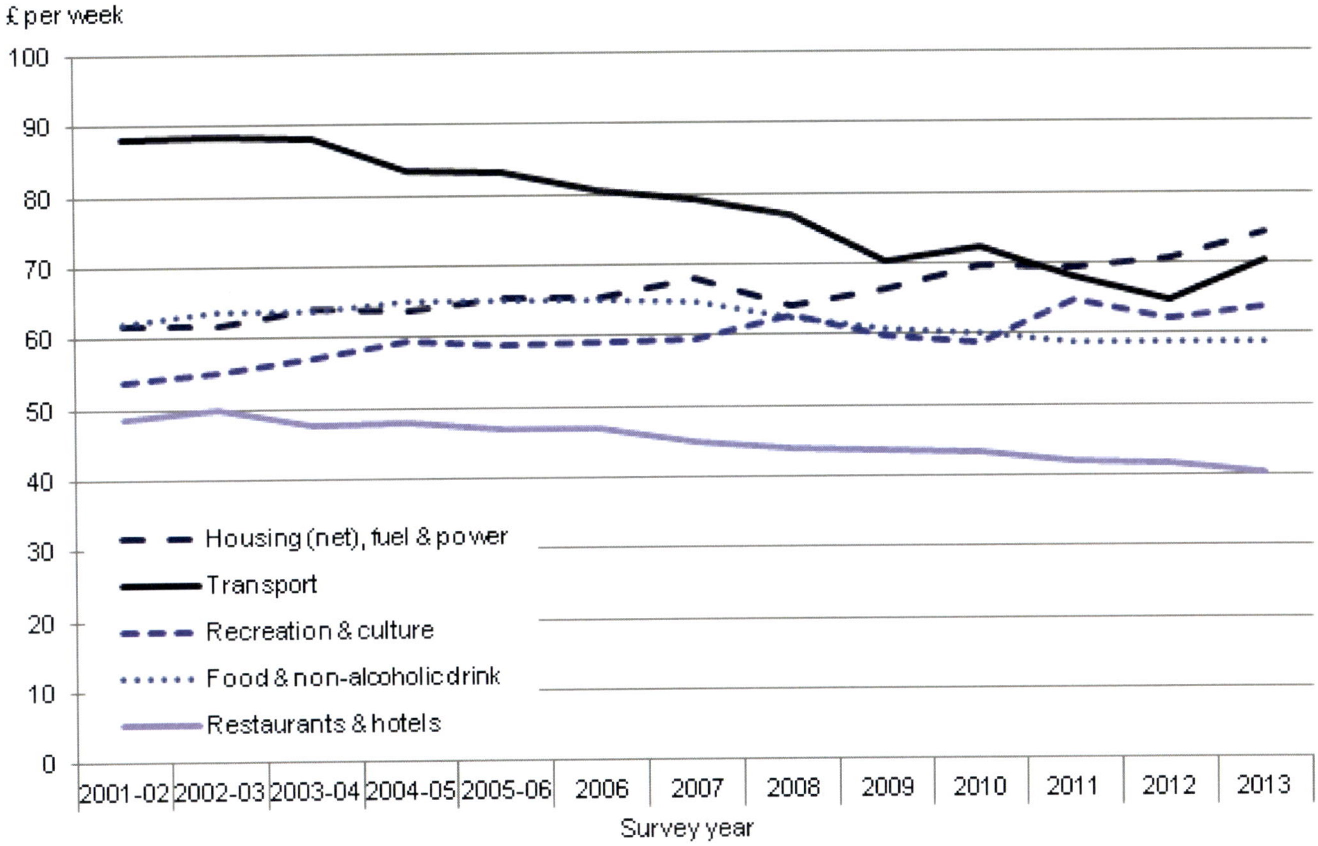

Source: Living Costs and Food Survey - Office for National Statistics

Notes:

1. Figures have been deflated to 2013 prices using deflators specific to the COICOP category.
2. In 2006, Family Spending changed to report for a calendar year instead of a financial year.
3. From 2001-02 to 2005-06, figures shown are calculated from weighted data using non-response weights based on the 1991 Census and population figures from the 1991 and 2001 Censuses. From 2006 onwards, figures shown are calculated from weighted data using non-response weights and population figures based on the 2001 Census.

Download chart

XLS XLS format
(80 Kb)

Spending on transport; housing (net), fuel and power; recreation and culture; food and non-alcoholic drink; and hotels and restaurants over the years 2001/2 to 2013 are shown in figure 1.3. The figures are adjusted for inflation, and shown at 2013 prices. The chart shows the different trends in spending for these categories over this period.

Notes

1. This increase was not found to be significant at the 95% confidence level.

Expenditure by region

Figure 1.4: Household expenditure by region, 2011 to 2013

United Kingdom

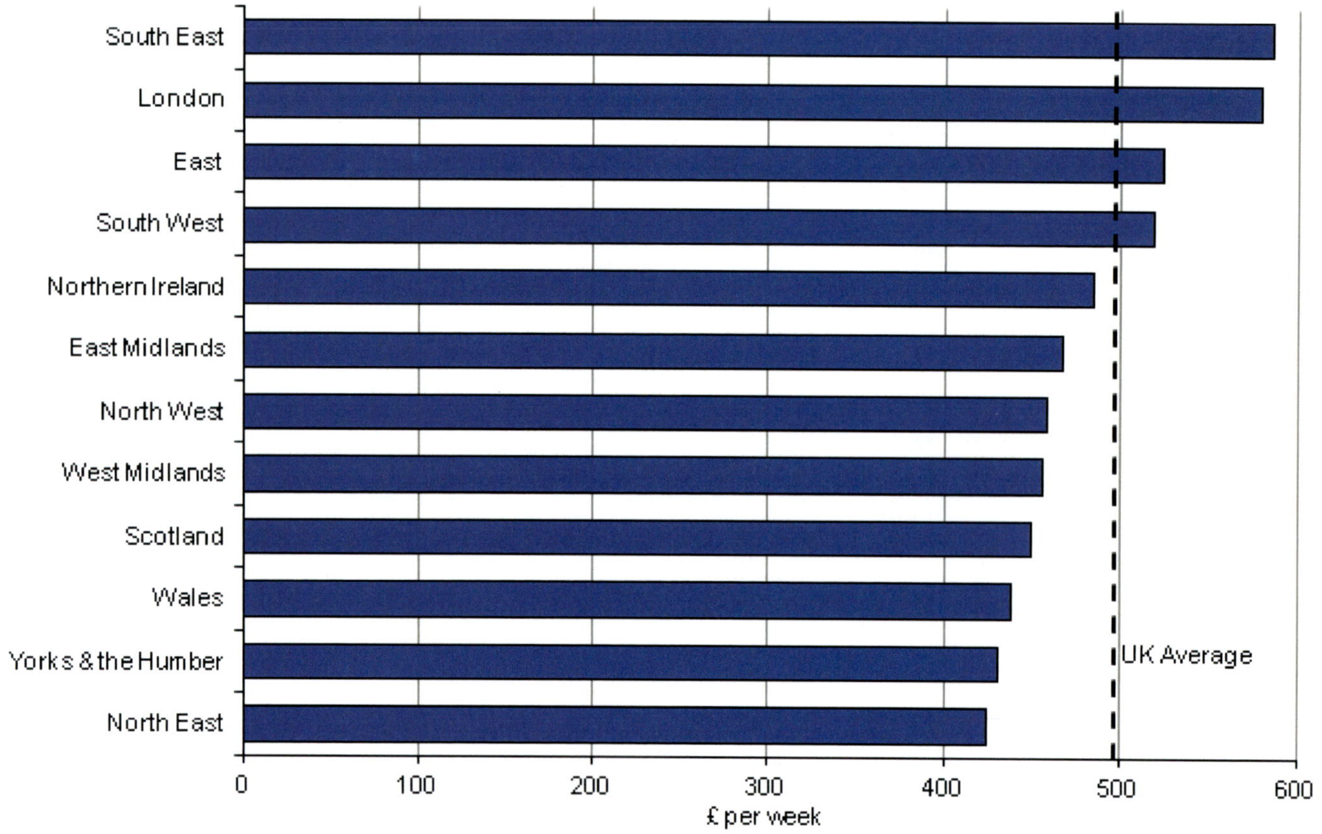

Source: Living Costs and Food Survey - Office for National Statistics

Download chart

XLS XLS format
(41 Kb)

Three years' data are combined when presenting spending figures broken down by country and region. This ensures the sample size is large enough to provide robust figures when below-UK levels of geography are considered. Detailed expenditure by region is shown in table A35 (103 Kb Excel sheet).

The average weekly household expenditure in the UK combined over the years 2011 to 2013 was £496.70. Four regions showed expenditure higher than the UK average; the two highest-spending regions, the South East and London, recorded very similar levels of expenditure. In descending order the top four regions are: the South East (£585.40), London (£579.60), the East (£523.40) and the South West (£518.20). At the opposite end of the scale with the lowest average expenditure are the North East (£424.60), Yorkshire and the Humber (£431.10) and Wales (£438.80). Average weekly expenditure in Scotland was £449.00.

For the three-year period 2011 to 2013, London was the highest spending region on housing (net), fuel and power (excluding mortgage payments), by a sizeable margin, at £103.20 per week, compared with the second highest average expenditure of £74.80 in the South East. As for previous years the major factor in London's large expenditure was net rent, at £62.50 per week. This was nearly twice the amount of the South East (£31.50); the second highest expenditure region on rent. Expenditure on rent is averaged across all households, including those that don't pay rent, so the higher rent figures for London reflect both the higher costs of rent, and the high proportion of householders who rent their accommodation.

Transport spending in the UK averaged £66.80 over the years 2011 to 2013. It was notably higher in the South East, at £84.50 per week. London's households spent lower than the UK average on transport, at £62.50 per week. London's relatively low spending on transport was most striking in operation of personal transport (fuel and running costs of vehicles), where London was the lowest spending area at £25.30 per week, compared with the UK average of £35.60. As a general pattern across the UK, expenditure on the purchase of new vehicles is almost double that spent on transport services such as train and bus fares. However, London reported a notably larger expenditure on transport services (£22.60) than new vehicles (£14.60). This lower expenditure on the purchase of new vehicles is reflected by the fact that only 61% of households owned a car/van in London over the years 2011 to 2013, compared to 75% of households in the UK as a whole (see table A48 (69.5 Kb Excel sheet)). The relatively low spending by London's households on personal transport may reflect the availability of public transport in London.

Average weekly household expenditure was higher for households in rural areas (£550.50) than urban areas (£481.70) over the years 2011 to 2013, as presented in table A36 (51 Kb Excel sheet). This difference was mirrored across most categories, and reversed only for housing (net), fuel and power, where spending was higher in urban areas (£69.70) than rural areas (£66.50). Transport showed the largest difference between spending in rural and urban areas. Rural areas recorded an average weekly expenditure of £85.50 on transport, whilst urban households averaged £61.40. This may be due to a number of factors, including the enhanced availability of public transport in urban areas compared with in rural areas. Another factor is the longer, and perhaps more frequent, journeys that are often required in rural areas to access services and amenities. Higher transport expenditure in rural areas may also interact with higher expenditure noted in other categories; for example, higher spending on recreation and culture may generate higher transport expenditure, due to greater travel costs incurred getting to venues for recreational activities.

Income

The lowest earning ten per cent of households spent an average of £189.80 per week, while the highest earning ten per cent of households spent an average of £1,119.50 per week. Figure 1.5 shows average household weekly expenditure, broken down by the gross income band of the household. Households have been ranked in ascending order of income and divided into ten equally-sized bands.

Figure 1.5: Household expenditure by gross income decile group, 2013

United Kingdom

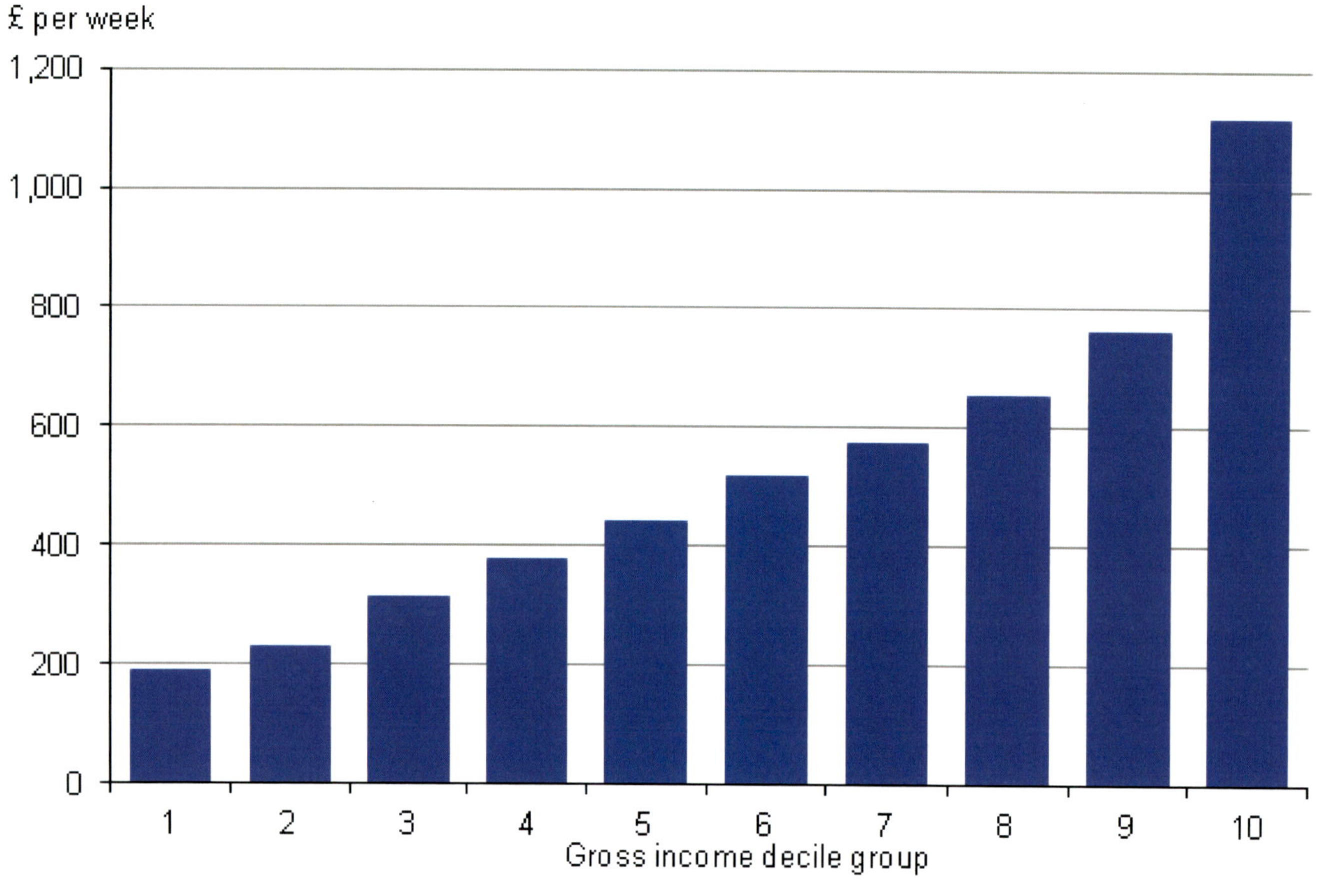

Source: Living Costs and Food Survey - Office for National Statistics

Download chart

XLS XLS format
(41.5 Kb)

Looking at spending patterns by total gross household income doesn't tell the whole story. Households of different sizes, and with different numbers of adults and children, need different levels of income in order to maintain a comparable standard of living. Chapter 3 examines expenditure patterns after income is adjusted to account for different demands on resources, by considering the household size and composition. Overall, this process, known as equivalisation, reduces the differences in income between the highest and lowest earning households and allows more meaningful comparisons to be made.

Households on lower incomes apportion their spending differently from those on higher incomes. For example, after adjusting income for household size and composition, expenditure on food and non-alcoholic drink as a proportion of total expenditure decreased as income increased; from 16% of expenditure for the ten per cent of households with the lowest incomes, to 8% of expenditure for the highest earning households. This reflects the necessity for all households to spend a certain amount on food and non-alcoholic drink, but, as income increases, there is a limit to how much households can consume, or are willing to spend, on food.

The opposite trend is seen for recreation and culture where the proportion of total expenditure increased as income increased (from 9% to 15%). This reflects the expectation that higher income households will have more income available to spend on non-essential items, such as package holidays abroad.

Computer ownership and internet connection at home

Family Spending also includes information on ownership of consumer durables, including ownership of a home computer and having access to the internet at home.

Overall, 83% of households have a home computer, and 82% are connected to the internet at home. This figure varies considerably for different types of households. For example, computer ownership increased steadily as household income increases (table A46 (61.5 Kb Excel sheet)). Virtually all of the households in the top ten-per-cent income bracket owned a computer (100%); but only just more than half (55%) of the lowest earning households did.

Other differences emerge when we examine ownership of home computers for different household compositions. Households with children showed the highest levels of computer ownership: 98% of households with two adults and two children, and 89% of households with one adult and two or more children, had home computers. The situation is very different for retired households. Among retired households mainly dependent on state pensions containing two adults, about two thirds (66%) owned a home computer. The figure was much lower still for retired households mainly dependent on state pensions containing one adult, where 27% had a home computer. Note that many retired households also have lower incomes.

The relatively high proportion of households with a home computer masks the fact that ownership is far lower among low income households and retired households. However, these types of households have been closing the gap in recent years. In 2003, only 15% of the lowest earning households had access to the internet at home, compared with 51% in 2013. Some of the increase may be due the increasing levels of smart-phone ownership, allowing relatively inexpensive access to the internet. There was already a high level of connectedness among the highest earning households in 2003/4 (90%), which increased to virtually all households in 2013 (100%).

Figure 1.6: Percentage of households with internet connection, by lowest and highest gross income decile groups and for all households, 2003/04 and 2013
United Kingdom

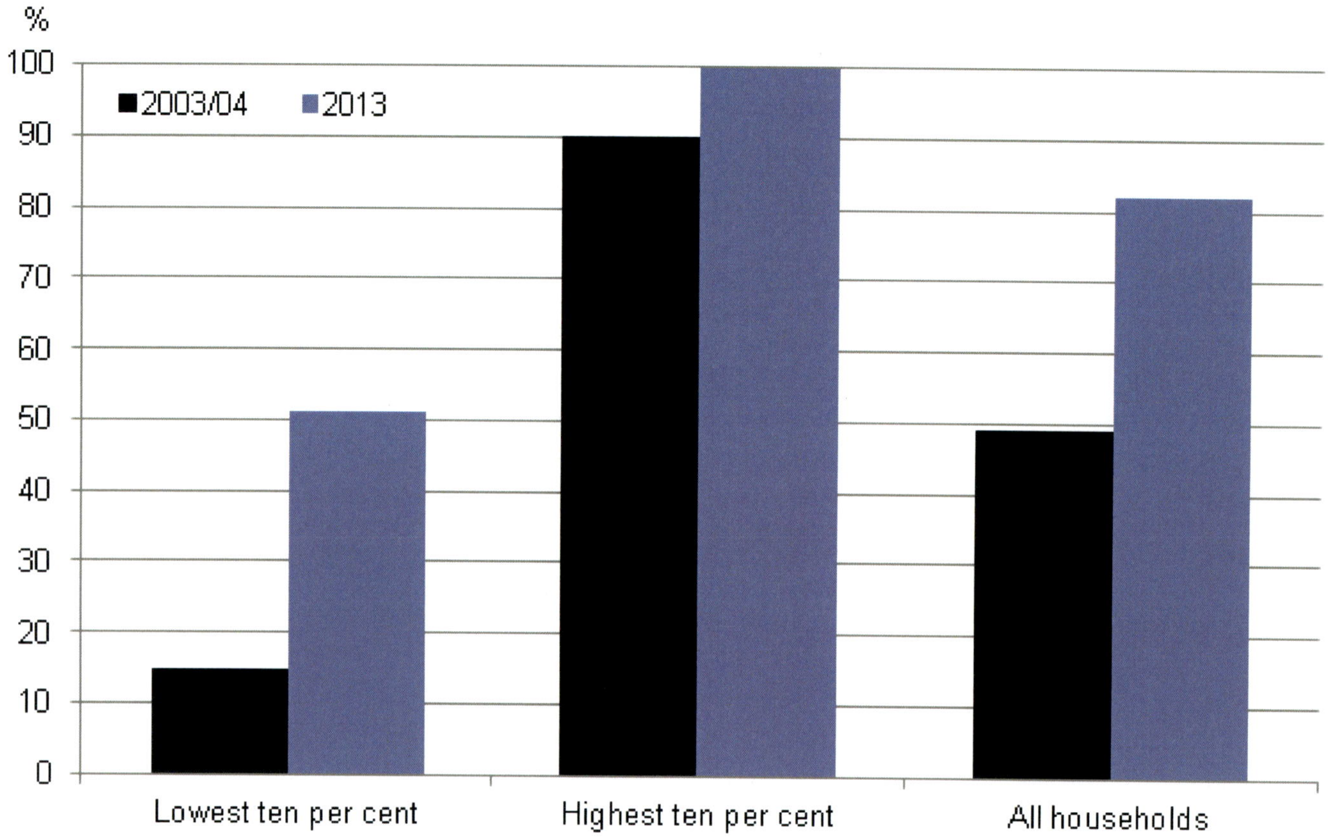

Source: Living Costs and Food Survey - Office for National Statistics

Download chart

XLS XLS format
(35.5 Kb)

Society increasingly utilises the internet to share information and provide services. In this context it is important to note that not all households own a home computer or have access to the internet at home. In addition, levels of ownership vary notably for different types of household: retired and low income households are far less likely than average to have access to the internet at home. However, households in these groups have caught up, to some extent, in recent years.

Background notes

1. **Symbols and conventions used in Family Spending 2014 edition**

   [ ] Figures should be used with extra caution because they are based on fewer than 20 reporting households.

.. The data is suppressed if the unweighted sample counts are less than 10 reporting households.

- No figures are available because there are no reporting households.

Rounding: Individual figures have been rounded independently. The sum of component items does not therefore necessarily add to the totals shown.

Averages: These are averages (means) for all households included in the column or row, and unless specified, are not restricted to those households reporting expenditure on a particular item or income of a particular type.

Period covered: Calendar year 2013 (1 January 2013 to 31 December 2013).

2. Contacts

For information about the content of this publication, contact ONS Social Surveys Data Advice and Relations Team.

Tel +44 (0)1633 455678

Email: socialsurveys@ons.gsi.gov.uk

Other customer enquiries

ONS Customer Contact Centre

Tel: 0845 601 3034

International: +44 (0) 1633 817521

Minicom: +44 (0)1633 815044

Email: info@ons.gsi.gov.uk

Fax: +44 (0)1633 652747

Post: Room D265, Government Buildings,

Cardiff Road, Newport, South Wales NP10 8XG

www.ons.gov.uk

Media enquiries

Tel: +44 (0)845 604 1858

Email: press.office@ons.gsi.gov.uk

Editor

Giles Horsfield

giles.horsfield@ons.gsi.gov.uk

3. **A National Statistics publication**

National Statistics are produced to high professional standards set out in the Code of Practice for Official Statistics. They are produced free from political influence.

4. **About us**

The Office for National Statistics

The Office for National Statistics (ONS) is the executive office of the UK Statistics Authority, a non-ministerial department which reports directly to Parliament. ONS is the UK government's single largest statistical producer. It compiles information about the UK's society and economy, and provides the evidence-base for policy and decision-making, the allocation of resources, and public accountability. The Director-General of ONS reports directly to the National Statistician who is the Authority's Chief Executive and the Head of the Government Statistical Service.

The Government Statistical Service

The Government Statistical Service (GSS) is a network of professional statisticians and their staff operating both within the Office for National Statistics and across more than 30 other government departments and agencies.

5. **Copyright and reproduction**

ISSN 2040-1647

6. Details of the policy governing the release of new data are available by visiting www.statisticsauthority.gov.uk/assessment/code-of-practice/index.html or from the Media Relations Office email: media.relations@ons.gsi.gov.uk

These National Statistics are produced to high professional standards and released according to the arrangements approved by the UK Statistics Authority.

Copyright

This document is also available on our website at www.ons.gov.uk.

Office for National Statistics

Chapter 2: Housing expenditure

Abstract

This chapter presents housing-related costs such as rent, mortgage payments, repairs and maintenance, and home improvements. The chapter examines housing expenditure: in 2013 and previous years, by region, income and household characteristics. It also explores housing costs for renters, and for mortgage holders in more depth. The final section outlines the definitions of housing expenditure: the Classification Of Individual COnsumption by Purpose (COICOP) definition, followed by the definition used in the analysis of this chapter, which includes expenditure not present in COICOP.

Key points

- UK households spent on average £147.90 a week on housing in 2013.
- Households in London recorded the highest housing expenditure in the UK, at £206.90 a week.
- Northern Ireland households had the lowest housing expenditure in the UK, 45% below the UK average at £81.00 per week.
- Among households with mortgages, the average weekly spend on mortgages was £145.40 a week. Among renting households, the average weekly spend on net rent was £92.10 per week. Net rent refers to the rent payments that the householders have to meet themselves, so benefits and rebates received by the household to help pay for rent have been subtracted.
- London has the highest expenditure both on mortgage payments and net rent. This reflects both high property prices in London and the large numbers of people renting. London's mortgage-holding households spent an average of £211.60 per week on mortgages, and its renting households spent an average of £141.60 on net rent.

Background

This chapter presents a more complete view of housing costs than the Classification Of Individual COnsumption by Purpose (COICOP) definition. The survey uses the COICOP definition for most reporting purposes because it is the internationally-recognised classification consistent with that used by UK National Accounts. However, it is interesting to consider also a fuller and more intuitive view of housing expenditure. Definitions of housing expenditure are included in the final section

'Definitions of housing expenditure'. This explains both the definition used under COICOP, and the different definition as used for this chapter summarised in table 2.1.

The definition of housing expenditure used in this chapter includes net rent, mortgage payments, repairs and maintenance, and home improvements but excludes expenditure on fuel and power. Net rent refers to the amount payable by the household, after benefits for housing costs have been deducted.

The first section examines the types of spending that make up housing expenditure and how these have changed over time. The remaining sections look at how spending on housing varies for different parts of the UK, and for different types of households.

Housing expenditure

Table 2.2 (77 Kb Excel sheet) shows expenditure on the items included in the comprehensive definition of housing expenditure used for this chapter. It also displays total household expenditure, which includes all expenditure items covered by the survey. The total expenditure figure reported here is therefore greater than the expenditure totals shown in the tables in appendix A, as these exclude certain goods and services not covered by the COICOP definition of expenditure.

Under the comprehensive definition of housing expenditure, UK households spent on average £147.90 a week on housing in 2013, which equates to about a fifth (21%) of total weekly expenditure.

The COICOP definition of housing expenditure (with fuel and power removed) on the other hand, gave an average of £47.80 per week for each household (as shown in table A1 in appendix A (153.5 Kb Excel sheet)).

Housing expenditure in 2013 and previous years

Figure 2.1: Housing expenditure items as a percentage of total housing expenditure, 2013

United Kingdom

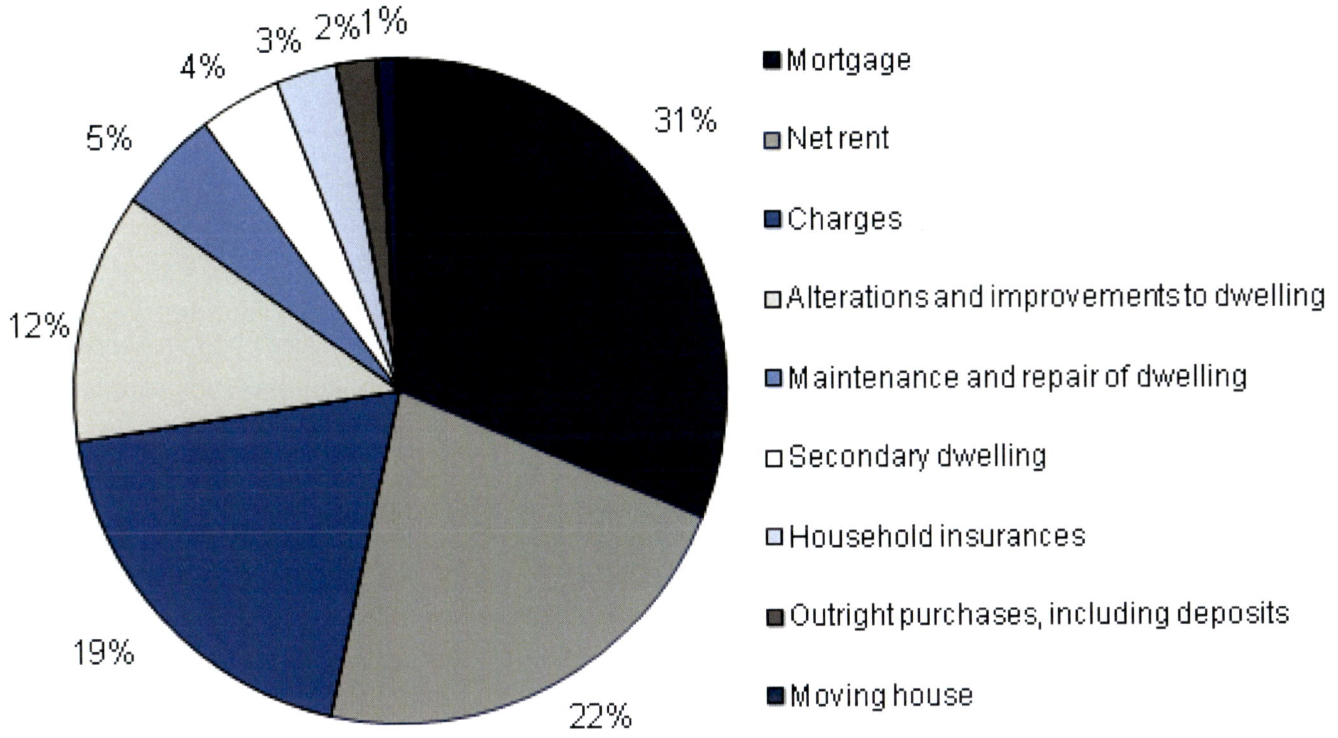

Source: Living Costs and Food Survey - Office for National Statistics

Download chart

XLS XLS format
(47.5 Kb)

This section considers the breakdown of housing expenditure, averaged across all households, regardless of whether or not they hold a mortgage or pay rent.

As shown in figure 2.1, mortgage payments accounted for 31% of housing expenditure in 2013; this includes interest payments, protection premiums and capital repayments. Net rent accounts for 22% of housing expenditure; this refers to the rent payments that the householders have to meet themselves, so benefits and rebates received by the household to help pay for rent have been subtracted.

Charges such as council tax, water charges and refuse collection made up 19% of housing-related expenditure. Alterations and improvements to the dwelling accounted for 12%; this category includes expenses such as installing central heating and double glazing. Maintenance and repair of the dwelling took up a much lower share of spending, at 5% of total housing expenditure; this category includes repairing central heating, and painting and wallpapering.

In terms of amounts spent, averaged across all households, £45.70 per week was spent on mortgages in 2013 and £32.00 on net rent, as shown in figure 2.2. The overall average amounts spent on rents and mortgages are partly determined by the proportions of households in each type of tenure. The survey records tenure type (see table A50 (50 Kb Excel sheet)), showing that in 2013:

- 35% of households rented
- 32% held mortgages
- 33% owned their properties outright

Interestingly, there has been a fall in the proportion of households with mortgages since 2006 (when 40% held mortgages) and a corresponding increase in the proportion renting (29% rented in 2006). A similar trend was reported by the English Housing Survey. This makes it useful to consider rent and mortgage payments only for the relevant households, and this is done in the section 'Analysis of housing costs for renters and mortgage holders'.

There was an average weekly spend of £28.80 on charges (council tax or domestic rates in Northern Ireland, water charges, refuse collection and other regular services). There has been little change on average spending on charges since 2011, when £28.00 per week was recorded. This is despite reported continued rises in the cost of water rates, along with other housing costs (Price Waterhouse Cooper, 2013). These charges on the dwelling constitute an important component of total housing related costs, alongside rent and mortgage payments.

Figure 2.2: Housing expenditure 2011 to 2013

United Kingdom

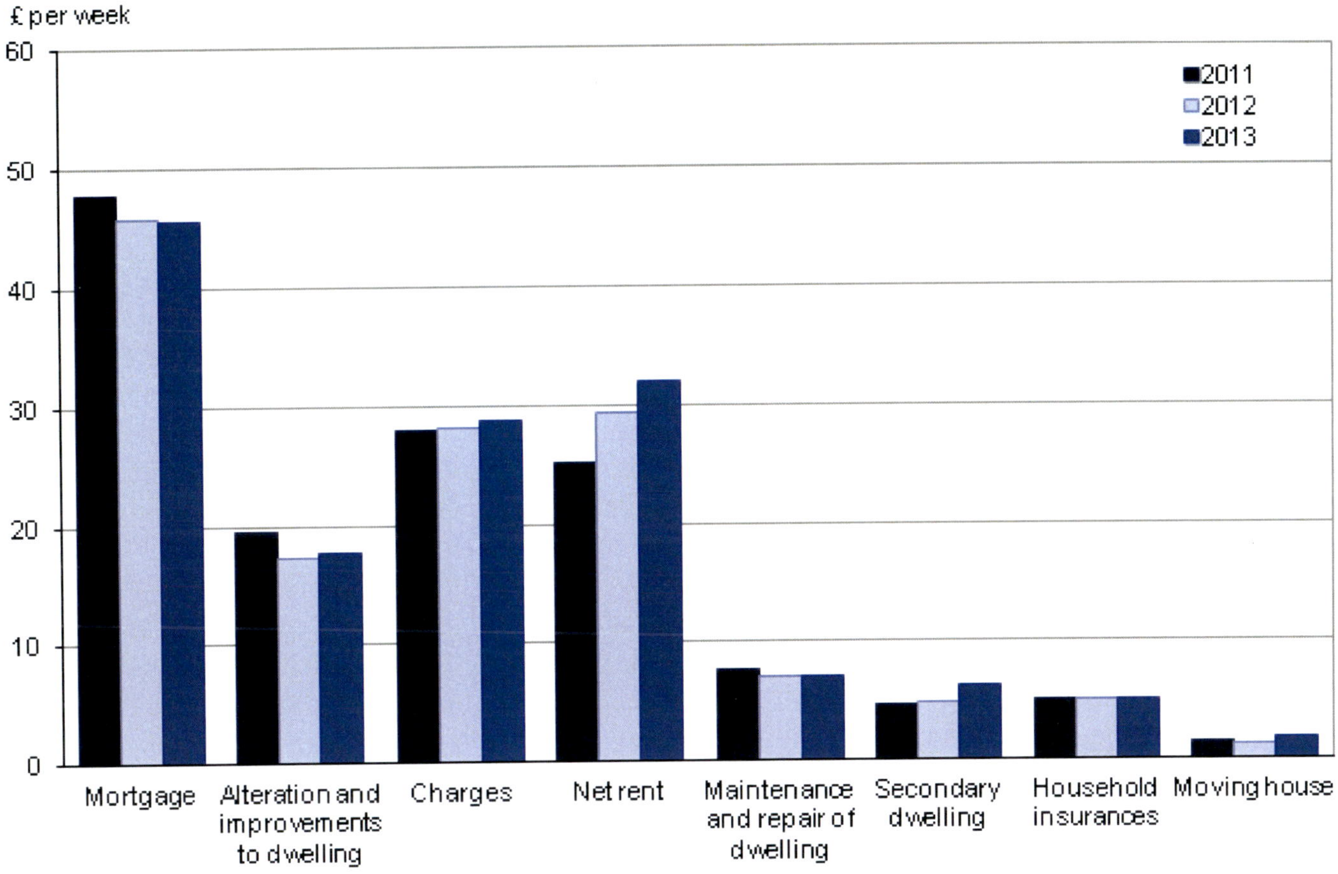

Source: Living Costs and Food Survey - Office for National Statistics

Download chart

XLS XLS format
(45 Kb)

Spending on alterations and improvements was £17.70 in 2013, compared with £19.60 in 2011 (without adjusting for inflation). Interestingly, there has recently been official encouragement for homeowners to improve their properties, such as one run by the Home Improvement Agency and the government revamped Green Deal. These schemes focus on ensuring existing housing is fit for purpose for elderly, disabled or low income home owners, by assisting financially in making homes more energy efficient or providing lists of reliable builders for any work required. This might be a factor in the absence of increased expenditure in this category in recent years.

Analysis of housing costs for renters and mortgage holders

The following section looks at average expenditure on net rent for households that report spending on rent and expenditure on mortgages for mortgage holders. This is the only place in this report where averages are not calculated across all households. This is because including only households that do pay rent or hold a mortgage provides a more informative picture of expenditure on these important elements of household expenditure.

Expenditure on net rent increased slightly in 2013 (table 2.8 (35.5 Kb Excel sheet)). On average renters spent £92.10 per week in 2013; this is an increase from 2012 (£86.40) and 2011 (£77.00) without adjusting for inflation. These findings are consistent with other sources such as the English Housing Survey where it was found that the average weekly rents in both the private and social rented sectors increased in 2012-13. The Index of Private Housing Rental Prices also found that between May 2012 and May 2013 private rental prices grew by 1.3% in Great Britain.

Expenditure on mortgages rose in 2013, without adjusting for inflation. The average weekly expenditure on mortgages by mortgage holders was £145.40 in 2013, compared with £138.60 in 2012 (table 2.9 (34.5 Kb Excel sheet)). Analysis of rent in this publication tends to focus on net rent, because this is what is used in calculations of total expenditure. Average spending on gross rent by renting households (£138.40 per week) is very similar to spending on mortgages by mortgage holders. Gross rent refers to the rent payable in total, including the elements that are met by benefits and rebates, rather than householders.

Figure 2.3 and table 2.10 (74 Kb Excel sheet) show mortgage payments by mortgage holders and net rent payments by renters broken down by income band. The first income decile comprises the tenth of households with the lowest income, the second decile the tenth of households with the next highest incomes, and so on. The figures should be treated with caution, because there are low numbers of renters, or mortgage holders in the survey sample for some income groups: relatively few low-income households hold mortgages and high income households rent.

Figure 2.3: Expenditure on net rent by renters, and mortgages by mortgage holders, by gross income decile group, 2013

United Kingdom

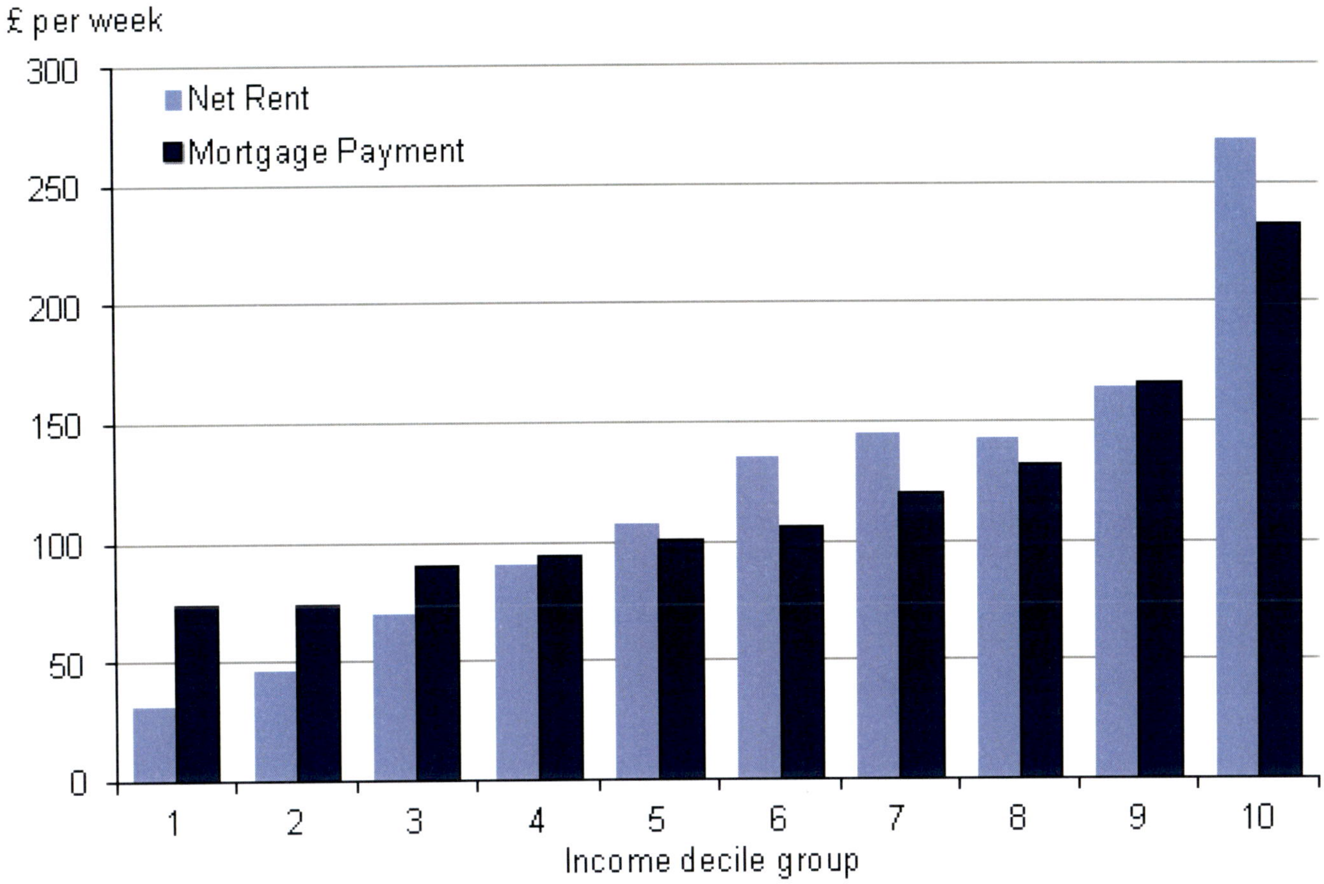

Source: Living Costs and Food Survey - Office for National Statistics

Download chart

XLS [XLS format](#)
(38 Kb)

As might be expected, spending both on mortgages (by mortgage holding households) and net rent (by rent paying households) increased as income increased. Among the lowest-income households, average spending on net rent (£31.70 per week) was much lower than mortgage payments (£74.20 per week). Among higher income groups the pattern was different, with spending on net rent higher than mortgage payments. For the tenth of households with the highest incomes, net rent expenditure averaged £268.60 and mortgage payments £233.20 per week. This pattern is largely due to housing benefits and rebates, which make renting markedly less expensive for lower-income households, but have almost no impact on higher earning households. Average weekly expenditure on gross rent was £118.10 for the lowest-income ten per cent of households, much higher than the £31.70 net rent figure.

Housing expenditure by socio-demographic characteristics

The relationship between income and housing expenditure was reflected in associated socio-demographic characteristics, such as socio-economic classification of the Household Reference Person (HRP, defined in appendix B), as shown in table 2.6 (78 Kb Excel sheet). Where the HRP was in an occupation defined as being "higher managerial or large employer", housing expenditure averaged £299.20 per week; this was much higher than £104.50 per week if the HRP was in a routine occupation.

Age is another important factor. Housing expenditure is presented in table 2.4 (60 Kb Excel sheet) by the age group of the HRP. Households where the HRP was aged between 30 and 49 spent the most on housing (£199.40 per week). Higher spending in this age group is driven largely by mortgage payments, which were £84.10 per week compared with £45.70 for all age groups combined. This is the age range where households tend to take up mortgages, and take the greatest responsibility for meeting the payments. By contrast, younger households, where the HRP was aged under 30, spent an average of £88.40 on net rent, much higher than the overall figure of £32.00. It's not surprising that households with younger HRPs tend to spend more on rent, as many people in this age group have not yet acquired the means or stability of lifestyle to maintain a mortgage.

Expenditure by region/country

There are large variations in average expenditure on housing across different regions of the UK, as shown in figure 2.4 and table 2.5 (54.5 Kb Excel sheet). The pattern is very similar to that recorded for total expenditure. The UK average household weekly expenditure on housing was £147.90 in 2013. London households spent the most at £206.90 per week; followed by the South East (£186.30) and the South West (£184.80). The lowest spending areas were Northern Ireland (£81.00) and the North East (£96.50). This is largely reflected in the average house price across different regions of the UK. The ONS House Price Index (HPI) showed house prices were most expensive in London in 2013 with an average of £424,000, followed by the South East (£300,000), whereas the UK average house price was £242,000; Northern Ireland was the least expensive region with an average of £130,000. The prices given are "mix-adjusted" prices, as explained in the HPI bulletin.

Figure 2.4: Housing expenditure by UK countries and regions, 2013

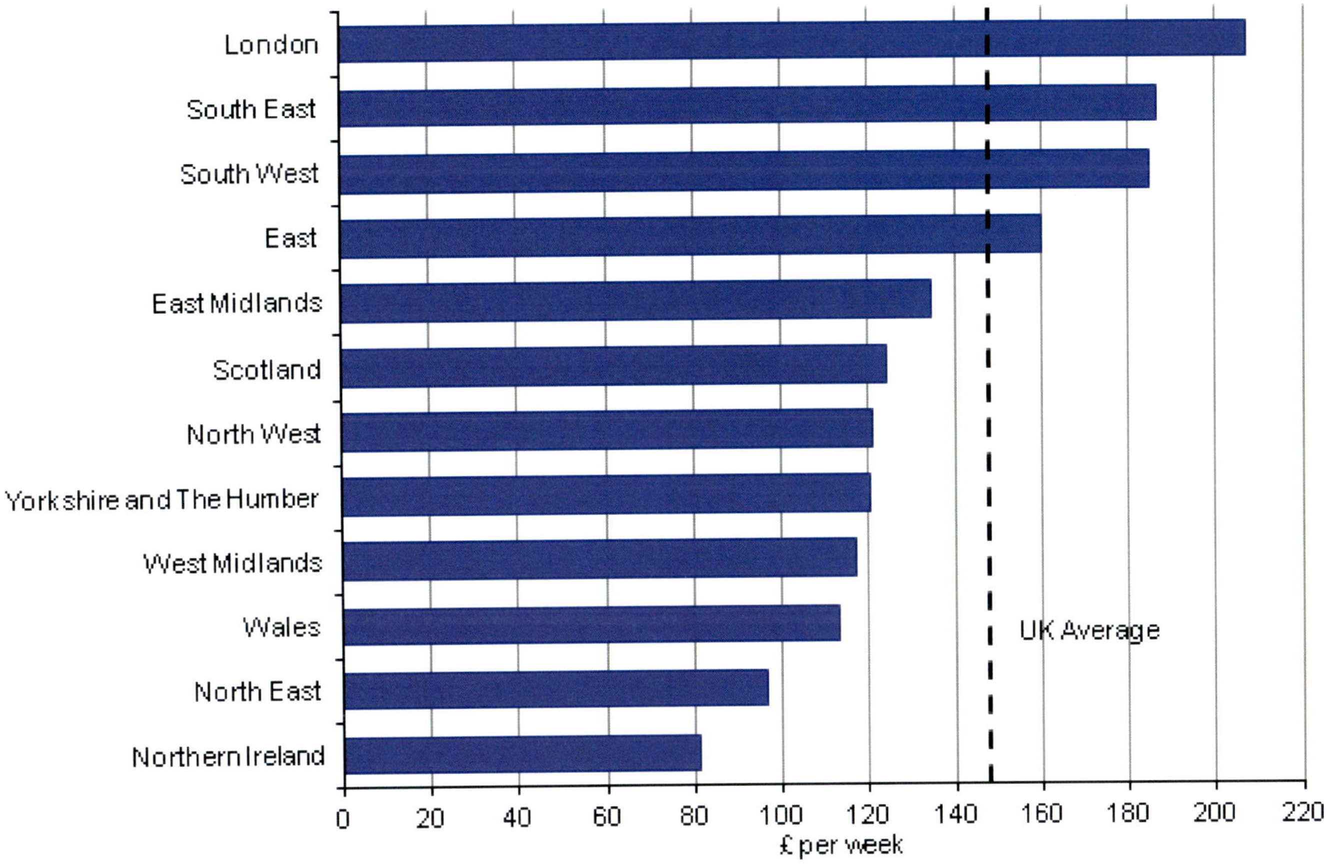

Source: Living Costs and Food Survey - Office for National Statistics

Download chart

XLS XLS format
(44.5 Kb)

These differences are reflected both in net rent and mortgage payments (although to different extents), averaged across all households, as shown in figure 2.5. Average household weekly expenditure on net rent in London (£64.70) was twice the UK average (£32.00), and much higher than the next highest area, the South East, at £37.60. The difference between London and the rest of the UK is much less pronounced for mortgages than for net rent, with an average spend of £58.00. This was very similar to that recorded in the South East (£57.00) and 27% above the UK average of £45.70.

Figure 2.5: Percentage difference compared with UK average for mortgage payments and net rent payments by UK countries and regions, 2013

United Kingdom

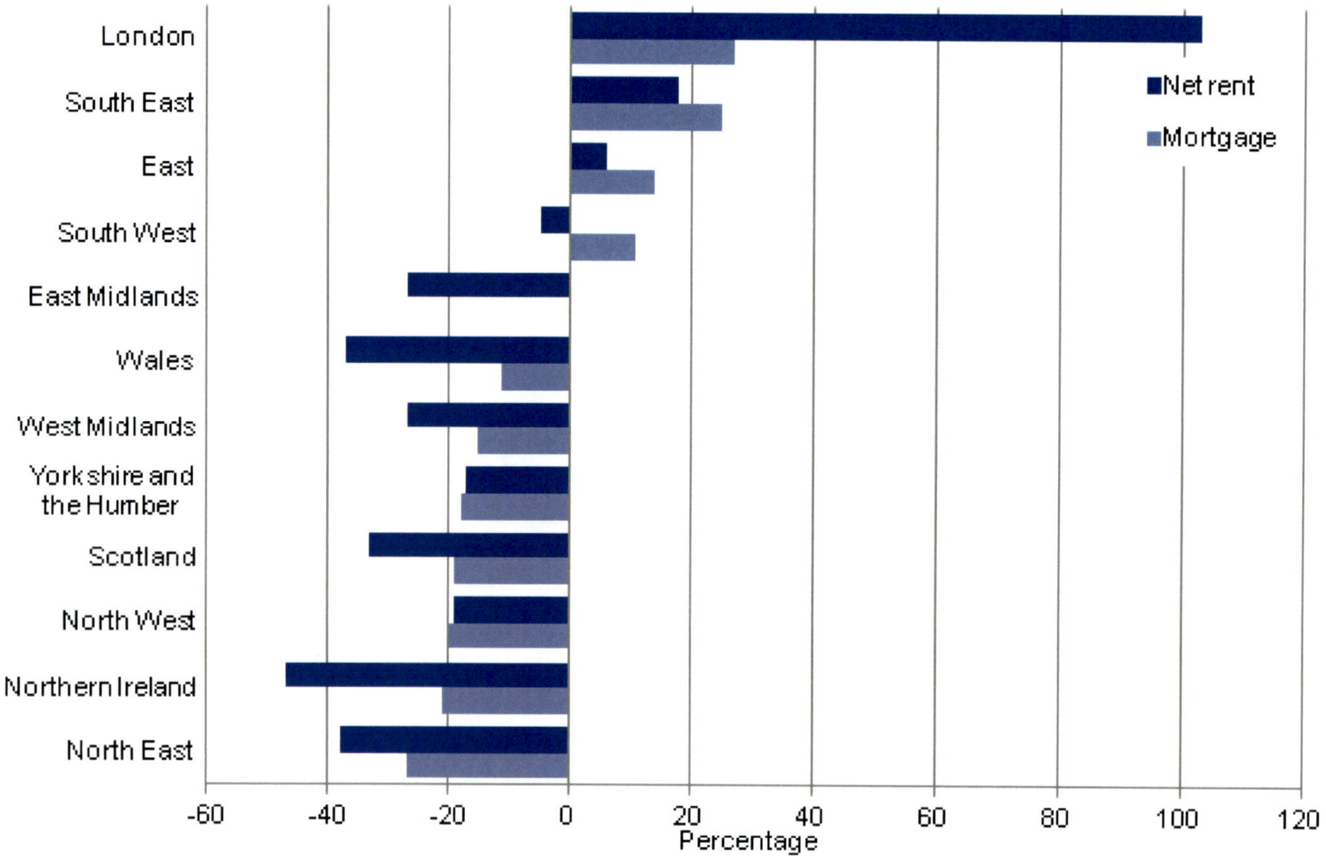

Source: Living Costs and Food Survey - Office for National Statistics

Download chart

XLS XLS format
(44.5 Kb)

A slightly different pattern emerges when considering only rent payers and mortgage holders, by region, as shown in table 2.11 (70.5 Kb Excel sheet). For net rent, London is less far ahead of other areas (£141.60, compared with the UK average of £92.10) than when rent figures are averaged across all households. This reflects the fact that higher average expenditure on rent in London is partly driven by the high proportion of renters in the capital. 2011 Census analysis established that London accounted for the largest percentage of renters at 50.4% of households. The other factor is rental prices, which are higher in London than other parts of the UK, as found by an Index of Housing Rental Prices (IHRP) report.

For mortgages, higher spending by London's households can be seen more clearly when looking at expenditure by mortgage holders only. The capital's spending averaged £211.80 per week; the next highest areas were the South East (£172.10) and the East (£158.90). The 2011 Census confirmed that London has a lower proportion of mortgage holding households than many other areas with just 27.1% of owner occupiers compared to the UK average of 32.7%, pushing down the spending averaged across all households. However, property prices are high in London (The ONS House Price Index, HPI) and its mortgage holding households paid considerably more than in other parts of the UK.

Expenditure on housing reflects both the characteristics of the geographic area of the household and of the household itself. There are complex interactions between these factors as house prices and rental costs are influenced by the demands of the local population and the perceived desirability of an area of residence. There are large differences in housing-related expenditure among regions of the UK, with London standing out as the area with the highest expenditure both on rent and mortgages.

Definitions of housing expenditure

The COICOP system has been used to classify expenditure on the Living Costs and Food Survey (LCF) and previously the Expenditure and Food Survey (EFS) since 2001/02.

COICOP is an internationally agreed system of classification for reporting consumption expenditure within National Accounts and is used by other household budget surveys across the European Union.

Further information on COICOP can be found on the United Nations Statistics Division website.

Under COICOP, household consumption expenditure is categorised into the following 12 headings:

1. Food and non-alcoholic drinks
2. Alcoholic drinks, tobacco and narcotics
3. Clothing and footwear
4. Housing (net), fuel and power
5. Household goods and services
6. Health
7. Transport
8. Communication
9. Recreation and culture
10. Education
11. Restaurants and hotels
12. Miscellaneous goods and services

It is important to note that COICOP classified housing costs do not include what is considered to be non-consumption expenditure, for example: mortgage interest payments, mortgage capital repayments, mortgage protection premiums, council tax and domestic rates.

In addition to the 12 COICOP expenditure categories, the tables contained in appendix A include a category called 'other expenditure items' under which certain non-consumption expenditures can be found. This category includes the following housing-related costs: mortgage interest payments, mortgage protection premiums, council tax, and domestic rates. Housing costs that are not included in the COICOP definition of housing or the 'other expenditure items' category are captured within the 'other items recorded' category that can be viewed in table A1 (153.5 Kb Excel sheet) in appendix A.

For the purpose of this chapter all data relating to housing expenditure have been combined to facilitate an understanding of total housing costs. This comprehensive definition of housing expenditure is made up from three types of expenditure detailed in table 2.1: expenditure included in COICOP, housing costs in the 'other expenditure items' and 'other items recorded' categories of this report.

Table 2.1: Definition of total housing expenditure

Costs which are included in the COICOP classification of housing expenditure:

- Actual rentals for housing
  - – net rent (gross rent less housing benefit, rebates and allowances received)
  - – second dwelling rent
- Maintenance and repair of dwelling
  - – central heating maintenance and repair
  - – house maintenance and repair
  - – paint, wallpaper, timber
  - – equipment hire, small materials
- Water supply and miscellaneous services relating to dwelling
  - – water charges
  - – other regular housing payments including service charge for rent
  - – refuse collection, including skip hire.

Housing costs which are included elsewhere in the COICOP classification:

Housing costs which are included as 'other expenditure items' but excluded from COICOP classification:

- Housing: mortgage interest payments etc.
  - – mortgage interest payments
  - – mortgage protection premiums
  - – council tax, domestic rates
  - – council tax, mortgage, insurance (second dwelling).

Housing costs which are included as 'other items recorded' and are excluded from COICOP classification:

- Purchase or alteration of dwellings (contracted out), mortgages
  - – outright purchase of houses, flats etc. including deposits
  - – capital repayment of mortgage
  - – central heating installation
  - – DIY improvements: double glazing, kitchen units, sheds etc.
  - – home improvements (contracted out)
  - – bathroom fittings

• Household Insurances	– structural insurance – contents insurance – insurance for household appliances.	– purchase of materials for capital improvements – purchase of second dwelling.

Table source: Office for National Statistics

Download table

XLS [XLS format](#)
(36 Kb)

Background notes

1. **Symbols and conventions used in Family Spending 2014 edition**

   [ ] Figures should be used with extra caution because they are based on fewer than 20 reporting households.

   .. The data is suppressed if the unweighted sample counts are less than 10 reporting households.

   \- No figures are available because there are no reporting households.

   Rounding: Individual figures have been rounded independently. The sum of component items does not therefore necessarily add to the totals shown.

   Averages: These are averages (means) for all households included in the column or row, and unless specified, are not restricted to those households reporting expenditure on a particular item or income of a particular type.

   Period covered: Calendar year 2013 (1 January 2013 to 31 December 2013).

2. **Contacts**

   For information about the content of this publication, contact ONS Social Surveys Data Advice and Relations Team.

Tel +44 (0)1633 455678

Email: socialsurveys@ons.gsi.gov.uk

Other customer enquiries

ONS Customer Contact Centre

Tel: 0845 601 3034

International: +44 (0) 1633 817521

Minicom: +44 (0)1633 815044

Email: info@ons.gsi.gov.uk

Fax: +44 (0)1633 652747

Post: Room D265, Government Buildings,

Cardiff Road, Newport, South Wales NP10 8XG

www.ons.gov.uk

Media enquiries

Tel: +44 (0)845 604 1858

Email: press.office@ons.gsi.gov.uk

Editor

Giles Horsfield

giles.horsfield@ons.gsi.gov.uk

3. A National Statistics publication

National Statistics are produced to high professional standards set out in the Code of Practice for Official Statistics. They are produced free from political influence.

4. About us

The Office for National Statistics

The Office for National Statistics (ONS) is the executive office of the UK Statistics Authority, a non-ministerial department which reports directly to Parliament. ONS is the UK government's single largest statistical producer. It compiles information about the UK's society and economy, and provides the evidence-base for policy and decision-making, the allocation of resources, and public accountability. The Director-General of ONS reports directly to the National Statistician who is the Authority's Chief Executive and the Head of the Government Statistical Service.

The Government Statistical Service

The Government Statistical Service (GSS) is a network of professional statisticians and their staff operating both within the Office for National Statistics and across more than 30 other government departments and agencies.

5. **Copyright and reproduction**

ISSN 2040-1647

6. Details of the policy governing the release of new data are available by visiting www.statisticsauthority.gov.uk/assessment/code-of-practice/index.html or from the Media Relations Office email: media.relations@ons.gsi.gov.uk

These National Statistics are produced to high professional standards and released according to the arrangements approved by the UK Statistics Authority.

Copyright

This document is also available on our website at www.ons.gov.uk.

Table 2.2
Housing expenditure, 2011 to 2013
United Kingdom

	2011			2012			2013		
	£ per week	% of total expend-iture	% of housing expend-iture	£ per week	% of total expend-iture	% of housing expend-iture	£ per week	% of total expend-iture	% of housing expend-iture
Weighted number of households (thousands)	26,110			26,410			26,840		
Total number of households in sample	5,690			5,600			5,140		
Total number of persons in sample	13,430			13,180			12,120		
Total number of adults in sample	10,330			10,200			9,350		
Weighted average number of persons per household	2.4			2.3			2.4		
Commodity or service	Average weekly household expenditure (£)								
Primary dwelling									
Rent	**40.60**	***6***	***29***	**46.10**	***7***	***33***	**48.00**	***7***	***32***
Gross rent	40.60	*6*	*29*	46.10	*7*	*33*	48.00	*7*	*32*
less *housing benefit, rebates and allowances received*	15.40	*2*	*11*	16.80	*2*	*12*	16.10	*2*	*11*
Net rent[1]	25.20	*4*	*18*	29.30	*4*	*21*	32.00	*4*	*22*
Mortgage	**47.90**	***7***	***34***	**45.80**	***7***	***33***	**45.70**	***6***	***31***
Mortgage interest payments	24.30	*4*	*17*	22.00	*3*	*16*	21.40	*3*	*14*
Mortgage protection premiums	1.30	*0*	*1*	1.20	*0*	*1*	1.00	*0*	*1*
Capital repayment of mortgage	22.40	*3*	*16*	22.50	*3*	*16*	23.20	*3*	*16*
Outright purchase, including deposits	**[0.30]**	***0***	***0***	**0.30**	***0***	***0***	**[3.60]**	***1***	***2***
Secondary dwelling	**4.60**	***1***	***3***	**4.80**	***1***	***3***	**6.20**	***1***	***4***
Rent	[0.10]	*0*	*0*	[0.10]	*0*	*0*	[0.10]	*0*	*0*
Council tax, mortgage, insurance (secondary dwelling)	2.40	*0*	*2*	2.00	*0*	*1*	1.80	*0*	*1*
Purchase of second dwelling	2.00	*0*	*1*	2.70	*0*	*2*	4.40	*1*	*3*
Charges	**28.00**	***4***	***20***	**28.20**	***4***	***20***	**28.80**	***4***	***19***
Council tax, domestic rates	19.80	*3*	*14*	19.70	*3*	*14*	20.10	*3*	*14*
Water charges	6.90	*1*	*5*	7.10	*1*	*5*	7.40	*1*	*5*
Other regular housing payments including service charge for rent	1.20	*0*	*1*	**1.20**	*0*	*1*	**1.30**	*0*	*1*
Refuse collection, including skip hire	[0.10]	*0*	*0*	[0.10]	*0*	*0*	[0.00]	*0*	*0*
Moving house	**1.50**	***0***	***1***	**1.30**	***0***	***1***	**1.80**	***0***	***1***
Property transaction - purchase and sale	0.70	*0*	*1*	0.70	*0*	*1*	0.70	*0*	*0*
Property transaction - sale only	0.30	*0*	*0*	0.20	*0*	*0*	0.60	*0*	*0*
Property transaction - purchase only	0.20	*0*	*0*	0.20	*0*	*0*	0.40	*0*	*0*
Property transaction - other payments	0.20	*0*	*0*	0.10	*0*	*0*	0.20	*0*	*0*
Maintenance and repair of dwelling	**7.70**	***1***	***5***	**7.00**	***1***	***5***	**7.10**	***1***	***5***
Central heating repairs	1.60	*0*	*1*	1.30	*0*	*1*	1.20	*0*	*1*
House maintenance etc.	4.20	*1*	*3*	3.90	*1*	*3*	4.00	*1*	*3*
Paint, wallpaper, timber	1.20	*0*	*1*	1.10	*0*	*1*	1.30	*0*	*1*
Equipment hire, small materials	0.60	*0*	*0*	0.60	*0*	*0*	0.50	*0*	*0*
Alterations and improvements to dwelling	**19.60**	***3***	***14***	**17.30**	***3***	***12***	**17.70**	***2***	***12***
Central heating installation	1.20	*0*	*1*	1.00	*0*	*1*	0.90	*0*	*1*
DIY improvements: double glazing, kitchen units, sheds etc.	1.60	*0*	*1*	1.30	*0*	*1*	0.80	*0*	*1*
Home improvements - contracted out	16.00	*2*	*11*	13.90	*2*	*10*	15.50	*2*	*11*
Bathroom fittings	0.60	*0*	*0*	0.70	*0*	*1*	0.30	*0*	*0*
Purchase of materials for Capital Improvements	0.20	*0*	*0*	0.30	*0*	*0*	0.10	*0*	*0*
Household insurances	**5.10**	***1***	***4***	**5.10**	***1***	***4***	**5.10**	***1***	***3***
Structure	2.50	*0*	*2*	2.50	*0*	*2*	2.40	*0*	*2*
Contents	2.40	*0*	*2*	2.40	*0*	*2*	2.40	*0*	*2*
Household appliances	0.10	*0*	*0*	0.10	*0*	*0*	0.20	*0*	*0*
Housing expenditure	**139.80**	***21***	***100***	**139.00**	***21***	***100***	**147.90**	***21***	***100***
Total expenditure[2]	**677.30**			**677.80**			**713.70**		

Please see background notes for symbols and conventions used in this report.

1 The figure included in total expenditure is net rent as opposed to gross rent.

2 This total includes all categories recorded in the LCF, including those outside the 'COICOP' total expenditure.

Table 2.3

Housing expenditure by gross income decile group, 2013

United Kingdom

	Gross income decile group										
	1	2	3	4	5	6	7	8	9	10	All
Weighted number of households (thousands)	2,690	2,680	2,690	2,690	2,680	2,690	2,680	2,680	2,690	2,680	26,840
Total number of households in sample	500	510	540	550	530	530	510	500	490	480	5,140
Total number of persons in sample	650	860	1,030	1,180	1,190	1,360	1,430	1,450	1,440	1,530	12,120
Total number of adults in sample	570	690	820	920	950	1,020	1,040	1,090	1,120	1,140	9,350
Weighted average number of persons per household	1.3	1.7	1.9	2.1	2.3	2.6	2.7	2.8	3.0	3.2	2.4
Commodity or service	Average weekly household expenditure (£)										
Primary dwelling											
Rent	**78.10**	**66.70**	**60.50**	**53.70**	**47.90**	**43.70**	**34.40**	**33.20**	**30.90**	**31.20**	**48.00**
Gross rent	78.10	66.70	60.50	53.70	47.90	43.70	34.40	33.20	30.90	31.20	48.00
less *housing benefit, rebates and allowances received*	57.20	42.00	28.60	16.50	9.30	4.00	1.10	0.90	[1.10]	[0.00]	16.10
Net rent[1]	20.90	24.80	32.00	37.20	38.50	39.70	33.30	32.30	29.80	31.20	32.00
Mortgage	**4.40**	**4.70**	**9.40**	**16.00**	**23.80**	**36.50**	**56.50**	**67.90**	**93.90**	**143.70**	**45.70**
Mortgage interest payments	2.60	2.40	4.70	6.80	10.70	16.90	27.00	30.90	41.70	70.50	21.40
Mortgage protection premiums	[0.00]	[0.10]	[0.20]	0.40	0.50	1.00	1.50	1.80	1.90	2.80	1.00
Capital repayment of mortgage	[1.70]	2.20	4.60	8.80	12.60	18.60	28.00	35.20	50.30	70.40	23.20
Outright purchase, including deposits	**[8.80]**	**-**	**[0.70]**	**-**	**[8.80]**	**-**	**[8.60]**	**[0.20]**	**[0.40]**	**[8.30]**	**[3.60]**
Secondary dwelling	**-**	**[0.10]**	**[0.10]**	**[0.90]**	**[8.70]**	**[1.70]**	**[7.30]**	**[2.30]**	**[2.80]**	**38.30**	**6.20**
Rent	-	-	-	-	-	-	[0.10]	[0.20]	-	[0.50]	[0.10]
Council tax, mortgage, insurance (secondary dwelling)	-	[0.10]	[0.10]	[0.90]	[0.30]	[0.30]	[2.20]	[1.50]	[1.60]	10.80	1.80
Purchase of second dwelling	-	-	-	[0.00]	[8.50]	[1.40]	[5.00]	[0.60]	[1.20]	[27.10]	4.40
Charges	**14.10**	**18.10**	**23.20**	**25.90**	**29.40**	**30.90**	**32.90**	**34.40**	**36.90**	**42.40**	**28.80**
Council tax, domestic rates	7.10	10.60	15.40	17.70	20.90	22.40	23.60	24.90	27.50	31.40	20.10
Water charges	5.90	6.00	6.50	6.80	7.30	7.40	8.30	8.10	8.20	9.30	7.40
Other regular housing payments including service charge for rent	1.20	1.50	1.10	1.40	1.30	1.10	1.00	1.20	1.10	1.70	1.30
Refuse collection, including skip hire	-	-	[0.20]	-	-	[0.00]	-	[0.10]	[0.10]	[0.00]	[0.00]
Moving house	**[0.80]**	**[0.50]**	**[0.30]**	**[1.30]**	**[1.10]**	**1.80**	**1.70**	**1.90**	**2.70**	**5.90**	**1.80**
Property transaction - purchase and sale	[0.20]	[0.10]	[0.20]	[0.80]	[0.90]	[0.90]	[1.00]	[0.40]	[1.30]	[0.80]	0.70
Property transaction - sale only	[0.50]	[0.40]	-	[0.10]	[0.00]	[0.60]	[0.20]	[0.60]	[0.40]	[3.00]	0.60
Property transaction - purchase only	-	[0.00]	[0.10]	[0.20]	[0.10]	[0.00]	[0.30]	[0.80]	[0.70]	[1.30]	0.40
Property transaction - other payments	[0.00]	[0.00]	[0.00]	[0.10]	[0.10]	[0.30]	[0.30]	[0.10]	[0.30]	0.80	0.20
Maintenance and repair of dwelling	**1.90**	**2.90**	**4.70**	**4.30**	**5.70**	**7.60**	**8.90**	**8.90**	**11.40**	**14.60**	**7.10**
Central heating repairs	0.30	0.60	1.00	0.90	1.10	1.10	1.40	2.20	1.50	2.30	1.20
House maintenance etc.	1.10	1.70	2.50	2.50	3.00	4.50	6.00	4.10	4.60	10.20	4.00
Paint, wallpaper, timber	0.40	0.50	0.80	0.60	1.20	1.30	1.10	1.90	4.10	1.00	1.30
Equipment hire, small materials	[0.10]	[0.10]	0.40	0.20	0.40	0.70	0.40	0.70	1.20	1.30	0.50
Alterations and improvements to dwelling	**3.60**	**6.30**	**5.60**	**5.90**	**8.60**	**15.50**	**21.50**	**22.70**	**24.00**	**63.40**	**17.70**
Central heating installation	[0.20]	[0.10]	[0.50]	[0.60]	[0.60]	[1.20]	[0.70]	[1.30]	[0.90]	2.70	0.90
DIY improvements: double glazing, kitchen units, sheds etc.	[0.10]	[0.00]	[0.60]	[0.00]	[1.00]	[1.10]	[0.40]	[0.70]	[0.50]	[3.50]	0.80
Home improvements - contracted out	3.20	6.10	4.40	5.10	7.00	12.20	19.50	19.60	22.00	56.30	15.50
Bathroom fittings	[0.00]	[0.00]	[0.10]	[0.10]	[0.00]	[0.70]	[0.70]	[0.80]	[0.40]	[0.30]	0.30
Purchase of materials for capital improvements	[0.10]	[0.00]	[0.00]	[0.10]	[0.10]	[0.20]	[0.10]	[0.30]	[0.00]	[0.50]	0.10
Household insurances	**1.90**	**3.60**	**3.70**	**3.90**	**4.70**	**5.30**	**5.70**	**6.20**	**6.60**	**9.10**	**5.10**
Structure	0.90	1.20	1.70	1.80	2.20	2.60	2.90	3.00	3.40	4.60	2.40
Contents	1.00	1.50	1.90	2.00	2.20	2.60	2.70	2.80	3.10	4.20	2.40
Household appliances	[0.00]	[0.80]	[0.10]	[0.10]	[0.30]	[0.10]	[0.10]	[0.40]	[0.10]	[0.20]	0.20
Housing expenditure	**56.50**	**61.00**	**79.70**	**95.30**	**129.50**	**138.90**	**176.50**	**176.70**	**208.30**	**357.00**	**147.90**
Total expenditure[2]	**207.60**	**244.30**	**347.80**	**431.60**	**544.70**	**646.20**	**772.40**	**905.40**	**1128.20**	**1910.70**	**713.70**

Please see background notes for symbols and conventions used in this report.

1 The figure included in total expenditure is net rent as opposed to gross rent.

2 This total includes all categories recorded in the LCF, including those outside the 'COICOP' total expenditure.

Table 2.4
Housing expenditure by age of household reference person, 2013
United Kingdom

	Under 30	30 to 49	50 to 64	65 to 74	75 or over	All
Weighted number of households (thousands)	2,610	9,640	7,100	3,850	3,640	26,840
Total number of households in sample	380	1,770	1,420	910	670	5,140
Total number of persons in sample	980	5,430	3,120	1,600	980	12,120
Total number of adults in sample	690	3,310	2,800	1,580	980	9,350
Weighted average number of persons per household	2.5	3.0	2.3	1.8	1.4	2.4
Commodity or service	Average weekly household expenditure (£)					
Primary dwelling						
Rent	**117.50**	**58.90**	**30.30**	**28.30**	**24.90**	**48.00**
Gross rent	117.50	58.90	30.30	28.30	24.90	48.00
less *housing benefit, rebates and allowances received*	29.10	16.70	11.80	15.20	14.30	16.10
Net rent[1]	88.40	42.20	18.50	13.10	10.60	32.00
Mortgage	**27.30**	**84.10**	**44.30**	**6.30**	**[1.50]**	**45.70**
Mortgage interest payments	14.60	41.00	17.90	2.50	[1.10]	21.40
Mortgage protection premiums	0.60	1.90	1.00	[0.10]	[0.00]	1.00
Capital repayment of mortgage	12.20	41.10	25.30	3.70	[0.40]	23.20
Outright purchase, including deposits	**[0.10]**	**[7.30]**	**[3.30]**	**[0.50]**	**-**	**[3.60]**
Secondary dwelling	**[2.80]**	**2.40**	**13.10**	**[5.80]**	**[5.80]**	**6.20**
Rent	[0.10]	[0.10]	[0.10]	-	-	[0.10]
Council tax, mortgage, insurance (secondary dwelling)	[2.20]	1.70	3.10	[1.00]	[0.10]	1.80
Purchase of second dwelling	[0.50]	[0.60]	[10.00]	[4.80]	[5.70]	4.40
Charges	**22.40**	**30.00**	**30.00**	**29.40**	**27.20**	**28.80**
Council tax, domestic rates	14.00	20.80	21.70	21.20	18.70	20.10
Water charges	6.90	8.00	7.60	6.90	6.10	7.40
Other regular housing payments including service charge for rent	1.50	1.20	0.80	1.20	2.30	1.30
Refuse collection, including skip hire	-	[0.10]	[0.00]	[0.20]	-	[0.00]
Moving house	**2.10**	**2.30**	**1.70**	**[1.20]**	**[1.00]**	**1.80**
Property transaction - purchase and sale	[0.20]	1.00	[0.40]	[0.30]	[1.00]	0.70
Property transaction - sale only	-	0.60	[1.00]	[0.70]	[0.00]	0.60
Property transaction - purchase only	[1.60]	0.30	[0.20]	[0.10]	-	0.40
Property transaction - other payments	0.30	0.30	[0.10]	[0.10]	[0.10]	0.20
Maintenance and repair of dwelling	**3.20**	**6.50**	**7.50**	**11.50**	**6.10**	**7.10**
Central heating repairs	[0.20]	1.10	1.20	1.80	1.80	1.20
House maintenance etc.	1.80	3.50	4.50	6.40	3.40	4.00
Paint, wallpaper, timber	0.90	1.20	1.20	2.80	0.60	1.30
Equipment hire, small materials	[0.30]	0.70	0.60	0.40	0.30	0.50
Alterations and improvements to dwelling	**2.20**	**19.70**	**22.40**	**20.50**	**11.40**	**17.70**
Central heating installation	[0.30]	0.90	1.10	[0.60]	[1.10]	0.90
DIY improvements: double glazing, kitchen units, sheds etc.	[0.20]	0.80	1.50	[0.70]	[0.00]	0.80
Home improvements - contracted out	[1.50]	17.40	19.20	18.90	10.20	15.50
Bathroom fittings	[0.20]	[0.50]	[0.40]	[0.10]	[0.00]	0.30
Purchase of materials for capital improvements	-	[0.20]	[0.30]	[0.10]	[0.00]	0.10
Household insurances	**1.90**	**4.90**	**5.80**	**5.80**	**5.50**	**5.10**
Structure	0.70	2.30	3.00	2.80	2.50	2.40
Contents	1.20	2.40	2.70	2.70	2.30	2.40
Household appliances	[0.00]	0.10	0.10	[0.30]	[0.70]	0.20
Housing expenditure	**150.40**	**199.40**	**146.70**	**94.10**	**69.10**	**147.90**
Total expenditure[2]	**575.10**	**893.80**	**798.20**	**553.50**	**341.10**	**713.70**

Please see background notes for symbols and conventions used in this report.

1 The figure included in total expenditure is net rent as opposed to gross rent.

2 This total includes all categories recorded in the LCF, including those outside the 'COICOP' total expenditure.

Table 2.5
Housing expenditure by UK Countries and regions, 2013

	North East	North West	Yorks & the Humber	East Midlands	West Midlands	East	London	South East	South West	England	Wales	Scotland	Northern Ireland	United Kingdom
Weighted number of households (thousands)	1,070	3,020	2,360	2,000	2,470	2,550	3,380	3,540	2,220	22,600	1,240	2,280	720	26,840
Total number of households in sample	250	590	460	420	530	500	480	680	430	4,340	250	410	150	5,140
Total number of persons in sample	590	1,350	1,030	980	1,270	1,160	1,190	1,630	1,000	10,190	600	930	400	12,120
Total number of adults in sample	450	1,050	820	770	940	900	880	1,260	780	7,860	460	740	300	9,350
Weighted average number of persons per household	2.3	2.3	2.2	2.3	2.3	2.3	2.5	2.4	2.4	2.4	2.5	2.3	2.5	2.4
Commodity or service	Average weekly household expenditure (£)													
Primary dwelling														
Rent	**43.60**	**41.90**	**39.20**	**36.50**	**40.80**	**45.80**	**96.70**	**52.10**	**38.40**	**51.00**	**32.20**	**34.10**	**26.80**	**48.00**
Gross rent	43.60	41.90	39.20	36.50	40.80	45.80	96.70	52.10	38.40	51.00	32.20	34.10	26.80	48.00
***less** housing benefit, rebates and allowances received*	23.90	15.90	12.50	13.20	17.70	11.80	32.00	14.50	8.10	16.80	12.10	12.60	9.90	16.10
Net rent[1]	19.70	26.00	26.70	23.30	23.20	34.00	64.70	37.60	30.30	34.20	20.10	21.50	17.00	32.00
Mortgage	**33.30**	**36.60**	**37.30**	**45.70**	**38.80**	**52.10**	**58.00**	**57.00**	**50.90**	**47.10**	**40.80**	**37.10**	**36.20**	**45.70**
Mortgage interest payments	14.30	16.10	15.40	21.50	18.50	25.20	29.90	27.70	23.90	22.40	18.20	16.50	12.70	21.40
Mortgage protection premiums	0.80	0.80	1.00	0.90	1.10	1.10	1.10	1.00	1.20	1.00	0.80	0.90	2.00	1.00
Capital repayment of mortgage	18.20	19.70	20.90	23.40	19.10	25.90	27.00	28.20	25.70	23.70	21.80	19.60	21.50	23.20
Outright purchase, including deposits	**[0.60]**	**[0.60]**	**-**	**[0.20]**	**-**	**-**	**[7.00]**	**[12.70]**	**[11.00]**	**[4.20]**	**-**	**-**	**-**	**[3.60]**
Secondary dwelling	**[2.00]**	**[6.10]**	**[9.30]**	**[3.20]**	**[7.60]**	**[1.70]**	**[2.70]**	**10.10**	**[4.20]**	**5.60**	**[0.10]**	**[17.90]**	**[0.70]**	**6.20**
Rent	-	-	-	[0.30]	-	[0.20]	-	-	[0.20]	[0.10]	[0.10]	[0.20]	-	[0.10]
Council tax, mortgage, insurance (secondary dwelling)	[1.60]	[0.80]	[0.80]	[1.20]	[0.80]	[0.90]	[2.10]	[2.40]	[3.20]	1.50	-	[5.40]	[0.50]	1.80
Purchase of second dwelling	[0.40]	[5.30]	[8.50]	[1.70]	[6.80]	[0.50]	[0.60]	[7.70]	[0.80]	3.90	-	[12.30]	[0.20]	4.40
Charges	**23.60**	**27.70**	**25.80**	**27.80**	**25.50**	**31.90**	**31.50**	**33.60**	**33.70**	**29.60**	**27.70**	**27.10**	**10.50**	**28.80**
Council tax, domestic rates	16.30	18.50	17.80	19.80	17.20	23.20	20.60	24.50	23.00	20.50	18.90	20.00	10.20	20.10
Water charges	7.00	8.10	7.60	7.30	7.00	7.70	7.20	7.60	9.10	7.70	8.40	6.30	0.00	7.40
Other regular housing payments including service charge for rent	[0.30]	1.00	0.50	[0.60]	1.10	1.00	3.70	1.40	1.30	1.40	[0.50]	0.70	0.30	1.30
Refuse collection, including skip hire	-	-	-	[0.10]	[0.10]	-	-	[0.00]	[0.30]	[0.10]	-	-	-	[0.00]
Moving house	**[1.50]**	**0.70**	**[0.90]**	**[1.60]**	**[1.20]**	**3.90**	**2.70**	**2.70**	**1.80**	**2.00**	**[0.80]**	**[1.10]**	**[0.70]**	**1.80**
Property transaction - purchase and sale	[0.80]	[0.30]	[0.20]	[0.10]	[0.50]	[2.20]	[0.70]	[0.70]	[0.60]	0.70	[0.40]	[0.50]	-	0.70
Property transaction - sale only	[0.40]	[0.20]	[0.40]	[0.90]	[0.10]	[0.50]	[1.00]	[1.20]	[0.70]	0.70	[0.20]	[0.00]	[0.70]	0.60
Property transaction - purchase only	[0.10]	[0.10]	[0.10]	[0.50]	[0.40]	[0.60]	[0.70]	[0.50]	[0.20]	0.40	[0.10]	[0.40]	-	0.40
Property transaction - other payments	[0.10]	[0.10]	[0.20]	[0.10]	[0.20]	[0.50]	[0.30]	[0.20]	[0.30]	0.20	-	[0.20]	-	0.20
Maintenance and repair of dwelling	**4.40**	**5.20**	**5.20**	**8.20**	**5.10**	**7.50**	**9.50**	**9.10**	**8.60**	**7.30**	**6.10**	**6.30**	**5.60**	**7.10**
Central heating repairs	0.90	1.30	0.90	1.30	1.20	1.60	1.00	1.40	2.00	1.30	0.80	1.00	0.70	1.20
House maintenance etc.	2.70	2.80	2.80	4.80	2.50	4.10	5.20	5.30	5.50	4.10	3.40	3.60	2.70	4.00
Paint, wallpaper, timber	[0.60]	0.60	1.20	1.30	1.30	0.80	2.90	1.50	0.60	1.30	1.20	1.30	[2.00]	1.30
Equipment hire, small materials	[0.20]	0.40	0.30	0.70	0.20	1.00	0.50	1.00	0.40	0.60	0.70	0.50	[0.20]	0.50
Alterations and improvements to dwelling	**7.40**	**13.30**	**10.20**	**19.80**	**11.00**	**23.70**	**25.70**	**17.90**	**38.90**	**19.30**	**12.30**	**8.90**	**[5.90]**	**17.70**
Central heating installation	[1.10]	[0.20]	[1.10]	[1.30]	[0.60]	[0.90]	[0.70]	[0.90]	[1.80]	0.90	[0.70]	[1.10]	[0.60]	0.90
DIY improvements: double glazing, kitchen units, sheds etc.	[0.50]	[0.30]	[0.20]	[0.50]	[0.50]	[2.70]	[1.90]	[0.40]	[0.10]	0.80	[0.10]	[0.90]	[0.50]	0.80
Home improvements - contracted out	5.80	12.70	8.70	17.90	9.40	19.80	22.30	16.10	36.20	17.10	[10.10]	6.80	[2.50]	15.50
Bathroom fittings	[0.00]	[0.00]	[0.20]	[0.10]	[0.40]	[0.00]	[0.60]	[0.30]	[0.80]	0.30	[0.20]	[0.00]	[2.30]	0.30
Purchase of materials for capital improvements	-	[0.00]	[0.00]	-	[0.20]	[0.20]	[0.10]	[0.10]	[0.00]	[0.10]	[1.30]	[0.10]	[0.00]	0.10
Household insurances	**3.90**	**5.10**	**5.20**	**4.60**	**4.60**	**5.40**	**5.10**	**5.70**	**5.50**	**5.10**	**5.20**	**4.60**	**4.40**	**5.10**
Structure	1.90	2.30	2.30	2.20	2.30	2.60	2.50	2.60	2.70	2.40	2.50	2.30	2.30	2.40
Contents	1.90	2.30	2.50	2.20	2.20	2.60	2.50	2.70	2.70	2.50	2.30	2.20	2.10	2.40
Household appliances	[0.10]	[0.50]	[0.30]	[0.20]	[0.10]	[0.20]	[0.00]	0.40	[0.20]	0.20	[0.30]	[0.10]	[0.00]	0.20
Housing expenditure	**96.50**	**121.10**	**120.60**	**134.50**	**117.10**	**160.00**	**206.90**	**186.30**	**184.80**	**154.30**	**113.10**	**124.50**	**81.00**	**147.90**
Total expenditure[2]	**561.70**	**617.20**	**610.70**	**666.10**	**590.20**	**766.40**	**920.20**	**839.40**	**761.90**	**726.40**	**627.00**	**667.20**	**613.70**	**713.70**

Please see background notes for symbols and conventions used in this report.

1 The figure included in total expenditure is net rent as opposed to gross rent.

2 This total includes all categories recorded in the LCF, including those outside the 'COICOP' total expenditure.

Table 2.6

Housing expenditure by socio-economic classification of household reference person, 2013

United Kingdom

	Large employers & higher managerial	Higher professional	Lower managerial & professional	Intermediate	Small employers	Lower supervisory	Semi-routine	Routine	Long-term unemployed[1]	Students	Occupation not stated[2] & not classifiable	All groups
Weighted number of households (thousands)	880	2,710	5,000	1,950	1,740	1,340	2,210	1,960	540	540	7,970	26,840
Total number of households in sample	170	490	930	370	320	250	420	380	100	80	1,640	5,140
Total number of persons in sample	490	1,370	2,440	910	860	700	1,080	1,050	250	210	2,760	12,120
Total number of adults in sample	360	970	1,810	650	630	500	750	720	160	180	2,630	9,350
Weighted average number of persons per household	2.9	2.7	2.6	2.5	2.7	2.8	2.6	2.8	2.3	2.6	1.7	2.4
Commodity or service	Average weekly household expenditure (£)											
Primary dwelling												
Rent	**[16.30]**	**39.30**	**38.60**	**57.20**	**52.80**	**54.30**	**71.20**	**69.50**	**106.10**	**149.60**	**33.60**	**48.00**
Gross rent	[16.30]	39.30	38.60	57.20	52.80	54.30	71.20	69.50	106.10	149.60	33.60	48.00
***less** housing benefit, rebates and allowances received*	[0.20]	0.70	4.70	15.00	14.60	10.80	24.10	27.50	81.40	20.50	21.90	16.10
Net rent[3]	[16.20]	38.60	33.90	42.20	38.20	43.50	47.00	42.00	24.70	129.10	11.70	32.00
Mortgage	**137.30**	**110.00**	**79.90**	**54.30**	**48.50**	**51.20**	**29.10**	**25.90**	**[3.30]**	**[11.80]**	**3.10**	**45.70**
Mortgage interest payments	65.60	52.80	39.30	24.50	21.20	20.00	12.80	10.70	[2.10]	[6.30]	1.60	21.40
Mortgage protection premiums	2.40	2.00	2.00	1.30	1.00	1.70	0.60	0.60	[0.00]	[0.60]	[0.10]	1.00
Capital repayment of mortgage	69.20	55.10	38.70	28.50	26.30	29.60	15.70	14.60	[1.20]	[4.90]	1.50	23.20
Outright purchase, including deposits	**[0.30]**	**-**	**[4.90]**	**[11.40]**	**[13.00]**	**[0.40]**	**[0.20]**	**[0.00]**	**[43.70]**	**-**	**[0.20]**	**[3.60]**
Secondary dwelling	**[21.80]**	**27.30**	**6.70**	**[2.10]**	**[2.90]**	**[1.00]**	**[0.50]**	**[0.20]**	**-**	**[5.10]**	**[3.30]**	**6.20**
Rent	[0.80]	-	[0.20]	[0.20]	-	-	-	-	-	-	-	0.10
Council tax, mortgage, insurance (secondary dwelling)	[1.90]	[7.70]	3.10	[0.90]	[1.70]	[1.00]	[0.10]	[0.00]	-	[3.30]	[0.20]	1.80
Purchase of second dwelling	[19.10]	[19.60]	[3.30]	[1.00]	[1.20]	-	[0.30]	[0.20]	-	[1.80]	[3.10]	4.40
Charges	**42.30**	**36.20**	**32.70**	**29.10**	**31.40**	**28.40**	**24.90**	**24.90**	**13.10**	**15.90**	**25.80**	**28.80**
Council tax, domestic rates	30.40	26.50	23.70	20.60	22.30	20.30	16.60	16.90	6.10	6.60	17.60	20.10
Water charges	9.40	8.30	7.70	7.40	7.90	7.60	7.20	7.40	6.60	6.60	6.60	7.40
Other regular housing payments including service charge for rent	[2.50]	1.40	1.30	0.90	1.20	[0.50]	0.90	0.60	[0.40]	[2.80]	1.50	1.30
Refuse collection, including skip hire	-	[0.00]	[0.00]	[0.10]	[0.00]	-	[0.20]	-	-	-	[0.10]	[0.00]
Moving house	**[3.10]**	**3.20**	**3.30**	**[1.00]**	**[1.40]**	**[0.40]**	**[0.90]**	**[0.60]**	**[1.00]**	**[0.60]**	**1.40**	**1.80**
Property transaction - purchase and sale	[0.50]	[0.80]	1.40	[0.50]	[0.60]	-	[0.10]	[0.20]	[0.90]	-	[0.60]	0.70
Property transaction - sale only	[0.40]	[1.20]	[0.80]	[0.10]	[0.50]	-	[0.30]	[0.10]	-	-	[0.70]	0.60
Property transaction - purchase only	[1.70]	[0.70]	[0.80]	[0.00]	[0.10]	[0.30]	[0.20]	[0.30]	[0.10]	[0.30]	[0.10]	0.40
Property transaction - other payments	[0.50]	[0.50]	0.30	[0.40]	[0.10]	[0.10]	[0.20]	[0.00]	[0.00]	[0.30]	[0.00]	0.20
Maintenance and repair of dwelling	**11.30**	**10.60**	**9.50**	**7.00**	**6.00**	**3.10**	**2.70**	**4.20**	**[1.60]**	**[0.40]**	**7.60**	**7.10**
Central heating repairs	1.50	1.50	1.50	1.20	0.90	0.60	0.70	0.60	[0.20]	[0.20]	1.60	1.20
House maintenance etc.	7.50	6.40	5.30	4.50	3.80	1.90	0.80	1.80	[1.20]	[0.10]	4.10	4.00
Paint, wallpaper, timber	[1.80]	1.30	1.90	0.70	1.00	[0.40]	0.60	1.40	[0.10]	[0.00]	1.60	1.30
Equipment hire, small materials	[0.50]	1.50	0.80	[0.50]	[0.30]	[0.30]	0.50	0.40	[0.00]	[0.10]	0.30	0.50
Alterations and improvements to dwelling	**58.60**	**38.10**	**21.90**	**17.50**	**23.50**	**10.20**	**3.40**	**3.60**	**[2.00]**	**[0.90]**	**13.30**	**17.70**
Central heating installation	[0.20]	[1.80]	1.10	[1.50]	[1.00]	[0.30]	[0.40]	[0.60]	0.50	0.30	0.80	0.90
DIY improvements: double glazing, kitchen units, sheds etc.	[1.00]	[2.00]	[1.30]	[0.30]	[2.20]	[0.10]	[0.30]	[0.10]	-	[0.30]	[0.40]	0.80
Home improvements - contracted out	56.80	32.30	18.80	15.40	20.30	9.30	2.70	2.70	[1.50]	[0.30]	11.90	15.50
Bathroom fittings	[0.50]	[1.30]	[0.60]	[0.20]	[0.10]	[0.30]	[0.00]	[0.10]	-	-	[0.10]	0.30
Purchase of materials for capital improvements	[0.20]	[0.60]	[0.10]	[0.10]	-	[0.20]	-	-	-	-	[0.10]	0.10
Household insurances	**8.60**	**7.10**	**6.00**	**4.70**	**5.30**	**4.80**	**3.00**	**3.00**	**1.20**	**1.60**	**5.00**	**5.10**
Structure	4.30	3.60	3.00	2.20	2.40	2.00	1.40	1.50	[0.50]	[0.40]	2.30	2.40
Contents	4.20	3.30	2.90	2.30	2.40	2.40	1.50	1.50	0.70	1.20	2.30	2.40
Household appliances	[0.10]	[0.10]	0.10	[0.20]	[0.50]	[0.40]	[0.10]	[0.00]	[0.00]	-	0.40	0.20
Housing expenditure	**299.20**	**271.10**	**198.80**	**169.30**	**170.20**	**143.10**	**111.60**	**104.50**	**90.60**	**165.30**	**71.60**	**147.90**
Total expenditure[4]	**1,547.30**	**1,265.90**	**970.30**	**716.30**	**683.50**	**678.60**	**506.40**	**510.10**	**316.70**	**696.90**	**420.50**	**713.70**

Note: Changes to categories of socio-economic classification were made from 2011. Please see Appendix B for details

Please see background notes for symbols and conventions used in this report

1 Includes those who have never worked.

2 Includes those who are economically inactive.

3 The figure included in total expenditure is net rent as opposed to gross rent

4 This total includes all categories recorded in the LCF, including those outside the 'COICOP' total expenditure

Table 2.7
Housing expenditure by household composition, 2013
United Kingdom

	Retired households		Non-retired		Retired and non-retired households			
	One Person	Two adults	One Person	Two adults	One adult with children	Two adults with children	Three or more adults without children	Three or more adults with children
Weighted number of households (thousands)	3,700	2,970	4,090	5,720	1,360	5,390	2,490	1,120
Total number of households in sample	700	700	740	1,080	300	1,050	390	200
Total number of persons in sample	700	1,410	740	2,150	780	4,050	1,340	970
Total number of adults in sample	700	1,410	740	2,150	300	2,090	1,340	640
Weighted average number of persons per household	1.0	2.0	1.0	2.0	2.6	3.8	3.5	4.9
Commodity or service	Average weekly household expenditure (£)							
Primary dwelling								
Rent	**35.50**	**19.50**	**58.20**	**45.90**	**98.40**	**54.40**	**48.40**	**46.50**
Gross rent	35.50	19.50	58.20	45.90	98.40	54.40	48.40	46.50
less *housing benefit, rebates & allowances received*	22.80	11.00	20.70	5.50	61.00	15.30	[6.90]	14.10
Net rent[1]	12.70	8.50	37.40	40.40	37.40	39.20	41.50	32.30
Mortgage	**[0.80]**	**2.80**	**32.00**	**54.80**	**31.40**	**97.00**	**46.80**	**77.60**
Mortgage interest payments	[0.50]	1.10	15.70	25.30	16.40	46.60	19.60	34.10
Mortgage protection premiums	-	[0.10]	0.70	1.10	0.60	2.30	1.00	1.90
Capital repayment of mortgage	[0.30]	[1.60]	15.70	28.40	14.40	48.10	26.20	41.60
Outright purchase, including deposits	**[0.50]**	**-**	**[5.80]**	**[0.00]**	**-**	**[13.10]**	**-**	**-**
Secondary dwelling	**[5.40]**	**[1.40]**	**[3.70]**	**6.60**	**[0.40]**	**2.90**	**[26.80]**	**[6.70]**
Rent	-	-	-	[0.10]	-	[0.20]	[0.30]	-
Council tax, mortgage, insurance (secondary dwelling)	[0.20]	[0.10]	[0.50]	2.40	[0.10]	2.20	[5.30]	[5.00]
Purchase of second dwelling	[5.30]	[1.30]	[3.20]	[4.10]	[0.30]	[0.50]	[21.30]	[1.70]
Charges	**21.80**	**32.60**	**21.70**	**32.90**	**19.10**	**32.60**	**32.60**	**32.60**
Council tax, domestic rates	13.80	24.00	13.50	24.00	11.00	23.30	23.60	23.40
Water charges	5.50	7.40	5.90	7.50	7.70	8.60	8.60	8.80
Other regular housing payments including service charge for rent	2.40	1.10	2.20	1.30	[0.40]	0.70	0.40	[0.10]
Refuse collection, including skip hire	[0.20]	-	[0.00]	[0.00]	-	[0.10]	-	[0.30]
Moving house	**[0.90]**	**[1.40]**	**1.90**	**2.20**	**[1.10]**	**2.20**	**[2.10]**	**[1.50]**
Property transaction - purchase and sale	[0.60]	[0.70]	[0.80]	[0.30]	[0.40]	1.30	[0.20]	[0.20]
Property transaction - sale only	[0.10]	[0.50]	[0.40]	[0.70]	[0.40]	[0.40]	[1.60]	[0.90]
Property transaction - purchase only	[0.10]	[0.10]	[0.50]	[0.80]	[0.00]	[0.20]	[0.30]	[0.10]
Property transaction - other payments	[0.00]	[0.10]	[0.10]	0.40	[0.30]	0.30	[0.10]	[0.30]
Maintenance and repair of dwelling	**6.00**	**10.60**	**5.60**	**9.10**	**2.70**	**6.50**	**6.80**	**5.20**
Central heating repairs	1.70	1.80	0.70	1.30	0.40	1.10	1.30	1.20
House maintenance etc.	3.50	5.10	3.60	5.40	1.00	3.60	3.70	2.80
Paint, wallpaper, timber	0.60	3.20	0.60	1.80	1.20	1.10	0.90	[0.70]
Equipment hire, small materials	0.20	0.40	0.70	0.60	[0.20]	0.60	0.90	[0.50]
Alterations and improvements to dwelling	**8.90**	**21.20**	**8.00**	**20.90**	**[6.80]**	**23.40**	**28.10**	**19.50**
Central heating installation	[0.90]	[1.00]	[0.50]	1.10	[0.50]	1.00	[1.30]	[0.40]
DIY improvements: double glazing, kitchen units, sheds etc.	[0.20]	[0.10]	[0.20]	[1.50]	[0.20]	[0.40]	[3.20]	[0.60]
Home improvements - contracted out	7.80	19.80	6.60	17.90	[6.20]	21.20	23.10	18.20
Bathroom fittings	[0.10]	[0.10]	[0.50]	[0.10]	-	[0.70]	[0.60]	[0.10]
Purchase of materials for capital improvements	[0.00]	[0.20]	[0.20]	[0.30]	-	[0.10]	-	[0.20]
Household insurances	**4.60**	**6.10**	**3.60**	**5.50**	**2.60**	**5.40**	**6.20**	**6.00**
Structure	2.00	3.10	1.60	2.70	1.20	2.70	2.90	3.00
Contents	2.00	2.80	1.90	2.70	1.40	2.60	2.90	2.50
Household appliances	[0.60]	[0.20]	[0.10]	0.10	[0.10]	0.10	[0.40]	[0.40]
Housing expenditure	**61.60**	**84.50**	**119.80**	**172.40**	**101.70**	**222.20**	**191.00**	**181.50**
Total expenditure[2]	**275.80**	**517.90**	**455.50**	**860.10**	**418.70**	**975.70**	**1101.80**	**1109.70**

Please see background notes for symbols and conventions used in this report.

1 The figure included in total expenditure is net rent as opposed to gross rent.

2 This total includes all categories recorded in the LCF, including those outside the 'COICOP' total expenditure.

Table 2.8

Expenditure on rent[1] by renters, 2011 to 2013
United Kingdom

	2011		2012		2013	
	£[2]	% of total expenditure	£[2]	% of total expenditure	£[2]	% of total expenditure
Weighted number of households (thousands)	8,540		8,950		9,320	
Total number of households in sample	1,760		1,760		1,640	
Total number of persons in sample	4,050		4,070		3,840	
Total number of adults in sample	2,890		2,920		2,750	
Weighted average number of persons per household	2.3		2.3		2.3	
Total expenditure for renters	**441.20**		**464.00**		**487.30**	
Rent	**124.30**	***28.2***	**136.00**	***29.3***	**138.40**	***28.4***
Gross rent	124.30	*28.2*	136.00	*29.3*	138.40	*28.4*
less *housing benefit, rebates and allowances received*	47.20	*10.7*	49.60	*10.7*	46.30	*9.5*
Net rent[3]	77.00	*17.5*	86.40	*18.6*	92.10	*18.9*

Please see background notes for symbols and conventions used in this report.

1 Primary dwelling.

2 Average weekly household expenditure (£).

3 The figure included in total expenditure is net rent as opposed to gross rent.

Table 2.9

Expenditure on mortgages[1] by mortgage holders, 2011 to 2013

United Kingdom

	2011		2012		2013	
	£[2]	% of total expenditure	£[2]	% of total expenditure	£[2]	% of total expenditure
Weighted number of households (thousands)	8,920		8,660		8,370	
Total number of households in sample	1,950		1,840		1,580	
Total number of persons in sample	5,570		5,270		4,600	
Total number of adults in sample	3,910		3,680		3,170	
Weighted average number of persons per household	2.8		2.8		2.9	
Total expenditure for mortgage payers	**1,006.20**		**999.30**		**1,071.20**	
Mortgage	**139.30**	***13.8***	**138.60**	***13.9***	**145.40**	***13.6***
Mortgage interest payments	70.60	*7.0*	66.70	*6.7*	68.10	*6.4*
Mortgage protection premiums	3.70	*0.4*	3.70	*0.4*	3.20	*0.3*
Capital repayment of mortgage	65.00	*6.5*	68.20	*6.8*	74.00	*6.9*

Please see background notes for symbols and conventions used in this report.

1 Primary dwelling.

2 Average weekly household expenditure (£).

Table 2.10

Expenditure on rent and mortgages[1] by renters and mortgage holders by gross income decile group, 2013

United Kingdom

	Gross income decile group										
	1	**2**	**3**	**4**	**5**	**6**	**7**	**8**	**9**	**10**	**All**
Weighted number of households (thousands)	1,780	1,440	1,220	1,110	960	790	610	610	490	310	9,320
Total number of households in sample	330	270	230	200	160	130	110	90	70	50	1,640
Total number of persons in sample	450	510	510	550	430	400	330	290	220	150	3,840
Total number of adults in sample	370	370	350	370	290	260	230	220	180	110	2,750
Weighted average number of persons per household	1.3	1.9	2.2	2.6	2.7	3.0	2.9	2.9	3.0	3.1	2.3
Commodity or service	Average weekly household expenditure (£)										
Rent for renters	**118.10**	**124.00**	**133.30**	**130.30**	**133.30**	**148.80**	**150.10**	**146.50**	**171.10**	**268.80**	**138.40**
Gross rent	118.10	124.00	133.30	130.30	133.30	148.80	150.10	146.50	171.10	268.80	138.40
less *housing benefit, rebates and allowances received*	*86.40*	*78.00*	*62.90*	*40.00*	*26.00*	*13.80*	*4.70*	*4.00*	*[6.20]*	*[0.20]*	*46.30*
Net rent[2]	31.70	46.00	70.50	90.30	107.30	135.00	145.40	142.50	164.80	268.60	92.10
Weighted number of households (thousands)	160	170	280	460	620	920	1,270	1,350	1,500	1,650	8,370
Total number of households in sample	30	40	60	90	120	180	240	260	280	290	1,580
Total number of persons in sample	40	70	120	200	300	500	720	810	860	970	4,600
Total number of adults in sample	40	60	80	140	220	340	470	550	610	680	3,170
Weighted average number of persons per household	1.4	2.2	2.1	2.1	2.4	2.7	3.0	3.1	3.1	3.3	2.9
Commodity or service	Average weekly household expenditure (£)										
Mortgage for mortgage holders	**74.20**	**73.80**	**89.50**	**93.80**	**101.10**	**105.70**	**119.80**	**132.10**	**166.60**	**233.20**	**145.40**
Mortgage interest payments	44.90	37.30	44.40	39.80	45.50	49.00	57.20	60.10	73.90	114.40	68.10
Mortgage protection premiums	[0.80]	[1.00]	[1.50]	2.40	2.00	2.90	3.20	3.30	3.30	4.60	3.20
Capital repayment of mortgage	[28.50]	35.50	43.70	51.60	53.60	53.90	59.40	68.70	89.40	114.30	74.00

Please see background notes for symbols and conventions used in this report.

1 Primary dwelling.

2 The figure included in total expenditure is net rent as opposed to gross rent.

Table 2.11
Expenditure on rent and mortgages[1] by renters and mortgage holders by UK Countries and regions, 2013

	North East	North West	Yorks & the Humber	East Midlands	West Midlands	East	London
Weighted number of households (thousands)	450	1,120	750	640	900	790	1,540
Total number of households in sample	100	200	140	130	180	140	210
Total number of persons in sample	230	450	300	300	420	340	540
Total number of adults in sample	150	330	220	220	280	250	360
Weighted average number of persons per household	2.2	2.2	2.1	2.3	2.2	2.3	2.5
Commodity or service	Average weekly household expenditure (£)						
Rent by renters	**102.50**	**112.80**	**123.00**	**115.00**	**112.10**	**148.50**	**211.60**
Gross rent	102.50	112.80	123.00	115.00	112.10	148.50	211.60
less *housing benefit, rebates and allowances received*	56.10	42.90	39.30	41.50	48.50	38.20	70.00
Net rent[2]	46.40	69.90	83.70	73.50	63.70	110.20	141.60
Weighted number of households (thousands)	300	970	700	660	690	820	910
Total number of households in sample	70	190	130	140	150	160	130
Total number of persons in sample	210	530	360	400	460	460	350
Total number of adults in sample	150	380	260	270	310	310	250
Weighted average number of persons per household	2.8	2.9	2.7	2.8	3.0	2.8	2.8
Commodity or service	Average weekly household expenditure (£)						
Mortgage by mortgage holders	**117.50**	**113.60**	**125.40**	**135.90**	**135.80**	**158.90**	**211.80**
Mortgage interest payments	50.50	49.90	51.70	63.90	65.00	76.60	109.30
Mortgage protection premiums	2.70	2.50	3.30	2.50	3.90	3.40	3.80
Capital repayment of mortgage	64.30	61.30	70.40	69.50	66.90	78.90	98.80

	South East	South West	England	Wales	Scotland	Northern Ireland	United Kingdom
Weighted number of households (thousands)	1,140	660	8,000	340	770	210	9,320
Total number of households in sample	200	120	1,410	60	130	40	1,640
Total number of persons in sample	480	290	3,320	150	280	80	3,840
Total number of adults in sample	340	210	2,360	110	220	60	2,750
Weighted average number of persons per household	2.5	2.4	2.3	2.4	2.2	2.1	2.3
Commodity or service	Average weekly household expenditure (£)						
Rent by renters	**161.40**	**128.70**	**144.10**	**118.10**	**100.80**	**91.70**	**138.40**
Gross rent	161.40	128.70	144.10	118.10	100.80	91.70	138.40
less *housing benefit, rebates and allowances received*	45.00	27.20	47.60	44.50	37.20	33.80	46.30
Net rent[2]	116.40	101.50	96.50	73.60	63.70	58.00	92.10
Weighted number of households (thousands)	1,160	760	6,990	420	720	230	8,370
Total number of households in sample	210	140	1,330	80	120	50	1,580
Total number of persons in sample	620	410	3,800	260	360	180	4,600
Total number of adults in sample	440	290	2,650	170	250	120	3,170
Weighted average number of persons per household	2.9	2.9	2.8	3.1	2.9	3.4	2.9
Commodity or service	Average weekly household expenditure (£)						
Mortgage by mortgage holders	**172.10**	**148.00**	**150.90**	**120.10**	**117.30**	**112.50**	**145.40**
Mortgage interest payments	83.70	69.70	71.60	53.40	52.30	39.60	68.10
Mortgage protection premiums	3.00	3.50	3.20	2.40	3.00	6.00	3.20
Capital repayment of mortgage	85.40	74.80	76.10	64.30	62.00	66.90	74.00

Please see background notes for symbols and conventions used in this report.

1 Primary dwelling.

2 The figure included in total expenditure is net rent as opposed to gross rent.

Office for National Statistics

Chapter 3: Equivalised income

Abstract

This chapter examines how expenditure varies with equivalised income. Equivalised income is household income that has been recalculated to take into account the fact that households with many members are likely to need a higher income to achieve the same standard of living as households with fewer members.

Key points

- Lower income households spend a higher proportion of their total expenditure on food and drink than higher income households (16% compared to 8%), although households in the highest income group spent £35 more per week than households in the lowest income group.
- The proportion of total expenditure on recreation and culture increased with income (9% to 15%). This reflects the expectation that higher income households have more income available to spend on discretionary items.
- Expenditure patterns differ between retired and non-retired households. For example, among one person households spending on clothing and footwear increased by £21.60 for non-retired households between the top and bottom income groups, compared to an increase of £2.40 for retired households.
- Spending on food and drink by income differed for one person households, in comparison to the overall pattern for all household types. There was little variation in spending by one person households as income increased (£10.20 for one person non-retired households, £6.00 for one person retired households, compared to £34.70 for all households).

Background

This chapter examines how expenditure varies with equivalised income, which refers to household income that has been recalculated to take into account differences in household size and composition.

Equivalisation is a standard methodology that adjusts household income to account for the different financial resource requirements of different household types. Household size is an important factor to consider because larger households usually need a higher income than smaller households to achieve a comparable standard of living. The composition of a household also affects resource needs, for example, living costs for adults are normally higher than for children. After equivalisation has been applied, households with the same equivalised income can be said to have a comparable standard of living.

Data for disposable income has been published and is reported on in this chapter. Gross income tables are available on request. Disposable income is defined as gross weekly cash income less the statutory deductions and payments of income tax and National Insurance contributions[1]. Most analysis looking at income and expenditure together looks at disposable rather than gross income. This is because disposable income is the amount that households have available to spend or save.

Full details of the equivalisation methodology used are given in the 'Equivalisation Methodology' section. Information on how the equivalisation process affects the distribution of income data for different household types is in the 'Equivalisation Results' section.

Notes

1. For other ONS and DWP publications, council tax and domestic rates (Northern Ireland) are also deducted from gross income to provide a measure of disposable income. For Family Spending council tax and domestic rates (Northern Ireland) are counted as expenditure within the total expenditure definition.

Income, expenditure and well-being

For many households, income is their most important economic resource for meeting everyday living expenses. However, it is the consumption of goods and services (best reflected by expenditure) that is pivotal in meeting a household's requirements. As highlighted in the remainder of this section evidence suggests that income and expenditure together represent a better determinant of economic well-being than income alone.

Expenditures change less than incomes when short term changes in incomes are encountered, and can therefore be considered a better proxy of living standards. Households can smooth expenditure by, for example, adjusting savings, drawing on wealth and borrowing, whereas incomes may be more volatile. This led to Friedman's 'permanent income hypothesis', which suggests that decisions made by consumers are based on long-term income expectations rather than their current income. Headey, Muffels and Wooden, 2004 describe expenditure as 'the most valid measure of current living standards' in their analysis of household finances and well-being.

In addition, recent ONS analysis shows that household spending matters more to many aspects of personal well-being than household income. As spending rises, average life satisfaction (the sense that what one does in life is worthwhile) and happiness also rise (Lewis, 2014).

The Commission on the Measurement of Economic Performance and Social Progress (Stiglitz, Sen and Fitoussi, 2009) recommended that greater prominence should be given to the distributions of income and expenditure across households.

For given levels of expenditure, and everything else being equal, people with higher income can be seen as having a higher level of well-being from a personal finance perspective than people with lower income. With higher income, they have greater opportunity to increase expenditure if they want, or to save income to finance expenditure in the future.

In light of this context, this chapter examines how expenditure varies with income.

Household expenditure by income

This section illustrates how separating the expenditure patterns for different types of goods and services provides a fuller picture of how households with different levels of income spend their money.

Tables 3.1 (422 Kb Excel sheet) and 3.1E (89 Kb Excel sheet) show expenditure, in total and for each of the Classification of Individual COnsumption by Purpose (COICOP) categories, by non-equivalised and equivalised disposable income decile groups respectively.

As shown in figure 3.1, there was an overall increase in total expenditure as equivalised income, and non-equivalised income increased. In 2012 there was a similar pattern, although the second equivalised income decile had a slightly lower expenditure than the bottom non-equivalised income decile. This is often referred to as an ‘expenditure tick’.

Figure 3.1: Household expenditure by non-equivalised and OECD-modified equivalised disposable income decile group, 2013

United Kingdom

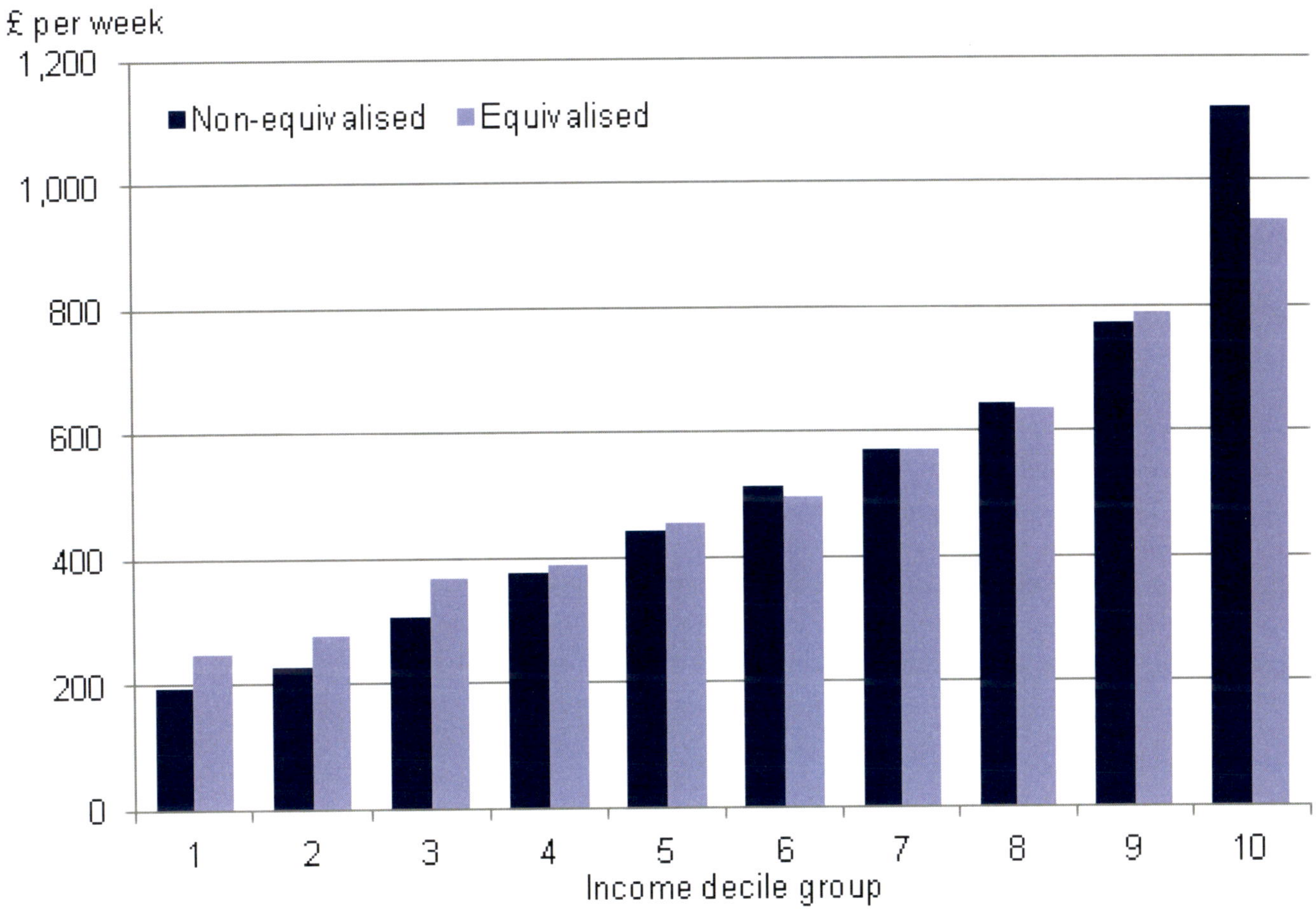

Source: Living Costs and Food Survey - Office for National Statistics

Download chart

XLS XLS format
(46 Kb)

In 2012 it was suggested that an 'expenditure tick' could be partly due to consumption smoothing. Consumption smoothing is caused by individuals who have a low income on a short-term basis but who have higher expenditure than expected for their level of income, such as students and the temporarily unemployed. The absence of the expenditure tick in 2013 could be due to the fall in the unemployment rate between 2012 and 2013 as reported in Labour Market Statistics, February 2014. The number of unemployed adults who were expecting to start work within the next few weeks fell, potentially reducing the impact of the temporarily unemployed whose spending may have been based on expected future income. However, as the Living Costs and Food Survey only collects information on households' current income sources, it is not possible to establish whether longer term income expectations account for the expenditure pattern observed.

Expenditure in the lower income decile groups increased after income was equivalised. This is due to the impact the equivalisation method has on the income positioning of households with children, and single adult households. Equivalisation increases the number of households with children in the lower income groups, whose spending is likely to be higher than households containing one adult. These households tend to move to a higher income decile group after income is equivalised. For more details see 'Equivalisation Results'.

Tables 3.2 (481 Kb Excel sheet) and table 3.2E (118.5 Kb Excel sheet) show the share of total expenditure on each COICOP category, by non-equivalised and equivalised income groups. The rest of this section compares the absolute spending and the share of total expenditure by equivalised disposable income for different categories of spending.

Expenditure on food and non-alcoholic drink rose with equivalised income, whilst the proportion of total expenditure on food and non-alcoholic drink decreased (see figure 3.2). Clearly all households have to spend a certain amount on food and non-alcoholic drink. However, as income rises households spend more in absolute terms on this category, but there is a limit to how much food households consume and the amount they are willing to spend overall. As a result of this, households in the higher equivalised disposable income decile groups spend a lower proportion of their expenditure on food and non-alcoholic drink than households in the lower income decile groups. As income rises from the lowest to the highest equivalised disposable income decile group, spending almost doubles from £40.70 to £75.40. However, for households in the bottom equivalised disposable income decile group food and non-alcoholic drinks accounted for 16% of total expenditure, compared to 8% for the top equivalised disposable income decile group.

Figure 3.2: Expenditure on food and non-alcoholic drinks (absolute expenditure and as a percentage of total expenditure) by OECD-modified equivalised disposable income decile group, 2013

United Kingdom

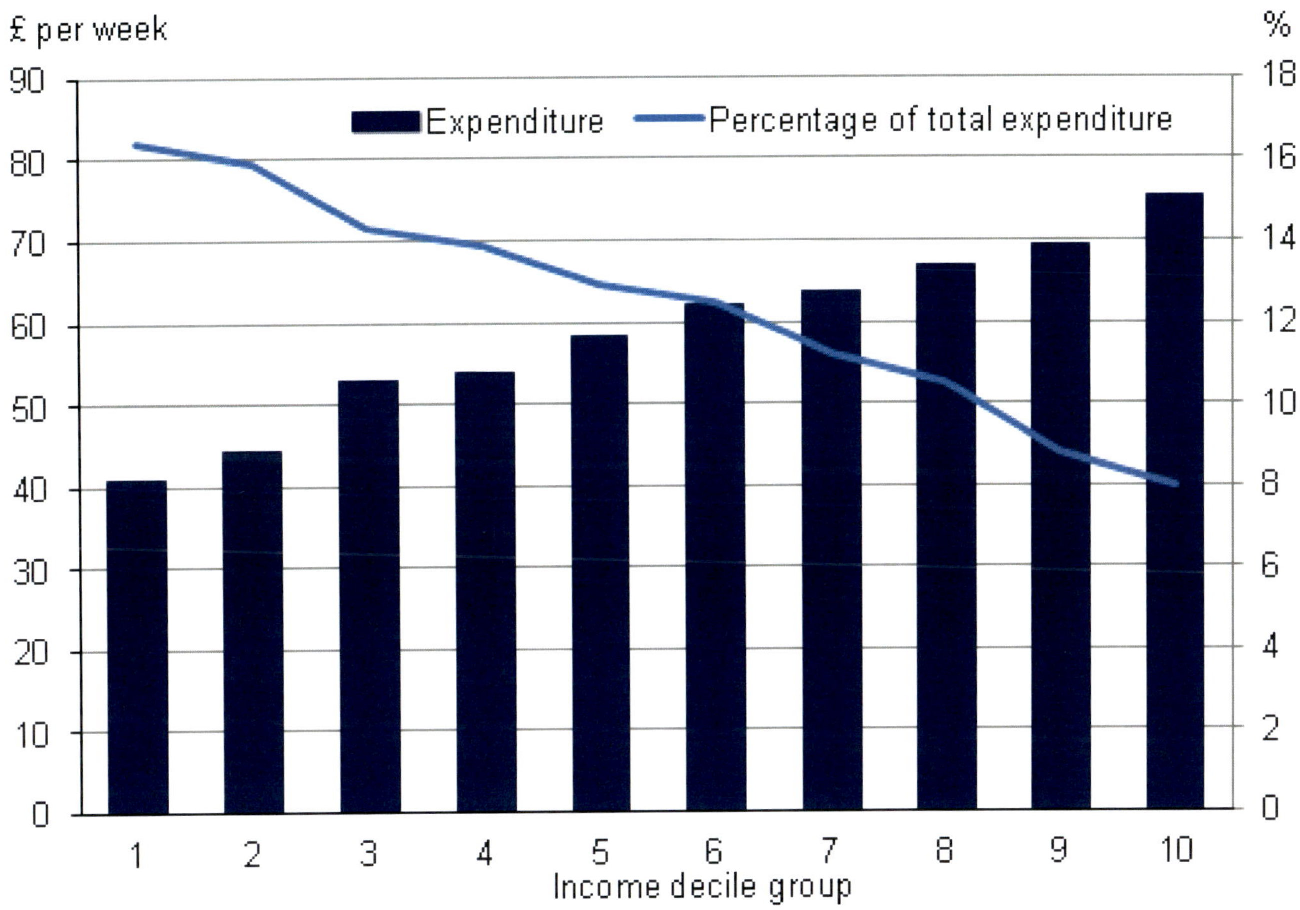

Source: Living Costs and Food Survey - Office for National Statistics

Download chart

XLS XLS format
(52 Kb)

For certain categories where spending can be seen as non-essential, the proportion of total expenditure increased, as well as the amount. An example of this is recreation and culture, which includes expenditures that are almost entirely non-essential (such as package holidays, sports admissions and audio-visual equipment). Higher income households may be expected to have more available to spend on recreational activities, for example, package holidays abroad where the pattern is particularly evident. Figure 3.3 shows the highest equivalised income households spent £137 per week on recreation and culture. This is around six times as much as households in the lowest equivalised income decile, which only spent £22 per week. The proportion of spending increases from 9% to 15%. Figure 3.4 shows a breakdown of selected lower-level items in recreation and culture, showing the pattern above for package holidays.

Figure 3.3: Expenditure on recreation and culture (absolute expenditure and as a percentage of total expenditure) by OECD-modified equivalised disposable income decile group, 2013

United Kingdom

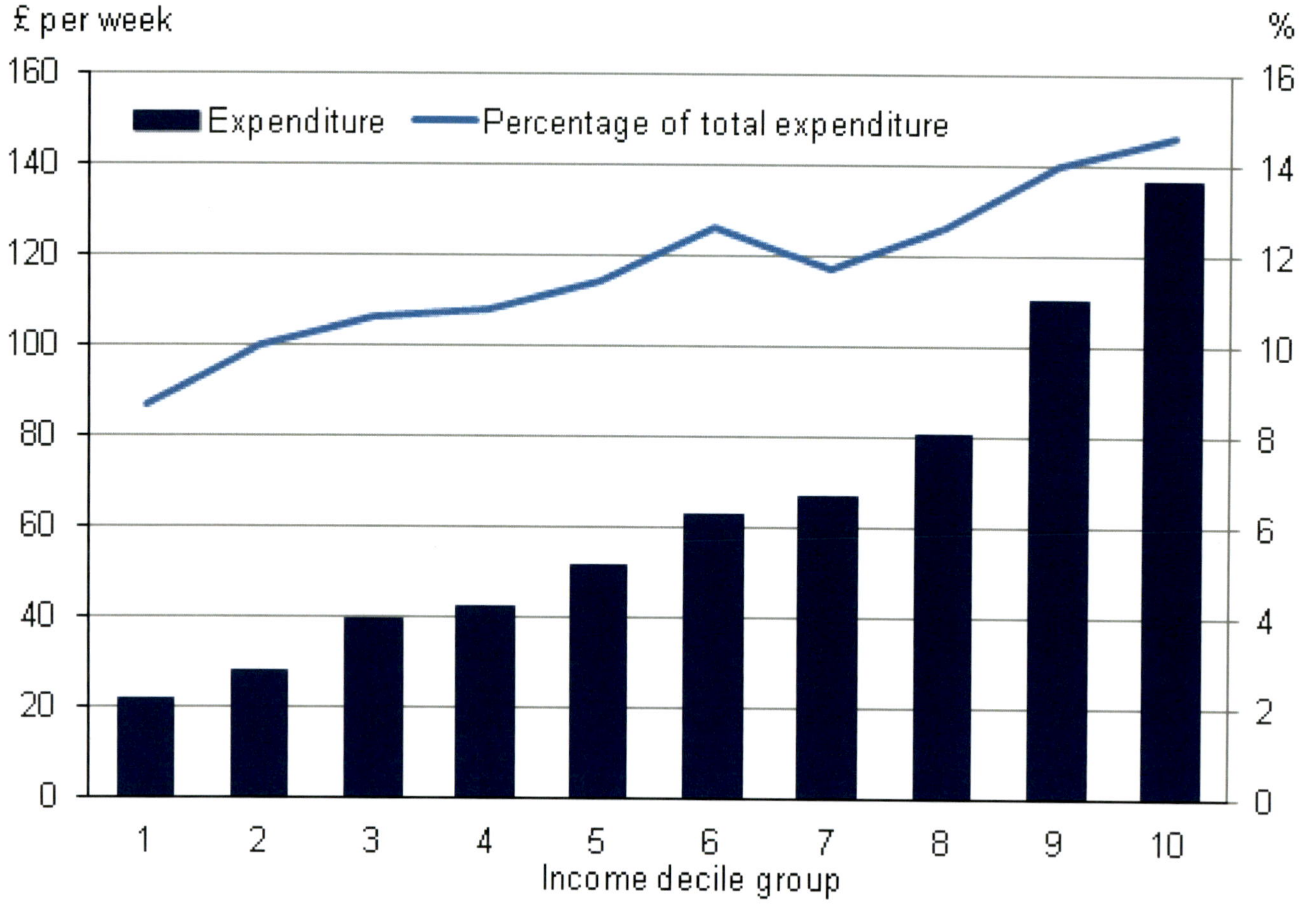

Source: Living Costs and Food Survey - Office for National Statistics

Download chart

XLS [XLS format](#)
(52 Kb)

Figure 3.4: Expenditure on recreation and culture and selected lower-level items by OECD-modified equivalised disposable income decile group, 2013

United Kingdom

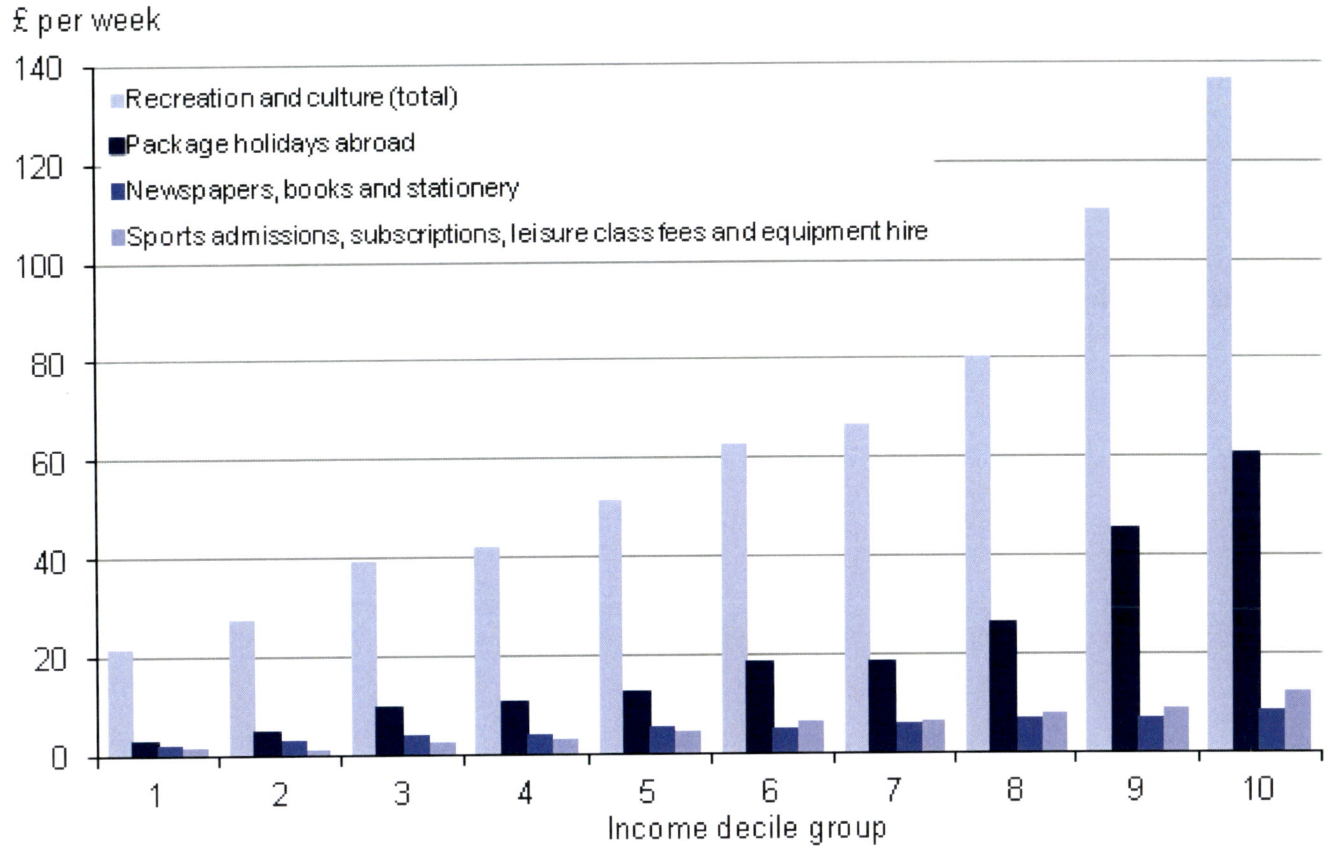

Source: Living Costs and Food Survey - Office for National Statistics

Download chart

XLS XLS format
(41 Kb)

Household expenditure by household composition and income

This section looks at how expenditure varies with income for retired and non-retired households containing one adult (see tables 3.3 to 3.10 and tables 3.3E to 3.10E). One adult retired and non-retired households have been chosen as an example of how expenditure varies with income for different household types. Retired households are those where the householder has reached state pension age, is not working or seeking work, and is mainly dependent on income sources other than the state pension (for example, occupational pension, income from investments, or annuities). Retired households mainly dependent on state pensions have been excluded from this analysis as they have low sample sizes.

As seen in figure 3.5, total expenditure for both non-retired and retired households containing one adult rose with equivalised disposable income quintile (these increased by £375 per week for non-retired households, and £308 per week for retired households). For each quintile group, absolute spending was higher for households containing one non-retired adult. Most individual expenditure categories showed a similar pattern, but for some categories the variation in spending with income was more or less marked.

Figure 3.5: Expenditure for one adult households by OECD-modified equivalised disposable income quintile group, 2013

United Kingdom

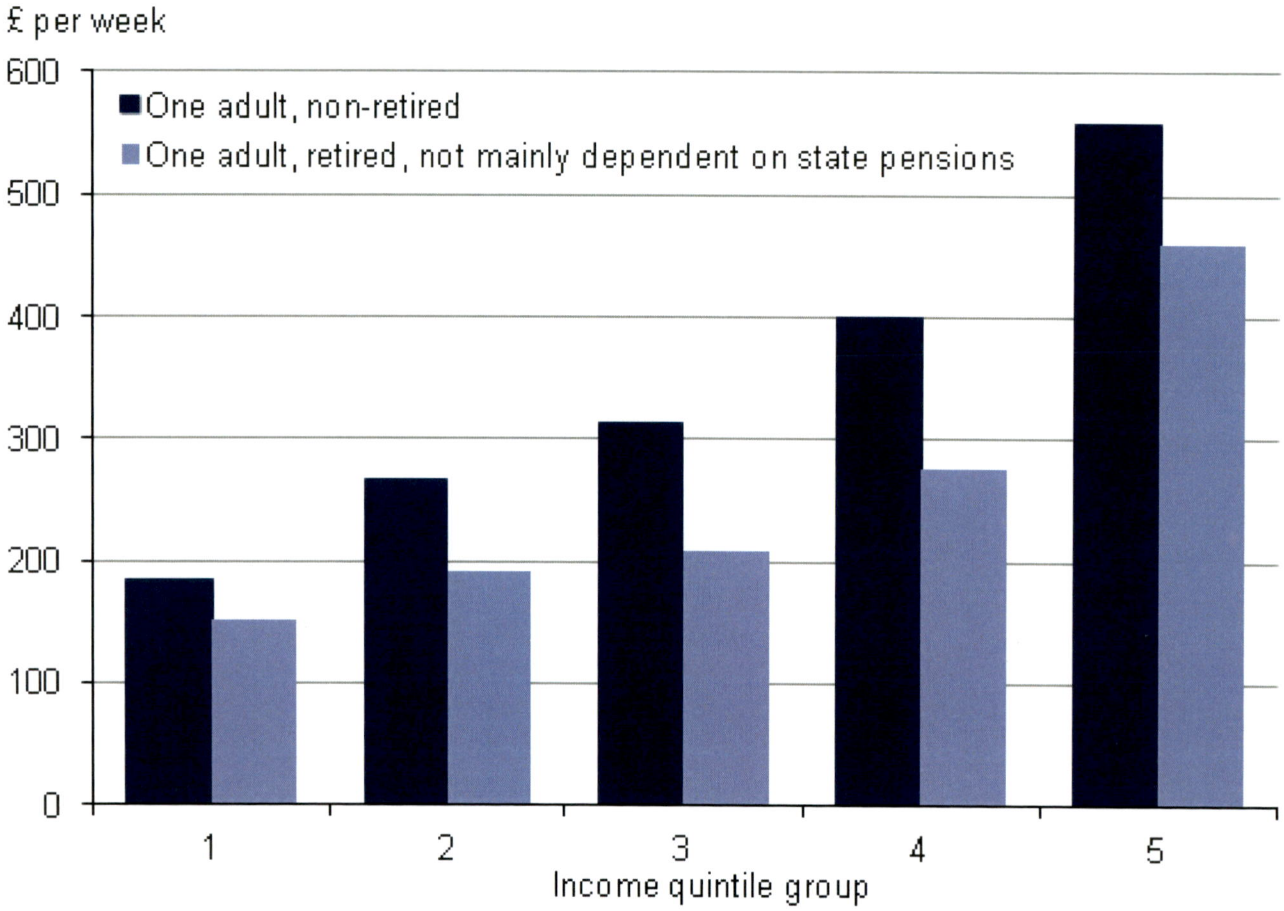

Source: Living Costs and Food Survey - Office for National Statistics

Download chart

XLS XLS format
(40 Kb)

Spending on food and non-alcoholic drink was similar for both types of household for the second to fifth income quintiles, as shown in figure 3.6. There is much less variation in spending between income quintile groups for both household types as compared to the overall picture of expenditure on food and non-alcoholic drink seen in figure 3.2, where there is a strong trend of expenditure increasing with income. This suggests spending additional income on food is less of a priority for one-person households than for other household types.

Figure 3.6: Expenditure on food and non-alcoholic drinks for one adult households by OECD-modified equivalised disposable income quintile group, 2013

United Kingdom

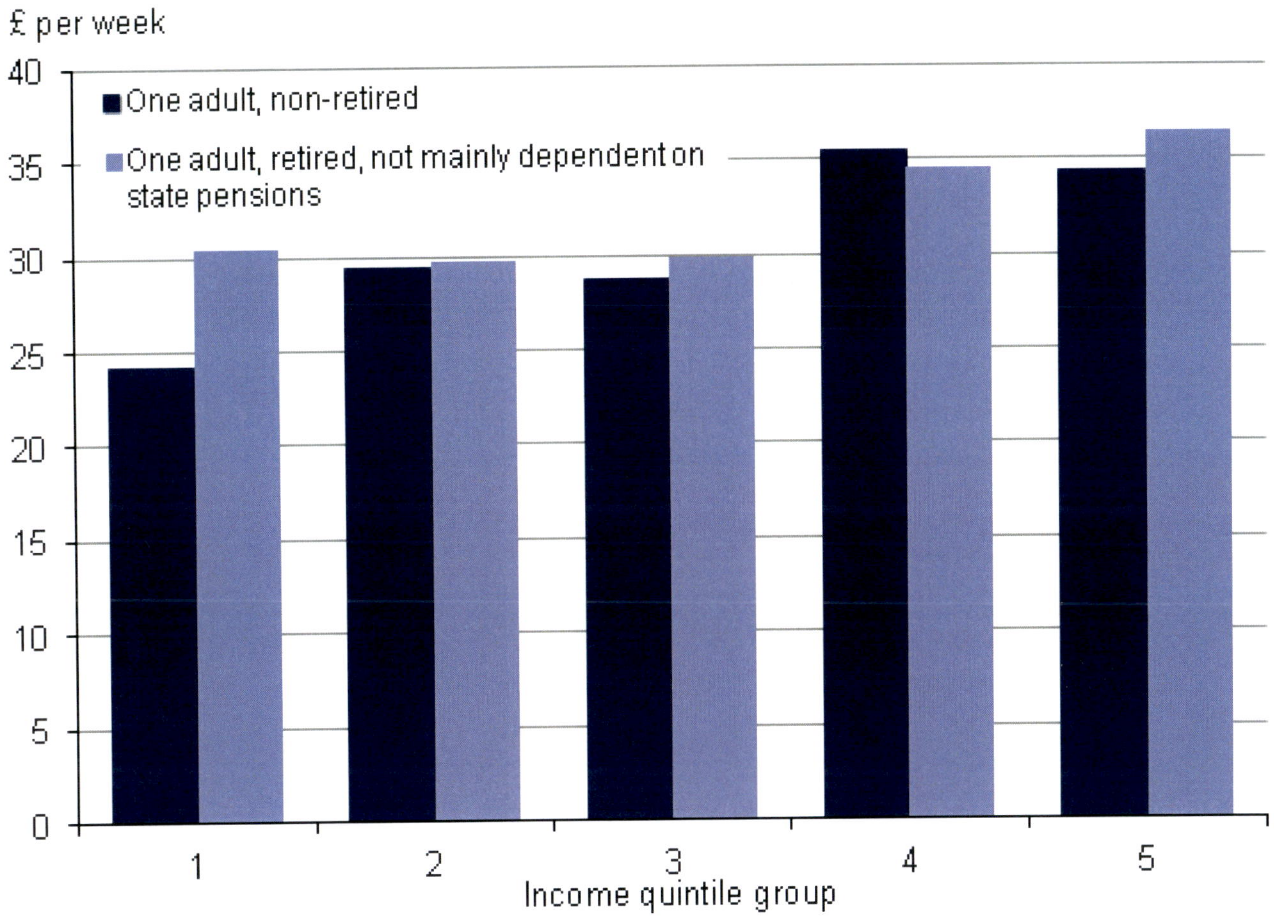

Source: Living Costs and Food Survey - Office for National Statistics

Download chart

XLS XLS format
(40.5 Kb)

For non-retired households made up of one adult, spending on clothing and footwear increased sharply as equivalised disposable income increased. However, there was very little increase among retired households. Spending on essential clothing is expected for all households but clothing offers a broad range of price. The pattern seen for one adult non-retired households may be due to higher income households choosing to buy more expensive items, or choosing to buy more new clothes. The contrasting pattern seen in one person retired higher income households may reflect a lower priority for buying expensive or new clothes compared to other categories of spending.

Figure 3.7: Expenditure on clothing and footwear for one adult households by OECD-modified equivalised disposable income quintile group, 2013

United Kingdom

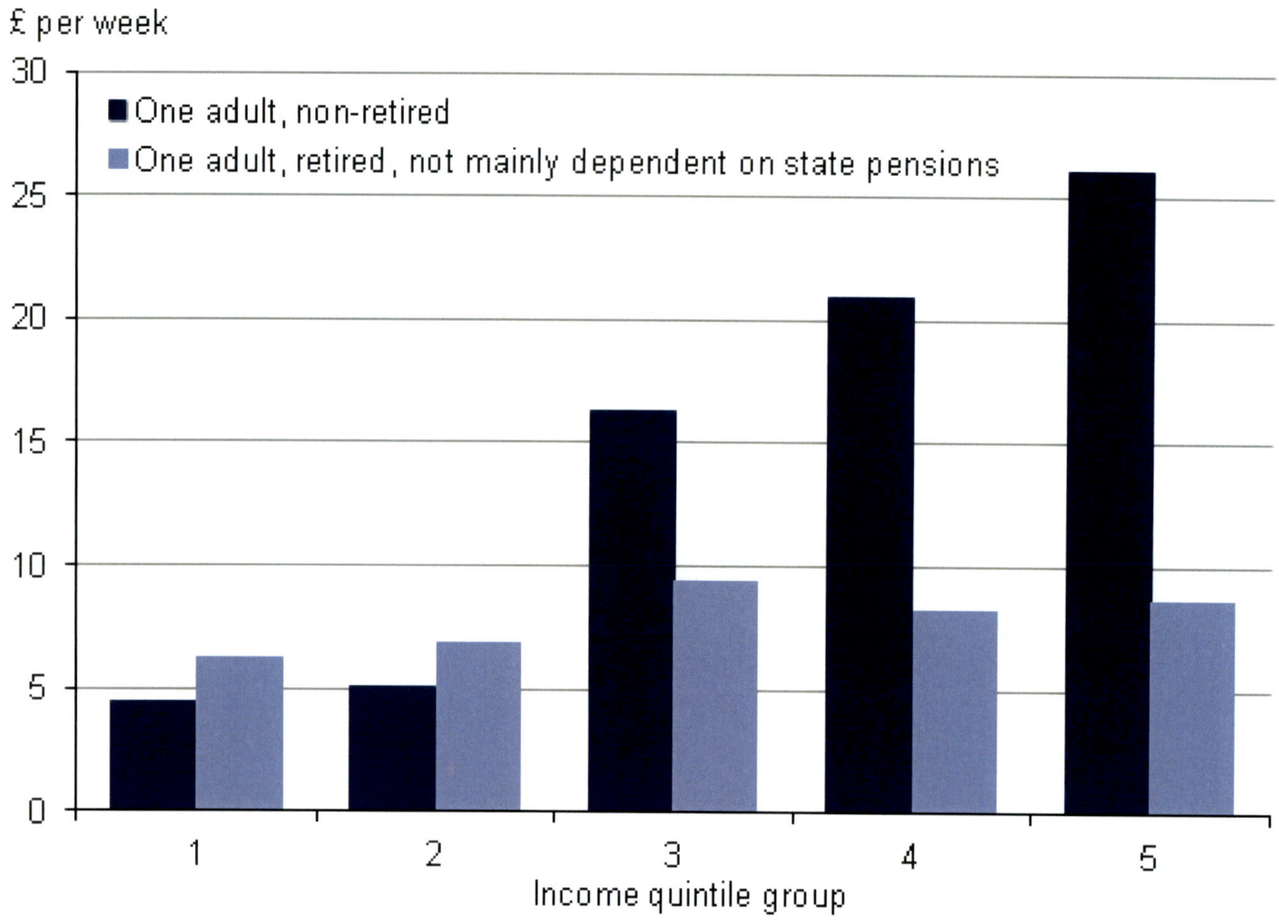

Source: Living Costs and Food Survey - Office for National Statistics

Download chart

XLS XLS format
(40.5 Kb)

Households containing one retired and non-retired adult have broadly similar levels and patterns of spending on household goods and services. Higher-earning retired and non-retired households spend more on items such as furniture, household appliances, and household garden tools. Non-retired households only spend notably more on these (arguably non-essential) expenditure items in the highest income quintile than retired households.

Figure 3.8: Expenditure on household goods and services for one adult households by OECD-modified equivalised income quintile group, 2013

United Kingdom

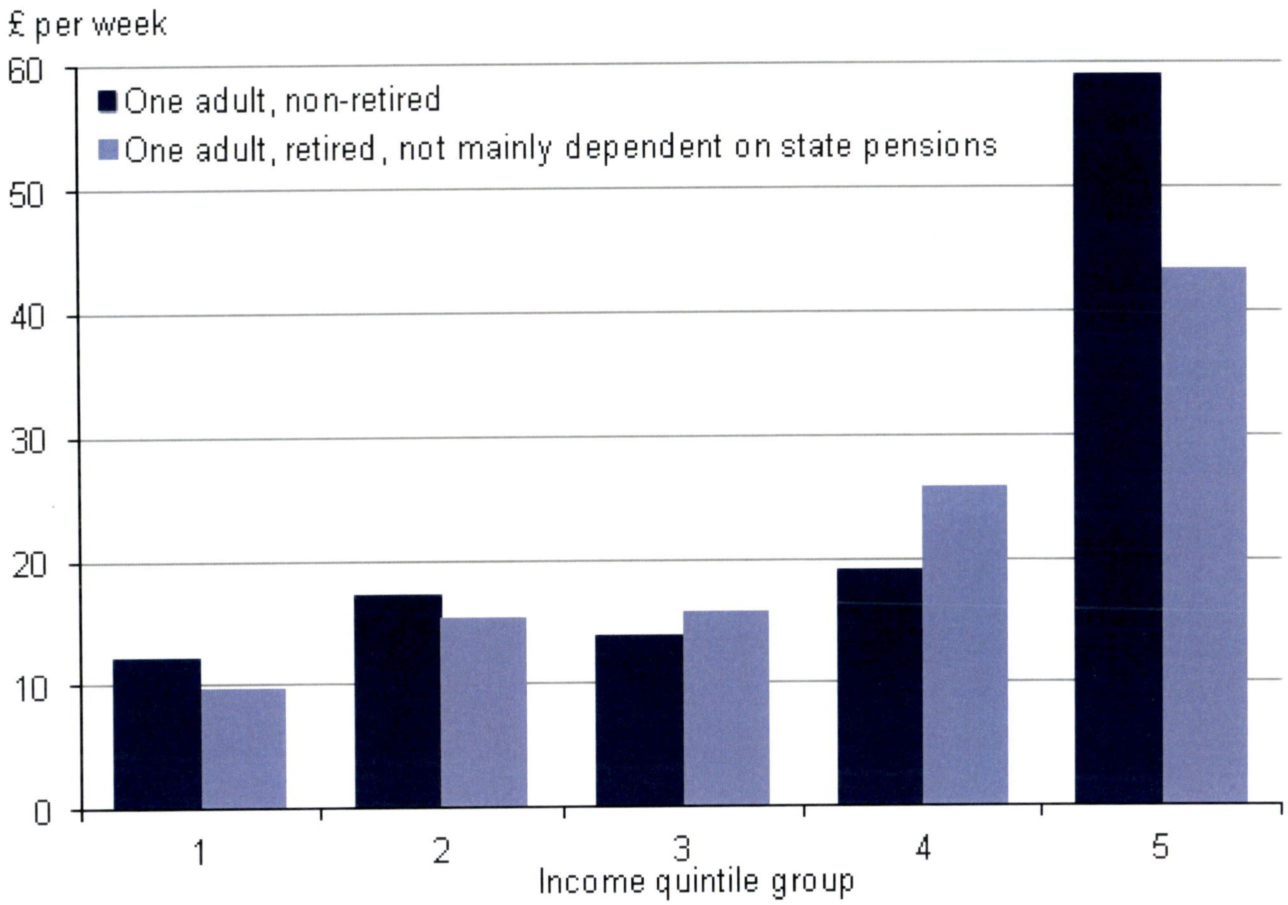

Source: Living Costs and Food Survey - Office for National Statistics

Download chart

XLS XLS format
(40.5 Kb)

As figure 3.9 shows, there is a general pattern of increasing expenditure on restaurants and hotels for both one adult non-retired and retired households, with non-retired households consistently spending more over income bands.

Figure 3.9: Expenditure on restaurants and hotels for one adult households by OECD-modified equivalised disposable income quintile group, 2013

United Kingdom

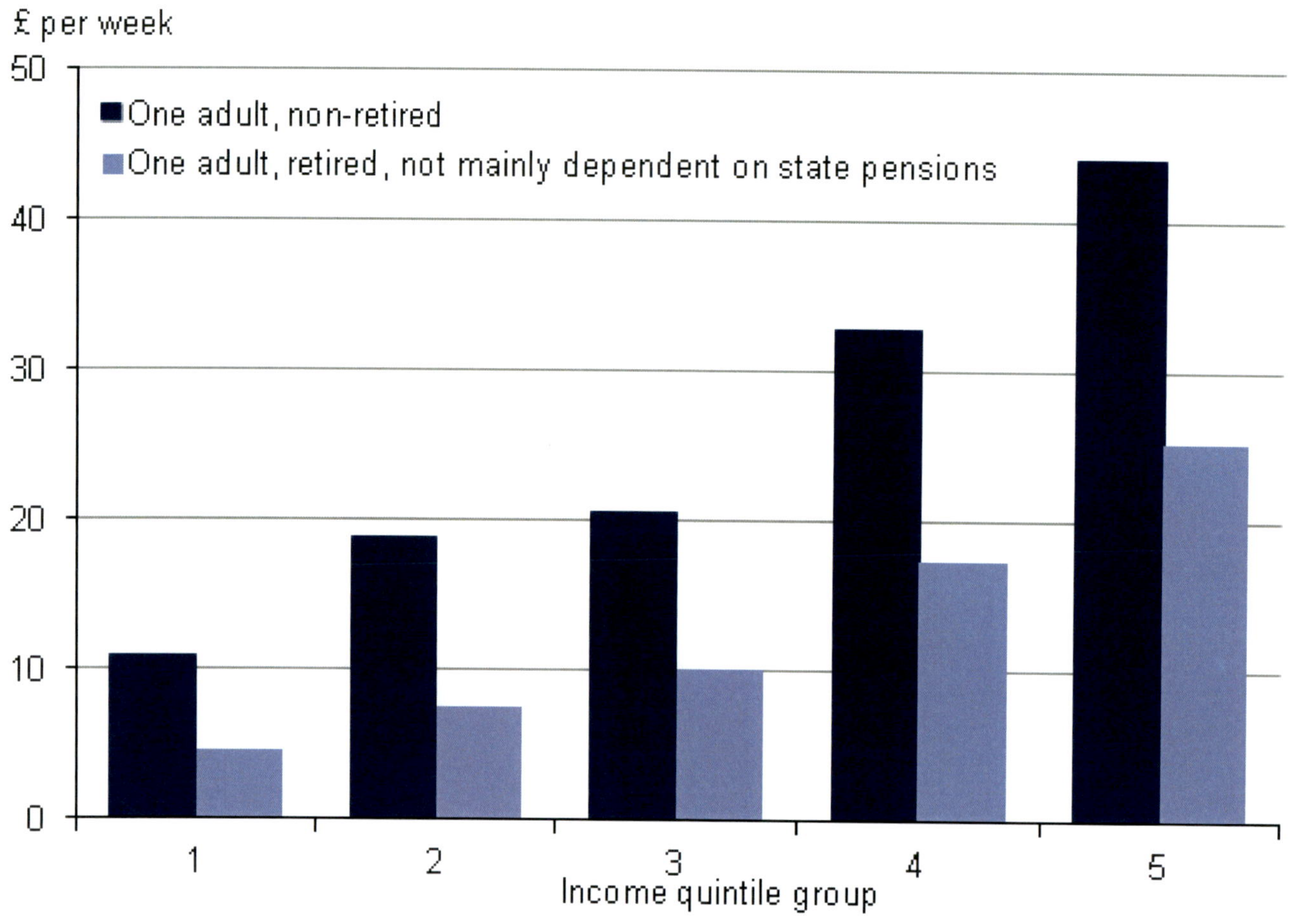

Source: Living Costs and Food Survey - Office for National Statistics

Download chart

XLS XLS format
(40.5 Kb)

These points illustrate how expenditure requirements differ between retired and non-retired households; note that non-retired households tend to have higher incomes. Income quintiles have been calculated separately for retired and non-retired households for this analysis, so patterns of expenditure within these groups can be explored meaningfully.

Examining spending patterns by income allows us to see how households prioritise spending on essentials, and how they balance this with enjoying some non-essential goods and services. The analysis above suggests that retired and non-retired households prioritise spending additional income differently for some spending categories. Equivalisation is a powerful tool to understand how income relates to the needs and choices of households of different sizes and compositions.

The complex findings give some clues as to what is important for well-being. Chapter 4 looks at how spending patterns have changed over time.

Equivalisation methodology

Equivalisation scales are used to adjust household income, taking into account household size and composition. There are various scales available, which differ in their complexity and methodology. The so-called OECD modified equivalence scale is used widely across Europe. It adjusts household income to reflect the different resource needs of single adults, any additional adults in the household, and children in various age groups.

The modified OECD equivalence scale is the standard scale for the Statistical Office of the European Union (Eurostat). It is also used by several government departments in the UK for key household income statistics. For example, the Department for Work and Pensions (DWP) use the modified OECD equivalence scale for their Households Below Average Income (HBAI) publication. ONS use it for the Effects of Taxes and Benefits on Household Income (ETB) analysis.

To calculate equivalised income using the modified OECD equivalence scale, each member of the household is first given an equivalence value. The modified OECD equivalence values are shown in table 3A. Single adult households are taken as the reference group and are given a value of one. For larger households, each additional adult is given a smaller value of 0.5 to reflect the economies of scale achieved when people live together. Economies of scale arise when households share resources such as water and electricity, which reduces the living costs per person. Children under the age of 14 are given a value of 0.3 to take account of their lower living costs, children aged 14 and over are given a value of 0.5 because their living costs are assumed to be the same as an adult.

Table 3A: OECD-modified equivalence scale as applied by household composition

Type of Household Member	Equivalence value
First adult	1.0
Additional adult	0.5
Child aged: 14 and over	0.5
Child aged: 0-13	0.3

Table source: Office for National Statistics

Download table

XLS XLS format
(30 Kb)

The equivalence values for each household member are summed to give a total equivalence number for the household. For example, the total equivalence value for a household with a married couple with two children aged 10 and 14 is calculated as follows:

1 (first adult) + 0.5 (second adult) + 0.5 (14-year-old child) + 0.3 (10-year-old child) = 2.3

The total equivalence value of 2.3 shows that the household needs more than twice the income of a single adult household in order to achieve a comparable standard of living.

In the final step of the calculation the total income for the household is divided by the equivalence value. For example, if the household described in the example above has an annual income of £30,000, their equivalised income is calculated as follows:

£30,000/2.3 = £13,043

For a single adult household with an income of £30,000, the equivalised income remains at £30,000. This is because the equivalence value for this household is equal to one. This demonstrates that a single adult household will have a higher standard of living than a larger household with the same level of income.

Equivalisation results

Equivalised household incomes were calculated for each household using the modified OECD equivalence scale. Household equivalised incomes were then ranked in ascending order and divided into ten equally-sized (decile) groups. Households with the lowest equivalised income make-up the first decile group. Non-equivalised disposable income data are presented in tables 3.1 to 3.11; equivalised disposable income data based on the modified OECD scale are shown in tables 3.1E to 3.11E.

The income decile groups can be seen in table 3B.

Table 3B: Income deciles for disposable weekly income and disposable weekly equivalised income, 2013

Income Decile	Disposable weekly income	Disposable weekly equivalised income (OECD-modified scale)
1	Up to £173	Up to £141
2	£174 to £255	£142 to £188
3	£256 to £332	£189 to £230
4	£333 to £416	£231 to £277
5	£417 to £503	£278 to £318
6	£504 to £599	£319 to £368
7	£600 to £719	£369 to £431
8	£720 to £881	£432 to £519
9	£882 to £1149	£520 to £663
10	£1,150 and over	£664 and over

Table source: Office for National Statistics

Download table

XLS XLS format
(31.5 Kb)

Table 3.12 (43.5 Kb Excel sheet) shows the household composition of the non-equivalised disposable income decile groups and the OECD-equivalised disposable income decile groups. Equivalisation has a large impact on the income positioning of households containing one adult without children. Households containing one non-retired adult accounted for only 3% of households in the highest non-equivalised disposable income decile group but when income was equivalised they accounted for 16%. These households tended to move to a higher income decile group after income was equivalised. These results demonstrate that when equivalisation is used to look at the incomes of all households on a comparable basis, single adult households tend to be better off than they appear pre-equivalisation.

The percentage of households where the household reference person is retired in each income group, before and after equivalisation is shown in figure 3.10. Equivalisation has a large effect on the proportion of retired households in the lowest income decile group. Before equivalisation, 15% of all retired households appeared in the lowest non-equivalised disposable income decile group; after equivalisation, only 7% of retired households appeared in this group. This result can largely be explained by the fact that a relatively high proportion of retired households contain only one adult. Therefore, as explained above, the incomes of single adult households are scaled up (relative to other households) when income is equivalised. The proportion of retired households in the second and third lowest income deciles also decreased after equivalisation, although the effect was much smaller. The opposite was true of the higher income decile groups; the proportion of retired households increased slightly after income was equivalised.

Figure 3.10: Percentage of retired households by non-equivalised and OECD-modified equivalised income decile group, 2013

United Kingdom

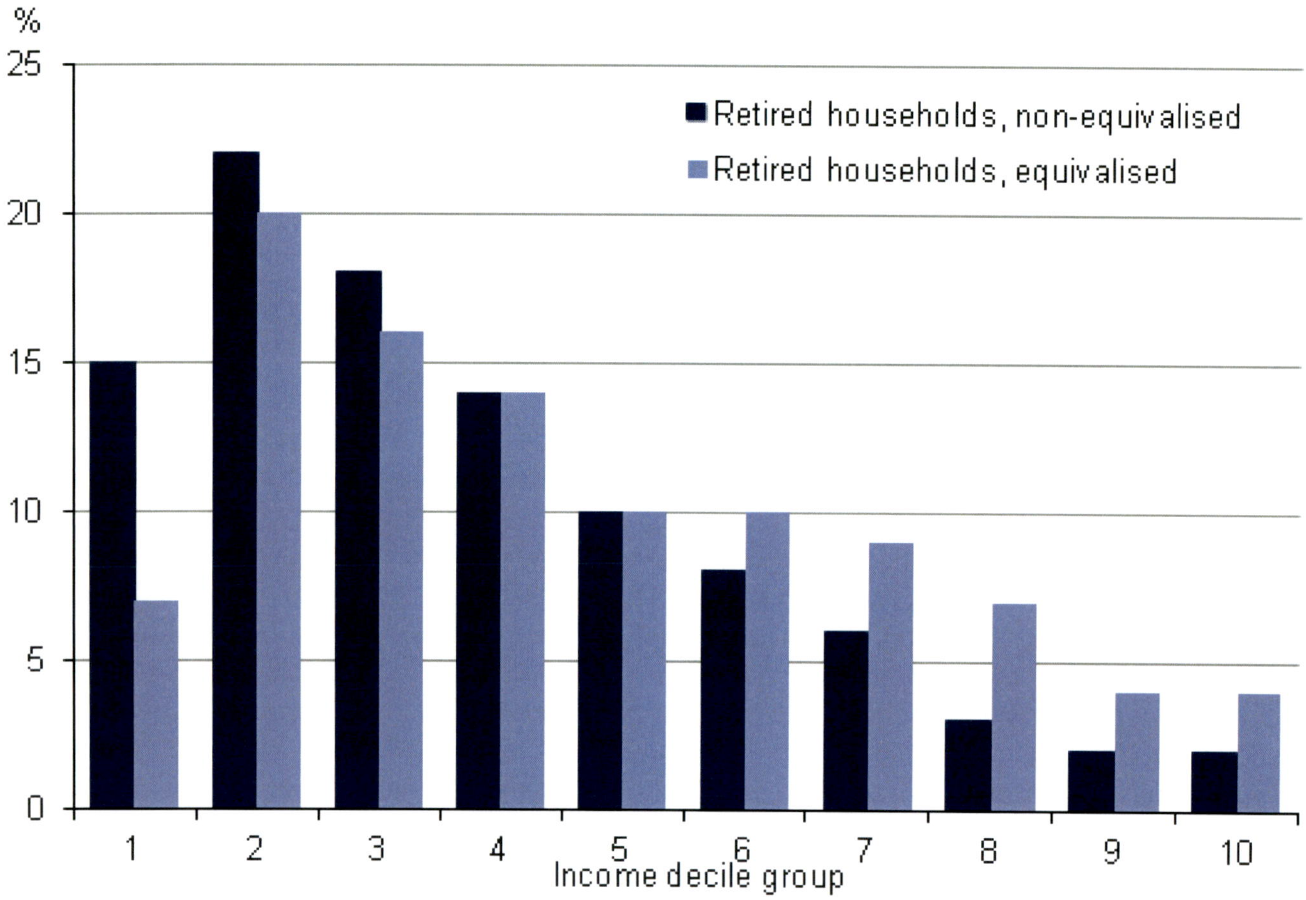

Source: Living Costs and Food Survey - Office for National Statistics

Download chart

XLS XLS format
(48 Kb)

Figure 3.11 shows the percentage of households with children in each income group, before and after income equivalisation. As non-equivalised disposable income increases, the proportion of households with children generally increases through the lower and middle income groups. Factoring in living costs for children as part of the equivalisation process brings about large changes in the income distribution. There are more households with children in the lower income groups and there is no longer an increase in the number of households with children as income increases.

Figure 3.11: Percentage of households with children in each non-equivalised and OECD-modified equivalised income decile group, 2013

United Kingdom

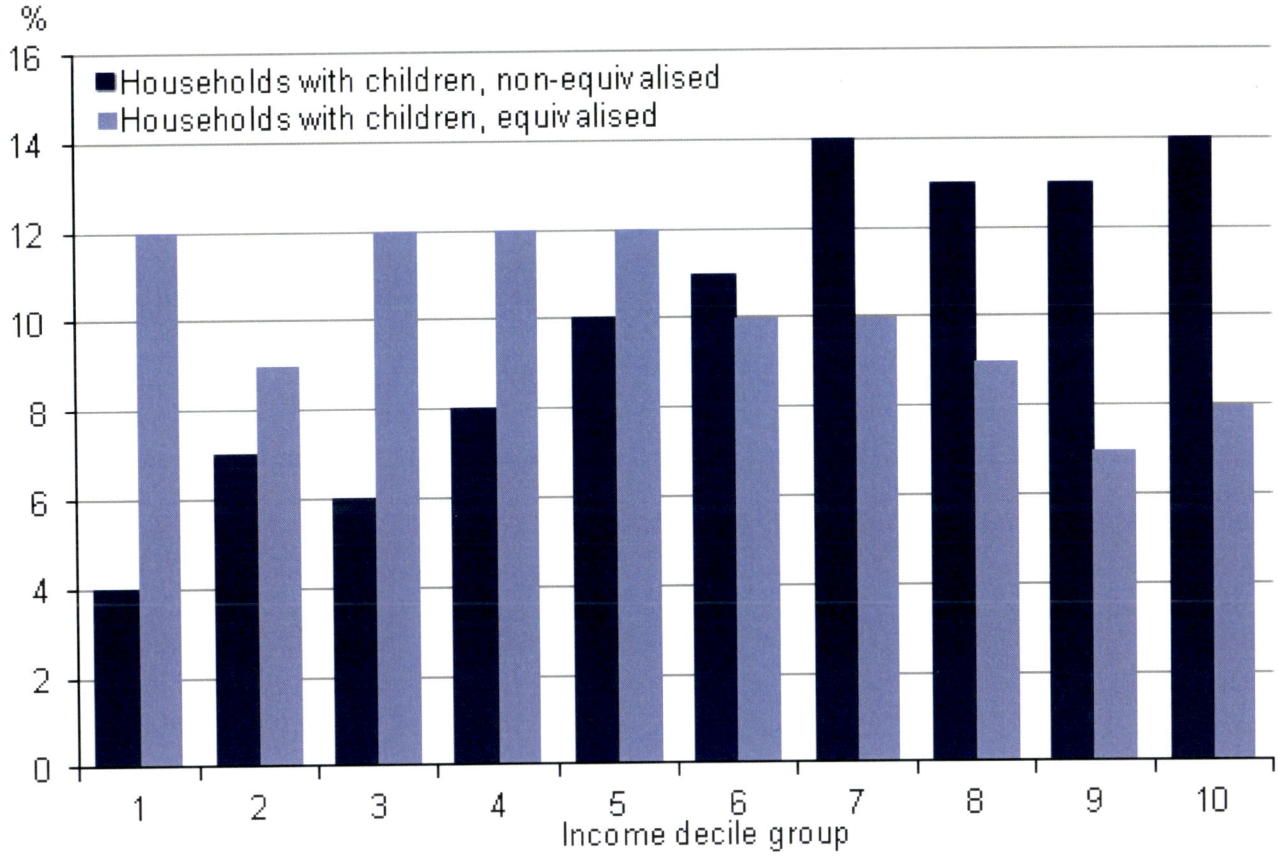

Source: Living Costs and Food Survey - Office for National Statistics

Download chart

XLS XLS format
(48.5 Kb)

Table 3.12 (43.5 Kb Excel sheet) also shows how equivalisation affects the average household size for each income decile group. As non-equivalised disposable income increases the average number of people in each household also increases. The average household size for the highest income group (3.2 people) was almost two and a half times that of the lowest income group (1.3 people). After income was equivalised, the average number of people in each household was more similar for each income decile group, with the average varying between 2.1 and 2.5. This pattern of results occurs because the equivalisation process scales up the income of households containing one adult (relative to other households) and scales down the income of households with more people.

This is the only chapter that presents equivalised income data. Other tables included in Family Spending are available on an equivalised income basis on request from ONS (see 'About this edition of Family Spending').

Background notes

1. **Symbols and conventions used in Family Spending 2014 edition**

[ ] Figures should be used with extra caution because they are based on fewer than 20 reporting households.

.. The data is suppressed if the unweighted sample counts are less than 10 reporting households.

- No figures are available because there are no reporting households.

Rounding: Individual figures have been rounded independently. The sum of component items does not therefore necessarily add to the totals shown.

Averages: These are averages (means) for all households included in the column or row, and unless specified, are not restricted to those households reporting expenditure on a particular item or income of a particular type.

Period covered: Calendar year 2013 (1 January 2013 to 31 December 2013).

2. **Contacts**

For information about the content of this publication, contact ONS Social Surveys Data Advice and Relations Team.

Tel +44 (0)1633 455678

Email: socialsurveys@ons.gsi.gov.uk

Other customer enquiries

ONS Customer Contact Centre

Tel: 0845 601 3034

International: +44 (0) 1633 817521

Minicom: +44 (0)1633 815044

Email: info@ons.gsi.gov.uk

Fax: +44 (0)1633 652747

Post: Room D265, Government Buildings,

Cardiff Road, Newport, South Wales NP10 8XG

www.ons.gov.uk

Media enquiries

Table 3.1
Detailed household expenditure by disposable income decile group, 2013
United Kingdom

	Lowest ten per cent	Second decile group	Third decile group	Fourth decile group	Fifth decile group	Sixth decile group	Seventh decile group	Eighth decile group	Ninth decile group	Highest ten per cent	All house-holds
Lower boundary of group (£ per week)		174	256	333	417	504	600	720	882	1,150	
Weighted number of households (thousands)	2,690	2,690	2,680	2,680	2,690	2,680	2,690	2,680	2,690	2,680	26,840
Total number of households in sample	500	510	550	530	530	540	520	500	500	480	5,140
Total number of persons in sample	660	830	970	1,130	1,250	1,340	1,490	1,420	1,490	1,540	12,120
Total number of adults in sample	570	670	790	890	960	1,020	1,060	1,080	1,150	1,170	9,350
Weighted average number of persons per household	1.3	1.6	1.7	2.1	2.3	2.5	2.9	2.8	3.0	3.2	2.4
Commodity or service	Average weekly household expenditure (£)										
1 Food & non-alcoholic drinks	**30.70**	**38.50**	**41.70**	**47.90**	**55.80**	**61.00**	**66.40**	**72.90**	**79.90**	**93.20**	**58.80**
1.1 Food	28.40	35.40	38.50	43.90	51.30	56.10	60.70	66.80	72.90	85.60	54.00
1.1.1 Bread, rice and cereals	3.10	3.80	4.00	4.70	5.80	5.50	6.40	7.00	7.40	7.90	5.60
1.1.2 Pasta products	0.20	0.20	0.30	0.30	0.40	0.40	0.50	0.60	0.70	0.80	0.40
1.1.3 Buns, cakes, biscuits etc.	1.80	2.70	2.60	3.00	3.70	3.80	4.10	4.40	4.50	5.30	3.60
1.1.4 Pastry (savoury)	0.40	0.40	0.50	0.60	0.80	0.90	1.00	1.00	1.20	1.50	0.80
1.1.5 Beef (fresh, chilled or frozen)	0.90	1.20	1.20	1.30	1.60	2.10	1.90	2.40	2.90	3.60	1.90
1.1.6 Pork (fresh, chilled or frozen)	0.40	0.50	0.60	0.60	0.60	0.70	0.80	0.90	0.70	0.80	0.70
1.1.7 Lamb (fresh, chilled or frozen)	0.40	0.50	0.60	0.60	0.60	0.60	0.50	0.90	0.80	1.10	0.70
1.1.8 Poultry (fresh, chilled or frozen)	1.10	1.20	1.50	1.80	2.00	2.90	2.60	3.20	3.50	4.40	2.40
1.1.9 Bacon and ham	0.50	0.70	0.80	0.90	0.90	1.10	1.10	1.30	1.30	1.60	1.00
1.1.10 Other meat and meat preparations	3.60	4.70	4.50	5.20	5.90	6.60	7.10	7.70	8.10	9.30	6.30
1.1.11 Fish and fish products	1.40	1.80	1.80	2.20	2.30	2.60	3.00	3.00	3.80	4.50	2.60
1.1.12 Milk	1.50	1.80	2.00	2.30	2.40	2.70	2.70	2.80	2.90	3.20	2.40
1.1.13 Cheese and curd	1.00	1.20	1.40	1.60	1.80	2.10	2.30	2.40	2.70	3.60	2.00
1.1.14 Eggs	0.50	0.50	0.60	0.60	0.70	0.70	0.80	0.90	1.00	1.20	0.70
1.1.15 Other milk products	1.00	1.30	1.40	1.60	2.00	2.10	2.50	2.50	2.60	3.40	2.10
1.1.16 Butter	0.30	0.30	0.30	0.40	0.50	0.50	0.50	0.60	0.70	0.70	0.50
1.1.17 Margarine, other vegetable fats and peanut butter	0.30	0.40	0.50	0.50	0.60	0.60	0.60	0.50	0.60	0.60	0.50
1.1.18 Cooking oils and fats	0.20	0.20	0.30	0.30	0.40	0.30	0.40	0.40	0.40	0.60	0.30
1.1.19 Fresh fruit	1.40	2.10	2.30	2.50	3.10	3.40	3.80	3.80	4.60	5.90	3.30
1.1.20 Other fresh, chilled or frozen fruits	0.20	0.20	0.30	0.30	0.30	0.30	0.40	0.60	0.50	0.80	0.40
1.1.21 Dried fruit and nuts	0.30	0.40	0.40	0.50	0.60	0.70	0.80	0.90	1.30	1.50	0.70
1.1.22 Preserved fruit and fruit based products	0.10	0.10	0.10	0.10	0.10	0.10	0.20	0.10	0.20	0.20	0.10
1.1.23 Fresh vegetables	2.30	2.50	3.00	3.30	3.90	4.40	4.70	5.50	6.30	7.50	4.30
1.1.24 Dried vegetables	[0.00]	[0.00]	[0.00]	[0.00]	0.10	0.00	0.10	0.10	0.10	0.10	0.10
1.1.25 Other preserved or processed vegetables	0.80	0.80	0.90	1.20	1.30	1.30	1.60	1.80	2.00	2.60	1.40
1.1.26 Potatoes	0.60	0.80	0.80	0.90	1.00	1.10	1.10	1.20	1.20	1.20	1.00
1.1.27 Other tubers and products of tuber vegetables	0.90	1.10	1.20	1.30	1.60	1.70	1.90	2.00	2.20	2.20	1.60
1.1.28 Sugar and sugar products	0.30	0.30	0.40	0.30	0.50	0.50	0.50	0.60	0.60	0.60	0.50
1.1.29 Jams, marmalades	0.20	0.20	0.30	0.20	0.30	0.30	0.30	0.30	0.30	0.40	0.30
1.1.30 Chocolate	0.80	1.00	1.20	1.60	1.60	1.90	2.10	2.30	2.60	2.70	1.80
1.1.31 Confectionery products	0.40	0.60	0.50	0.50	0.70	0.70	0.80	0.90	0.90	0.90	0.70
1.1.32 Edible ices and ice cream	0.30	0.40	0.40	0.50	0.60	0.70	0.70	0.70	0.70	0.90	0.60
1.1.33 Other food products	1.30	1.50	1.80	2.20	2.50	2.80	2.80	3.60	3.70	4.40	2.70
1.2 Non-alcoholic drinks	2.30	3.10	3.20	4.10	4.60	4.80	5.70	6.10	7.00	7.60	4.90
1.2.1 Coffee	0.40	0.60	0.60	0.70	0.60	0.70	0.80	0.80	1.00	1.20	0.70
1.2.2 Tea	0.30	0.40	0.40	0.40	0.50	0.50	0.50	0.50	0.50	0.60	0.50
1.2.3 Cocoa and powdered chocolate	0.10	0.10	0.10	0.10	0.10	0.10	0.10	0.10	0.20	0.20	0.10
1.2.4 Fruit and vegetable juices (inc. fruit squash)	0.50	0.70	0.70	0.90	1.10	1.20	1.50	1.70	1.90	2.40	1.20
1.2.5 Mineral or spring waters	0.10	0.20	0.20	0.20	0.20	0.30	0.30	0.30	0.40	0.70	0.30
1.2.6 Soft drinks (inc. fizzy and ready to drink fruit drinks)	0.90	1.10	1.30	1.70	2.00	2.10	2.60	2.70	3.00	2.60	2.00

Note: The commodity and service categories are not comparable to those in publications before 2001-02.
The numbering system is sequential, it does not use actual COICOP codes.
Please see background notes for symbols and conventions used in this report.

Table 3.1
Detailed household expenditure by disposable income decile group, 2013 (cont.)
United Kingdom

		Lowest ten per cent	Second decile group	Third decile group	Fourth decile group	Fifth decile group	Sixth decile group	Seventh decile group	Eighth decile group	Ninth decile group	Highest ten per cent	All house-holds
Commodity or service		Average weekly household expenditure (£)										
2	**Alcoholic drink, tobacco & narcotics**	**7.10**	**6.90**	**9.60**	**10.50**	**10.70**	**12.20**	**15.50**	**13.50**	**15.30**	**18.90**	**12.00**
2.1	Alcoholic drinks	3.50	3.30	4.50	5.10	6.10	7.70	9.30	9.80	12.10	15.50	7.70
2.1.1	Spirits and liqueurs (brought home)	1.20	1.00	1.30	1.20	1.50	1.50	1.90	1.60	2.00	2.30	1.60
2.1.2	Wines, fortified wines (brought home)	1.20	1.40	1.90	1.90	2.90	3.90	4.50	5.20	7.20	9.80	4.00
2.1.3	Beer, lager, ciders and perry (brought home)	1.00	0.90	1.30	2.00	1.70	2.20	2.80	2.90	2.90	3.30	2.10
2.1.4	Alcopops (brought home)	[0.10]	[0.00]	[0.00]	[0.00]	[0.00]	[0.10]	[0.00]	[0.00]	[0.00]	[0.10]	0.00
2.2	Tobacco and narcotics	3.60	3.60	5.10	5.40	4.60	4.40	6.20	3.70	3.30	3.40	4.30
2.2.1	Cigarettes	2.40	2.80	4.30	4.60	3.60	3.50	5.20	3.10	2.80	2.80	3.50
2.2.2	Cigars, other tobacco products and narcotics	1.20	0.80	0.80	0.70	1.00	1.00	1.00	0.60	0.50	0.70	0.80
3	**Clothing & footwear**	**6.70**	**7.10**	**10.10**	**15.80**	**17.10**	**24.20**	**28.40**	**31.30**	**37.10**	**48.20**	**22.60**
3.1	Clothing	5.50	5.70	8.00	13.00	13.20	19.90	22.50	24.70	30.70	39.40	18.30
3.1.1	Men's outer garments	1.10	1.00	1.30	3.60	3.20	5.60	6.10	6.30	8.10	10.30	4.70
3.1.2	Men's under garments	[0.10]	[0.10]	0.30	0.30	0.40	0.50	0.70	0.50	0.70	0.60	0.40
3.1.3	Women's outer garments	2.50	2.30	3.50	5.40	5.30	8.70	8.60	10.60	13.00	18.10	7.80
3.1.4	Women's under garments	0.60	0.50	0.70	0.70	0.70	1.10	1.40	1.40	2.00	2.40	1.10
3.1.5	Boys' outer garments (5-15)	[0.30]	[0.20]	0.60	0.60	1.10	1.00	1.30	0.90	1.30	1.10	0.80
3.1.6	Girls' outer garments (5-15)	[0.20]	0.40	0.50	0.60	0.70	0.60	1.50	1.10	1.60	2.00	0.90
3.1.7	Infants' outer garments (under 5)	[0.10]	0.30	0.40	0.50	0.70	0.70	0.90	1.50	1.30	1.20	0.80
3.1.8	Children's under garments (under 16)	[0.10]	0.30	0.10	0.50	0.20	0.40	0.60	0.50	0.70	0.70	0.40
3.1.9	Accessories	0.30	0.20	0.40	0.50	0.70	0.90	1.10	1.10	1.30	1.80	0.80
3.1.10	Haberdashery and clothing hire	[0.10]	[0.20]	0.20	0.20	0.20	0.20	0.20	0.30	0.20	0.40	0.20
3.1.11	Dry cleaners, laundry and dyeing	[0.20]	[0.20]	[0.10]	[0.20]	[0.10]	[0.20]	[0.20]	0.50	0.40	0.70	0.30
3.2	Footwear	1.30	1.50	2.10	2.70	3.80	4.30	5.90	6.60	6.40	8.90	4.30
4	**Housing (net)[1], fuel & power**	**51.00**	**57.40**	**66.00**	**75.40**	**81.20**	**77.60**	**78.10**	**80.70**	**81.90**	**94.50**	**74.40**
4.1	Actual rentals for housing	77.40	64.40	56.70	58.40	52.50	38.40	35.70	34.70	30.80	32.20	48.10
4.1.1	Gross rent	77.40	64.40	56.70	58.40	52.50	38.40	35.60	34.50	30.80	31.70	48.00
4.1.2	*less housing benefit, rebates & allowances rec'd*	55.20	40.30	25.50	20.60	10.50	4.60	2.00	[0.60]	[1.30]	[0.10]	16.10
4.1.3	Net rent[2]	22.20	24.20	31.20	37.80	42.00	33.80	33.60	33.80	29.50	31.60	32.00
4.1.4	Second dwelling rent	-	-	-	-	-	-	[0.10]	[0.20]	-	[0.50]	[0.10]
4.2	Maintenance and repair of dwelling	1.60	3.30	5.00	4.20	5.50	8.90	7.20	9.10	11.80	14.30	7.10
4.3	Water supply and miscellaneous services relating to the dwelling	6.90	7.60	7.50	8.30	9.00	8.30	9.50	9.50	9.30	10.90	8.70
4.4	Electricity, gas and other fuels[3]	20.40	22.30	22.30	25.00	24.70	26.60	27.60	28.20	31.30	37.20	26.50
4.4.1	Electricity	9.60	10.60	10.50	11.70	11.70	12.00	12.40	12.90	13.50	16.00	12.10
4.4.2	Gas	9.20	10.00	10.70	12.30	11.90	12.40	13.20	13.40	14.10	17.20	12.40
4.4.3	Other fuels	[1.50]	1.70	1.00	1.10	1.10	2.20	2.10	1.90	3.70	4.10	2.00

Note: The commodity and service categories are not comparable to those in publications before 2001-02.
The numbering system is sequential, it does not use actual COICOP codes.
Please see background notes for symbols and conventions used in this report.
1 Excluding mortgage interest payments, council tax and Northern Ireland rates.
2 The figure included in total expenditure is net rent as opposed to gross rent.
3 Recording of expenditure on gas and electricity via combined payment packages was changed in 2013. Recording of expenditure via slot meters was also changed.

Table 3.1
Detailed household expenditure by disposable income decile group, 2013 (cont.)
United Kingdom

Commodity or service		Lowest ten per cent	Second decile group	Third decile group	Fourth decile group	Fifth decile group	Sixth decile group	Seventh decile group	Eighth decile group	Ninth decile group	Highest ten per cent	All house-holds
		Average weekly household expenditure (£)										
5	**Household goods & services**	**13.80**	**15.30**	**20.40**	**23.90**	**26.00**	**36.20**	**34.20**	**38.70**	**43.30**	**80.00**	**33.10**
5.1	Furniture and furnishings, carpets and other floor coverings[4]	7.00	8.00	9.50	11.90	12.40	22.50	15.90	20.50	23.70	50.70	18.20
5.1.1	Furniture and furnishings	5.80	6.00	7.90	9.20	9.60	18.80	12.20	16.80	18.80	43.40	14.80
5.1.2	Floor coverings	1.10	2.00	1.60	2.70	2.80	3.70	3.70	3.60	4.90	7.30	3.40
5.2	Household textiles	0.90	0.60	0.80	1.40	2.50	1.40	2.30	2.90	2.60	3.10	1.80
5.3	Household appliances	2.00	1.50	2.40	3.10	2.90	3.70	3.80	3.70	2.50	5.00	3.10
5.4	Glassware, tableware and household utensils	0.50	0.50	0.80	0.90	1.40	1.30	1.50	2.20	2.10	4.40	1.60
5.5	Tools and equipment for house and garden	0.80	0.60	1.30	1.40	1.90	2.00	4.10	3.30	4.90	3.40	2.40
5.6	Goods and services for routine household maintenance	2.70	4.00	5.50	5.20	4.80	5.30	6.50	6.10	7.50	13.40	6.10
5.6.1	Cleaning materials	1.30	1.50	1.70	2.00	2.20	2.20	2.90	2.90	3.30	3.80	2.40
5.6.2	Household goods and hardware	0.70	1.10	0.90	1.10	1.20	1.70	1.60	1.60	1.90	2.60	1.40
5.6.3	Domestic services, carpet cleaning, hire/repair of furniture/furnishings	0.70	1.40	2.90	2.20	1.50	1.50	2.10	1.70	2.30	7.00	2.30
6	**Health**	**1.90**	**2.60**	**3.10**	**4.40**	**4.20**	**7.60**	**7.80**	**11.30**	**8.90**	**10.40**	**6.20**
6.1	Medical products, appliances and equipment	1.10	2.00	1.60	2.50	2.80	5.30	4.70	8.60	4.80	6.30	4.00
6.1.1	Medicines, prescriptions, healthcare products etc.	0.90	1.30	1.00	1.50	1.80	2.90	2.30	5.60	2.60	2.60	2.30
6.1.2	Spectacles, lenses, accessories and repairs	[0.20]	[0.70]	0.50	1.00	1.00	2.40	2.30	3.00	2.20	3.70	1.70
6.2	Hospital services	[0.80]	0.60	1.50	1.90	1.40	2.40	3.20	2.70	4.10	4.10	2.30
7	**Transport**	**16.30**	**19.10**	**33.30**	**41.70**	**60.00**	**72.80**	**79.00**	**96.80**	**117.60**	**167.80**	**70.40**
7.1	Purchase of vehicles	4.20	3.60	7.50	9.80	18.20	23.70	23.90	29.70	37.80	52.70	21.10
7.1.1	Purchase of new cars and vans	[2.20]	[1.00]	[2.70]	3.50	7.30	10.00	6.30	11.90	12.40	25.70	8.30
7.1.2	Purchase of second hand cars or vans	1.90	2.60	4.70	6.20	10.20	12.80	16.70	16.80	23.10	24.80	12.00
7.1.3	Purchase of motorcycles and other vehicles	[0.10]	-	[0.00]	[0.10]	[0.60]	[0.90]	[0.80]	[1.00]	[2.30]	[2.20]	0.80
7.2	Operation of personal transport	7.30	10.60	18.20	22.80	30.50	36.70	39.80	49.30	54.30	70.80	34.00
7.2.1	Spares and accessories	[0.50]	[0.40]	0.90	0.40	2.80	2.20	3.00	3.20	2.20	7.20	2.30
7.2.2	Petrol, diesel and other motor oils	5.00	7.60	13.00	16.30	19.50	25.50	29.00	34.90	38.90	45.30	23.50
7.2.3	Repairs and servicing	1.30	2.10	2.80	4.00	5.70	6.60	5.40	7.90	9.00	12.50	5.70
7.2.4	Other motoring costs	0.50	0.50	1.40	2.10	2.50	2.40	2.30	3.30	4.20	5.70	2.50
7.3	Transport services[5]	4.80	4.90	7.70	9.20	11.30	12.50	15.30	17.90	25.50	44.40	15.30
7.3.1	Rail and tube fares	1.00	0.60	0.90	1.80	2.40	2.30	3.20	4.50	8.30	13.60	3.90
7.3.2	Bus and coach fares	1.20	1.10	1.30	1.40	1.30	2.40	2.20	1.80	1.90	1.50	1.60
7.3.3	Combined fares	[0.00]	[0.00]	[0.20]	[1.00]	[0.60]	[0.70]	[0.30]	[1.10]	1.70	2.30	0.80
7.3.4	Other travel and transport	2.50	3.20	5.30	4.90	7.00	7.00	9.70	10.50	13.60	27.00	9.10
8	**Communication**	**7.10**	**8.10**	**10.60**	**11.80**	**13.70**	**16.10**	**16.50**	**18.30**	**20.30**	**22.00**	**14.50**
8.1	Postal services	0.30	0.30	0.40	0.50	0.60	0.50	0.60	0.70	1.00	1.20	0.60
8.2	Telephone and telefax equipment	[0.10]	[0.20]	[0.40]	[0.50]	[0.10]	1.20	0.50	0.50	0.90	0.80	0.50
8.3	Telephone and telefax services	5.30	6.20	7.70	8.30	10.20	11.20	12.20	13.70	15.00	16.00	10.60
8.4	Internet subscription fees	1.40	1.50	2.00	2.50	2.80	3.20	3.30	3.40	3.50	4.10	2.80

Note: The commodity and service categories are not comparable to those in publications before 2001-02.
The numbering system is sequential, it does not use actual COICOP codes.
Please see background notes for symbols and conventions used in this report.
4 Recording of expenditure on furniture was changed in 2013.
5 Recording of expenditure on flights was changed in 2013.

Table 3.1
Detailed household expenditure by disposable income decile group, 2013 (cont.)
United Kingdom

	Commodity or service	Lowest ten per cent	Second decile group	Third decile group	Fourth decile group	Fifth decile group	Sixth decile group	Seventh decile group	Eighth decile group	Ninth decile group	Highest ten per cent	All house-holds
		Average weekly household expenditure (£)										
9	**Recreation & culture**	**18.30**	**22.20**	**32.30**	**39.30**	**53.20**	**62.80**	**70.10**	**81.10**	**99.80**	**160.40**	**63.90**
9.1	Audio-visual, photographic and information processing equipment	2.10	1.20	2.50	3.10	3.70	5.20	6.70	6.30	8.40	12.20	5.10
9.1.1	Audio equipment and accessories, CD players	[0.30]	0.10	0.20	0.30	0.90	0.80	2.00	1.20	1.30	2.10	0.90
9.1.2	TV, video and computers	1.80	1.10	2.10	2.70	2.40	4.00	4.60	4.90	6.80	9.00	3.90
9.1.3	Photographic, cine and optical equipment	[0.00]	[0.00]	[0.20]	[0.10]	[0.40]	[0.40]	[0.10]	[0.20]	[0.30]	[1.10]	0.30
9.2	Other major durables for recreation and culture	[0.30]	[0.70]	[0.80]	[1.00]	[0.30]	[0.60]	[1.80]	[1.80]	[5.40]	8.10	2.10
9.3	Other recreational items and equipment, gardens and pets	4.00	4.10	6.00	7.80	8.80	10.60	12.40	14.80	15.70	20.40	10.40
9.3.1	Games, toys and hobbies	0.60	0.80	1.00	1.20	2.00	2.20	2.60	3.60	3.80	5.00	2.30
9.3.2	Computer software and games	[0.30]	[0.20]	[0.30]	0.50	0.80	1.00	1.40	0.60	1.40	1.80	0.80
9.3.3	Equipment for sport, camping and open-air recreation	[0.30]	[0.10]	[0.30]	0.60	0.50	1.10	1.40	1.30	1.90	1.30	0.90
9.3.4	Horticultural goods, garden equipment and plants	0.90	1.00	1.70	1.60	2.10	2.30	2.20	2.50	3.30	4.00	2.20
9.3.5	Pets and pet food	1.90	1.90	2.70	3.90	3.40	3.90	4.80	6.80	5.30	8.30	4.30
9.4	Recreational and cultural services	6.70	8.00	11.80	12.30	14.90	18.90	22.30	26.00	28.20	36.80	18.60
9.4.1	Sports admissions, subscriptions, leisure class fees and equipment hire	0.90	1.00	2.20	2.50	3.10	6.50	5.80	8.70	9.40	15.30	5.50
9.4.2	Cinema, theatre and museums etc.	[0.30]	0.40	1.00	1.10	2.10	1.50	3.20	3.30	4.80	5.60	2.30
9.4.3	TV, video, satellite rental, cable subscriptions and TV licences	3.60	4.10	5.00	5.90	6.50	7.20	7.60	8.60	8.60	9.50	6.70
9.4.4	Miscellaneous entertainments	0.30	0.50	0.50	0.50	0.90	0.90	2.00	1.80	2.00	2.90	1.20
9.4.5	Development of film, deposit for film development, passport photos, holiday and school photos	[0.00]	[0.10]	[0.20]	[0.10]	[0.20]	[0.20]	0.20	0.60	0.30	0.40	0.20
9.4.6	Gambling payments	1.50	2.00	2.90	2.20	2.20	2.60	3.50	3.00	3.10	3.00	2.60
9.5	Newspapers, books and stationery	2.20	3.10	3.90	3.90	5.10	5.60	5.60	6.80	7.50	9.10	5.30
9.5.1	Books	0.30	0.30	0.60	0.80	1.10	0.90	1.00	1.60	1.80	2.40	1.10
9.5.2	Diaries, address books, cards etc.	0.60	0.80	1.10	1.10	1.60	1.90	2.00	2.60	2.90	4.00	1.90
9.5.3	Newspapers	0.90	1.40	1.60	1.50	1.70	1.80	1.60	1.70	1.90	1.50	1.60
9.5.4	Magazines and periodicals	0.40	0.50	0.60	0.50	0.80	1.00	1.00	0.90	0.90	1.10	0.80
9.6	Package holidays[6]	3.00	5.00	7.30	11.20	20.40	21.90	21.30	25.60	34.60	73.90	22.40
9.6.1	Package holidays - UK	[0.50]	0.90	1.20	1.70	2.00	1.20	0.90	1.50	2.40	2.10	1.40
9.6.2	Package holidays - abroad	2.40	4.10	6.10	9.50	18.40	20.70	20.40	24.00	32.20	71.80	21.00
10	**Education**	**[4.30]**	**[1.80]**	**[3.90]**	**[14.40]**	**7.20**	**1.90**	**3.20**	**6.50**	**21.40**	**23.40**	**8.80**
10.1	Education fees	[4.30]	[1.70]	[3.60]	[14.30]	[6.80]	1.60	2.70	6.20	20.80	22.80	8.50
10.2	Payments for school trips, other ad-hoc expenditure	[0.00]	[0.10]	[0.30]	[0.10]	[0.40]	[0.30]	0.60	[0.30]	[0.60]	[0.50]	0.30
11	**Restaurants & hotels**	**10.60**	**12.00**	**19.40**	**26.50**	**30.00**	**38.80**	**47.10**	**54.40**	**71.40**	**93.60**	**40.40**
11.1	Catering services	9.20	10.50	17.00	22.40	24.60	32.50	41.20	46.70	59.20	72.30	33.50
11.1.1	Restaurant and café meals	4.30	5.20	8.30	11.10	11.60	14.80	18.70	21.30	28.40	35.40	15.90
11.1.2	Alcoholic drinks (away from home)	2.00	1.90	3.20	4.30	4.90	7.10	8.70	10.70	12.60	16.00	7.10
11.1.3	Take away meals eaten at home	1.40	1.50	2.60	3.20	3.40	4.30	5.80	5.80	6.80	7.10	4.20
11.1.4	Other take-away and snack food	1.20	1.40	2.10	2.60	3.00	4.40	5.20	6.40	8.00	9.50	4.40
11.1.5	Contract catering (food) and canteens	0.30	0.50	0.70	1.20	1.70	1.90	2.80	2.50	3.40	4.30	1.90
11.2	Accommodation services	1.40	1.50	2.40	4.10	5.40	6.30	5.90	7.70	12.30	21.30	6.80
11.2.1	Holiday in the UK	1.20	1.00	1.90	2.70	4.30	4.50	3.80	4.40	7.80	8.80	4.00
11.2.2	Holiday abroad	[0.20]	[0.50]	[0.50]	[1.30]	[1.10]	1.80	2.00	3.30	4.20	12.30	2.70
11.2.3	Room hire	[0.00]	[0.00]	[0.00]	[0.00]	[0.00]	[0.00]	[0.00]	[0.00]	[0.30]	[0.20]	[0.10]

Note: The commodity and service categories are not comparable to those in publications before 2001-02.
The numbering system is sequential, it does not use actual COICOP codes.
Please see background notes for symbols and conventions used in this report.
6 Recording of expenditure on package holidays was changed in 2013.

Table 3.1
Detailed household expenditure by disposable income decile group, 2013 (cont.)
United Kingdom

Commodity or service	Lowest ten per cent	Second decile group	Third decile group	Fourth decile group	Fifth decile group	Sixth decile group	Seventh decile group	Eighth decile group	Ninth decile group	Highest ten per cent	All house-holds
	Average weekly household expenditure (£)										
12 Miscellaneous goods & services	**12.00**	**15.20**	**23.10**	**24.60**	**32.90**	**37.50**	**46.70**	**52.70**	**58.20**	**88.30**	**39.10**
12.1 Personal care	4.10	5.00	7.30	8.50	7.90	11.20	14.20	14.70	16.60	22.00	11.20
12.1.1 Hairdressing, beauty treatment	1.20	1.50	2.70	2.70	2.00	3.50	4.30	4.60	5.10	6.90	3.40
12.1.2 Toilet paper	0.50	0.60	0.60	0.70	0.80	0.90	1.00	1.00	0.90	1.40	0.80
12.1.3 Toiletries and soap	1.10	1.30	1.60	2.00	2.10	2.30	2.90	3.40	3.70	4.40	2.50
12.1.4 Baby toiletries and accessories (disposable)	0.20	0.30	0.30	0.40	0.70	0.70	0.90	0.70	0.90	1.10	0.60
12.1.5 Hair products, cosmetics and related electrical appliances	1.20	1.30	2.10	2.80	2.30	3.80	5.10	4.90	6.00	8.30	3.80
12.2 Personal effects	0.50	1.10	1.30	1.50	2.50	2.70	4.20	4.50	3.70	8.10	3.00
12.3 Social protection	[0.40]	[0.70]	[1.50]	[0.30]	3.70	[1.50]	4.60	9.10	7.40	11.40	4.10
12.4 Insurance	5.40	7.40	10.00	12.20	15.90	17.50	19.90	21.00	24.40	34.20	16.80
12.4.1 Household insurances - structural, contents and appliances	2.00	3.60	3.70	3.90	4.60	5.30	5.50	5.70	7.40	8.80	5.10
12.4.2 Medical insurance premiums	[0.30]	0.20	0.50	0.60	1.30	2.00	2.20	2.60	2.70	7.80	2.00
12.4.3 Vehicle insurance including boat insurance	2.90	3.60	5.70	7.40	9.90	10.20	12.10	12.70	14.20	16.50	9.50
12.4.4 Non-package holiday, other travel insurance	[0.20]	-	[0.00]	[0.30]	[0.00]	[0.00]	[0.10]	[0.00]	[0.20]	[1.10]	0.20
12.5 Other services	1.60	1.00	3.10	2.00	2.90	4.70	3.80	3.40	6.10	12.50	4.10
12.5.1 Moving house	[1.00]	[0.70]	[0.90]	0.90	1.80	2.10	2.10	1.30	3.50	7.00	2.10
12.5.2 Bank, building society, post office, credit card charges	0.20	0.20	0.30	0.30	0.50	0.50	0.60	0.70	0.60	1.10	0.50
12.5.3 Other services and professional fees	[0.30]	[0.10]	1.90	0.80	0.60	2.00	1.10	1.50	2.00	4.40	1.50
1-12 All expenditure groups	**179.90**	**206.10**	**273.60**	**336.10**	**391.80**	**448.80**	**493.10**	**558.40**	**655.20**	**900.80**	**444.30**
13 Other expenditure items	**16.40**	**23.20**	**35.00**	**40.30**	**50.80**	**65.60**	**79.00**	**84.60**	**117.20**	**218.30**	**73.00**
13.1 Housing: mortgage interest payments, council tax etc.	10.10	14.30	21.30	25.10	33.00	39.90	54.10	60.20	73.80	111.70	44.30
13.2 Licences, fines and transfers	1.00	1.30	2.10	2.90	2.70	3.70	5.20	4.90	8.10	6.30	3.80
13.3 Holiday spending	[1.70]	[2.30]	[3.30]	[3.20]	[3.80]	5.20	5.80	7.10	13.10	73.10	11.80
13.4 Money transfers and credit	3.60	5.30	8.30	9.00	11.40	16.80	14.00	12.50	22.20	27.20	13.00
13.4.1 Money, cash gifts given to children	[0.00]	[0.00]	[0.00]	[0.00]	[0.30]	[0.10]	[0.20]	[0.10]	0.30	[0.20]	0.10
13.4.2 Cash gifts and donations[7]	3.20	5.00	7.80	8.20	9.70	15.80	12.10	9.90	20.50	24.80	11.70
13.4.3 Club instalment payments (child) and interest on credit cards	0.40	0.20	0.50	0.80	1.40	1.00	1.60	2.40	1.40	2.20	1.20
Total expenditure	**196.30**	**229.30**	**308.60**	**376.40**	**442.70**	**514.40**	**572.10**	**643.00**	**772.40**	**1119.10**	**517.30**
14 Other items recorded											
14.1 Life assurance and contributions to pension funds	1.40	1.80	3.40	4.40	9.40	11.50	18.00	27.30	41.10	80.40	19.90
14.2 Other insurance inc. friendly societies	0.20	0.20	0.50	0.70	1.20	1.30	3.10	1.40	2.20	3.10	1.40
14.3 Income tax, payments *less* refunds	3.60	4.60	16.10	27.20	42.60	55.30	79.10	107.80	164.50	385.00	88.50
14.4 National insurance contributions	0.60	0.90	4.50	9.00	16.30	20.40	33.00	44.90	63.60	89.50	28.30
14.5 Purchase or alteration of dwellings, mortgages	14.30	9.50	11.30	14.30	39.60	37.30	61.10	56.60	76.90	168.20	48.90
14.6 Savings and investments	[0.90]	0.50	1.30	1.70	2.80	4.20	3.70	8.20	9.40	23.90	5.70
14.7 Pay off loan to clear other debt	[0.10]	[0.40]	0.80	2.00	3.00	1.80	4.20	4.10	5.80	4.30	2.60
14.8 Windfall receipts from gambling etc[8]	0.90	0.70	1.10	0.90	1.00	0.80	1.10	2.10	0.90	2.10	1.20

Note: The commodity and service categories are not comparable to those in publications before 2001-02.
The numbering system is sequential, it does not use actual COICOP codes.
Please see background notes for symbols and conventions used in this report.
7 Recording of expenditure on money sent abroad was changed in 2013.
8 Expressed as an income figure as opposed to an expenditure figure.

Table 3.1E
Detailed household expenditure by equivalised disposable income decile group, 2013
United Kingdom

	Lowest ten per cent	Second decile group	Third decile group	Fourth decile group	Fifth decile group	Sixth decile group	Seventh decile group	Eighth decile group	Ninth decile group	Highest ten per cent	All house-holds
Lower boundary of group (£ per week)		142	189	231	278	319	369	432	520	664	
Weighted number of households (thousands)	2,690	2,680	2,680	2,690	2,680	2,680	2,690	2,680	2,690	2,680	26,840
Total number of households in sample	500	520	530	530	530	520	520	510	500	490	5,140
Total number of persons in sample	1,060	1,140	1,300	1,310	1,300	1,230	1,250	1,240	1,170	1,120	12,120
Total number of adults in sample	730	840	920	950	970	990	1,010	1,010	1,000	950	9,350
Weighted average number of persons per household	2.1	2.2	2.4	2.4	2.5	2.4	2.4	2.5	2.4	2.3	2.4
Commodity or service	Average weekly household expenditure (£)										
1 Food & non-alcoholic drinks	**40.70**	**44.40**	**52.80**	**53.90**	**58.40**	**62.20**	**63.80**	**66.90**	**69.50**	**75.40**	**58.80**
1.1 Food	37.30	40.80	48.30	49.30	53.50	57.00	58.50	61.50	64.20	69.20	54.00
1.1.1 Bread, rice and cereals	4.20	4.60	5.50	5.30	5.90	5.90	5.90	6.20	5.80	6.20	5.60
1.1.2 Pasta products	0.30	0.30	0.40	0.40	0.40	0.50	0.40	0.50	0.50	0.60	0.40
1.1.3 Buns, cakes, biscuits etc.	2.50	2.90	3.50	3.40	3.70	3.80	3.90	3.90	3.90	4.30	3.60
1.1.4 Pastry (savoury)	0.50	0.60	0.70	0.70	0.80	0.90	0.90	0.90	1.10	1.10	0.80
1.1.5 Beef (fresh, chilled or frozen)	1.30	1.20	1.40	1.70	1.80	2.10	2.00	2.30	2.80	2.70	1.90
1.1.6 Pork (fresh, chilled or frozen)	0.40	0.60	0.80	0.70	0.70	0.70	0.70	0.80	0.70	0.60	0.70
1.1.7 Lamb (fresh, chilled or frozen)	0.60	0.50	0.60	0.70	0.60	0.50	0.60	0.60	1.00	0.80	0.70
1.1.8 Poultry (fresh, chilled or frozen)	1.50	1.60	2.00	2.10	2.40	2.50	2.70	3.00	2.80	3.40	2.40
1.1.9 Bacon and ham	0.60	0.80	0.90	1.00	1.00	1.10	1.00	1.20	1.30	1.20	1.00
1.1.10 Other meat and meat preparations	4.50	4.90	5.80	5.70	6.60	6.80	6.80	7.00	7.10	7.40	6.30
1.1.11 Fish and fish products	1.90	1.70	1.90	2.30	2.40	2.60	2.90	3.10	3.60	4.10	2.60
1.1.12 Milk	2.00	2.30	2.50	2.40	2.70	2.50	2.60	2.30	2.50	2.50	2.40
1.1.13 Cheese and curd	1.20	1.40	1.70	1.70	2.00	2.00	2.20	2.50	2.40	2.80	2.00
1.1.14 Eggs	0.50	0.60	0.60	0.70	0.70	0.90	0.70	0.90	0.90	0.90	0.70
1.1.15 Other milk products	1.30	1.50	2.00	1.80	2.00	2.30	2.30	2.20	2.40	2.70	2.10
1.1.16 Butter	0.30	0.40	0.40	0.40	0.50	0.50	0.60	0.60	0.60	0.60	0.50
1.1.17 Margarine, other vegetable fats and peanut butter	0.40	0.50	0.60	0.60	0.60	0.50	0.50	0.50	0.50	0.50	0.50
1.1.18 Cooking oils and fats	0.30	0.30	0.30	0.40	0.30	0.40	0.30	0.30	0.40	0.50	0.30
1.1.19 Fresh fruit	2.00	2.10	2.70	2.90	3.00	3.40	3.60	4.00	4.10	5.10	3.30
1.1.20 Other fresh, chilled or frozen fruits	0.20	0.20	0.30	0.30	0.30	0.40	0.40	0.50	0.60	0.60	0.40
1.1.21 Dried fruit and nuts	0.40	0.40	0.50	0.60	0.60	0.70	0.90	0.80	1.10	1.40	0.70
1.1.22 Preserved fruit and fruit based products	0.10	0.10	0.10	0.10	0.10	0.10	0.10	0.20	0.20	0.10	0.10
1.1.23 Fresh vegetables	2.80	3.20	3.30	3.60	3.80	4.40	4.60	5.50	5.60	6.50	4.30
1.1.24 Dried vegetables	[0.00]	0.10	0.10	0.00	0.00	[0.00]	0.10	0.10	0.10	0.10	0.10
1.1.25 Other preserved or processed vegetables	1.00	1.00	1.00	1.10	1.30	1.50	1.50	1.60	1.90	2.20	1.40
1.1.26 Potatoes	0.70	0.90	1.00	1.00	1.10	1.10	1.10	1.10	1.10	0.90	1.00
1.1.27 Other tubers and products of tuber vegetables	1.20	1.40	1.60	1.80	1.70	1.80	1.80	1.70	1.60	1.50	1.60
1.1.28 Sugar and sugar products	0.40	0.50	0.40	0.40	0.40	0.60	0.50	0.40	0.50	0.50	0.50
1.1.29 Jams, marmalades	0.20	0.20	0.30	0.20	0.30	0.20	0.40	0.30	0.40	0.30	0.30
1.1.30 Chocolate	1.10	1.10	1.80	1.70	2.00	1.80	2.10	1.90	2.10	2.30	1.80
1.1.31 Confectionery products	0.50	0.60	0.70	0.60	0.70	0.80	0.80	0.70	0.70	0.60	0.70
1.1.32 Edible ices and ice cream	0.40	0.40	0.70	0.60	0.70	0.70	0.60	0.60	0.50	0.70	0.60
1.1.33 Other food products	1.90	1.90	2.10	2.20	2.50	3.00	2.90	3.20	3.50	3.40	2.70
1.2 Non-alcoholic drinks	3.50	3.60	4.50	4.70	4.90	5.20	5.30	5.40	5.30	6.20	4.90
1.2.1 Coffee	0.50	0.60	0.70	0.70	0.70	0.70	0.80	0.80	0.90	1.10	0.70
1.2.2 Tea	0.40	0.40	0.50	0.50	0.40	0.50	0.50	0.50	0.50	0.50	0.50
1.2.3 Cocoa and powdered chocolate	0.10	0.10	0.10	0.10	0.10	0.20	0.10	0.10	0.10	0.20	0.10
1.2.4 Fruit and vegetable juices (inc. fruit squash)	0.80	0.70	1.00	1.10	1.30	1.30	1.40	1.50	1.50	1.90	1.20
1.2.5 Mineral or spring waters	0.30	0.20	0.20	0.20	0.20	0.30	0.40	0.30	0.30	0.60	0.30
1.2.6 Soft drinks (inc. fizzy and ready to drink fruit drinks)	1.50	1.60	1.90	2.10	2.20	2.20	2.20	2.20	2.00	2.00	2.00

Note: The commodity and service categories are not comparable to those in publications before 2001-02.
The numbering system is sequential, it does not use actual COICOP codes.
Please see background notes for symbols and conventions used in this report.

Table 3.1E
Detailed household expenditure by equivalised disposable income decile group, 2013 (cont.)
United Kingdom

Commodity or service	Lowest ten per cent	Second decile group	Third decile group	Fourth decile group	Fifth decile group	Sixth decile group	Seventh decile group	Eighth decile group	Ninth decile group	Highest ten per cent	All house-holds
	Average weekly household expenditure (£)										
2 Alcoholic drink, tobacco & narcotics	**8.40**	**9.40**	**9.80**	**9.10**	**10.80**	**15.00**	**12.00**	**15.20**	**14.00**	**16.60**	**12.00**
2.1 Alcoholic drinks	3.50	4.20	4.60	5.20	6.20	9.40	8.40	10.40	10.60	14.30	7.70
2.1.1 Spirits and liqueurs (brought home)	1.10	1.20	1.30	1.00	1.50	2.00	1.60	2.00	1.60	2.30	1.60
2.1.2 Wines, fortified wines (brought home)	1.30	1.70	1.80	2.20	3.10	4.40	4.00	5.70	6.30	9.50	4.00
2.1.3 Beer, lager, ciders and perry (brought home)	1.10	1.30	1.40	2.00	1.60	3.00	2.70	2.70	2.70	2.40	2.10
2.1.4 Alcopops (brought home)	[0.10]	[0.00]	[0.00]	[0.10]	[0.10]	[0.00]	[0.10]	[0.00]	[0.00]	[0.00]	0.00
2.2 Tobacco and narcotics	4.80	5.20	5.20	3.80	4.60	5.60	3.60	4.80	3.30	2.40	4.30
2.2.1 Cigarettes	3.30	3.80	4.30	3.30	3.90	4.80	2.80	4.00	2.80	2.00	3.50
2.2.2 Cigars, other tobacco products and narcotics	1.50	1.40	0.90	0.50	0.70	0.80	0.90	0.70	0.50	[0.40]	0.80
3 Clothing & footwear	**9.50**	**11.10**	**15.10**	**14.60**	**21.00**	**25.30**	**26.50**	**29.70**	**35.70**	**37.50**	**22.60**
3.1 Clothing	7.60	8.30	12.10	11.60	16.80	19.50	22.20	24.30	29.10	31.00	18.30
3.1.1 Men's outer garments	1.60	1.50	2.80	2.60	3.60	5.90	5.10	6.60	7.90	9.00	4.70
3.1.2 Men's under garments	0.20	[0.10]	0.40	0.40	0.50	0.40	0.60	0.60	0.60	0.50	0.40
3.1.3 Women's outer garments	2.50	3.60	4.30	4.70	7.20	7.50	10.00	10.20	13.90	14.00	7.80
3.1.4 Women's under garments	0.50	0.50	0.90	0.90	1.00	1.20	1.20	1.70	1.70	1.90	1.10
3.1.5 Boys' outer garments (5-15)	0.70	0.60	1.40	0.40	1.10	1.10	1.10	0.70	0.60	0.70	0.80
3.1.6 Girls' outer garments (5-15)	0.70	0.50	0.70	0.80	1.00	1.00	1.00	1.10	1.00	1.50	0.90
3.1.7 Infants' outer garments (under 5)	0.20	0.60	0.70	0.60	1.00	0.60	0.90	1.00	1.10	0.80	0.80
3.1.8 Children's under garments (under 16)	0.30	0.30	0.30	0.30	0.40	0.40	0.70	0.30	0.40	0.50	0.40
3.1.9 Accessories	0.40	0.30	0.50	0.50	0.70	1.10	0.90	1.30	1.40	1.20	0.80
3.1.10 Haberdashery and clothing hire	[0.10]	0.20	[0.10]	0.20	0.20	0.10	0.40	0.40	0.20	0.30	0.20
3.1.11 Dry cleaners, laundry and dyeing	[0.30]	[0.10]	[0.00]	[0.10]	[0.10]	[0.20]	0.30	0.40	[0.40]	0.80	0.30
3.2 Footwear	1.90	2.70	3.00	3.00	4.20	5.80	4.30	5.40	6.60	6.50	4.30
4 Housing (net)[1], fuel & power	**62.10**	**63.90**	**76.30**	**70.40**	**72.70**	**72.20**	**72.40**	**79.90**	**73.40**	**100.60**	**74.40**
4.1 Actual rentals for housing	95.30	76.90	63.20	44.60	39.90	34.10	30.40	34.30	24.70	37.90	48.10
4.1.1 Gross rent	95.30	76.90	63.20	44.60	39.80	34.10	30.40	34.10	24.50	37.60	48.00
4.1.2 *less housing benefit, rebates & allowances rec'd*	65.90	45.90	23.50	11.70	7.00	2.30	2.60	1.20	[0.20]	[0.30]	16.10
4.1.3 Net rent[2]	29.40	31.00	39.60	32.90	32.70	31.70	27.80	32.90	24.20	37.40	32.00
4.1.4 Second dwelling rent	-	-	-	-	[0.10]	-	[0.00]	[0.20]	[0.20]	[0.30]	[0.10]
4.2 Maintenance and repair of dwelling	1.60	2.40	4.00	4.30	5.50	6.30	9.30	8.80	11.00	17.60	7.10
4.3 Water supply and miscellaneous services relating to the dwelling	7.30	7.50	8.00	8.40	8.40	8.90	8.50	9.30	9.40	11.20	8.70
4.4 Electricity, gas and other fuels[3]	23.80	22.90	24.70	24.80	25.90	25.30	26.70	28.70	28.50	34.20	26.50
4.4.1 Electricity	11.20	11.00	11.80	12.00	12.10	11.40	12.10	12.50	12.40	14.30	12.10
4.4.2 Gas	10.90	10.70	11.50	11.50	12.60	12.20	12.40	13.40	13.80	15.30	12.40
4.4.3 Other fuels	1.70	1.20	1.40	1.20	1.20	1.70	2.20	2.80	2.30	4.50	2.00

Note: The commodity and service categories are not comparable to those in publications before 2001-02.
The numbering system is sequential, it does not use actual COICOP codes.
Please see background notes for symbols and conventions used in this report.
1 Excluding mortgage interest payments, council tax and Northern Ireland rates.
2 The figure included in total expenditure is net rent as opposed to gross rent.
3 Recording of expenditure on gas and electricity via combined payment packages was changed in 2013. Recording of expenditure via slot meters was also changed.

Table 3.1E
Detailed household expenditure by equivalised disposable income decile group, 2013 (cont.)
United Kingdom

	Commodity or service	Lowest ten per cent	Second decile group	Third decile group	Fourth decile group	Fifth decile group	Sixth decile group	Seventh decile group	Eighth decile group	Ninth decile group	Highest ten per cent	All house-holds
		Average weekly household expenditure (£)										
5	**Household goods & services**	**15.40**	**13.90**	**26.20**	**24.10**	**27.80**	**30.40**	**31.90**	**42.10**	**50.30**	**69.40**	**33.10**
5.1	Furniture and furnishings, carpets and other floor coverings[4]	8.30	6.40	15.10	11.40	14.20	14.80	17.10	22.00	30.40	42.30	18.20
5.1.1	Furniture and furnishings	7.40	4.60	12.40	8.20	10.80	11.60	14.00	17.60	25.60	36.20	14.80
5.1.2	Floor coverings	0.90	1.80	2.80	3.10	3.40	3.10	3.10	4.40	4.80	6.10	3.40
5.2	Household textiles	0.80	0.90	1.50	1.70	1.70	1.80	2.00	2.00	3.10	3.00	1.80
5.3	Household appliances	1.70	1.40	2.70	2.30	3.10	3.50	3.50	4.60	4.30	3.50	3.10
5.4	Glassware, tableware and household utensils	0.60	0.80	1.00	1.00	1.30	1.70	1.60	2.20	2.00	3.60	1.60
5.5	Tools and equipment for house and garden	0.90	0.70	1.50	2.10	1.80	2.50	1.70	4.60	3.40	4.60	2.40
5.6	Goods and services for routine household maintenance	3.30	3.70	4.30	5.70	5.80	6.20	5.90	6.70	7.10	12.50	6.10
5.6.1	Cleaning materials	1.60	1.80	2.10	2.20	2.50	2.70	2.50	2.60	2.70	3.00	2.40
5.6.2	Household goods and hardware	1.10	1.00	1.10	1.20	1.50	1.30	1.40	1.80	1.70	2.10	1.40
5.6.3	Domestic services, carpet cleaning, hire/repair of furniture/furnishings	0.50	1.00	1.10	2.30	1.70	2.20	1.90	2.20	2.70	7.40	2.30
6	**Health**	**1.80**	**2.60**	**3.20**	**4.30**	**5.00**	**8.50**	**9.70**	**7.00**	**10.10**	**10.00**	**6.20**
6.1	Medical products, appliances and equipment	1.30	1.70	1.90	2.90	3.20	6.00	6.50	4.10	6.20	5.90	4.00
6.1.1	Medicines, prescriptions, healthcare products etc.	1.10	1.10	1.30	1.80	1.90	4.20	3.00	2.20	3.90	2.10	2.30
6.1.2	Spectacles, lenses, accessories and repairs	[0.20]	[0.60]	0.60	1.20	1.30	1.80	3.50	1.90	2.30	3.70	1.70
6.2	Hospital services	[0.60]	0.90	1.30	1.40	1.80	2.50	3.20	2.90	3.90	4.10	2.30
7	**Transport**	**24.50**	**24.80**	**43.10**	**49.00**	**63.20**	**64.30**	**86.20**	**92.50**	**113.10**	**144.00**	**70.40**
7.1	Purchase of vehicles	6.00	3.20	9.80	13.60	17.30	19.40	28.80	27.30	38.30	47.20	21.10
7.1.1	Purchase of new cars and vans	[3.00]	[0.30]	[3.10]	[3.50]	5.70	9.90	9.00	7.90	19.90	20.80	8.30
7.1.2	Purchase of second hand cars or vans	2.90	3.00	6.60	9.70	10.80	9.10	18.60	18.50	17.30	23.40	12.00
7.1.3	Purchase of motorcycles and other vehicles	[0.10]	[0.00]	[0.10]	[0.40]	[0.80]	[0.40]	[1.10]	[0.90]	[1.00]	[3.00]	0.80
7.2	Operation of personal transport	11.30	14.70	23.40	25.30	33.80	32.80	43.50	45.40	53.00	56.80	34.00
7.2.1	Spares and accessories	[0.30]	0.70	1.70	0.70	2.60	2.00	3.40	2.80	2.30	6.50	2.30
7.2.2	Petrol, diesel and other motor oils	8.50	11.10	15.90	18.10	24.00	23.40	29.50	31.90	37.60	35.20	23.50
7.2.3	Repairs and servicing	1.80	2.20	3.90	4.80	4.90	5.00	7.30	7.50	9.40	10.40	5.70
7.2.4	Other motoring costs	0.70	0.80	1.80	1.60	2.30	2.50	3.20	3.30	3.80	4.70	2.50
7.3	Transport services[5]	7.20	6.80	9.80	10.10	12.00	12.00	13.90	19.80	21.80	39.90	15.30
7.3.1	Rail and tube fares	1.70	0.90	1.50	1.90	2.10	2.60	3.40	5.60	6.70	12.30	3.90
7.3.2	Bus and coach fares	2.40	1.40	1.60	2.10	1.70	1.70	1.10	2.00	1.40	0.80	1.60
7.3.3	Combined fares	[0.10]	[0.40]	[0.80]	[0.50]	[0.50]	[0.50]	[0.90]	[0.90]	1.50	1.80	0.80
7.3.4	Other travel and transport	3.00	4.10	5.80	5.70	7.70	7.20	8.60	11.40	12.20	25.00	9.10
8	**Communication**	**8.60**	**9.90**	**12.90**	**13.30**	**14.70**	**14.20**	**16.30**	**17.50**	**18.80**	**18.50**	**14.50**
8.1	Postal services	0.20	0.30	0.50	0.50	0.50	0.60	0.70	0.50	1.00	1.20	0.60
8.2	Telephone and telefax equipment	[0.10]	[0.20]	[0.40]	[0.60]	0.60	[0.50]	[0.50]	1.00	1.00	[0.40]	0.50
8.3	Telephone and telefax services	6.40	7.60	9.60	9.70	10.90	10.40	12.10	12.80	13.10	13.20	10.60
8.4	Internet subscription fees	1.80	1.80	2.30	2.50	2.80	2.70	3.10	3.20	3.70	3.70	2.80

Note: The commodity and service categories are not comparable to those in publications before 2001-02.
The numbering system is sequential, it does not use actual COICOP codes.
Please see background notes for symbols and conventions used in this report.
4 Recording of expenditure on furniture was changed in 2013.
5 Recording of expenditure on flights was changed in 2013.

Table 3.1E
Detailed household expenditure by equivalised disposable income decile group, 2013 (cont.)
United Kingdom

Commodity or service	Lowest ten per cent	Second decile group	Third decile group	Fourth decile group	Fifth decile group	Sixth decile group	Seventh decile group	Eighth decile group	Ninth decile group	Highest ten per cent	All house-holds
	Average weekly household expenditure (£)										
9 Recreation & culture	**21.50**	**27.80**	**39.30**	**42.20**	**51.60**	**62.70**	**66.90**	**80.50**	**110.30**	**136.70**	**63.90**
9.1 Audio-visual, photographic and information processing equipment	2.00	2.60	4.00	3.20	5.10	5.10	5.10	4.20	7.90	12.20	5.10
9.1.1 Audio equipment and accessories, CD players	0.40	0.10	0.60	0.50	1.30	1.20	1.40	0.90	1.30	1.50	0.90
9.1.2 TV, video and computers	1.60	2.20	3.40	2.40	3.60	3.70	3.10	3.20	6.40	9.70	3.90
9.1.3 Photographic, cine and optical equipment	[0.00]	[0.20]	[0.10]	[0.40]	[0.10]	[0.20]	[0.50]	[0.10]	[0.20]	[1.00]	0.30
9.2 Other major durables for recreation and culture	[0.80]	[0.80]	[0.10]	[1.00]	[0.80]	[0.40]	[0.40]	[6.00]	[4.30]	6.30	2.10
9.3 Other recreational items and equipment, gardens and pets	4.80	5.80	7.50	7.90	9.60	11.30	12.70	11.30	16.60	16.90	10.40
9.3.1 Games, toys and hobbies	1.00	1.20	1.80	1.60	2.20	2.30	3.60	2.20	3.00	3.90	2.30
9.3.2 Computer software and games	0.50	[0.50]	0.50	0.70	0.90	1.00	0.90	[0.90]	1.50	0.80	0.80
9.3.3 Equipment for sport, camping and open-air recreation	0.30	[0.40]	0.50	0.70	1.10	0.70	1.10	0.70	1.30	1.90	0.90
9.3.4 Horticultural goods, garden equipment and plants	0.90	1.00	1.90	1.80	1.70	2.30	2.20	2.70	3.20	3.90	2.20
9.3.5 Pets and pet food	2.10	2.60	2.90	3.10	3.70	5.00	4.90	4.80	7.60	6.40	4.30
9.4 Recreational and cultural services	8.70	9.70	12.70	14.40	17.30	20.20	21.80	23.90	26.60	30.60	18.60
9.4.1 Sports admissions, subscriptions, leisure class fees and equipment hire	1.50	1.30	2.50	3.00	4.60	6.50	6.70	8.10	9.10	12.40	5.50
9.4.2 Cinema, theatre and museums etc.	0.40	0.80	1.30	1.90	2.30	2.40	2.70	2.80	4.10	4.80	2.30
9.4.3 TV, video, satellite rental, cable subscriptions and TV licences	4.60	4.80	5.50	5.70	6.70	6.70	7.60	7.90	8.40	8.60	6.70
9.4.4 Miscellaneous entertainments	0.40	0.50	0.80	1.00	1.30	0.90	1.60	1.90	1.60	2.20	1.20
9.4.5 Development of film, deposit for film development, passport photos, holiday and school photos	[0.10]	[0.10]	[0.10]	[0.10]	0.20	0.20	[0.10]	0.10	0.70	[0.30]	0.20
9.4.6 Gambling payments	1.70	2.20	2.50	2.70	2.30	3.50	3.00	3.20	2.70	2.30	2.60
9.5 Newspapers, books and stationery	2.30	3.20	3.90	4.00	5.40	5.00	6.20	7.20	6.80	8.60	5.30
9.5.1 Books	0.30	0.50	0.60	0.70	1.10	0.90	1.20	1.60	1.60	2.20	1.10
9.5.2 Diaries, address books, cards etc.	0.90	0.80	1.20	1.30	1.90	1.80	2.20	2.40	2.60	3.70	1.90
9.5.3 Newspapers	0.70	1.30	1.50	1.40	1.60	1.60	1.70	2.30	1.80	1.60	1.60
9.5.4 Magazines and periodicals	0.40	0.50	0.50	0.60	0.70	0.70	1.10	0.90	0.90	1.10	0.80
9.6 Package holidays[6]	2.90	5.70	11.10	11.70	13.50	20.70	20.80	27.90	48.00	62.00	22.40
9.6.1 Package holidays - UK	[0.30]	[0.90]	1.30	1.20	[0.80]	2.00	2.20	1.50	2.80	[1.40]	1.40
9.6.2 Package holidays - abroad	2.70	4.80	9.80	10.50	12.70	18.60	18.60	26.40	45.30	60.60	21.00
10 Education	**5.50**	**[15.50]**	**3.00**	**6.00**	**6.10**	**9.60**	**9.00**	**6.40**	**6.50**	**20.60**	**8.80**
10.1 Education fees	[5.30]	[15.10]	[2.70]	[5.70]	[5.50]	9.20	8.60	6.00	6.20	20.50	8.50
10.2 Payments for school trips, other ad-hoc expenditure	[0.10]	[0.30]	[0.30]	[0.30]	0.60	[0.30]	[0.40]	[0.40]	[0.20]	[0.10]	0.30
11 Restaurants & hotels	**14.60**	**15.40**	**25.50**	**27.00**	**33.20**	**38.00**	**47.40**	**54.20**	**66.40**	**82.00**	**40.40**
11.1 Catering services	12.80	14.00	22.20	23.70	28.20	32.50	39.50	45.40	53.90	63.20	33.50
11.1.1 Restaurant and café meals	5.00	6.00	10.00	10.40	12.90	14.70	20.50	20.90	26.80	32.00	15.90
11.1.2 Alcoholic drinks (away from home)	2.00	2.60	4.00	4.10	5.70	6.70	7.90	10.80	12.40	15.30	7.10
11.1.3 Take away meals eaten at home	2.50	2.40	3.40	4.10	4.30	4.80	4.90	5.10	5.10	5.30	4.20
11.1.4 Other take-away and snack food	2.50	2.10	3.30	3.50	3.70	3.90	4.40	6.10	7.10	7.10	4.40
11.1.5 Contract catering (food) and canteens	0.80	0.90	1.60	1.70	1.60	2.50	1.80	2.50	2.50	3.40	1.90
11.2 Accommodation services	1.80	1.40	3.30	3.30	4.90	5.50	7.90	8.90	12.50	18.80	6.80
11.2.1 Holiday in the UK	1.30	1.00	2.40	2.10	4.00	3.60	4.70	6.00	6.90	8.30	4.00
11.2.2 Holiday abroad	[0.40]	[0.40]	[0.90]	[1.10]	[0.90]	1.80	3.10	2.80	5.20	10.40	2.70
11.2.3 Room hire	[0.00]	-	[0.00]	[0.00]	[0.00]	[0.00]	[0.00]	[0.00]	[0.40]	[0.10]	[0.10]

Note: The commodity and service categories are not comparable to those in publications before 2001-02.
The numbering system is sequential, it does not use actual COICOP codes.
Please see background notes for symbols and conventions used in this report.
6 Recording of expenditure on package holidays was changed in 2013.

Table 3.1E
Detailed household expenditure by equivalised disposable income decile group, 2013 (cont.)
United Kingdom

	Lowest ten per cent	Second decile group	Third decile group	Fourth decile group	Fifth decile group	Sixth decile group	Seventh decile group	Eighth decile group	Ninth decile group	Highest ten per cent	All house-holds
Commodity or service	Average weekly household expenditure (£)										
12 Miscellaneous goods & services	**16.20**	**16.30**	**25.50**	**29.10**	**34.70**	**35.90**	**43.00**	**59.10**	**58.00**	**73.40**	**39.10**
12.1 Personal care	5.80	6.20	8.20	8.50	10.50	10.80	13.30	14.80	14.90	18.70	11.20
12.1.1 Hairdressing, beauty treatment	1.50	1.50	2.50	2.30	2.80	3.30	3.90	4.70	5.20	6.70	3.40
12.1.2 Toilet paper	0.60	0.70	0.80	0.80	0.80	0.90	0.90	1.00	0.90	1.00	0.80
12.1.3 Toiletries and soap	1.30	1.60	2.00	2.00	2.50	2.60	2.80	3.10	3.20	3.50	2.50
12.1.4 Baby toiletries and accessories (disposable)	0.50	0.50	0.60	0.70	0.80	0.50	0.80	0.60	0.70	0.70	0.60
12.1.5 Hair products, cosmetics and related electrical appliances	1.90	1.90	2.30	2.70	3.50	3.50	4.90	5.40	4.90	6.80	3.80
12.2 Personal effects	1.00	0.70	2.10	2.00	2.30	3.50	3.00	3.60	6.10	5.90	3.00
12.3 Social protection	[0.90]	[0.40]	[1.30]	2.90	1.90	2.00	4.10	13.60	6.10	7.50	4.10
12.4 Insurance	6.80	8.10	11.90	14.00	16.10	15.90	20.00	21.60	23.50	30.10	16.80
12.4.1 Household insurances - structural, contents and appliances	1.90	2.90	4.00	4.30	4.90	5.20	5.80	6.40	6.40	8.80	5.10
12.4.2 Medical insurance premiums	[0.30]	[0.20]	0.30	0.50	1.20	0.90	2.20	3.70	3.70	7.20	2.00
12.4.3 Vehicle insurance including boat insurance	4.40	5.00	7.50	9.10	9.90	9.80	11.70	11.40	13.30	13.00	9.50
12.4.4 Non-package holiday, other travel insurance	[0.10]	[0.00]	-	[0.10]	[0.00]	[0.00]	[0.20]	[0.10]	[0.20]	[1.00]	0.20
12.5 Other services	1.80	0.90	2.10	1.90	4.00	3.70	2.70	5.60	7.30	11.20	4.10
12.5.1 Moving house	[1.20]	0.50	[0.50]	[1.00]	2.20	0.80	1.10	3.60	4.80	5.50	2.10
12.5.2 Bank, building society, post office, credit card charges	0.20	0.20	0.40	0.30	0.50	0.50	0.60	0.80	0.70	1.00	0.50
12.5.3 Other services and professional fees	0.40	0.20	1.20	0.60	1.30	2.30	1.00	1.20	1.80	4.80	1.50
1-12 All expenditure groups	**228.90**	**254.90**	**332.70**	**343.10**	**399.30**	**438.20**	**485.00**	**550.90**	**626.00**	**784.70**	**444.30**
13 Other expenditure items	**19.70**	**24.60**	**36.50**	**46.10**	**54.90**	**59.10**	**85.40**	**85.70**	**164.20**	**154.20**	**73.00**
13.1 Housing: mortgage interest payments, council tax etc.	12.50	14.80	24.20	31.10	39.00	39.70	50.00	57.00	77.20	98.10	44.30
13.2 Licences, fines and transfers	1.40	2.70	2.40	3.30	3.20	3.20	6.50	4.70	5.20	5.60	3.80
13.3 Holiday spending	[2.00]	[3.40]	[2.70]	[5.20]	[2.90]	5.80	6.00	10.40	57.00	22.90	11.80
13.4 Money transfers and credit	3.90	3.70	7.30	6.50	9.70	10.40	22.90	13.60	24.70	27.60	13.00
13.4.1 Money, cash gifts given to children	[0.10]	[0.10]	[0.00]	[0.20]	[0.30]	[0.10]	[0.20]	[0.20]	[0.10]	[0.00]	0.10
13.4.2 Cash gifts and donations[7]	3.50	3.20	6.50	5.40	8.20	8.90	21.30	11.10	23.10	25.80	11.70
13.4.3 Club instalment payments (child) and interest on credit cards	0.40	0.30	0.70	0.90	1.20	1.30	1.40	2.30	1.50	1.80	1.20
Total expenditure	**248.70**	**279.40**	**369.20**	**389.20**	**454.20**	**497.40**	**570.40**	**636.70**	**790.10**	**938.90**	**517.30**
14 Other items recorded											
14.1 Life assurance and contributions to pension funds	1.80	2.30	5.50	6.60	10.80	11.60	18.10	26.10	42.10	73.80	19.90
14.2 Other insurance inc. friendly societies	0.20	0.30	0.60	0.70	1.10	1.20	3.10	1.80	2.20	2.50	1.40
14.3 Income tax, payments *less* refunds	4.80	5.30	17.60	27.10	42.60	58.10	83.90	113.00	161.50	372.00	88.50
14.4 National insurance contributions	0.90	2.10	7.20	11.80	18.30	23.80	33.00	45.70	60.00	80.00	28.30
14.5 Purchase or alteration of dwellings, mortgages	15.10	11.00	26.70	19.30	31.50	40.20	45.90	64.10	101.10	134.10	48.90
14.6 Savings and investments	[0.80]	0.80	0.90	1.70	2.50	2.70	4.20	6.90	11.50	24.60	5.70
14.7 Pay off loan to clear other debt	[0.10]	[0.40]	1.70	2.50	2.00	3.60	3.10	5.10	4.10	3.70	2.60
14.8 Windfall receipts from gambling etc[8]	1.00	0.50	0.80	1.20	0.80	1.30	1.20	2.00	0.80	1.90	1.20

Note: The commodity and service categories are not comparable to those in publications before 2001-02.
The numbering system is sequential, it does not use actual COICOP codes.
Please see background notes for symbols and conventions used in this report.
7 Recording of expenditure on money sent abroad was changed in 2013.
8 Expressed as an income figure as opposed to an expenditure figure.

Table 3.2
Detailed household expenditure as a percentage of total expenditure by disposable income decile group, 2013
United Kingdom

	Lowest ten per cent	Second decile group	Third decile group	Fourth decile group	Fifth decile group	Sixth decile group	Seventh decile group	Eighth decile group	Ninth decile group	Highest ten per cent	All house-holds
Lower boundary of group (£ per week)		174	256	333	417	504	600	720	882	1,150	
Weighted number of households (thousands)	2,690	2,690	2,680	2,680	2,690	2,680	2,690	2,680	2,690	2,680	26,840
Total number of households in sample	500	510	550	530	530	540	520	500	500	480	5,140
Total number of persons in sample	660	830	970	1,130	1,250	1,340	1,490	1,420	1,490	1,540	12,120
Total number of adults in sample	570	670	790	890	960	1,020	1,060	1,080	1,150	1,170	9,350
Weighted average number of persons per household	1.3	1.6	1.7	2.1	2.3	2.5	2.9	2.8	3.0	3.2	2.4
Commodity or service						Percentage of total expenditure					
1 Food & non-alcoholic drinks	***15.7***	***16.8***	***13.5***	***12.7***	***12.6***	***11.9***	***11.6***	***11.3***	***10.3***	***8.3***	***11.4***
1.1 Food	*14.5*	*15.4*	*12.5*	*11.7*	*11.6*	*10.9*	*10.6*	*10.4*	*9.4*	*7.6*	*10.4*
1.1.1 Bread, rice and cereals	*1.6*	*1.7*	*1.3*	*1.2*	*1.3*	*1.1*	*1.1*	*1.1*	*1.0*	*0.7*	*1.1*
1.1.2 Pasta products	*0.1*	*0.1*	*0.1*	*0.1*	*0.1*	*0.1*	*0.1*	*0.1*	*0.1*	*0.1*	*0.1*
1.1.3 Buns, cakes, biscuits etc.	*0.9*	*1.2*	*0.8*	*0.8*	*0.8*	*0.7*	*0.7*	*0.7*	*0.6*	*0.5*	*0.7*
1.1.4 Pastry (savoury)	*0.2*	*0.2*	*0.2*	*0.2*	*0.2*	*0.2*	*0.2*	*0.2*	*0.2*	*0.1*	*0.2*
1.1.5 Beef (fresh, chilled or frozen)	*0.5*	*0.5*	*0.4*	*0.4*	*0.4*	*0.4*	*0.3*	*0.4*	*0.4*	*0.3*	*0.4*
1.1.6 Pork (fresh, chilled or frozen)	*0.2*	*0.2*	*0.2*	*0.2*	*0.1*	*0.1*	*0.1*	*0.1*	*0.1*	*0.1*	*0.1*
1.1.7 Lamb (fresh, chilled or frozen)	*0.2*	*0.2*	*0.2*	*0.2*	*0.1*	*0.1*	*0.1*	*0.1*	*0.1*	*0.1*	*0.1*
1.1.8 Poultry (fresh, chilled or frozen)	*0.5*	*0.5*	*0.5*	*0.5*	*0.5*	*0.6*	*0.5*	*0.5*	*0.5*	*0.4*	*0.5*
1.1.9 Bacon and ham	*0.3*	*0.3*	*0.3*	*0.2*	*0.2*	*0.2*	*0.2*	*0.2*	*0.2*	*0.1*	*0.2*
1.1.10 Other meat and meat preparations	*1.9*	*2.1*	*1.5*	*1.4*	*1.3*	*1.3*	*1.2*	*1.2*	*1.0*	*0.8*	*1.2*
1.1.11 Fish and fish products	*0.7*	*0.8*	*0.6*	*0.6*	*0.5*	*0.5*	*0.5*	*0.5*	*0.5*	*0.4*	*0.5*
1.1.12 Milk	*0.8*	*0.8*	*0.6*	*0.6*	*0.5*	*0.5*	*0.5*	*0.4*	*0.4*	*0.3*	*0.5*
1.1.13 Cheese and curd	*0.5*	*0.5*	*0.4*	*0.4*	*0.4*	*0.4*	*0.4*	*0.4*	*0.4*	*0.3*	*0.4*
1.1.14 Eggs	*0.2*	*0.2*	*0.2*	*0.2*	*0.2*	*0.1*	*0.1*	*0.1*	*0.1*	*0.1*	*0.1*
1.1.15 Other milk products	*0.5*	*0.6*	*0.5*	*0.4*	*0.5*	*0.4*	*0.4*	*0.4*	*0.3*	*0.3*	*0.4*
1.1.16 Butter	*0.1*	*0.1*	*0.1*	*0.1*	*0.1*	*0.1*	*0.1*	*0.1*	*0.1*	*0.1*	*0.1*
1.1.17 Margarine, other vegetable fats and peanut butter	*0.2*	*0.2*	*0.1*	*0.1*	*0.1*	*0.1*	*0.1*	*0.1*	*0.1*	*0.1*	*0.1*
1.1.18 Cooking oils and fats	*0.1*	*0.1*	*0.1*	*0.1*	*0.1*	*0.1*	*0.1*	*0.1*	*0.1*	*0.0*	*0.1*
1.1.19 Fresh fruit	*0.7*	*0.9*	*0.7*	*0.7*	*0.7*	*0.7*	*0.7*	*0.6*	*0.6*	*0.5*	*0.6*
1.1.20 Other fresh, chilled or frozen fruits	*0.1*	*0.1*	*0.1*	*0.1*	*0.1*	*0.1*	*0.1*	*0.1*	*0.1*	*0.1*	*0.1*
1.1.21 Dried fruit and nuts	*0.1*	*0.2*	*0.1*	*0.1*	*0.1*	*0.1*	*0.1*	*0.1*	*0.2*	*0.1*	*0.1*
1.1.22 Preserved fruit and fruit based products	*0.1*	*0.1*	*0.0*	*0.0*	*0.0*	*0.0*	*0.0*	*0.0*	*0.0*	*0.0*	*0.0*
1.1.23 Fresh vegetables	*1.2*	*1.1*	*1.0*	*0.9*	*0.9*	*0.9*	*0.8*	*0.9*	*0.8*	*0.7*	*0.8*
1.1.24 Dried vegetables	*[0.0]*	*[0.0]*	*[0.0]*	*[0.0]*	*0.0*	*0.0*	*0.0*	*0.0*	*0.0*	*0.0*	*0.0*
1.1.25 Other preserved or processed vegetables	*0.4*	*0.3*	*0.3*	*0.3*	*0.3*	*0.3*	*0.3*	*0.3*	*0.3*	*0.2*	*0.3*
1.1.26 Potatoes	*0.3*	*0.3*	*0.3*	*0.2*	*0.2*	*0.2*	*0.2*	*0.2*	*0.2*	*0.1*	*0.2*
1.1.27 Other tubers and products of tuber vegetables	*0.4*	*0.5*	*0.4*	*0.4*	*0.4*	*0.3*	*0.3*	*0.3*	*0.3*	*0.2*	*0.3*
1.1.28 Sugar and sugar products	*0.1*	*0.1*	*0.1*	*0.1*	*0.1*	*0.1*	*0.1*	*0.1*	*0.1*	*0.1*	*0.1*
1.1.29 Jams, marmalades	*0.1*	*0.1*	*0.1*	*0.1*	*0.1*	*0.1*	*0.0*	*0.1*	*0.0*	*0.0*	*0.1*
1.1.30 Chocolate	*0.4*	*0.4*	*0.4*	*0.4*	*0.4*	*0.4*	*0.4*	*0.4*	*0.3*	*0.2*	*0.3*
1.1.31 Confectionery products	*0.2*	*0.2*	*0.2*	*0.1*	*0.2*	*0.1*	*0.1*	*0.1*	*0.1*	*0.1*	*0.1*
1.1.32 Edible ices and ice cream	*0.1*	*0.2*	*0.1*	*0.1*	*0.1*	*0.1*	*0.1*	*0.1*	*0.1*	*0.1*	*0.1*
1.1.33 Other food products	*0.7*	*0.7*	*0.6*	*0.6*	*0.6*	*0.5*	*0.5*	*0.6*	*0.5*	*0.4*	*0.5*
1.2 Non-alcoholic drinks	*1.2*	*1.4*	*1.0*	*1.1*	*1.0*	*0.9*	*1.0*	*1.0*	*0.9*	*0.7*	*0.9*
1.2.1 Coffee	*0.2*	*0.2*	*0.2*	*0.2*	*0.1*	*0.1*	*0.1*	*0.1*	*0.1*	*0.1*	*0.1*
1.2.2 Tea	*0.1*	*0.2*	*0.1*	*0.1*	*0.1*	*0.1*	*0.1*	*0.1*	*0.1*	*0.1*	*0.1*
1.2.3 Cocoa and powdered chocolate	*0.0*	*0.0*	*0.0*	*0.0*	*0.0*	*0.0*	*0.0*	*0.0*	*0.0*	*0.0*	*0.0*
1.2.4 Fruit and vegetable juices (inc. fruit squash)	*0.3*	*0.3*	*0.2*	*0.2*	*0.3*	*0.2*	*0.3*	*0.3*	*0.2*	*0.2*	*0.2*
1.2.5 Mineral or spring waters	*0.1*	*0.1*	*0.1*	*0.1*	*0.0*	*0.1*	*0.1*	*0.1*	*0.0*	*0.1*	*0.1*
1.2.6 Soft drinks (inc. fizzy and ready to drink fruit drinks)	*0.4*	*0.5*	*0.4*	*0.4*	*0.4*	*0.4*	*0.4*	*0.4*	*0.4*	*0.2*	*0.4*

Note: The commodity and service categories are not comparable to those in publications before 2001-02.
The numbering system is sequential, it does not use actual COICOP codes.
Please see background notes for symbols and conventions used in this report.

Table 3.2
Detailed household expenditure as a percentage of total expenditure by disposable income decile group, 2013
United Kingdom

		Lowest ten per cent	Second decile group	Third decile group	Fourth decile group	Fifth decile group	Sixth decile group	Seventh decile group	Eighth decile group	Ninth decile group	Highest ten per cent	All house-holds
Commodity or service		Percentage of total expenditure										
2	**Alcoholic drink, tobacco & narcotics**	**3.6**	**3.0**	**3.1**	**2.8**	**2.4**	**2.4**	**2.7**	**2.1**	**2.0**	**1.7**	**2.3**
2.1	Alcoholic drinks	1.8	1.4	1.5	1.4	1.4	1.5	1.6	1.5	1.6	1.4	1.5
	2.1.1 Spirits and liqueurs (brought home)	0.6	0.4	0.4	0.3	0.3	0.3	0.3	0.3	0.3	0.2	0.3
	2.1.2 Wines, fortified wines (brought home)	0.6	0.6	0.6	0.5	0.6	0.8	0.8	0.8	0.9	0.9	0.8
	2.1.3 Beer, lager, ciders and perry (brought home)	0.5	0.4	0.4	0.5	0.4	0.4	0.5	0.5	0.4	0.3	0.4
	2.1.4 Alcopops (brought home)	[0.0]	[0.0]	[0.0]	[0.0]	[0.0]	[0.0]	[0.0]	[0.0]	[0.0]	[0.0]	0.0
2.2	Tobacco and narcotics	1.8	1.6	1.6	1.4	1.0	0.9	1.1	0.6	0.4	0.3	0.8
	2.2.1 Cigarettes	1.2	1.2	1.4	1.2	0.8	0.7	0.9	0.5	0.4	0.2	0.7
	2.2.2 Cigars, other tobacco products and narcotics	0.6	0.3	0.3	0.2	0.2	0.2	0.2	0.1	0.1	0.1	0.2
3	**Clothing & footwear**	**3.4**	**3.1**	**3.3**	**4.2**	**3.9**	**4.7**	**5.0**	**4.9**	**4.8**	**4.3**	**4.4**
3.1	Clothing	2.8	2.5	2.6	3.5	3.0	3.9	3.9	3.8	4.0	3.5	3.5
	3.1.1 Men's outer garments	0.6	0.4	0.4	0.9	0.7	1.1	1.1	1.0	1.1	0.9	0.9
	3.1.2 Men's under garments	[0.0]	[0.0]	0.1	0.1	0.1	0.1	0.1	0.1	0.1	0.1	0.1
	3.1.3 Women's outer garments	1.2	1.0	1.1	1.4	1.2	1.7	1.5	1.7	1.7	1.6	1.5
	3.1.4 Women's under garments	0.3	0.2	0.2	0.2	0.2	0.2	0.2	0.2	0.3	0.2	0.2
	3.1.5 Boys' outer garments (5-15)	[0.1]	[0.1]	0.2	0.2	0.2	0.2	0.2	0.1	0.2	0.1	0.2
	3.1.6 Girls' outer garments (5-15)	[0.1]	0.2	0.2	0.2	0.2	0.1	0.3	0.2	0.2	0.2	0.2
	3.1.7 Infants' outer garments (under 5)	[0.0]	0.1	0.1	0.1	0.2	0.1	0.2	0.2	0.2	0.1	0.1
	3.1.8 Children's under garments (under 16)	[0.1]	0.1	0.0	0.1	0.1	0.1	0.1	0.1	0.1	0.1	0.1
	3.1.9 Accessories	0.1	0.1	0.1	0.1	0.2	0.2	0.2	0.2	0.2	0.2	0.2
	3.1.10 Haberdashery and clothing hire	[0.1]	[0.1]	0.1	0.0	0.0	0.0	0.0	0.1	0.0	0.0	0.0
	3.1.11 Dry cleaners, laundry and dyeing	[0.1]	[0.1]	[0.0]	[0.0]	[0.0]	[0.0]	[0.0]	0.1	0.1	0.1	0.1
3.2	Footwear	0.6	0.6	0.7	0.7	0.9	0.8	1.0	1.0	0.8	0.8	0.8
4	**Housing (net)[1], fuel & power**	**26.0**	**25.0**	**21.4**	**20.0**	**18.3**	**15.1**	**13.6**	**12.6**	**10.6**	**8.4**	**14.4**
4.1	Actual rentals for housing	39.4	28.1	18.4	15.5	11.9	7.5	6.2	5.4	4.0	2.9	9.3
	4.1.1 Gross rent	39.4	28.1	18.4	15.5	11.9	7.5	6.2	5.4	4.0	2.8	9.3
	4.1.2 *less housing benefit, rebates & allowances rec'c*	28.1	17.6	8.3	5.5	2.4	0.9	0.3	[0.1]	[0.2]	[0.0]	3.1
	4.1.3 Net rent[2]	11.3	10.5	10.1	10.0	9.5	6.6	5.9	5.3	3.8	2.8	6.2
	4.1.4 Second dwelling rent	-	-	-	-	-	-	[0.0]	[0.0]	-	[0.0]	[0.0]
4.2	Maintenance and repair of dwelling	0.8	1.4	1.6	1.1	1.2	1.7	1.3	1.4	1.5	1.3	1.4
4.3	Water supply and miscellaneous services relating to the dwelling	3.5	3.3	2.4	2.2	2.0	1.6	1.7	1.5	1.2	1.0	1.7
4.4	Electricity, gas and other fuels[3]	10.4	9.7	7.2	6.6	5.6	5.2	4.8	4.4	4.1	3.3	5.1
	4.4.1 Electricity	4.9	4.6	3.4	3.1	2.6	2.3	2.2	2.0	1.8	1.4	2.3
	4.4.2 Gas	4.7	4.4	3.5	3.3	2.7	2.4	2.3	2.1	1.8	1.5	2.4
	4.4.3 Other fuels	[0.8]	0.7	0.3	0.3	0.2	0.4	0.4	0.3	0.5	0.4	0.4

Note: The commodity and service categories are not comparable to those in publications before 2001-02.
The numbering system is sequential, it does not use actual COICOP codes.
Please see background notes for symbols and conventions used in this report.
1 Excluding mortgage interest payments, council tax and Northern Ireland rates.
2 The figure included in total expenditure is net rent as opposed to gross rent.
3 Recording of expenditure on gas and electricity via combined payment packages was changed in 2013. Recording of expenditure via slot meters was also changed.

Table 3.2
Detailed household expenditure as a percentage of total expenditure by disposable income decile group, 2013
United Kingdom

Commodity or service		Lowest ten per cent	Second decile group	Third decile group	Fourth decile group	Fifth decile group	Sixth decile group	Seventh decile group	Eighth decile group	Ninth decile group	Highest ten per cent	All house-holds
		Percentage of total expenditure										
5	**Household goods & services**	***7.0***	***6.7***	***6.6***	***6.3***	***5.9***	***7.0***	***6.0***	***6.0***	***5.6***	***7.1***	***6.4***
5.1	Furniture and furnishings, carpets and other floor coverings[4]	*3.6*	*3.5*	*3.1*	*3.2*	*2.8*	*4.4*	*2.8*	*3.2*	*3.1*	*4.5*	*3.5*
5.1.1	Furniture and furnishings	*3.0*	*2.6*	*2.6*	*2.4*	*2.2*	*3.6*	*2.1*	*2.6*	*2.4*	*3.9*	*2.9*
5.1.2	Floor coverings	*0.6*	*0.9*	*0.5*	*0.7*	*0.6*	*0.7*	*0.7*	*0.6*	*0.6*	*0.7*	*0.6*
5.2	Household textiles	*0.4*	*0.3*	*0.3*	*0.4*	*0.6*	*0.3*	*0.4*	*0.4*	*0.3*	*0.3*	*0.4*
5.3	Household appliances	*1.0*	*0.6*	*0.8*	*0.8*	*0.6*	*0.7*	*0.7*	*0.6*	*0.3*	*0.4*	*0.6*
5.4	Glassware, tableware and household utensils	*0.3*	*0.2*	*0.3*	*0.2*	*0.3*	*0.3*	*0.3*	*0.3*	*0.3*	*0.4*	*0.3*
5.5	Tools and equipment for house and garden	*0.4*	*0.3*	*0.4*	*0.4*	*0.4*	*0.4*	*0.7*	*0.5*	*0.6*	*0.3*	*0.5*
5.6	Goods and services for routine household maintenance	*1.4*	*1.8*	*1.8*	*1.4*	*1.1*	*1.0*	*1.1*	*1.0*	*1.0*	*1.2*	*1.2*
5.6.1	Cleaning materials	*0.6*	*0.7*	*0.6*	*0.5*	*0.5*	*0.4*	*0.5*	*0.4*	*0.4*	*0.3*	*0.5*
5.6.2	Household goods and hardware	*0.4*	*0.5*	*0.3*	*0.3*	*0.3*	*0.3*	*0.3*	*0.2*	*0.2*	*0.2*	*0.3*
5.6.3	Domestic services, carpet cleaning, hire/repair of furniture/furnishings	*0.3*	*0.6*	*0.9*	*0.6*	*0.3*	*0.3*	*0.4*	*0.3*	*0.3*	*0.6*	*0.4*
6	**Health**	***1.0***	***1.1***	***1.0***	***1.2***	***1.0***	***1.5***	***1.4***	***1.8***	***1.2***	***0.9***	***1.2***
6.1	Medical products, appliances and equipment	*0.6*	*0.9*	*0.5*	*0.7*	*0.6*	*1.0*	*0.8*	*1.3*	*0.6*	*0.6*	*0.8*
6.1.1	Medicines, prescriptions, healthcare products etc.	*0.5*	*0.6*	*0.3*	*0.4*	*0.4*	*0.6*	*0.4*	*0.9*	*0.3*	*0.2*	*0.4*
6.1.2	Spectacles, lenses, accessories and repairs	*[0.1]*	*[0.3]*	*0.2*	*0.3*	*0.2*	*0.5*	*0.4*	*0.5*	*0.3*	*0.3*	*0.3*
6.2	Hospital services	*[0.4]*	*0.3*	*0.5*	*0.5*	*0.3*	*0.5*	*0.6*	*0.4*	*0.5*	*0.4*	*0.4*
7	**Transport**	***8.3***	***8.3***	***10.8***	***11.1***	***13.6***	***14.2***	***13.8***	***15.1***	***15.2***	***15.0***	***13.6***
7.1	Purchase of vehicles	*2.1*	*1.6*	*2.4*	*2.6*	*4.1*	*4.6*	*4.2*	*4.6*	*4.9*	*4.7*	*4.1*
7.1.1	Purchase of new cars and vans	*[1.1]*	*[0.4]*	*[0.9]*	*0.9*	*1.7*	*2.0*	*1.1*	*1.9*	*1.6*	*2.3*	*1.6*
7.1.2	Purchase of second hand cars or vans	*1.0*	*1.1*	*1.5*	*1.6*	*2.3*	*2.5*	*2.9*	*2.6*	*3.0*	*2.2*	*2.3*
7.1.3	Purchase of motorcycles and other vehicles	*[0.0]*	-	*[0.0]*	*[0.0]*	*[0.1]*	*[0.2]*	*[0.1]*	*[0.1]*	*[0.3]*	*[0.2]*	*0.2*
7.2	Operation of personal transport	*3.7*	*4.6*	*5.9*	*6.1*	*6.9*	*7.1*	*7.0*	*7.7*	*7.0*	*6.3*	*6.6*
7.2.1	Spares and accessories	*[0.3]*	*[0.2]*	*0.3*	*0.1*	*0.6*	*0.4*	*0.5*	*0.5*	*0.3*	*0.6*	*0.4*
7.2.2	Petrol, diesel and other motor oils	*2.6*	*3.3*	*4.2*	*4.3*	*4.4*	*5.0*	*5.1*	*5.4*	*5.0*	*4.0*	*4.5*
7.2.3	Repairs and servicing	*0.7*	*0.9*	*0.9*	*1.1*	*1.3*	*1.3*	*0.9*	*1.2*	*1.2*	*1.1*	*1.1*
7.2.4	Other motoring costs	*0.3*	*0.2*	*0.4*	*0.6*	*0.6*	*0.5*	*0.4*	*0.5*	*0.5*	*0.5*	*0.5*
7.3	Transport services[5]	*2.4*	*2.1*	*2.5*	*2.4*	*2.6*	*2.4*	*2.7*	*2.8*	*3.3*	*4.0*	*3.0*
7.3.1	Rail and tube fares	*0.5*	*0.3*	*0.3*	*0.5*	*0.5*	*0.5*	*0.6*	*0.7*	*1.1*	*1.2*	*0.7*
7.3.2	Bus and coach fares	*0.6*	*0.5*	*0.4*	*0.4*	*0.3*	*0.5*	*0.4*	*0.3*	*0.2*	*0.1*	*0.3*
7.3.3	Combined fares	*[0.0]*	*[0.0]*	*[0.1]*	*[0.3]*	*[0.1]*	*[0.1]*	*[0.1]*	*[0.2]*	*0.2*	*0.2*	*0.2*
7.3.4	Other travel and transport	*1.3*	*1.4*	*1.7*	*1.3*	*1.6*	*1.4*	*1.7*	*1.6*	*1.8*	*2.4*	*1.8*
8	**Communication**	***3.6***	***3.5***	***3.4***	***3.1***	***3.1***	***3.1***	***2.9***	***2.8***	***2.6***	***2.0***	***2.8***
8.1	Postal services	*0.1*	*0.1*	*0.1*	*0.1*	*0.1*	*0.1*	*0.1*	*0.1*	*0.1*	*0.1*	*0.1*
8.2	Telephone and telefax equipment	*[0.1]*	*[0.1]*	*[0.1]*	*[0.1]*	*[0.0]*	*0.2*	*0.1*	*0.1*	*0.1*	*0.1*	*0.1*
8.3	Telephone and telefax services	*2.7*	*2.7*	*2.5*	*2.2*	*2.3*	*2.2*	*2.1*	*2.1*	*1.9*	*1.4*	*2.0*
8.4	Internet subscription fees	*0.7*	*0.6*	*0.7*	*0.7*	*0.6*	*0.6*	*0.6*	*0.5*	*0.5*	*0.4*	*0.5*

Note: The commodity and service categories are not comparable to those in publications before 2001-02.
The numbering system is sequential, it does not use actual COICOP codes.
Please see background notes for symbols and conventions used in this report.
4 Recording of expenditure on furniture was changed in 2013.
5 Recording of expenditure on flights was changed in 2013.

Table 3.2
Detailed household expenditure as a percentage of total expenditure by disposable income decile group, 2013
United Kingdom

Commodity or service	Lowest ten per cent	Second decile group	Third decile group	Fourth decile group	Fifth decile group	Sixth decile group	Seventh decile group	Eighth decile group	Ninth decile group	Highest ten per cent	All house-holds
	Percentage of total expenditure										
9 Recreation & culture	***9.3***	***9.7***	***10.5***	***10.4***	***12.0***	***12.2***	***12.2***	***12.6***	***12.9***	***14.3***	***12.4***
9.1 Audio-visual, photographic and information processing equipment	*1.1*	*0.5*	*0.8*	*0.8*	*0.8*	*1.0*	*1.2*	*1.0*	*1.1*	*1.1*	*1.0*
9.1.1 Audio equipment and accessories, CD players	*[0.1]*	*0.1*	*0.1*	*0.1*	*0.2*	*0.2*	*0.3*	*0.2*	*0.2*	*0.2*	*0.2*
9.1.2 TV, video and computers	*0.9*	*0.5*	*0.7*	*0.7*	*0.5*	*0.8*	*0.8*	*0.8*	*0.9*	*0.8*	*0.8*
9.1.3 Photographic, cine and optical equipment	*[0.0]*	*[0.0]*	*[0.1]*	*[0.0]*	*[0.1]*	*[0.1]*	*[0.0]*	*[0.0]*	*[0.0]*	*[0.1]*	*0.1*
9.2 Other major durables for recreation and culture	*[0.1]*	*[0.3]*	*[0.3]*	*[0.3]*	*[0.1]*	*[0.1]*	*[0.3]*	*[0.3]*	*[0.7]*	*0.7*	*0.4*
9.3 Other recreational items and equipment, gardens and pets	*2.1*	*1.8*	*1.9*	*2.1*	*2.0*	*2.1*	*2.2*	*2.3*	*2.0*	*1.8*	*2.0*
9.3.1 Games, toys and hobbies	*0.3*	*0.4*	*0.3*	*0.3*	*0.5*	*0.4*	*0.5*	*0.6*	*0.5*	*0.4*	*0.4*
9.3.2 Computer software and games	*[0.2]*	*[0.1]*	*[0.1]*	*0.1*	*0.2*	*0.2*	*0.2*	*0.1*	*0.2*	*0.2*	*0.2*
9.3.3 Equipment for sport, camping and open-air recreation	*[0.2]*	*[0.1]*	*[0.1]*	*0.1*	*0.1*	*0.2*	*0.2*	*0.2*	*0.2*	*0.1*	*0.2*
9.3.4 Horticultural goods, garden equipment and plants	*0.4*	*0.4*	*0.6*	*0.4*	*0.5*	*0.5*	*0.4*	*0.4*	*0.4*	*0.4*	*0.4*
9.3.5 Pets and pet food	*1.0*	*0.8*	*0.9*	*1.0*	*0.8*	*0.8*	*0.8*	*1.1*	*0.7*	*0.7*	*0.8*
9.4 Recreational and cultural services	*3.4*	*3.5*	*3.8*	*3.3*	*3.4*	*3.7*	*3.9*	*4.0*	*3.7*	*3.3*	*3.6*
9.4.1 Sports admissions, subscriptions, leisure class fees and equipment hire	*0.4*	*0.4*	*0.7*	*0.7*	*0.7*	*1.3*	*1.0*	*1.3*	*1.2*	*1.4*	*1.1*
9.4.2 Cinema, theatre and museums etc.	*[0.2]*	*0.2*	*0.3*	*0.3*	*0.5*	*0.3*	*0.6*	*0.5*	*0.6*	*0.5*	*0.5*
9.4.3 TV, video, satellite rental, cable subscriptions and TV licences	*1.9*	*1.8*	*1.6*	*1.6*	*1.5*	*1.4*	*1.3*	*1.3*	*1.1*	*0.8*	*1.3*
9.4.4 Miscellaneous entertainments	*0.2*	*0.2*	*0.2*	*0.1*	*0.2*	*0.2*	*0.3*	*0.3*	*0.3*	*0.3*	*0.2*
9.4.5 Development of film, deposit for film development, passport photos, holiday and school photos	*[0.0]*	*[0.0]*	*[0.1]*	*[0.0]*	*[0.0]*	*[0.0]*	*0.0*	*0.1*	*0.0*	*0.0*	*0.0*
9.4.6 Gambling payments	*0.8*	*0.9*	*1.0*	*0.6*	*0.5*	*0.5*	*0.6*	*0.5*	*0.4*	*0.3*	*0.5*
9.5 Newspapers, books and stationery	*1.1*	*1.3*	*1.3*	*1.0*	*1.2*	*1.1*	*1.0*	*1.1*	*1.0*	*0.8*	*1.0*
9.5.1 Books	*0.2*	*0.2*	*0.2*	*0.2*	*0.2*	*0.2*	*0.2*	*0.3*	*0.2*	*0.2*	*0.2*
9.5.2 Diaries, address books, cards etc.	*0.3*	*0.4*	*0.3*	*0.3*	*0.4*	*0.4*	*0.4*	*0.4*	*0.4*	*0.4*	*0.4*
9.5.3 Newspapers	*0.5*	*0.6*	*0.5*	*0.4*	*0.4*	*0.3*	*0.3*	*0.3*	*0.2*	*0.1*	*0.3*
9.5.4 Magazines and periodicals	*0.2*	*0.2*	*0.2*	*0.1*	*0.2*	*0.2*	*0.2*	*0.1*	*0.1*	*0.1*	*0.1*
9.6 Package holidays[6]	*1.5*	*2.2*	*2.4*	*3.0*	*4.6*	*4.3*	*3.7*	*4.0*	*4.5*	*6.6*	*4.3*
9.6.1 Package holidays - UK	*[0.3]*	*0.4*	*0.4*	*0.4*	*0.4*	*0.2*	*0.2*	*0.2*	*0.3*	*0.2*	*0.3*
9.6.2 Package holidays - abroad	*1.2*	*1.8*	*2.0*	*2.5*	*4.2*	*4.0*	*3.6*	*3.7*	*4.2*	*6.4*	*4.1*
10 Education	***[2.2]***	***[0.8]***	***[1.3]***	***[3.8]***	***1.6***	***0.4***	***0.6***	***1.0***	***2.8***	***2.1***	***1.7***
10.1 Education fees	*[2.2]*	*[0.8]*	*[1.2]*	*[3.8]*	*[1.5]*	*0.3*	*0.5*	*1.0*	*2.7*	*2.0*	*1.6*
10.2 Payments for school trips, other ad-hoc expenditure	*[0.0]*	*[0.0]*	*[0.1]*	*[0.0]*	*[0.1]*	*[0.1]*	*0.1*	*[0.1]*	*[0.1]*	*[0.0]*	*0.1*
11 Restaurants & hotels	***5.4***	***5.2***	***6.3***	***7.0***	***6.8***	***7.5***	***8.2***	***8.5***	***9.2***	***8.4***	***7.8***
11.1 Catering services	*4.7*	*4.6*	*5.5*	*6.0*	*5.6*	*6.3*	*7.2*	*7.3*	*7.7*	*6.5*	*6.5*
11.1.1 Restaurant and café meals	*2.2*	*2.2*	*2.7*	*2.9*	*2.6*	*2.9*	*3.3*	*3.3*	*3.7*	*3.2*	*3.1*
11.1.2 Alcoholic drinks (away from home)	*1.0*	*0.8*	*1.0*	*1.2*	*1.1*	*1.4*	*1.5*	*1.7*	*1.6*	*1.4*	*1.4*
11.1.3 Take away meals eaten at home	*0.7*	*0.7*	*0.8*	*0.8*	*0.8*	*0.8*	*1.0*	*0.9*	*0.9*	*0.6*	*0.8*
11.1.4 Other take-away and snack food	*0.6*	*0.6*	*0.7*	*0.7*	*0.7*	*0.8*	*0.9*	*1.0*	*1.0*	*0.8*	*0.8*
11.1.5 Contract catering (food) and canteens	*0.1*	*0.2*	*0.2*	*0.3*	*0.4*	*0.4*	*0.5*	*0.4*	*0.4*	*0.4*	*0.4*
11.2 Accommodation services	*0.7*	*0.7*	*0.8*	*1.1*	*1.2*	*1.2*	*1.0*	*1.2*	*1.6*	*1.9*	*1.3*
11.2.1 Holiday in the UK	*0.6*	*0.4*	*0.6*	*0.7*	*1.0*	*0.9*	*0.7*	*0.7*	*1.0*	*0.8*	*0.8*
11.2.2 Holiday abroad	*[0.1]*	*[0.2]*	*[0.2]*	*[0.4]*	*[0.2]*	*0.3*	*0.4*	*0.5*	*0.5*	*1.1*	*0.5*
11.2.3 Room hire	*[0.0]*	*[0.0]*	*[0.0]*	*[0.0]*	*[0.0]*	*[0.0]*	*[0.0]*	*[0.0]*	*[0.0]*	*[0.0]*	*[0.0]*

Note: The commodity and service categories are not comparable to those in publications before 2001-02.
The numbering system is sequential, it does not use actual COICOP codes.
Please see background notes for symbols and conventions used in this report.
6 Recording of expenditure on package holidays was changed in 2013.

Table 3.2
Detailed household expenditure as a percentage of total expenditure by disposable income decile group, 2013
United Kingdom

Commodity or service	Lowest ten per cent	Second decile group	Third decile group	Fourth decile group	Fifth decile group	Sixth decile group	Seventh decile group	Eighth decile group	Ninth decile group	Highest ten per cent	All house-holds
	Percentage of total expenditure										
12 Miscellaneous goods & services	**6.1**	**6.6**	**7.5**	**6.5**	**7.4**	**7.3**	**8.2**	**8.2**	**7.5**	**7.9**	**7.6**
12.1 Personal care	2.1	2.2	2.4	2.3	1.8	2.2	2.5	2.3	2.2	2.0	2.2
12.1.1 Hairdressing, beauty treatment	0.6	0.7	0.9	0.7	0.4	0.7	0.7	0.7	0.7	0.6	0.7
12.1.2 Toilet paper	0.3	0.2	0.2	0.2	0.2	0.2	0.2	0.2	0.1	0.1	0.2
12.1.3 Toiletries and soap	0.6	0.6	0.5	0.5	0.5	0.4	0.5	0.5	0.5	0.4	0.5
12.1.4 Baby toiletries and accessories (disposable)	0.1	0.2	0.1	0.1	0.2	0.1	0.2	0.1	0.1	0.1	0.1
12.1.5 Hair products, cosmetics and related electrical appliances	0.6	0.6	0.7	0.7	0.5	0.7	0.9	0.8	0.8	0.7	0.7
12.2 Personal effects	0.3	0.5	0.4	0.4	0.6	0.5	0.7	0.7	0.5	0.7	0.6
12.3 Social protection	[0.2]	[0.3]	[0.5]	[0.1]	0.8	[0.3]	0.8	1.4	1.0	1.0	0.8
12.4 Insurance	2.7	3.2	3.2	3.2	3.6	3.4	3.5	3.3	3.2	3.1	3.2
12.4.1 Household insurances - structural, contents and appliances	1.0	1.6	1.2	1.0	1.0	1.0	1.0	0.9	1.0	0.8	1.0
12.4.2 Medical insurance premiums	[0.2]	0.1	0.2	0.2	0.3	0.4	0.4	0.4	0.3	0.7	0.4
12.4.3 Vehicle insurance including boat insurance	1.5	1.6	1.9	2.0	2.2	2.0	2.1	2.0	1.8	1.5	1.8
12.4.4 Non-package holiday, other travel insurance	[0.1]	-	[0.0]	[0.1]	[0.0]	[0.0]	[0.0]	[0.0]	[0.0]	[0.1]	0.0
12.5 Other services	0.8	0.4	1.0	0.5	0.7	0.9	0.7	0.5	0.8	1.1	0.8
12.5.1 Moving house	[0.5]	[0.3]	[0.3]	0.3	0.4	0.4	0.4	0.2	0.5	0.6	0.4
12.5.2 Bank, building society, post office, credit card charges	0.1	0.1	0.1	0.1	0.1	0.1	0.1	0.1	0.1	0.1	0.1
12.5.3 Other services and professional fees	[0.2]	[0.1]	0.6	0.2	0.1	0.4	0.2	0.2	0.3	0.4	0.3
1-12 All expenditure groups	**91.6**	**89.9**	**88.7**	**89.3**	**88.5**	**87.2**	**86.2**	**86.8**	**84.8**	**80.5**	**85.9**
13 Other expenditure items	**8.4**	**10.1**	**11.3**	**10.7**	**11.5**	**12.8**	**13.8**	**13.2**	**15.2**	**19.5**	**14.1**
13.1 Housing: mortgage interest payments, council tax etc.	5.1	6.2	6.9	6.7	7.5	7.7	9.5	9.4	9.6	10.0	8.6
13.2 Licences, fines and transfers	0.5	0.6	0.7	0.8	0.6	0.7	0.9	0.8	1.0	0.6	0.7
13.3 Holiday spending	[0.9]	[1.0]	[1.1]	[0.8]	[0.9]	1.0	1.0	1.1	1.7	6.5	2.3
13.4 Money transfers and credit	1.8	2.3	2.7	2.4	2.6	3.3	2.4	1.9	2.9	2.4	2.5
13.4.1 Money, cash gifts given to children	[0.0]	[0.0]	[0.0]	[0.0]	[0.1]	[0.0]	[0.0]	[0.0]	0.0	[0.0]	0.0
13.4.2 Cash gifts and donations[7]	1.6	2.2	2.5	2.2	2.2	3.1	2.1	1.5	2.7	2.2	2.3
13.4.3 Club instalment payments (child) and interest on credit cards	0.2	0.1	0.2	0.2	0.3	0.2	0.3	0.4	0.2	0.2	0.2
Total expenditure	**100.0**	**100.0**	**100.0**	**100.0**	**100.0**	**100.0**	**100.0**	**100.0**	**100.0**	**100.0**	**100.0**

Note: The commodity and service categories are not comparable to those in publications before 2001-02.
The numbering system is sequential, it does not use actual COICOP codes.
Please see background notes for symbols and conventions used in this report.
7 Recording of expenditure on money sent abroad was changed in 2013.

Table 3.2E

Detailed household expenditure as a percentage of total expenditure by equivalised disposable income decile group, 2013 United Kingdom

	Lowest ten per cent	Second decile group	Third decile group	Fourth decile group	Fifth decile group	Sixth decile group	Seventh decile group	Eighth decile group	Ninth decile group	Highest ten per cent	All house-holds
Lower boundary of group (£ per week)		142	189	231	278	319	369	432	520	664	
Weighted number of households (thousands)	2,690	2,680	2,680	2,690	2,680	2,680	2,690	2,680	2,690	2,680	26,840
Total number of households in sample	500	520	530	530	530	520	520	510	500	490	5,140
Total number of persons in sample	1,060	1,140	1,300	1,310	1,300	1,230	1,250	1,240	1,170	1,120	12,120
Total number of adults in sample	730	840	920	950	970	990	1,010	1,010	1,000	950	9,350
Weighted average number of persons per household	2.1	2.2	2.4	2.4	2.5	2.4	2.4	2.5	2.4	2.3	2.4
Commodity or service	Percentage of total expenditure										
1 Food & non-alcoholic drinks	***16.4***	***15.9***	***14.3***	***13.9***	***12.9***	***12.5***	***11.2***	***10.5***	***8.8***	***8.0***	***11.4***
1.1 Food	*15.0*	*14.6*	*13.1*	*12.7*	*11.8*	*11.5*	*10.3*	*9.7*	*8.1*	*7.4*	*10.4*
1.1.1 Bread, rice and cereals	*1.7*	*1.6*	*1.5*	*1.4*	*1.3*	*1.2*	*1.0*	*1.0*	*0.7*	*0.7*	*1.1*
1.1.2 Pasta products	*0.1*	*0.1*	*0.1*	*0.1*	*0.1*	*0.1*	*0.1*	*0.1*	*0.1*	*0.1*	*0.1*
1.1.3 Buns, cakes, biscuits etc.	*1.0*	*1.0*	*1.0*	*0.9*	*0.8*	*0.8*	*0.7*	*0.6*	*0.5*	*0.5*	*0.7*
1.1.4 Pastry (savoury)	*0.2*	*0.2*	*0.2*	*0.2*	*0.2*	*0.2*	*0.1*	*0.1*	*0.1*	*0.1*	*0.2*
1.1.5 Beef (fresh, chilled or frozen)	*0.5*	*0.4*	*0.4*	*0.4*	*0.4*	*0.4*	*0.3*	*0.4*	*0.4*	*0.3*	*0.4*
1.1.6 Pork (fresh, chilled or frozen)	*0.1*	*0.2*	*0.2*	*0.2*	*0.1*	*0.1*	*0.1*	*0.1*	*0.1*	*0.1*	*0.1*
1.1.7 Lamb (fresh, chilled or frozen)	*0.2*	*0.2*	*0.2*	*0.2*	*0.1*	*0.1*	*0.1*	*0.1*	*0.1*	*0.1*	*0.1*
1.1.8 Poultry (fresh, chilled or frozen)	*0.6*	*0.6*	*0.6*	*0.5*	*0.5*	*0.5*	*0.5*	*0.5*	*0.4*	*0.4*	*0.5*
1.1.9 Bacon and ham	*0.2*	*0.3*	*0.2*	*0.3*	*0.2*	*0.2*	*0.2*	*0.2*	*0.2*	*0.1*	*0.2*
1.1.10 Other meat and meat preparations	*1.8*	*1.7*	*1.6*	*1.5*	*1.4*	*1.4*	*1.2*	*1.1*	*0.9*	*0.8*	*1.2*
1.1.11 Fish and fish products	*0.7*	*0.6*	*0.5*	*0.6*	*0.5*	*0.5*	*0.5*	*0.5*	*0.5*	*0.4*	*0.5*
1.1.12 Milk	*0.8*	*0.8*	*0.7*	*0.6*	*0.6*	*0.5*	*0.5*	*0.4*	*0.3*	*0.3*	*0.5*
1.1.13 Cheese and curd	*0.5*	*0.5*	*0.5*	*0.4*	*0.4*	*0.4*	*0.4*	*0.4*	*0.3*	*0.3*	*0.4*
1.1.14 Eggs	*0.2*	*0.2*	*0.2*	*0.2*	*0.1*	*0.2*	*0.1*	*0.1*	*0.1*	*0.1*	*0.1*
1.1.15 Other milk products	*0.5*	*0.5*	*0.5*	*0.5*	*0.4*	*0.5*	*0.4*	*0.3*	*0.3*	*0.3*	*0.4*
1.1.16 Butter	*0.1*	*0.2*	*0.1*	*0.1*	*0.1*	*0.1*	*0.1*	*0.1*	*0.1*	*0.1*	*0.1*
1.1.17 Margarine, other vegetable fats and peanut butter	*0.2*	*0.2*	*0.2*	*0.1*	*0.1*	*0.1*	*0.1*	*0.1*	*0.1*	*0.0*	*0.1*
1.1.18 Cooking oils and fats	*0.1*	*0.1*	*0.1*	*0.1*	*0.1*	*0.1*	*0.1*	*0.1*	*0.0*	*0.0*	*0.1*
1.1.19 Fresh fruit	*0.8*	*0.8*	*0.7*	*0.8*	*0.7*	*0.7*	*0.6*	*0.6*	*0.5*	*0.5*	*0.6*
1.1.20 Other fresh, chilled or frozen fruits	*0.1*	*0.1*	*0.1*	*0.1*	*0.1*	*0.1*	*0.1*	*0.1*	*0.1*	*0.1*	*0.1*
1.1.21 Dried fruit and nuts	*0.1*	*0.1*	*0.1*	*0.1*	*0.1*	*0.1*	*0.2*	*0.1*	*0.1*	*0.1*	*0.1*
1.1.22 Preserved fruit and fruit based products	*0.0*	*0.0*	*0.0*	*0.0*	*0.0*	*0.0*	*0.0*	*0.0*	*0.0*	*0.0*	*0.0*
1.1.23 Fresh vegetables	*1.1*	*1.1*	*0.9*	*0.9*	*0.8*	*0.9*	*0.8*	*0.9*	*0.7*	*0.7*	*0.8*
1.1.24 Dried vegetables	*[0.0]*	*0.0*	*0.0*	*0.0*	*0.0*	*[0.0]*	*0.0*	*0.0*	*0.0*	*0.0*	*0.0*
1.1.25 Other preserved or processed vegetables	*0.4*	*0.3*	*0.3*	*0.3*	*0.3*	*0.3*	*0.3*	*0.3*	*0.2*	*0.2*	*0.3*
1.1.26 Potatoes	*0.3*	*0.3*	*0.3*	*0.3*	*0.2*	*0.2*	*0.2*	*0.2*	*0.1*	*0.1*	*0.2*
1.1.27 Other tubers and products of tuber vegetables	*0.5*	*0.5*	*0.4*	*0.5*	*0.4*	*0.4*	*0.3*	*0.3*	*0.2*	*0.2*	*0.3*
1.1.28 Sugar and sugar products	*0.2*	*0.2*	*0.1*	*0.1*	*0.1*	*0.1*	*0.1*	*0.1*	*0.1*	*0.1*	*0.1*
1.1.29 Jams, marmalades	*0.1*	*0.1*	*0.1*	*0.1*	*0.1*	*0.1*	*0.1*	*0.0*	*0.0*	*0.0*	*0.1*
1.1.30 Chocolate	*0.4*	*0.4*	*0.5*	*0.4*	*0.4*	*0.4*	*0.4*	*0.3*	*0.3*	*0.2*	*0.3*
1.1.31 Confectionery products	*0.2*	*0.2*	*0.2*	*0.2*	*0.2*	*0.2*	*0.1*	*0.1*	*0.1*	*0.1*	*0.1*
1.1.32 Edible ices and ice cream	*0.2*	*0.1*	*0.2*	*0.1*	*0.1*	*0.1*	*0.1*	*0.1*	*0.1*	*0.1*	*0.1*
1.1.33 Other food products	*0.8*	*0.7*	*0.6*	*0.6*	*0.6*	*0.6*	*0.5*	*0.5*	*0.4*	*0.4*	*0.5*
1.2 Non-alcoholic drinks	*1.4*	*1.3*	*1.2*	*1.2*	*1.1*	*1.0*	*0.9*	*0.8*	*0.7*	*0.7*	*0.9*
1.2.1 Coffee	*0.2*	*0.2*	*0.2*	*0.2*	*0.1*	*0.1*	*0.1*	*0.1*	*0.1*	*0.1*	*0.1*
1.2.2 Tea	*0.1*	*0.1*	*0.1*	*0.1*	*0.1*	*0.1*	*0.1*	*0.1*	*0.1*	*0.1*	*0.1*
1.2.3 Cocoa and powdered chocolate	*0.0*	*0.0*	*0.0*	*0.0*	*0.0*	*0.0*	*0.0*	*0.0*	*0.0*	*0.0*	*0.0*
1.2.4 Fruit and vegetable juices (inc. fruit squash)	*0.3*	*0.3*	*0.3*	*0.3*	*0.3*	*0.3*	*0.2*	*0.2*	*0.2*	*0.2*	*0.2*
1.2.5 Mineral or spring waters	*0.1*	*0.1*	*0.1*	*0.1*	*0.0*	*0.1*	*0.1*	*0.0*	*0.0*	*0.1*	*0.1*
1.2.6 Soft drinks (inc. fizzy and ready to drink fruit drinks)	*0.6*	*0.6*	*0.5*	*0.5*	*0.5*	*0.4*	*0.4*	*0.4*	*0.3*	*0.2*	*0.4*

Note: The commodity and service categories are not comparable to those in publications before 2001-02
The numbering system is sequential, it does not use actual COICOP codes
Please see background notes for symbols and conventions used in this report

Table 3.2E
Detailed household expenditure as a percentage of total expenditure by equivalised disposable income decile group, 2013 United Kingdom

	Lowest ten per cent	Second decile group	Third decile group	Fourth decile group	Fifth decile group	Sixth decile group	Seventh decile group	Eighth decile group	Ninth decile group	Highest ten per cent	All house-holds
Commodity or service	Percentage of total expenditure										
2 Alcoholic drink, tobacco & narcotics	***3.4***	***3.3***	***2.7***	***2.3***	***2.4***	***3.0***	***2.1***	***2.4***	***1.8***	***1.8***	***2.3***
2.1 Alcoholic drinks	*1.4*	*1.5*	*1.2*	*1.3*	*1.4*	*1.9*	*1.5*	*1.6*	*1.3*	*1.5*	*1.5*
2.1.1 Spirits and liqueurs (brought home)	*0.4*	*0.4*	*0.4*	*0.3*	*0.3*	*0.4*	*0.3*	*0.3*	*0.2*	*0.2*	*0.3*
2.1.2 Wines, fortified wines (brought home)	*0.5*	*0.6*	*0.5*	*0.6*	*0.7*	*0.9*	*0.7*	*0.9*	*0.8*	*1.0*	*0.8*
2.1.3 Beer, lager, ciders and perry (brought home)	*0.5*	*0.5*	*0.4*	*0.5*	*0.4*	*0.6*	*0.5*	*0.4*	*0.3*	*0.3*	*0.4*
2.1.4 Alcopops (brought home)	*[0.0]*	*[0.0]*	*[0.0]*	*[0.0]*	*[0.0]*	*[0.0]*	*[0.0]*	*[0.0]*	*[0.0]*	*[0.0]*	*0.0*
2.2 Tobacco and narcotics	*1.9*	*1.9*	*1.4*	*1.0*	*1.0*	*1.1*	*0.6*	*0.7*	*0.4*	*0.3*	*0.8*
2.2.1 Cigarettes	*1.3*	*1.4*	*1.2*	*0.9*	*0.9*	*1.0*	*0.5*	*0.6*	*0.4*	*0.2*	*0.7*
2.2.2 Cigars, other tobacco products and narcotics	*0.6*	*0.5*	*0.3*	*0.1*	*0.1*	*0.2*	*0.2*	*0.1*	*0.1*	*[0.0]*	*0.2*
3 Clothing & footwear	***3.8***	***4.0***	***4.1***	***3.8***	***4.6***	***5.1***	***4.6***	***4.7***	***4.5***	***4.0***	***4.4***
3.1 Clothing	*3.1*	*3.0*	*3.3*	*3.0*	*3.7*	*3.9*	*3.9*	*3.8*	*3.7*	*3.3*	*3.5*
3.1.1 Men's outer garments	*0.7*	*0.5*	*0.8*	*0.7*	*0.8*	*1.2*	*0.9*	*1.0*	*1.0*	*1.0*	*0.9*
3.1.2 Men's under garments	*0.1*	*[0.0]*	*0.1*	*0.1*	*0.1*	*0.1*	*0.1*	*0.1*	*0.1*	*0.1*	*0.1*
3.1.3 Women's outer garments	*1.0*	*1.3*	*1.2*	*1.2*	*1.6*	*1.5*	*1.7*	*1.6*	*1.8*	*1.5*	*1.5*
3.1.4 Women's under garments	*0.2*	*0.2*	*0.2*	*0.2*	*0.2*	*0.2*	*0.2*	*0.3*	*0.2*	*0.2*	*0.2*
3.1.5 Boys' outer garments (5-15)	*0.3*	*0.2*	*0.4*	*0.1*	*0.2*	*0.2*	*0.2*	*0.1*	*0.1*	*0.1*	*0.2*
3.1.6 Girls' outer garments (5-15)	*0.3*	*0.2*	*0.2*	*0.2*	*0.2*	*0.2*	*0.2*	*0.2*	*0.1*	*0.2*	*0.2*
3.1.7 Infants' outer garments (under 5)	*0.1*	*0.2*	*0.2*	*0.2*	*0.2*	*0.1*	*0.2*	*0.2*	*0.1*	*0.1*	*0.1*
3.1.8 Children's under garments (under 16)	*0.1*	*0.1*	*0.1*	*0.1*	*0.1*	*0.1*	*0.1*	*0.1*	*0.0*	*0.0*	*0.1*
3.1.9 Accessories	*0.1*	*0.1*	*0.1*	*0.1*	*0.1*	*0.2*	*0.2*	*0.2*	*0.2*	*0.1*	*0.2*
3.1.10 Haberdashery and clothing hire	*[0.0]*	*0.1*	*[0.0]*	*0.0*	*0.0*	*0.0*	*0.1*	*0.1*	*0.0*	*0.0*	*0.0*
3.1.11 Dry cleaners, laundry and dyeing	*[0.1]*	*[0.0]*	*[0.0]*	*[0.0]*	*[0.0]*	*[0.0]*	*0.1*	*0.1*	*[0.0]*	*0.1*	*0.1*
3.2 Footwear	*0.8*	*1.0*	*0.8*	*0.8*	*0.9*	*1.2*	*0.8*	*0.8*	*0.8*	*0.7*	*0.8*
4 Housing (net)[1], fuel & power	***25.0***	***22.9***	***20.7***	***18.1***	***16.0***	***14.5***	***12.7***	***12.5***	***9.3***	***10.7***	***14.4***
4.1 Actual rentals for housing	*38.3*	*27.5*	*17.1*	*11.5*	*8.8*	*6.8*	*5.3*	*5.4*	*3.1*	*4.0*	*9.3*
4.1.1 Gross rent	*38.3*	*27.5*	*17.1*	*11.5*	*8.8*	*6.8*	*5.3*	*5.4*	*3.1*	*4.0*	*9.3*
4.1.2 *less housing benefit, rebates & allowances rec'c*	*26.5*	*16.4*	*6.4*	*3.0*	*1.5*	*0.5*	*0.5*	*0.2*	*[0.0]*	*[0.0]*	*3.1*
4.1.3 Net rent[2]	*11.8*	*11.1*	*10.7*	*8.5*	*7.2*	*6.4*	*4.9*	*5.2*	*3.1*	*4.0*	*6.2*
4.1.4 Second dwelling rent	-	-	-	-	*[0.0]*	-	*[0.0]*	*[0.0]*	*[0.0]*	*[0.0]*	*[0.0]*
4.2 Maintenance and repair of dwelling	*0.7*	*0.9*	*1.1*	*1.1*	*1.2*	*1.3*	*1.6*	*1.4*	*1.4*	*1.9*	*1.4*
4.3 Water supply and miscellaneous services relating to the dwelling	*2.9*	*2.7*	*2.2*	*2.2*	*1.8*	*1.8*	*1.5*	*1.5*	*1.2*	*1.2*	*1.7*
4.4 Electricity, gas and other fuels[3]	*9.6*	*8.2*	*6.7*	*6.4*	*5.7*	*5.1*	*4.7*	*4.5*	*3.6*	*3.6*	*5.1*
4.4.1 Electricity	*4.5*	*3.9*	*3.2*	*3.1*	*2.7*	*2.3*	*2.1*	*2.0*	*1.6*	*1.5*	*2.3*
4.4.2 Gas	*4.4*	*3.8*	*3.1*	*3.0*	*2.8*	*2.5*	*2.2*	*2.1*	*1.8*	*1.6*	*2.4*
4.4.3 Other fuels	*0.7*	*0.4*	*0.4*	*0.3*	*0.3*	*0.3*	*0.4*	*0.4*	*0.3*	*0.5*	*0.4*

Note: The commodity and service categories are not comparable to those in publications before 2001-02
The numbering system is sequential, it does not use actual COICOP codes
Please see background notes for symbols and conventions used in this report
1 Excluding mortgage interest payments, council tax and Northern Ireland rates
2 The figure included in total expenditure is net rent as opposed to gross rent
3 Recording of expenditure on gas and electricity via combined payment packages was changed in 2013. Recording of expenditure via slot meters was also changed

Table 3.2E
Detailed household expenditure as a percentage of total expenditure by equivalised disposable income decile group, 2013 United Kingdom

		Lowest ten per cent	Second decile group	Third decile group	Fourth decile group	Fifth decile group	Sixth decile group	Seventh decile group	Eighth decile group	Ninth decile group	Highest ten per cent	All house-holds
Commodity or service		Percentage of total expenditure										
5	**Household goods & services**	***6.2***	***5.0***	***7.1***	***6.2***	***6.1***	***6.1***	***5.6***	***6.6***	***6.4***	***7.4***	***6.4***
5.1	Furniture and furnishings, carpets and other floor coverings[4]	*3.3*	*2.3*	*4.1*	*2.9*	*3.1*	*3.0*	*3.0*	*3.5*	*3.9*	*4.5*	*3.5*
5.1.1	Furniture and furnishings	*3.0*	*1.6*	*3.4*	*2.1*	*2.4*	*2.3*	*2.5*	*2.8*	*3.2*	*3.9*	*2.9*
5.1.2	Floor coverings	*0.4*	*0.6*	*0.7*	*0.8*	*0.7*	*0.6*	*0.5*	*0.7*	*0.6*	*0.6*	*0.6*
5.2	Household textiles	*0.3*	*0.3*	*0.4*	*0.4*	*0.4*	*0.4*	*0.4*	*0.3*	*0.4*	*0.3*	*0.4*
5.3	Household appliances	*0.7*	*0.5*	*0.7*	*0.6*	*0.7*	*0.7*	*0.6*	*0.7*	*0.5*	*0.4*	*0.6*
5.4	Glassware, tableware and household utensils	*0.2*	*0.3*	*0.3*	*0.2*	*0.3*	*0.3*	*0.3*	*0.3*	*0.2*	*0.4*	*0.3*
5.5	Tools and equipment for house and garden	*0.4*	*0.3*	*0.4*	*0.5*	*0.4*	*0.5*	*0.3*	*0.7*	*0.4*	*0.5*	*0.5*
5.6	Goods and services for routine household maintenance	*1.3*	*1.3*	*1.2*	*1.5*	*1.3*	*1.2*	*1.0*	*1.0*	*0.9*	*1.3*	*1.2*
5.6.1	Cleaning materials	*0.7*	*0.6*	*0.6*	*0.6*	*0.6*	*0.5*	*0.4*	*0.4*	*0.3*	*0.3*	*0.5*
5.6.2	Household goods and hardware	*0.4*	*0.3*	*0.3*	*0.3*	*0.3*	*0.3*	*0.3*	*0.3*	*0.2*	*0.2*	*0.3*
5.6.3	Domestic services, carpet cleaning, hire/repair of furniture/furnishings	*0.2*	*0.4*	*0.3*	*0.6*	*0.4*	*0.4*	*0.3*	*0.3*	*0.3*	*0.8*	*0.4*
6	**Health**	***0.7***	***0.9***	***0.9***	***1.1***	***1.1***	***1.7***	***1.7***	***1.1***	***1.3***	***1.1***	***1.2***
6.1	Medical products, appliances and equipment	*0.5*	*0.6*	*0.5*	*0.8*	*0.7*	*1.2*	*1.1*	*0.6*	*0.8*	*0.6*	*0.8*
6.1.1	Medicines, prescriptions, healthcare products etc.	*0.4*	*0.4*	*0.4*	*0.5*	*0.4*	*0.8*	*0.5*	*0.3*	*0.5*	*0.2*	*0.4*
6.1.2	Spectacles, lenses, accessories and repairs	*[0.1]*	*[0.2]*	*0.2*	*0.3*	*0.3*	*0.4*	*0.6*	*0.3*	*0.3*	*0.4*	*0.3*
6.2	Hospital services	*[0.2]*	*0.3*	*0.3*	*0.4*	*0.4*	*0.5*	*0.6*	*0.5*	*0.5*	*0.4*	*0.4*
7	**Transport**	***9.8***	***8.9***	***11.7***	***12.6***	***13.9***	***12.9***	***15.1***	***14.5***	***14.3***	***15.3***	***13.6***
7.1	Purchase of vehicles	*2.4*	*1.2*	*2.7*	*3.5*	*3.8*	*3.9*	*5.1*	*4.3*	*4.8*	*5.0*	*4.1*
7.1.1	Purchase of new cars and vans	*[1.2]*	*[0.1]*	*[0.8]*	*[0.9]*	*1.2*	*2.0*	*1.6*	*1.2*	*2.5*	*2.2*	*1.6*
7.1.2	Purchase of second hand cars or vans	*1.2*	*1.1*	*1.8*	*2.5*	*2.4*	*1.8*	*3.3*	*2.9*	*2.2*	*2.5*	*2.3*
7.1.3	Purchase of motorcycles and other vehicles	*[0.0]*	*[0.0]*	*[0.0]*	*[0.1]*	*[0.2]*	*[0.1]*	*[0.2]*	*[0.1]*	*[0.1]*	*[0.3]*	*0.2*
7.2	Operation of personal transport	*4.5*	*5.3*	*6.3*	*6.5*	*7.4*	*6.6*	*7.6*	*7.1*	*6.7*	*6.0*	*6.6*
7.2.1	Spares and accessories	*[0.1]*	*0.3*	*0.5*	*0.2*	*0.6*	*0.4*	*0.6*	*0.4*	*0.3*	*0.7*	*0.4*
7.2.2	Petrol, diesel and other motor oils	*3.4*	*4.0*	*4.3*	*4.7*	*5.3*	*4.7*	*5.2*	*5.0*	*4.8*	*3.8*	*4.5*
7.2.3	Repairs and servicing	*0.7*	*0.8*	*1.1*	*1.2*	*1.1*	*1.0*	*1.3*	*1.2*	*1.2*	*1.1*	*1.1*
7.2.4	Other motoring costs	*0.3*	*0.3*	*0.5*	*0.4*	*0.5*	*0.5*	*0.6*	*0.5*	*0.5*	*0.5*	*0.5*
7.3	Transport services[5]	*2.9*	*2.4*	*2.7*	*2.6*	*2.7*	*2.4*	*2.4*	*3.1*	*2.8*	*4.3*	*3.0*
7.3.1	Rail and tube fares	*0.7*	*0.3*	*0.4*	*0.5*	*0.5*	*0.5*	*0.6*	*0.9*	*0.8*	*1.3*	*0.7*
7.3.2	Bus and coach fares	*0.9*	*0.5*	*0.4*	*0.5*	*0.4*	*0.3*	*0.2*	*0.3*	*0.2*	*0.1*	*0.3*
7.3.3	Combined fares	*[0.0]*	*[0.1]*	*[0.2]*	*[0.1]*	*[0.1]*	*[0.1]*	*[0.2]*	*[0.1]*	*0.2*	*0.2*	*0.2*
7.3.4	Other travel and transport	*1.2*	*1.5*	*1.6*	*1.5*	*1.7*	*1.5*	*1.5*	*1.8*	*1.5*	*2.7*	*1.8*
8	**Communication**	***3.5***	***3.5***	***3.5***	***3.4***	***3.2***	***2.9***	***2.9***	***2.7***	***2.4***	***2.0***	***2.8***
8.1	Postal services	*0.1*	*0.1*	*0.1*	*0.1*	*0.1*	*0.1*	*0.1*	*0.1*	*0.1*	*0.1*	*0.1*
8.2	Telephone and telefax equipment	*[0.1]*	*[0.1]*	*[0.1]*	*[0.1]*	*0.1*	*[0.1]*	*[0.1]*	*0.2*	*0.1*	*[0.0]*	*0.1*
8.3	Telephone and telefax services	*2.6*	*2.7*	*2.6*	*2.5*	*2.4*	*2.1*	*2.1*	*2.0*	*1.7*	*1.4*	*2.0*
8.4	Internet subscription fees	*0.7*	*0.6*	*0.6*	*0.7*	*0.6*	*0.6*	*0.5*	*0.5*	*0.5*	*0.4*	*0.5*

Note: The commodity and service categories are not comparable to those in publications before 2001-02
The numbering system is sequential, it does not use actual COICOP codes
Please see background notes for symbols and conventions used in this report
4 Recording of expenditure on furniture was changed in 2013
5 Recording of expenditure on flights was changed in 2013

Table 3.2E
Detailed household expenditure as a percentage of total expenditure by equivalised disposable income decile group, 2013 United Kingdom

Commodity or service	Lowest ten per cent	Second decile group	Third decile group	Fourth decile group	Fifth decile group	Sixth decile group	Seventh decile group	Eighth decile group	Ninth decile group	Highest ten per cent	All house-holds
	Percentage of total expenditure										
9 Recreation & culture	***8.7***	***10.0***	***10.6***	***10.8***	***11.4***	***12.6***	***11.7***	***12.6***	***14.0***	***14.6***	***12.4***
9.1 Audio-visual, photographic and information processing equipment	*0.8*	*0.9*	*1.1*	*0.8*	*1.1*	*1.0*	*0.9*	*0.7*	*1.0*	*1.3*	*1.0*
9.1.1 Audio equipment and accessories, CD players	*0.2*	*0.0*	*0.2*	*0.1*	*0.3*	*0.2*	*0.2*	*0.1*	*0.2*	*0.2*	*0.2*
9.1.2 TV, video and computers	*0.6*	*0.8*	*0.9*	*0.6*	*0.8*	*0.7*	*0.5*	*0.5*	*0.8*	*1.0*	*0.8*
9.1.3 Photographic, cine and optical equipment	*[0.0]*	*[0.1]*	*[0.0]*	*[0.1]*	*[0.0]*	*[0.0]*	*[0.1]*	*[0.0]*	*[0.0]*	*[0.1]*	*0.1*
9.2 Other major durables for recreation and culture	*[0.3]*	*[0.3]*	*[0.0]*	*[0.2]*	*[0.2]*	*[0.1]*	*[0.1]*	*[0.9]*	*[0.5]*	*0.7*	*0.4*
9.3 Other recreational items and equipment, gardens and pets	*1.9*	*2.1*	*2.0*	*2.0*	*2.1*	*2.3*	*2.2*	*1.8*	*2.1*	*1.8*	*2.0*
9.3.1 Games, toys and hobbies	*0.4*	*0.4*	*0.5*	*0.4*	*0.5*	*0.5*	*0.6*	*0.3*	*0.4*	*0.4*	*0.4*
9.3.2 Computer software and games	*0.2*	*[0.2]*	*0.1*	*0.2*	*0.2*	*0.2*	*0.2*	*[0.1]*	*0.2*	*0.1*	*0.2*
9.3.3 Equipment for sport, camping and open-air recreation	*0.1*	*[0.2]*	*0.1*	*0.2*	*0.2*	*0.2*	*0.2*	*0.1*	*0.2*	*0.2*	*0.2*
9.3.4 Horticultural goods, garden equipment and plants	*0.3*	*0.4*	*0.5*	*0.5*	*0.4*	*0.5*	*0.4*	*0.4*	*0.4*	*0.4*	*0.4*
9.3.5 Pets and pet food	*0.8*	*0.9*	*0.8*	*0.8*	*0.8*	*1.0*	*0.9*	*0.7*	*1.0*	*0.7*	*0.8*
9.4 Recreational and cultural services	*3.5*	*3.5*	*3.4*	*3.7*	*3.8*	*4.1*	*3.8*	*3.8*	*3.4*	*3.3*	*3.6*
9.4.1 Sports admissions, subscriptions, leisure class fees and equipment hire	*0.6*	*0.5*	*0.7*	*0.8*	*1.0*	*1.3*	*1.2*	*1.3*	*1.1*	*1.3*	*1.1*
9.4.2 Cinema, theatre and museums etc.	*0.2*	*0.3*	*0.3*	*0.5*	*0.5*	*0.5*	*0.5*	*0.4*	*0.5*	*0.5*	*0.5*
9.4.3 TV, video, satellite rental, cable subscriptions and TV licences	*1.8*	*1.7*	*1.5*	*1.5*	*1.5*	*1.4*	*1.3*	*1.2*	*1.1*	*0.9*	*1.3*
9.4.4 Miscellaneous entertainments	*0.2*	*0.2*	*0.2*	*0.3*	*0.3*	*0.2*	*0.3*	*0.3*	*0.2*	*0.2*	*0.2*
9.4.5 Development of film, deposit for film development, passport photos, holiday and school photos	*[0.0]*	*[0.0]*	*[0.0]*	*[0.0]*	*0.0*	*0.0*	*[0.0]*	*0.0*	*0.1*	*[0.0]*	*0.0*
9.4.6 Gambling payments	*0.7*	*0.8*	*0.7*	*0.7*	*0.5*	*0.7*	*0.5*	*0.5*	*0.3*	*0.2*	*0.5*
9.5 Newspapers, books and stationery	*0.9*	*1.1*	*1.0*	*1.0*	*1.2*	*1.0*	*1.1*	*1.1*	*0.9*	*0.9*	*1.0*
9.5.1 Books	*0.1*	*0.2*	*0.2*	*0.2*	*0.2*	*0.2*	*0.2*	*0.3*	*0.2*	*0.2*	*0.2*
9.5.2 Diaries, address books, cards etc.	*0.4*	*0.3*	*0.3*	*0.3*	*0.4*	*0.4*	*0.4*	*0.4*	*0.3*	*0.4*	*0.4*
9.5.3 Newspapers	*0.3*	*0.5*	*0.4*	*0.4*	*0.4*	*0.3*	*0.3*	*0.4*	*0.2*	*0.2*	*0.3*
9.5.4 Magazines and periodicals	*0.2*	*0.2*	*0.1*	*0.2*	*0.2*	*0.1*	*0.2*	*0.1*	*0.1*	*0.1*	*0.1*
9.6 Package holidays[6]	*1.2*	*2.0*	*3.0*	*3.0*	*3.0*	*4.2*	*3.6*	*4.4*	*6.1*	*6.6*	*4.3*
9.6.1 Package holidays - UK	*[0.1]*	*[0.3]*	*0.4*	*0.3*	*[0.2]*	*0.4*	*0.4*	*0.2*	*0.3*	*[0.2]*	*0.3*
9.6.2 Package holidays - abroad	*1.1*	*1.7*	*2.6*	*2.7*	*2.8*	*3.7*	*3.3*	*4.1*	*5.7*	*6.5*	*4.1*
10 Education	**2.2**	**[5.5]**	**0.8**	**1.5**	**1.3**	**1.9**	**1.6**	**1.0**	**0.8**	**2.2**	**1.7**
10.1 Education fees	*[2.1]*	*[5.4]*	*[0.7]*	*[1.5]*	*[1.2]*	*1.9*	*1.5*	*0.9*	*0.8*	*2.2*	*1.6*
10.2 Payments for school trips, other ad-hoc expenditure	*[0.1]*	*[0.1]*	*[0.1]*	*[0.1]*	*0.1*	*[0.1]*	*[0.1]*	*[0.1]*	*[0.0]*	*[0.0]*	*0.1*
11 Restaurants & hotels	**5.9**	**5.5**	**6.9**	**6.9**	**7.3**	**7.6**	**8.3**	**8.5**	**8.4**	**8.7**	**7.8**
11.1 Catering services	*5.2*	*5.0*	*6.0*	*6.1*	*6.2*	*6.5*	*6.9*	*7.1*	*6.8*	*6.7*	*6.5*
11.1.1 Restaurant and café meals	*2.0*	*2.1*	*2.7*	*2.7*	*2.8*	*2.9*	*3.6*	*3.3*	*3.4*	*3.4*	*3.1*
11.1.2 Alcoholic drinks (away from home)	*0.8*	*0.9*	*1.1*	*1.1*	*1.3*	*1.3*	*1.4*	*1.7*	*1.6*	*1.6*	*1.4*
11.1.3 Take away meals eaten at home	*1.0*	*0.9*	*0.9*	*1.0*	*1.0*	*1.0*	*0.9*	*0.8*	*0.6*	*0.6*	*0.8*
11.1.4 Other take-away and snack food	*1.0*	*0.8*	*0.9*	*0.9*	*0.8*	*0.8*	*0.8*	*1.0*	*0.9*	*0.8*	*0.8*
11.1.5 Contract catering (food) and canteens	*0.3*	*0.3*	*0.4*	*0.4*	*0.4*	*0.5*	*0.3*	*0.4*	*0.3*	*0.4*	*0.4*
11.2 Accommodation services	*0.7*	*0.5*	*0.9*	*0.8*	*1.1*	*1.1*	*1.4*	*1.4*	*1.6*	*2.0*	*1.3*
11.2.1 Holiday in the UK	*0.5*	*0.4*	*0.7*	*0.5*	*0.9*	*0.7*	*0.8*	*0.9*	*0.9*	*0.9*	*0.8*
11.2.2 Holiday abroad	*[0.2]*	*[0.1]*	*[0.2]*	*[0.3]*	*[0.2]*	*0.4*	*0.5*	*0.4*	*0.7*	*1.1*	*0.5*
11.2.3 Room hire	*[0.0]*	*-*	*[0.0]*	*[0.0]*	*[0.0]*	*[0.0]*	*[0.0]*	*[0.0]*	*[0.0]*	*[0.0]*	*[0.0]*

Note: The commodity and service categories are not comparable to those in publications before 2001-02
The numbering system is sequential, it does not use actual COICOP codes
Please see background notes for symbols and conventions used in this report
6 Recording of expenditure on package holidays was changed in 2013

Table 3.2E

Detailed household expenditure as a percentage of total expenditure by equivalised disposable income decile group, 2013 United Kingdom

Commodity or service		Lowest ten per cent	Second decile group	Third decile group	Fourth decile group	Fifth decile group	Sixth decile group	Seventh decile group	Eighth decile group	Ninth decile group	Highest ten per cent	All house-holds
		Percentage of total expenditure										
12	**Miscellaneous goods & services**	***6.5***	***5.8***	***6.9***	***7.5***	***7.6***	***7.2***	***7.5***	***9.3***	***7.3***	***7.8***	***7.6***
12.1	Personal care	*2.3*	*2.2*	*2.2*	*2.2*	*2.3*	*2.2*	*2.3*	*2.3*	*1.9*	*2.0*	*2.2*
	12.1.1 Hairdressing, beauty treatment	*0.6*	*0.5*	*0.7*	*0.6*	*0.6*	*0.7*	*0.7*	*0.7*	*0.7*	*0.7*	*0.7*
	12.1.2 Toilet paper	*0.2*	*0.2*	*0.2*	*0.2*	*0.2*	*0.2*	*0.2*	*0.2*	*0.1*	*0.1*	*0.2*
	12.1.3 Toiletries and soap	*0.5*	*0.6*	*0.5*	*0.5*	*0.6*	*0.5*	*0.5*	*0.5*	*0.4*	*0.4*	*0.5*
	12.1.4 Baby toiletries and accessories (disposable)	*0.2*	*0.2*	*0.2*	*0.2*	*0.2*	*0.1*	*0.1*	*0.1*	*0.1*	*0.1*	*0.1*
	12.1.5 Hair products, cosmetics and related electrical appliances	*0.7*	*0.7*	*0.6*	*0.7*	*0.8*	*0.7*	*0.9*	*0.8*	*0.6*	*0.7*	*0.7*
12.2	Personal effects	*0.4*	*0.3*	*0.6*	*0.5*	*0.5*	*0.7*	*0.5*	*0.6*	*0.8*	*0.6*	*0.6*
12.3	Social protection	*[0.4]*	*[0.1]*	*[0.3]*	*0.7*	*0.4*	*0.4*	*0.7*	*2.1*	*0.8*	*0.8*	*0.8*
12.4	Insurance	*2.7*	*2.9*	*3.2*	*3.6*	*3.5*	*3.2*	*3.5*	*3.4*	*3.0*	*3.2*	*3.2*
	12.4.1 Household insurances - structural, contents and appliances	*0.8*	*1.0*	*1.1*	*1.1*	*1.1*	*1.0*	*1.0*	*1.0*	*0.8*	*0.9*	*1.0*
	12.4.2 Medical insurance premiums	*[0.1]*	*[0.1]*	*0.1*	*0.1*	*0.3*	*0.2*	*0.4*	*0.6*	*0.5*	*0.8*	*0.4*
	12.4.3 Vehicle insurance including boat insurance	*1.8*	*1.8*	*2.0*	*2.3*	*2.2*	*2.0*	*2.1*	*1.8*	*1.7*	*1.4*	*1.8*
	12.4.4 Non-package holiday, other travel insurance	*[0.1]*	*[0.0]*	-	*[0.0]*	*[0.0]*	*[0.0]*	*[0.0]*	*[0.0]*	*[0.0]*	*[0.1]*	*0.0*
12.5	Other services	*0.7*	*0.3*	*0.6*	*0.5*	*0.9*	*0.7*	*0.5*	*0.9*	*0.9*	*1.2*	*0.8*
	12.5.1 Moving house	*[0.5]*	*0.2*	*[0.1]*	*[0.2]*	*0.5*	*0.2*	*0.2*	*0.6*	*0.6*	*0.6*	*0.4*
	12.5.2 Bank, building society, post office, credit card charges	*0.1*	*0.1*	*0.1*	*0.1*	*0.1*	*0.1*	*0.1*	*0.1*	*0.1*	*0.1*	*0.1*
	12.5.3 Other services and professional fees	*0.1*	*0.1*	*0.3*	*0.2*	*0.3*	*0.5*	*0.2*	*0.2*	*0.2*	*0.5*	*0.3*
1-12	**All expenditure groups**	***92.1***	***91.2***	***90.1***	***88.2***	***87.9***	***88.1***	***85.0***	***86.5***	***79.2***	***83.6***	***85.9***
13	**Other expenditure items**	***7.9***	***8.8***	***9.9***	***11.8***	***12.1***	***11.9***	***15.0***	***13.5***	***20.8***	***16.4***	***14.1***
13.1	Housing: mortgage interest payments, council tax etc.	*5.0*	*5.3*	*6.5*	*8.0*	*8.6*	*8.0*	*8.8*	*9.0*	*9.8*	*10.4*	*8.6*
13.2	Licences, fines and transfers	*0.6*	*1.0*	*0.6*	*0.8*	*0.7*	*0.7*	*1.1*	*0.7*	*0.7*	*0.6*	*0.7*
13.3	Holiday spending	*[0.8]*	*[1.2]*	*[0.7]*	*[1.3]*	*[0.6]*	*1.2*	*1.0*	*1.6*	*7.2*	*2.4*	*2.3*
13.4	Money transfers and credit	*1.6*	*1.3*	*2.0*	*1.7*	*2.1*	*2.1*	*4.0*	*2.1*	*3.1*	*2.9*	*2.5*
	13.4.1 Money, cash gifts given to children	*[0.0]*	*[0.1]*	*[0.0]*	*[0.0]*	*[0.1]*	*[0.0]*	*[0.0]*	*[0.0]*	*[0.0]*	*[0.0]*	*0.0*
	13.4.2 Cash gifts and donations[7]	*1.4*	*1.2*	*1.8*	*1.4*	*1.8*	*1.8*	*3.7*	*1.7*	*2.9*	*2.7*	*2.3*
	13.4.3 Club instalment payments (child) and interest on credit cards	*0.1*	*0.1*	*0.2*	*0.2*	*0.3*	*0.3*	*0.3*	*0.4*	*0.2*	*0.2*	*0.2*
Total expenditure		***100.0***	***100.0***	***100.0***	***100.0***	***100.0***	***100.0***	***100.0***	***100.0***	***100.0***	***100.0***	***100.0***

Note: The commodity and service categories are not comparable to those in publications before 2001-02
The numbering system is sequential, it does not use actual COICOP codes
Please see background notes for symbols and conventions used in this report
7 Recording of expenditure on money sent abroad was changed in 2013.

Table 3.3
Expenditure of one adult non-retired households by disposable income quintile group, 2013
United Kingdom

	Lowest twenty per cent	Second quintile group	Third quintile group	Fourth quintile group	Highest twenty per cent	All house-holds
Lower boundary of group (£ per week)[1]		315	496	688	960	
Weighted number of households (thousands)	2,050	1,090	550	280	130	4,090
Total number of households in sample	380	200	100	50	20	740
Total number of persons in sample	380	200	100	50	20	740
Total number of adults in sample	380	200	100	50	20	740
Weighted average number of persons per household	1.0	1.0	1.0	1.0	1.0	1.0
Commodity or service	Average weekly household expenditure (£)					
1 Food & non-alcoholic drinks	25.80	32.50	32.80	34.20	39.10	29.50
2 Alcoholic drinks, tobacco & narcotics	8.60	10.10	10.50	10.90	[6.30]	9.40
3 Clothing & footwear	5.10	17.20	31.00	13.60	[38.10]	13.40
4 Housing (net)[2], fuel & power	60.30	71.20	84.90	106.30	80.50	70.30
5 Household goods & services	13.60	16.60	55.00	21.10	[81.70]	22.60
6 Health	1.80	3.70	4.00	[3.20]	[4.50]	2.80
7 Transport	21.80	40.90	61.00	56.80	[113.60]	37.40
8 Communication	7.80	10.70	15.60	10.50	15.80	10.00
9 Recreation & culture	16.70	32.00	58.20	71.50	[98.30]	32.60
10 Education	[5.00]	[0.40]	[0.80]	[0.20]	[1.30]	[2.80]
11 Restaurants & hotels	13.60	24.30	40.30	39.30	68.90	23.50
12 Miscellaneous goods & services	12.70	23.80	41.60	23.70	[41.20]	21.20
1-12 All expenditure groups	192.90	283.40	435.60	391.20	589.30	275.40
13 Other expenditure items	25.40	55.90	76.20	90.20	143.50	48.40
Total expenditure	**218.30**	**339.30**	**511.80**	**481.40**	**732.80**	**323.80**
Average weekly expenditure per person (£)						
Total expenditure	**218.30**	**339.30**	**511.80**	**481.40**	**732.80**	**323.80**

Note: The commodity and service categories are not comparable to those in publications before 2001-02.
Please see background notes for symbols and conventions used in this report.
1 Quintile groups have been calculated separately for retired and non-retired households.
2 Excluding mortgage interest payments, council tax and Northern Ireland rates.

Table 3.3E
Expenditure of one adult non-retired households by disposable equivalised income quintile group (OECD-modified scale), 2013
United Kingdom

		Lowest twenty per cent	Second quintile group	Third quintile group	Fourth quintile group	Highest twenty per cent	All house-holds
Lower boundary of group (£ per week)[1]			198	299	404	561	
Weighted number of households (thousands)		1,310	590	770	710	710	4,090
Total number of households in sample		240	110	140	120	120	740
Total number of persons in sample		240	110	140	120	120	740
Total number of adults in sample		240	110	140	120	120	740
Weighted average number of persons per household		1.0	1.0	1.0	1.0	1.0	1.0
Commodity or service		Average weekly household expenditure (£)					
1	Food & non-alcoholic drinks	24.20	29.40	28.70	35.40	34.40	29.50
2	Alcoholic drinks, tobacco & narcotics	8.30	8.40	11.00	10.00	9.60	9.40
3	Clothing & footwear	4.50	5.10	16.30	20.90	26.10	13.40
4	Housing (net)[2], fuel & power	56.40	63.20	68.90	82.80	90.40	70.30
5	Household goods & services	12.10	17.30	13.80	19.10	59.00	22.60
6	Health	1.30	3.30	3.60	3.10	4.00	2.80
7	Transport	15.00	33.80	34.50	52.60	69.30	37.40
8	Communication	6.20	10.20	10.20	13.00	13.80	10.00
9	Recreation & culture	13.00	21.10	30.40	38.50	74.50	32.60
10	Education	[6.50]	[2.70]	[0.50]	[0.30]	[0.90]	[2.80]
11	Restaurants & hotels	11.00	18.80	20.50	32.80	44.20	23.50
12	Miscellaneous goods & services	9.90	15.70	23.50	29.50	35.40	21.20
1-12	All expenditure groups	168.50	229.10	262.00	338.00	461.60	275.40
13	Other expenditure items	16.00	38.20	52.20	62.70	97.70	48.40
Total expenditure		**184.50**	**267.30**	**314.20**	**400.80**	**559.30**	**323.80**
Average weekly expenditure per person (£)							
Total expenditure		**184.50**	**267.30**	**314.20**	**400.80**	**559.30**	**323.80**

Note: The commodity and service categories are not comparable to those in publications before 2001-02.

Please see background notes for symbols and conventions used in this report.

1 Quintile groups have been calculated separately for retired and non-retired households.

2 Excluding mortgage interest payments, council tax and Northern Ireland Rates.

Table 3.4

Expenditure of one person retired households not mainly dependent on state pensions[1] by disposable income quintile group, 2013

United Kingdom

		Lowest twenty per cent	Second quintile group	Third quintile group	Fourth quintile group	Highest twenty per cent	All house-holds
Lower boundary of group (£ per week)[2]			193	277	379	555	
Weighted number of households (thousands)		820	740	640	440	190	2,830
Total number of households in sample		160	140	120	90	40	550
Total number of persons in sample		160	140	120	90	40	550
Total number of adults in sample		160	140	120	90	40	550
Weighted average number of persons per household		1.0	1.0	1.0	1.0	1.0	1.0
Commodity or service		Average weekly household expenditure (£)					
1	Food & non-alcoholic drinks	29.40	30.60	33.90	36.60	35.80	32.30
2	Alcoholic drinks, tobacco & narcotics	6.20	4.20	7.40	6.00	17.10	6.70
3	Clothing & footwear	6.30	8.80	8.60	10.00	[4.90]	7.90
4	Housing (net)[3], fuel & power	41.20	47.10	50.20	61.90	64.90	49.60
5	Household goods & services	11.40	16.50	22.90	30.80	67.10	22.10
6	Health	1.60	3.20	6.40	7.00	14.40	4.80
7	Transport	7.90	12.30	25.00	35.40	91.50	22.90
8	Communication	6.50	7.20	8.50	9.80	10.90	8.00
9	Recreation & culture	19.30	22.30	31.20	39.80	72.50	29.60
10	Education	-	-	-	[0.30]	-	[0.00]
11	Restaurants & hotels	5.40	9.00	16.00	25.00	23.80	13.10
12	Miscellaneous goods & services	10.70	14.70	19.10	46.00	60.00	22.50
1-12	All expenditure groups	145.90	176.00	229.20	308.60	463.00	219.60
13	Other expenditure items	13.60	25.40	33.60	57.00	178.70	39.20
Total expenditure		**159.50**	**201.40**	**262.80**	**365.60**	**641.70**	**258.90**
Average weekly expenditure per person (£)							
Total expenditure		**159.50**	**201.40**	**262.80**	**365.60**	**641.70**	**258.90**

Note: The commodity and service categories are not comparable to those in publications before 2001-02.
Please see background notes for symbols and conventions used in this report.
1 Mainly dependent on state pension and not economically active - see Appendix B.
2 Quintile groups have been calculated separately for retired and non-retired households.
3 Excluding mortgage interest payments, council tax and Northern Ireland rates.

Table 3.4E

Expenditure of one person retired households not mainly dependent on state pensions[1] by disposable equivalised income quintile group (OECD-modified scale), 2013

United Kingdom

		Lowest twenty per cent	Second quintile group	Third quintile group	Fourth quintile group	Highest twenty per cent	All house-holds
Lower boundary of group (£ per week)[2]			177	228	298	390	
Weighted number of households (thousands)		580	540	590	530	590	2,830
Total number of households in sample		110	100	110	100	110	550
Total number of persons in sample		110	100	110	100	110	550
Total number of adults in sample		110	100	110	100	110	550
Weighted average number of persons per household		1.0	1.0	1.0	1.0	1.0	1.0
Commodity or service		Average weekly household expenditure (£)					
1	Food & non-alcoholic drinks	30.50	29.80	29.90	34.60	36.50	32.30
2	Alcoholic drinks, tobacco & narcotics	7.00	4.20	4.40	8.40	9.40	6.70
3	Clothing & footwear	6.30	6.90	9.40	8.30	8.70	7.90
4	Housing (net)[3], fuel & power	36.50	51.10	45.10	53.10	62.60	49.60
5	Household goods & services	9.70	15.40	15.90	25.90	43.40	22.10
6	Health	1.50	2.70	3.50	6.70	9.60	4.80
7	Transport	7.60	9.70	14.20	29.20	53.00	22.90
8	Communication	6.40	7.30	7.30	9.10	9.80	8.00
9	Recreation & culture	20.00	17.90	24.90	33.70	50.80	29.60
10	Education	-	-	-	-	[0.20]	[0.00]
11	Restaurants & hotels	4.60	7.60	10.20	17.40	25.40	13.10
12	Miscellaneous goods & services	9.80	13.60	15.10	20.30	52.70	22.50
1-12	All expenditure groups	139.90	166.40	179.90	246.70	362.10	219.60
13	Other expenditure items	11.60	24.60	29.40	30.50	97.50	39.20
Total expenditure		**151.60**	**191.10**	**209.30**	**277.20**	**459.60**	**258.90**
Average weekly expenditure per person (£)							
Total expenditure		**151.60**	**191.10**	**209.30**	**277.20**	**459.60**	**258.90**

Note: The commodity and service categories are not comparable to those in publications before 2001-02.

Please see background notes for symbols and conventions used in this report.

1 Mainly dependent on state pension and not economically active - see Appendix B.

2 Quintile groups have been calculated separately for retired and non-retired households.

3 Excluding mortgage interest payments, council tax and Northern Ireland rates.

Table 3.5
Expenditure of two adult households with children by disposable income quintile group, 2013
United Kingdom

	Lowest twenty per cent	Second quintile group	Third quintile group	Fourth quintile group	Highest twenty per cent	All house-holds
Lower boundary of group (£ per week)		256	417	600	882	
Weighted number of households (thousands)	270	630	1,230	1,640	1,620	5,390
Total number of households in sample	50	120	240	330	310	1,050
Total number of persons in sample	170	460	920	1,300	1,190	4,050
Total number of adults in sample	100	240	480	660	630	2,090
Weighted average number of persons per household	3.5	3.7	3.8	3.9	3.8	3.8
Commodity or service	Average weekly household expenditure (£)					
1 Food & non-alcoholic drinks	70.20	59.50	68.90	77.70	94.70	78.30
2 Alcoholic drinks, tobacco & narcotics	10.40	11.80	10.20	11.90	15.20	12.40
3 Clothing & footwear	18.30	18.20	24.60	33.70	42.10	31.60
4 Housing (net)[1], fuel & power	79.40	101.90	86.50	73.10	88.40	84.40
5 Household goods & services	20.10	21.00	28.20	33.20	51.00	35.30
6 Health	1.40	1.50	3.10	8.70	7.50	5.90
7 Transport	28.80	52.30	68.90	94.10	133.60	92.10
8 Communication	9.20	15.30	17.20	19.20	20.80	18.30
9 Recreation & culture	32.10	41.60	50.70	70.30	131.10	78.80
10 Education	[2.70]	[9.50]	2.70	3.90	38.40	14.60
11 Restaurants & hotels	21.30	24.00	33.50	49.40	72.50	48.40
12 Miscellaneous goods & services	18.70	28.80	35.40	55.60	89.80	56.30
1-12 All expenditure groups	312.50	385.50	430.00	530.60	785.10	556.30
13 Other expenditure items	26.50	41.80	63.80	99.20	187.30	107.20
Total expenditure	**339.00**	**427.40**	**493.80**	**629.80**	**972.40**	**663.50**
Average weekly expenditure per person (£)						
Total expenditure	**95.80**	**114.10**	**129.10**	**162.50**	**257.50**	**174.50**

Note: The commodity and service categories are not comparable to those in publications before 2001-02.
Please see background notes for symbols and conventions used in this report.
1 Excluding mortgage interest payments, council tax and Northern Ireland rates.

Table 3.5E
Expenditure of two adult households with children by disposable equivalised income quintile group (OECD-modified scale), 2013
United Kingdom

		Lowest twenty per cent	Second quintile group	Third quintile group	Fourth quintile group	Highest twenty per cent	All house-holds
Lower boundary of group (£ per week)			189	278	369	520	
Weighted number of households (thousands)		830	1,200	1,220	1,170	980	5,390
Total number of households in sample		160	240	240	230	190	1,050
Total number of persons in sample		640	990	890	840	670	4,050
Total number of adults in sample		310	480	470	450	370	2,090
Weighted average number of persons per household		4.0	4.0	3.7	3.7	3.6	3.8
Commodity or service		Average weekly household expenditure (£)					
1	Food & non-alcoholic drinks	65.80	71.10	76.30	80.20	98.00	78.30
2	Alcoholic drinks, tobacco & narcotics	12.20	9.50	12.00	13.90	14.90	12.40
3	Clothing & footwear	19.70	23.40	31.90	35.30	46.80	31.60
4	Housing (net)[1], fuel & power	92.40	90.60	74.00	68.60	101.90	84.40
5	Household goods & services	17.80	29.90	34.90	35.80	56.80	35.30
6	Health	1.70	4.40	8.00	6.80	7.40	5.90
7	Transport	42.80	72.90	83.40	113.30	143.00	92.10
8	Communication	13.40	18.10	18.30	20.40	19.80	18.30
9	Recreation & culture	35.90	60.50	59.60	89.70	149.00	78.80
10	Education	[8.00]	3.70	3.70	21.10	39.30	14.60
11	Restaurants & hotels	22.80	34.30	44.70	59.00	79.10	48.40
12	Miscellaneous goods & services	25.30	35.30	49.00	71.60	99.30	56.30
1-12	All expenditure groups	357.80	453.60	495.90	615.50	855.30	556.30
13	Other expenditure items	35.30	67.70	91.40	145.10	191.30	107.20
Total expenditure		**393.10**	**521.30**	**587.30**	**760.60**	**1046.60**	**663.50**
Average weekly expenditure per person (£)							
Total expenditure		**97.90**	**129.20**	**158.00**	**208.20**	**288.70**	**174.50**

Note: The commodity and service categories are not comparable to those in publications before 2001-02.
Please see background notes for symbols and conventions used in this report.
1 Excluding mortgage interest payments, council tax and Northern Ireland Rates.

Table 3.6
Expenditure of one adult households with children by disposable income quintile group, 2013
United Kingdom

	Lowest twenty per cent	Second quintile group	Third quintile group	Fourth quintile group	Highest twenty per cent	All house-holds
Lower boundary of group (£ per week)		256	417	600	882	
Weighted number of households (thousands)	520	460	260	100	30	1,360
Total number of households in sample	110	100	60	20	10	300
Total number of persons in sample	270	270	160	50	20	780
Total number of adults in sample	110	100	60	20	10	300
Weighted average number of persons per household	2.4	2.6	2.9	2.5	3.3	2.6
Commodity or service	Average weekly household expenditure (£)					
1 Food & non-alcoholic drinks	40.60	47.50	62.80	53.60	[85.40]	48.90
2 Alcoholic drinks, tobacco & narcotics	8.10	8.30	13.20	[7.90]	[44.70]	9.80
3 Clothing & footwear	9.40	19.60	20.50	[35.60]	[20.80]	17.00
4 Housing (net)[1], fuel & power	62.10	78.70	86.60	65.00	[164.30]	74.50
5 Household goods & services	15.90	16.80	30.20	34.20	[50.10]	20.90
6 Health	0.60	1.60	1.50	[2.20]	[32.00]	1.80
7 Transport	16.00	29.50	46.90	89.20	[152.50]	34.30
8 Communication	8.90	12.20	17.00	[18.50]	[22.00]	12.50
9 Recreation & culture	16.20	32.40	59.00	111.80	[141.50]	39.10
10 Education	[2.10]	[2.80]	[2.80]	[11.60]	[51.70]	4.10
11 Restaurants & hotels	10.30	20.40	38.40	[52.50]	[44.90]	22.80
12 Miscellaneous goods & services	13.20	23.00	53.20	46.20	[77.80]	27.80
1-12 All expenditure groups	203.30	292.60	432.00	528.20	[887.80]	313.50
13 Other expenditure items	11.40	33.00	50.70	125.80	[104.30]	36.10
Total expenditure	**214.70**	**325.60**	**482.70**	**654.00**	**[992.00]**	**349.60**
Average weekly expenditure per person (£)						
Total expenditure	**89.80**	**124.10**	**168.00**	**256.90**	**[298.70]**	**135.00**

Note: The commodity and service categories are not comparable to those in publications before 2001-02.
Please see background notes for symbols and conventions used in this report.
1 Excluding mortgage interest payments, council tax and Northern Ireland rates.

Table 3.6E
Expenditure of one adult households with children by disposable equivalised income quintile group (OECD-modified scale), 2013
United Kingdom

		Lowest twenty per cent	Second quintile group	Third quintile group	Fourth quintile group	Highest twenty per cent	All house-holds
Lower boundary of group (£ per week)			189	278	369	520	
Weighted number of households (thousands)		610	400	210	90	50	1,360
Total number of households in sample		130	90	50	20	10	300
Total number of persons in sample		360	230	110	50	30	780
Total number of adults in sample		130	90	50	20	10	300
Weighted average number of persons per household		2.6	2.7	2.4	2.5	2.5	2.6
Commodity or service		Average weekly household expenditure (£)					
1	Food & non-alcoholic drinks	42.30	54.70	53.40	50.90	[62.70]	48.90
2	Alcoholic drinks, tobacco & narcotics	9.00	7.60	14.50	[5.20]	[29.40]	9.80
3	Clothing & footwear	11.50	18.00	23.40	[27.40]	[30.50]	17.00
4	Housing (net)[1], fuel & power	63.50	86.60	77.50	85.50	[79.30]	74.50
5	Household goods & services	16.10	20.80	26.90	[27.10]	[44.80]	20.90
6	Health	0.70	1.60	[1.70]	[2.60]	[18.50]	1.80
7	Transport	16.90	34.40	45.40	88.60	[105.30]	34.30
8	Communication	8.80	14.70	15.70	[14.40]	[23.80]	12.50
9	Recreation & culture	21.50	33.10	56.70	100.60	[119.80]	39.10
10	Education	[2.70]	[2.80]	[2.50]	[1.10]	[48.80]	4.10
11	Restaurants & hotels	12.50	24.50	34.80	49.90	[34.00]	22.80
12	Miscellaneous goods & services	14.40	31.10	39.10	64.50	[49.10]	27.80
1-12	All expenditure groups	219.90	330.00	391.60	517.60	[646.00]	313.50
13	Other expenditure items	12.50	35.10	52.00	120.10	[116.20]	36.10
Total expenditure		**232.50**	**365.10**	**443.50**	**637.70**	**[762.20]**	**349.60**
Average weekly expenditure per person (£)							
Total expenditure		**89.10**	**136.40**	**183.60**	**250.30**	**[307.10]**	**135.00**

Note: The commodity and service categories are not comparable to those in publications before 2001-02.
Please see background notes for symbols and conventions used in this report.
1 Excluding mortgage interest payments, council tax and Northern Ireland Rates.

Table 3.7

Expenditure of two adult non-retired households by disposable income quintile group, 2013

United Kingdom

		Lowest twenty per cent	Second quintile group	Third quintile group	Fourth quintile group	Highest twenty per cent	All house-holds
Lower boundary of group (£ per week)[1]			315	496	688	960	
Weighted number of households (thousands)		650	1,090	1,290	1,420	1,280	5,720
Total number of households in sample		130	200	250	260	230	1,080
Total number of persons in sample		250	410	500	520	470	2,150
Total number of adults in sample		250	410	500	520	470	2,150
Weighted average number of persons per household		2.0	2.0	2.0	2.0	2.0	2.0
Commodity or service		Average weekly household expenditure (£)					
1	Food & non-alcoholic drinks	46.70	50.90	56.80	64.90	67.60	58.90
2	Alcoholic drinks, tobacco & narcotics	10.80	12.80	15.70	15.10	15.00	14.30
3	Clothing & footwear	10.30	11.40	22.00	32.80	35.40	24.30
4	Housing (net)[2], fuel & power	62.70	89.60	87.80	81.60	94.10	85.20
5	Household goods & services	26.60	31.50	37.80	38.60	61.40	40.80
6	Health	5.40	3.30	10.70	12.40	6.60	8.20
7	Transport	46.00	57.60	79.40	102.40	152.00	93.40
8	Communication	10.50	13.70	16.30	17.60	18.90	16.10
9	Recreation & culture	37.90	44.30	69.10	83.10	124.00	76.60
10	Education	[6.40]	[8.00]	[2.20]	[5.70]	[7.00]	5.70
11	Restaurants & hotels	21.40	27.20	39.50	63.50	88.80	52.10
12	Miscellaneous goods & services	22.50	27.10	33.80	50.40	64.40	42.20
1-12	All expenditure groups	307.50	377.30	471.20	567.90	735.10	517.70
13	Other expenditure items	39.00	44.80	61.70	81.60	141.60	78.70
Total expenditure		**346.50**	**422.10**	**532.80**	**649.50**	**876.70**	**596.30**
Average weekly expenditure per person (£)							
Total expenditure		**173.20**	**211.00**	**266.40**	**324.80**	**438.40**	**298.20**

Note: The commodity and service categories are not comparable to those in publications before 2001-02.
Please see background notes for symbols and conventions used in this report.
1 Quintile groups have been calculated separately for retired and non-retired households.
2 Excluding mortgage interest payments, council tax and Northern Ireland rates.

Table 3.7E
Expenditure of two adult non-retired households by disposable equivalised income quintile group (OECD-modified scale), 2013
United Kingdom

		Lowest twenty per cent	Second quintile group	Third quintile group	Fourth quintile group	Highest twenty per cent	All house-holds
Lower boundary of group (£ per week)[1]			198	299	404	561	
Weighted number of households (thousands)		570	810	1,180	1,290	1,870	5,720
Total number of households in sample		110	150	230	240	340	1,080
Total number of persons in sample		220	300	470	470	690	2,150
Total number of adults in sample		220	300	470	470	690	2,150
Weighted average number of persons per household		2.0	2.0	2.0	2.0	2.0	2.0
Commodity or service		Average weekly household expenditure (£)					
1	Food & non-alcoholic drinks	45.00	48.70	57.70	61.50	66.60	58.90
2	Alcoholic drinks, tobacco & narcotics	11.10	12.90	14.00	15.30	15.30	14.30
3	Clothing & footwear	10.00	10.50	19.10	27.20	36.00	24.30
4	Housing (net)[2], fuel & power	63.80	88.90	84.50	87.80	88.60	85.20
5	Household goods & services	25.50	32.10	35.10	37.50	55.20	40.80
6	Health	5.50	3.10	8.70	11.20	8.90	8.20
7	Transport	44.70	52.20	75.80	92.00	138.10	93.40
8	Communication	10.30	13.80	15.40	16.60	18.90	16.10
9	Recreation & culture	36.40	45.00	60.80	78.40	111.20	76.60
10	Education	[7.20]	[8.50]	[2.50]	[1.90]	8.70	5.70
11	Restaurants & hotels	19.80	27.90	32.10	52.20	84.90	52.10
12	Miscellaneous goods & services	21.00	26.90	32.50	46.60	58.40	42.20
1-12	All expenditure groups	300.30	370.60	438.30	528.30	690.80	517.70
13	**Other expenditure items**	**37.30**	**42.50**	**52.60**	**75.80**	**125.40**	**78.70**
Total expenditure		**337.70**	**413.10**	**490.90**	**604.00**	**816.10**	**596.30**
Average weekly expenditure per person (£)							
Total expenditure		**168.80**	**206.60**	**245.40**	**302.00**	**408.10**	**298.20**

Note: The commodity and service categories are not comparable to those in publications before 2001-02.
Please see background notes for symbols and conventions used in this report.
1 Quintile groups have been calculated separately for retired and non-retired households.
2 Excluding mortgage interest payments, council tax and Northern Ireland Rates.

Table 3.8

Expenditure of one person retired households mainly dependent on state pensions[1] by disposable income quintile group, 2013

United Kingdom

		Lowest twenty per cent	Second quintile group	Third quintile group	Fourth quintile group	Highest twenty per cent	All house-holds
Lower boundary of group (£ per week)[2]			193	277	379	555	
Weighted number of households (thousands)		560	260	50	0	0	870
Total number of households in sample		100	50	..	0	0	150
Total number of persons in sample		100	50	..	0	0	150
Total number of adults in sample		100	50	..	0	0	150
Weighted average number of persons per household		1.0	1.0	1.0	0	0	1.0
Commodity or service		Average weekly household expenditure (£)					
1	Food & non-alcoholic drinks	29.30	28.40	[26.90]	-	-	28.90
2	Alcoholic drinks, tobacco & narcotics	2.00	[3.80]	[2.50]	-	-	2.60
3	Clothing & footwear	5.20	[2.20]	[0.90]	-	-	4.00
4	Housing (net)[3], fuel & power	41.90	46.80	[48.70]	-	-	43.80
5	Household goods & services	10.70	14.80	[3.30]	-	-	11.40
6	Health	2.30	[2.10]	[0.50]	-	-	2.10
7	Transport	7.90	10.50	[3.20]	-	-	8.40
8	Communication	7.00	7.30	[4.00]	-	-	6.90
9	Recreation & culture	16.70	18.70	[17.40]	-	-	17.30
10	Education	-	-	-	-	-	-
11	Restaurants & hotels	7.10	[9.70]	[2.00]	-	-	7.60
12	Miscellaneous goods & services	14.50	16.50	[6.80]	-	-	14.60
1-12	All expenditure groups	144.70	160.80	[116.00]	-	-	147.70
13	Other expenditure items	14.60	17.70	[20.10]	-	-	15.80
Total expenditure		**159.20**	**178.50**	**[136.10]**	-	-	**163.50**
Average weekly expenditure per person (£)							
Total expenditure		**159.20**	**178.50**	**[136.10]**	-	-	**163.50**

Note: The commodity and service categories are not comparable to those in publications before 2001-02.

Please see background notes for symbols and conventions used in this report.

1 Mainly dependent on state pension and not economically active - see Appendix B.

2 Quintile groups have been calculated separately for retired and non-retired households.

3 Excluding mortgage interest payments, council tax and Northern Ireland rates.

Table 3.8E

Expenditure of one person retired households mainly dependent on state pensions[1] by disposable equivalised income quintile group (OECD-modified scale), 2013

United Kingdom

		Lowest twenty per cent	Second quintile group	Third quintile group	Fourth quintile group	Highest twenty per cent	All house-holds
Lower boundary of group (£ per week)[2]			177	228	298	390	
Weighted number of households (thousands)		420	290	130	30	0	870
Total number of households in sample		80	50	20	..	0	150
Total number of persons in sample		80	50	20	..	0	150
Total number of adults in sample		80	50	20	..	0	150
Weighted average number of persons per household		1.0	1.0	1.0	1.0	0	1.0
Commodity or service		Average weekly household expenditure (£)					
1	Food & non-alcoholic drinks	28.60	30.60	25.70	[29.90]	-	28.90
2	Alcoholic drinks, tobacco & narcotics	2.40	[1.80]	[4.80]	[3.20]	-	2.60
3	Clothing & footwear	4.60	[4.90]	[1.10]	-	-	4.00
4	Housing (net)[3], fuel & power	38.10	53.80	38.80	[45.70]	-	43.80
5	Household goods & services	10.20	10.60	[19.60]	[1.00]	-	11.40
6	Health	2.40	1.90	[2.10]	[0.60]	-	2.10
7	Transport	8.20	6.40	[14.30]	[5.00]	-	8.40
8	Communication	6.50	7.50	7.60	[2.20]	-	6.90
9	Recreation & culture	15.70	18.90	17.50	[23.30]	-	17.30
10	Education	-	-	-	-	-	-
11	Restaurants & hotels	6.30	9.80	[8.30]	[1.10]	-	7.60
12	Miscellaneous goods & services	11.00	17.50	21.20	[7.70]	-	14.60
1-12	All expenditure groups	134.20	163.80	160.80	[119.60]	-	147.70
13	Other expenditure items	13.90	16.90	17.50	[26.40]	-	15.80
Total expenditure		**148.10**	**180.70**	**178.30**	**[146.00]**	-	**163.50**
Average weekly expenditure per person (£)							
Total expenditure		**148.10**	**180.70**	**178.30**	**[146.00]**	-	**163.50**

Note: The commodity and service categories are not comparable to those in publications before 2001-02.

Please see background notes for symbols and conventions used in this report.

1 Mainly dependent on state pension and not economically active - see Appendix B.

2 Quintile groups have been calculated separately for retired and non-retired households.

3 Excluding mortgage interest payments, council tax and Northern Ireland rates.

Table 3.9

Expenditure of two adult retired households mainly dependent on state pensions[1] by disposable income quintile group, 2013

United Kingdom

		Lowest twenty per cent	Second quintile group	Third quintile group	Fourth quintile group	Highest twenty per cent	All house-holds
Lower boundary of group (£ per week)[2]			193	277	379	555	
Weighted number of households (thousands)		10	180	210	40	..	450
Total number of households in sample		..	50	50	10	..	110
Total number of persons in sample		..	90	100	20	..	230
Total number of adults in sample		..	90	100	20	..	230
Weighted average number of persons per household		2.0	2.0	2.0	2.0	2.0	2.0
Commodity or service		Average weekly household expenditure (£)					
1	Food & non-alcoholic drinks	[67.40]	57.60	54.90	[70.40]	[59.70]	57.90
2	Alcoholic drinks, tobacco & narcotics	[2.40]	[9.30]	6.50	[9.60]	[13.90]	7.90
3	Clothing & footwear	[4.60]	[7.90]	8.60	[15.20]	[2.70]	8.70
4	Housing (net)[3], fuel & power	[40.70]	47.90	48.60	[38.30]	[29.90]	46.80
5	Household goods & services	[12.50]	20.30	26.30	[15.80]	[5.00]	22.10
6	Health	[2.60]	[5.60]	6.10	[4.80]	[0.60]	5.60
7	Transport	[152.40]	25.20	40.00	[31.80]	[51.00]	36.80
8	Communication	[14.40]	8.30	8.50	[8.30]	[10.50]	8.60
9	Recreation & culture	[30.80]	46.40	42.50	[75.40]	[33.00]	46.70
10	Education	-	-	-	[1.80]	-	[0.20]
11	Restaurants & hotels	[5.50]	19.40	25.60	[34.60]	[15.80]	23.20
12	Miscellaneous goods & services	[23.10]	20.00	32.20	[32.80]	[23.00]	26.90
1-12	All expenditure groups	[356.40]	267.70	299.90	[338.90]	[245.10]	291.50
13	Other expenditure items	[54.60]	27.90	34.90	[27.40]	[30.00]	31.90
Total expenditure		**[411.00]**	**295.60**	**334.80**	**[366.40]**	**[275.00]**	**323.40**
Average weekly expenditure per person (£) **Total expenditure**		**[205.50]**	**147.80**	**167.40**	**[183.20]**	**[137.50]**	**161.70**

Note: The commodity and service categories are not comparable to those in publications before 2001-02.

Please see background notes for symbols and conventions used in this report.

1 Mainly dependent on state pension and not economically active - see Appendix B.

2 Quintile groups have been calculated separately for retired and non-retired households.

3 Excluding mortgage interest payments, council tax and Northern Ireland rates.

Table 3.9E

Expenditure of two adult retired households mainly dependent on state pensions[1] by disposable equivalised income quintile group (OECD-modified scale), 2013

United Kingdom

		Lowest twenty per cent	Second quintile group	Third quintile group	Fourth quintile group	Highest twenty per cent	All house-holds
Lower boundary of group (£ per week)[2]			177	228	298	390	
Weighted number of households (thousands)		170	190	60	30	..	450
Total number of households in sample		40	50	20	..	..	110
Total number of persons in sample		90	90	30	10	..	230
Total number of adults in sample		90	90	30	10	..	230
Weighted average number of persons per household		2.0	2.0	2.0	2.0	2.0	2.0
Commodity or service		Average weekly household expenditure (£)					
1	Food & non-alcoholic drinks	58.40	52.90	[68.70]	[67.40]	[47.10]	57.90
2	Alcoholic drinks, tobacco & narcotics	9.00	[6.80]	[7.70]	[6.50]	[27.00]	7.90
3	Clothing & footwear	8.30	7.80	[13.60]	[7.90]	[1.30]	8.70
4	Housing (net)[3], fuel & power	49.10	47.60	[47.60]	[27.70]	[29.70]	46.80
5	Household goods & services	14.70	29.50	[28.30]	[7.90]	[2.80]	22.10
6	Health	4.00	5.20	[12.10]	[5.10]	-	5.60
7	Transport	36.00	32.00	[53.80]	[35.60]	[53.50]	36.80
8	Communication	8.80	8.20	[10.10]	[7.80]	[4.90]	8.60
9	Recreation & culture	46.10	45.10	[45.40]	[65.90]	[34.60]	46.70
10	Education	-	-	-	[2.80]	-	[0.20]
11	Restaurants & hotels	18.40	26.10	[23.00]	[34.10]	[25.80]	23.20
12	Miscellaneous goods & services	19.50	32.40	[25.80]	[40.00]	[12.40]	26.90
1-12	All expenditure groups	272.40	293.60	[336.20]	[308.80]	[238.80]	291.50
13	Other expenditure items	29.80	34.50	[32.60]	[26.40]	[22.80]	31.90
Total expenditure		**302.30**	**328.10**	**[368.80]**	**[335.20]**	**[261.70]**	**323.40**
Average weekly expenditure per person (£)							
Total expenditure		**151.10**	**164.10**	**[184.40]**	**[167.60]**	**[130.80]**	**161.70**

Note: The commodity and service categories are not comparable to those in publications before 2001-02.

Please see background notes for symbols and conventions used in this report.

1 Mainly dependent on state pension and not economically active - see Appendix B.

2 Quintile groups have been calculated separately for retired and non-retired households.

3 Excluding mortgage interest payments, council tax and Northern Ireland rates.

Table 3.10

Expenditure of two adult retired households not mainly dependent on state pensions[1] by disposable income quintile group, 2013

United Kingdom

	Lowest twenty per cent	Second quintile group	Third quintile group	Fourth quintile group	Highest twenty per cent	All house-holds
Lower boundary of group (£ per week)[2]		193	277	379	555	
Weighted number of households (thousands)	30	240	500	870	870	2,510
Total number of households in sample	..	50	120	210	210	590
Total number of persons in sample	10	90	230	420	420	1,180
Total number of adults in sample	10	90	230	420	420	1,180
Weighted average number of persons per household	2.0	2.0	2.0	2.0	2.0	2.0
Commodity or service	Average weekly household expenditure (£)					
1 Food & non-alcoholic drinks	[63.70]	52.50	56.90	58.40	71.80	62.30
2 Alcoholic drinks, tobacco & narcotics	[3.80]	11.50	10.90	11.20	14.60	12.20
3 Clothing & footwear	[6.80]	6.40	11.20	15.00	25.20	16.90
4 Housing (net)[3], fuel & power	[73.00]	55.50	53.20	51.80	64.70	57.20
5 Household goods & services	[16.80]	11.10	32.70	29.10	52.30	35.90
6 Health	[2.80]	1.60	4.30	9.50	15.10	9.60
7 Transport	[12.60]	26.70	34.50	55.40	82.30	57.30
8 Communication	[10.90]	8.30	8.70	10.70	11.50	10.40
9 Recreation & culture	[40.50]	26.40	44.70	79.40	110.50	77.80
10 Education	-	-	-	[4.90]	[5.30]	[3.50]
11 Restaurants & hotels	[18.70]	18.30	24.00	34.20	52.30	36.70
12 Miscellaneous goods & services	[16.70]	20.60	24.40	30.60	52.50	35.80
1-12 All expenditure groups	[266.30]	238.90	305.30	390.20	558.20	415.50
13 Other expenditure items	[39.60]	14.10	30.90	38.80	75.00	47.40
Total expenditure	**[305.90]**	**253.00**	**336.20**	**429.00**	**633.20**	**462.90**
Average weekly expenditure per person (£)						
Total expenditure	**[153.00]**	**126.50**	**168.10**	**214.50**	**316.60**	**231.50**

Note: The commodity and service categories are not comparable to those in publications before 2001-02.
Please see background notes for symbols and conventions used in this report.
1 Mainly dependent on state pension and not economically active - see Appendix B.
2 Quintile groups have been calculated separately for retired and non-retired households.
3 Excluding mortgage interest payments, council tax and Northern Ireland Rates.

Table 3.10E
Expenditure of two adult retired households not mainly dependent on state pensions[1] by disposable equivalised income quintile group (OECD-modified scale), 2013

United Kingdom

		Lowest twenty per cent	Second quintile group	Third quintile group	Fourth quintile group	Highest twenty per cent	All house-holds
Lower boundary of group (£ per week)[2]			177	228	298	390	
Weighted number of households (thousands)		240	350	550	660	710	2,510
Total number of households in sample		50	80	130	160	170	590
Total number of persons in sample		90	160	270	330	340	1,180
Total number of adults in sample		90	160	270	330	340	1,180
Weighted average number of persons per household		2.0	2.0	2.0	2.0	2.0	2.0
Commodity or service		Average weekly household expenditure (£)					
1	Food & non-alcoholic drinks	53.30	55.60	57.30	62.70	72.10	62.30
2	Alcoholic drinks, tobacco & narcotics	11.50	12.60	9.00	11.40	15.60	12.20
3	Clothing & footwear	6.30	9.50	13.00	17.90	26.20	16.90
4	Housing (net)[3], fuel & power	59.30	52.50	53.80	49.70	68.30	57.20
5	Household goods & services	12.70	31.10	23.90	32.90	58.50	35.90
6	Health	1.70	3.60	5.30	12.50	15.80	9.60
7	Transport	18.90	39.20	48.70	64.90	78.90	57.30
8	Communication	8.50	9.00	9.60	11.10	11.60	10.40
9	Recreation & culture	25.50	45.40	60.70	85.70	117.40	77.80
10	Education	-	-	[7.60]	[0.20]	[6.40]	[3.50]
11	Restaurants & hotels	18.20	24.90	26.70	40.70	52.90	36.70
12	Miscellaneous goods & services	20.40	23.70	26.40	35.50	54.70	35.80
1-12	All expenditure groups	236.20	307.10	342.10	425.10	578.40	415.50
13	Other expenditure items	17.90	28.20	31.70	51.10	75.70	47.40
Total expenditure		**254.10**	**335.30**	**373.80**	**476.30**	**654.10**	**462.90**
Average weekly expenditure per person (£)							
Total expenditure		**127.10**	**167.70**	**186.90**	**238.10**	**327.10**	**231.50**

Note: The commodity and service categories are not comparable to those in publications before 2001-02.

Please see background notes for symbols and conventions used in this report.

1 Mainly dependent on state pension and not economically active - see Appendix B.

2 Quintile groups have been calculated separately for retired and non-retired households.

3 Excluding mortgage interest payments, council tax and Northern Ireland Rates.

Table 3.11
Income and source of income by disposable income quintile group, 2013
United Kingdom

Disposable income quintile group	Weighted number of households	Number of households in the sample	Weekly household income: Disposable	Weekly household income: Gross	Source of income: Wages and salaries	Self employment	Investments	Annuities and pensions[1]	Social security benefits[2]	Other sources
	(000s)	Number	£	£	Percentage of gross weekly household income					
Lowest twenty per cent	5,380	1,010	164	170	*13*	*4*	*2*	*9*	*70*	*1*
Second quintile group	5,360	1,070	335	365	*36*	*4*	*2*	*16*	*39*	*2*
Third quintile group	5,370	1,070	505	577	*55*	*5*	*2*	*15*	*21*	*2*
Fourth quintile group	5,370	1,010	726	868	*72*	*7*	*2*	*9*	*9*	*2*
Highest twenty per cent	5,370	980	1,341	1,715	*76*	*9*	*5*	*6*	*3*	*1*

Please see background notes for symbols and conventions used in this report.
1 Other than social security benefits.
2 Excluding housing benefit and council tax benefit (rates rebate in Northern Ireland) - see Appendix B.

Table 3.11E
Income and source of income by disposable equivalised income quintile group (OECD-modified scale), 2013
United Kingdom

Disposable equivalised income quintile group	Weighted number of households	Number of households in the sample	Weekly household income: Disposable	Weekly household income: Gross	Source of income: Wages and salaries	Self employment	Investments	Annuities and pensions[1]	Social security benefits[2]	Other sources
	(000s)	Number	£	£	Percentage of gross weekly household income					
Lowest twenty per cent	5,370	1,030	195	202	*22*	*5*	*1*	*4*	*65*	*2*
Second quintile group	5,370	1,060	376	410	*46*	*5*	*1*	*10*	*36*	*2*
Third quintile group	5,370	1,050	528	605	*61*	*6*	*2*	*11*	*18*	*3*
Fourth quintile group	5,370	1,030	721	868	*71*	*6*	*2*	*11*	*9*	*1*
Highest twenty per cent	5,360	980	1,252	1,609	*74*	*9*	*6*	*8*	*3*	*0*

Please see background notes for symbols and conventions used in this report.
1 Other than social security benefits.
2 Excluding housing benefit and council tax benefit (rates rebate in Northern Ireland) - see Appendix B.

Table 3.12
Percentage of households by composition in each disposable and equivalised income decile group (OECD-modified scale), 2013
United Kingdom

Percentages

	Income decile group									
	Lowest ten per cent		Second		Third		Fourth		Fifth	
	Disposable	Equivalised	Disposable	Equivalised	Disposable	Equivalised	Disposable	Equivalised	Disposable	Equivalised
Lower boundary of group (£ per week)			174	142	256	189	333	231	417	278
Average size of household	**1.3**	**2.1**	**1.6**	**2.2**	**1.7**	**2.4**	**2.1**	**2.4**	**2.3**	**2.5**
One adult retired mainly dependent on state pensions[1]	15	6	14	13	[3]	8	[1]	[4]	-	[1]
One adult, other retired	20	7	29	21	24	14	14	16	8	12
One adult, non-retired	42	35	18	11	25	9	18	10	15	14
One adult, one child	7	9	5	[3]	4	4	4	[3]	[2]	[3]
One adult, two or more children	[2]	6	5	5	4	4	5	4	4	[2]
Two adults, retired mainly dependent on state pensions[1]	-	[1]	5	6	7	6	3	[1]	[1]	[1]
Two adults, other retired	[1]	[3]	7	8	12	11	17	14	17	12
Two adults, non-retired	9	11	7	8	9	10	17	14	24	17
Two adults, one child	[1]	6	[4]	6	5	6	6	9	9	10
Two adults, two children	[0]	5	[3]	5	[3]	8	5	9	6	12
Two adults, three children	[1]	[4]	[1]	[2]	[2]	5	[2]	5	[4]	[3]
Two adults, four or more children	-	[1]	-	[2]	[0]	[3]	[0]	[1]	[1]	[1]
Three adults	[1]	[1]	-	[2]	[1]	6	[4]	[4]	6	4
Three adults, one or more children	-	[3]	[1]	[3]	[1]	[4]	[2]	[2]	[2]	4
All other households without children	[1]	[2]	-	[3]	[0]	[1]	[2]	[3]	[1]	[4]
All other households with children	-	[1]	-	[1]	-	[1]	[0]	[2]	[0]	[1]

	Income decile group									
	Sixth		Seventh		Eighth		Ninth		Highest ten per cent	
	Disposable	Equivalised	Disposable	Equivalised	Disposable	Equivalised	Disposable	Equivalised	Disposable	Equivalised
Lower boundary of group (£ per week)	504	319	600	369	720	432	882	520	1,150	664
Average size of household	**2.5**	**2.4**	**2.9**	**2.4**	**2.8**	**2.5**	**3.0**	**2.4**	**3.2**	**2.3**
One adult retired mainly dependent on state pensions[1]	-	[0]	-	[0]	-	-	-	-	-	-
One adult, other retired	6	11	[2]	8	[1]	7	[0]	5	[1]	[4]
One adult, non-retired	13	15	10	13	7	15	[3]	16	[3]	16
One adult, one child	[1]	[2]	[1]	[1]	[1]	[1]	-	[1]	[0]	[0]
One adult, two or more children	[2]	[2]	[1]	[1]	[0]	[1]	[0]	[0]	[1]	[0]
Two adults, retired mainly dependent on state pensions[1]	[0]	[0]	-	[0]	[0]	-	-	[0]	-	-
Two adults, other retired	15	13	12	14	6	9	5	5	[2]	5
Two adults, non-retired	27	21	25	23	34	28	33	38	28	43
Two adults, one child	13	9	10	10	11	9	12	8	10	9
Two adults, two children	8	10	16	11	13	10	16	7	15	9
Two adults, three children	4	[1]	5	[2]	[2]	[2]	[2]	[2]	5	[2]
Two adults, four or more children	[2]	[0]	[2]	[0]	[1]	[0]	[1]	-	[0]	-
Three adults	5	8	8	8	12	11	12	8	10	7
Three adults, one or more children	[3]	5	[3]	[3]	6	[3]	6	[3]	8	[2]
All other households without children	[1]	[3]	[3]	[4]	[4]	5	7	7	14	[2]
All other households with children	[1]	[2]	[2]	[1]	[1]	[1]	[2]	[0]	[3]	[1]

Please see background notes for symbols and conventions used in this report.

1 Mainly dependent on state pension and not economically active - see Appendix B.

Office for
National Statistics

Chapter 4: Trends in household expenditure over time

Abstract

This chapter examines trends in household expenditure over time. Table 4.1 and table 4.2 (see tables section) represent expenditure for the years 2001/02 to 2013, adjusted to take account of inflation mainly using the Consumer Prices Index (CPI). This enables a comparison of expenditure to be made between survey years that allows for changing prices. More detail on this is given in the Background section. Year-on-year comparisons must be treated with caution, because each year the LCF is reviewed and changes are made to keep it up to date. Expenditure over the same period is also shown without adjusting for inflation in table 4.3 (see tables section).

Key points

- Household average weekly expenditure has decreased since 2006, once inflation has been taken into account.
- Spending declined to £517.30 in 2013, from its peak in 2006 (adjusted to 2013 prices) when households spent an average of £539.80 per week.
- Between 2001/2 and 2006, average expenditure was at a higher level than that seen since 2006.
- Housing (net), fuel and power accounted for the highest average weekly spending in 2013, at £74.40, an increase from £70.70 in 2012 (adjusted to 2013 prices). Renting was the biggest area of expenditure in this category, followed by electricity gas and other fuels (it does not include mortgage payments, council tax or Northern Ireland rates). This category accounted for 14% of household expenditure, on average, in 2013.
- Transport remains the second highest expenditure category, averaging £70.40 per week in 2013. This was an increase from £64.80 per week in 2012, driven by an increase in the sales of new cars. However, transport expenditure has decreased in recent years from £88.00 in 2001/2 (adjusted for inflation).

The results show slight increases across a range of expenditure categories. However, these findings should be treated with caution due to changes to the way the survey recorded certain types of expenditure in 2013.

About this chapter

This chapter examines trends in household expenditure over time. Table 4.1 (82.5 Kb Excel sheet) and table 4.2 (91.5 Kb Excel sheet) present expenditure for the years 2001/2 to 2013, adjusted to take account of inflation using mainly the Consumer Prices Index (CPI). This enables a comparison of expenditure to be made between survey years that allows for changing prices. Expenditure over the same period is also shown without adjusting for inflation (table 4.3 (82 Kb Excel sheet)).

Changes and differences mentioned in the text have been found to be statistically significant at the 95% confidence level, unless stated. There is more detail in the background section.

Trends in average household spending

This section discusses some of the trends seen in average household weekly spending since 2001/2, once the effects of inflation have been taken into account.

Figure 4.1: Total household expenditure based on COICOP classification, 2001-02 to 2013, at 2013 prices [1]

United Kingdom

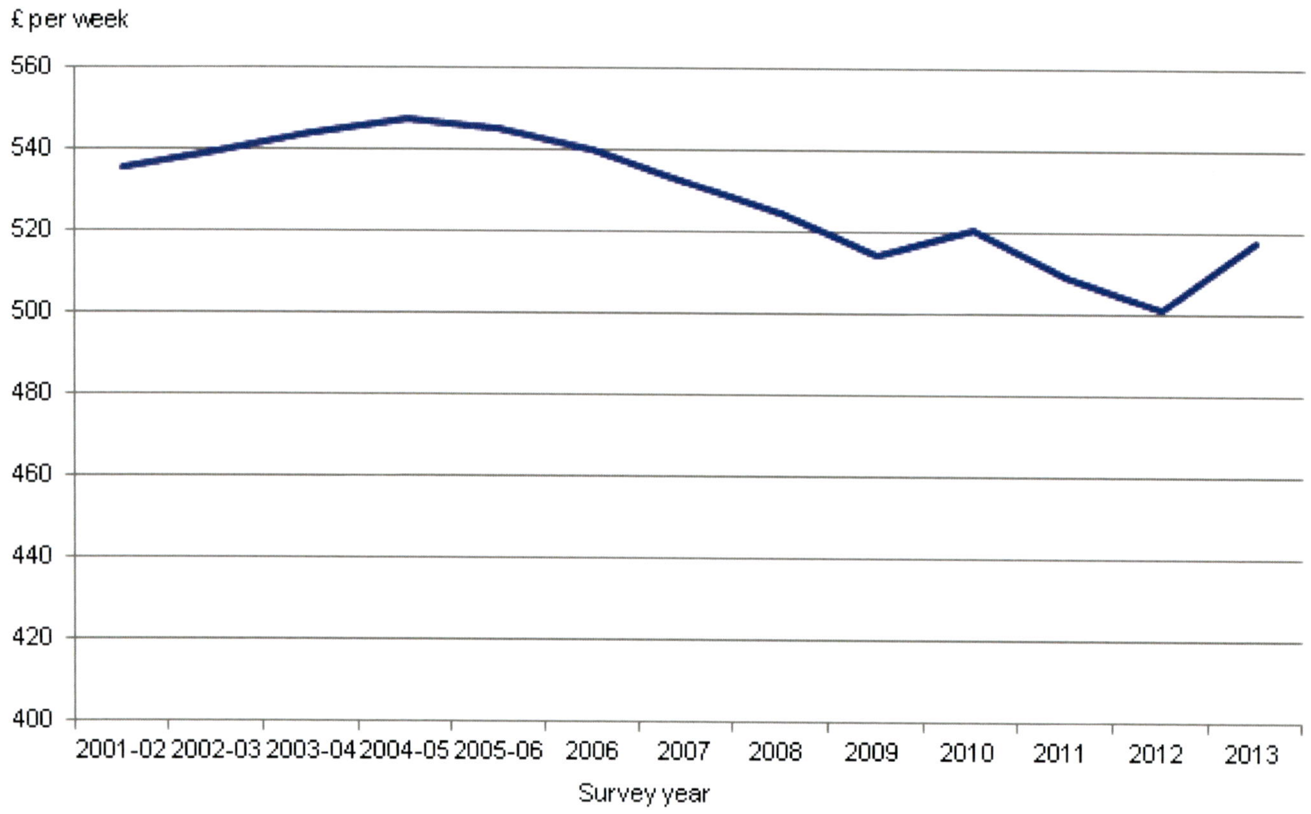

Source: Living Costs and Food Survey - Office for National Statistics

Notes:

1. Figures have been deflated to 2013 prices using deflators specific to the COICOP category.
2. In 2006, Family Spending changed to report for a calendar year instead of a financial year.

3. From 2001-02 to 2005-06, figures shown are calculated from weighted data using non-response weights based on the 1991 Census and population figures from the 1991 and 2001 Censuses. From 2006 onwards, figures shown are calculated from weighted data using non-response weights and population figures based on the 2001 Census.

Download chart

XLS XLS format
(75.5 Kb)

Figure 4.1 shows total expenditure over the years from 2001/2 to 2013. The figures have been adjusted to 2013 prices, to allow for the effects of inflation. Average weekly household spending was £539.80 in 2006, and started declining, just before the economic downturn, in 2007 (when £531.70 per week was recorded). Average spending decreased further to £501.00 in 2012, and then increased to £517.30 in 2013[1]. Table 4.1 (82.5 Kb Excel sheet) shows that household income declined slightly later than expenditure, following the start of the downturn. Disposable household income peaked in 2008 at £676 (adjusted to 2013 prices), declining to £612 in 2012 and £614 in 2013[2].

The trend observed in household spending after 2008 is broadly consistent with the wider economic context. Between 2008 quarter 1 and 2009 quarter 2, Gross Domestic Product (GDP) fell by 6.0%, marking the deepest economic downturn since ONS records began in 1948. The latest downturn is similar to the 5.9% fall in the early 1980s, while output fell by 2.4% in the early 1990s. The subsequent recovery has also been the slowest. However, the UK economy showed signs of increasing momentum throughout 2013 with GDP growing by 1.7%. The UK economy is now estimated to have surpassed the quarter 1 2008 pre-downturn peak in the quarter 3 2013. These figures can be found on the Office for National Statistics website.

If spending is considered without adjusting for inflation we see a different trend. Household spending, at the prices at the time the surveys were carried out, has increased from £398.30 in 2001/2 to £517.30 in 2013.

Notes

1. This increase was not found to be significant at the 95% confidence level; refer to the background section of the chapter for further details.

2. Standard errors are not calculated for income estimates in Family Spending. Therefore this change has not been tested for statistical significance at the 95% confidence level; refer to the background section of the chapter for further details.

Trends in spending patterns

Figure 4.2: Expenditure on selected categories based on COICOP classification, 2001-02 to 2013, at 2013 prices [1]

United Kingdom

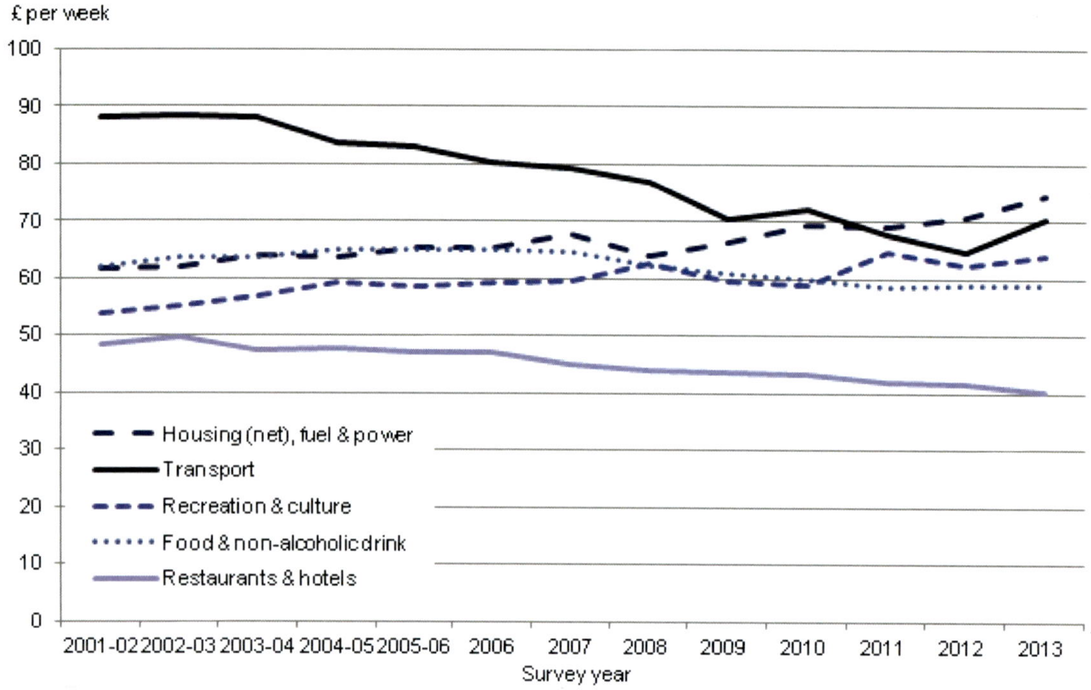

Source: Living Costs and Food Survey - Office for National Statistics

Notes:

1. Figures have been deflated to 2013 prices using deflators specific to the COICOP category.
2. In 2006, Family Spending changed to report for a calendar year instead of a financial year.
3. From 2001-02 to 2005-06, figures shown are calculated from weighted data using non-response weights based on the 1991 Census and population figures from the 1991 and 2001 Censuses. From 2006 onwards, figures shown are calculated from weighted data using non-response weights and population figures based on the 2001 Census.

Download chart

XLS XLS format
(80.5 Kb)

Figure 4.2 shows the total household expenditure from 2001/2 to 2013 on housing (net), fuel and power, transport, recreation and culture, food and non-alcoholic drink and restaurants and hotels adjusted to 2013 prices. These were the five categories with the highest spending over this period. The household expenditure trends for these categories are discussed in more detail below.

Housing (net), fuel and power has again accounted for the highest average spending in 2013. This category is mainly made up of:

- net rent: £32.00 per week in 2013

- electricity gas and other fuels: £26.50 in 2013
- maintenance and repair of dwelling: £7.10 in 2013
- water supply and miscellaneous charges: £8.70 in 2013.

Note: these figures are averaged across all households, for example, whether they pay rent or not.

The category housing (net), fuel and power does not include mortgage payments. Mortgage interest payments are included within the “other expenditure items” category. Spending in this category has fluctuated over time, decreasing overall from £78.30 in 2001/2 (adjusted for inflation) to £73.00 in 2013[1] (table 4.1 (82.5 Kb Excel sheet)). Capital repayment of mortgages for 2013 is detailed in section 14 (“other items recorded”) of table A1 (153.5 Kb Excel sheet) of this report. A full picture of housing related expenditure is provided in Chapter 2, including those, such as mortgage payments, that fall outside the Classification of Individual COnsumption by Purpose (COICOP) classification.

Rent payments make up the largest proportion of household expenditure in the category housing (net), fuel and power. The number of households renting accommodation has increased over recent years, as reported by the English Housing Survey. This is supported by figures published in table A50 (50 Kb Excel sheet) of Family Spending for 2013, and the corresponding table for 2006, which showed the proportion of households renting increased, from 29% in 2006 to 35% in 2013[2]. Therefore, the increased proportion of households renting has contributed to higher spending on housing (net), fuel and power.

Average household spending on transport decreased between 2001/2 (adjusted to 2013 prices) and 2013. However, it increased to £70.40 in 2013, from £64.80 per week in 2012. Households allocated an average of 14% of total expenditure to transport in 2013. Higher average household expenditure on transport between 2012 and 2013 can partly be attributed to increased purchase of new cars. Vehicle purchases were recorded as being at a six-year high with 1,074,622 new private cars registered.

Purchasing new cars is an area where households could moderate or defer expenditure, which may lead to demand building up over time. This is sometimes referred to as “pent up demand”. This may have fuelled the increase in sales of new cars seen in 2013, with consumers replacing vehicles they kept hold of through the recent downturn.

Recent years have seen the price of petrol and diesel increase substantially, with costs rising above the overall rate of inflation in 2012. However, between 2012 and 2013 prices decreased slightly so the increase in transport expenditure in 2013 cannot be attributed to spending on fuel.

Decreases in expenditure have been seen in categories that include some elements of discretionary spending, but not all. For example, spending on restaurants and hotels has gradually decreased to £40.40 in 2013, from £48.50 in 2001/2. This suggests that, in less favourable economic conditions, households are prepared to limit their spending on hotel stays and restaurant visits.

In contrast, overall spending on recreation and culture increased between 2001/2 and 2013, from £53.80 (adjusted for inflation) to £63.90 on average per week. This category includes a wide range of expenditure, including: information processing equipment, games, gardening items, sport, cinema and theatre admissions, and package holidays. A common feature of these products and services is that they would generally be considered to constitute discretionary spending (though see discussion below), so it is interesting that these types of expenditures have held up over time. For example, package holidays abroad accounted for an average of £21.00 per week of household expenditure in 2013[3]. This reflects the continued growth of the UK cruise market, with the number of people taking an ocean cruise continuing to grow by 1.5% in 2013. Expenditure on items such as TV, video, computers and recreational activities has also held up over time, showing the high priority placed on these goods and services by many households, regardless of economic circumstances.

There has been a slight decrease in the average weekly expenditure on alcoholic drinks, tobacco and narcotics in 2013 compared with 2012. Average weekly expenditure has gone down from £18.20 in 2001/2 to £12.00 in 2013, once inflation has been taken into account. Another likely factor is the well-documented decrease in the proportion of people who smoke; latest smoking figures show that the proportion of people smoking has decreased to 19% in 2013, from 27% in 2000.

Expenditure on clothing and footwear has fluctuated only slightly over the years 2011 to 2013 (when a weekly average of £22.60 was recorded). This is following a substantial increase from £15.40 in 2001/2 (adjusted for inflation). Spending on food and non-alcoholic drink remained very similar for the years 2011 to 2013 (£58.80 in 2013), having fallen from £65.00 in 2006.

The trend in expenditure after 2008 is broadly consistent with the wider economic context. There has been an overall reduction in weekly spending from 2001/2 to 2013 in real terms, but a slight (not-statistically significant) increase between 2012 and 2013. GDP is estimated to have increased by 1.7% in 2013, compared with 2012, showing signs of the economic recovery building momentum.

The trends for different types of spending show that consumers may be remaining price conscious following the economic downturn. For example, consumers are continuing to spend less on certain items that may be considered discretionary such as restaurants and hotels, and alcohol and tobacco. The picture is not straightforward, however, as decreases have not been observed over time on clothing and footwear, and goods and services in the recreation and culture category. This highlights that the label “discretionary” should be treated with caution since items or services that may have traditionally been considered discretionary, may be considered essential by many households after they get used to having these products. By contrast, other goods, such as tobacco, may become considered less desirable over time.

The economy has witnessed signs of economic recovery, despite consumers remaining price conscious. There is evidence that consumer confidence is increasing slowly; increases in household expenditure are largely focused on items such as housing. However, the results have also seen an increase in expenditure on big ticket items, such as new cars in 2013, indicating that pent up demand is being realised.

The year-on-year changes presented in this chapter should be treated with caution because changes in recording expenditure were implemented by the Living Costs and Food (LCF) survey in 2013.

Notes

1. This increase was not found to be significant at the 95% confidence level; refer to the background section of the chapter for further details

2. Standard errors are not calculated for table A50 of the Family Spending report 2013. Therefore this change has not been tested for statistical significance at the 95% confidence level; refer to the background section of the chapter for further details.

3. Recording of spending on package holidays was also subject to questionnaire changes in 2013.

Background

This chapter presents household expenditure data over time using the Classification of Individual COnsumption by Purpose (COICOP) classification. The expenditure figures have been deflated to allow comparison of expenditure in real terms across survey years.

The figures and tables present figures that have been deflated to 2013 prices using the consumer prices index (CPI), using indices specific to each major COICOP category. This is with the exception of specific items to which the CPI is not applicable: for mortgage interest payment and council tax payments the Retail Prices Index (RPI) was used. The approach used to deflate figures to 2013 prices is consistent with the approach used for Family Spending, 2012. However, it is different from editions previous to this, when the all-items RPI was used.

Tables based on the Family Expenditure Survey (FES) classification, used by the survey for years prior to 2001/2, have been reported in previous editions. They are not presented here, but can be made available on request. The time series presented, based on COICOP, has been increased to include 2001/2 to 2013; the range of years on which the survey has reported on COICOP.

The LCF is reviewed every year and changes are made to keep it up to date. Therefore, year-on-year changes should be interpreted with caution. This is particularly relevant for 2013 data; substantial changes were made to the questionnaire following research and testing. These changes included recording of household utility expenses, purchase of furniture and spending on air fares. It is important to continue to review the survey, to make sure it captures all types of spending as fully as possible, in an environment where products and methods of payment change rapidly. A detailed breakdown of the items that feed into each COICOP heading can be found in table A1 (153.5 Kb Excel sheet).

Standard errors for categories with lower levels of spending tend to be higher, so trends for these categories need to be treated with a degree of caution. Standard errors have been calculated for the data presented in this chapter; including the figures that have been deflated to 2013 prices (standard errors are discussed in more detail in appendix B). These calculations have been taken into account in the testing for statistical significance. This testing indicates the probability with which we are confident that the difference between the estimates under examination did not occur by chance.

Changes and differences mentioned have been found to be statistically significant at the 95% confidence level, unless stated. This means that the probability that the difference occurred by chance is low (1 in 20 or lower). Note that spending on certain items, notably tobacco and alcohol, may be under-reported.

COICOP time series data in this publication are not directly comparable with UK National Accounts household expenditure data, published in Consumer Trends (this publication can be downloaded from the Office for National Statistics website). National Accounts figures draw on a number of sources in addition to the LCF (Consumer Trends guidance has more details) and may be more appropriate for finding long term trends on expenditure.

Background notes

1. **Symbols and conventions used in Family Spending 2014 edition**

   [ ] Figures should be used with extra caution because they are based on fewer than 20 reporting households.

   .. The data is suppressed if the unweighted sample counts are less than 10 reporting households.

   \- No figures are available because there are no reporting households.

   Rounding: Individual figures have been rounded independently. The sum of component items does not therefore necessarily add to the totals shown.

   Averages: These are averages (means) for all households included in the column or row, and unless specified, are not restricted to those households reporting expenditure on a particular item or income of a particular type.

   Period covered: Calendar year 2013 (1 January 2013 to 31 December 2013).

2. **Contacts**

   For information about the content of this publication, contact ONS Social Surveys Data Advice and Relations Team.

   Tel +44 (0)1633 455678

   Email: socialsurveys@ons.gsi.gov.uk

   Other customer enquiries

ONS Customer Contact Centre

Tel: 0845 601 3034

International: +44 (0) 1633 817521

Minicom: +44 (0)1633 815044

Email: info@ons.gsi.gov.uk

Fax: +44 (0)1633 652747

Post: Room D265, Government Buildings,

Cardiff Road, Newport, South Wales NP10 8XG

www.ons.gov.uk

Media enquiries

Tel: +44 (0)845 604 1858

Email: press.office@ons.gsi.gov.uk

Editor

Giles Horsfield

giles.horsfield@ons.gsi.gov.uk

3. **A National Statistics publication**

National Statistics are produced to high professional standards set out in the Code of Practice for Official Statistics. They are produced free from political influence.

4. **About us**

The Office for National Statistics

The Office for National Statistics (ONS) is the executive office of the UK Statistics Authority, a non-ministerial department which reports directly to Parliament. ONS is the UK government's single largest statistical producer. It compiles information about the UK's society and economy, and provides the evidence-base for policy and decision-making, the allocation of resources, and public accountability. The Director-General of ONS reports directly to the National Statistician who is the Authority's Chief Executive and the Head of the Government Statistical Service.

The Government Statistical Service

The Government Statistical Service (GSS) is a network of professional statisticians and their staff operating both within the Office for National Statistics and across more than 30 other government departments and agencies.

5. **Copyright and reproduction**

ISSN 2040-1647

6. Details of the policy governing the release of new data are available by visiting www.statisticsauthority.gov.uk/assessment/code-of-practice/index.html or from the Media Relations Office email: media.relations@ons.gsi.gov.uk

These National Statistics are produced to high professional standards and released according to the arrangements approved by the UK Statistics Authority.

Copyright

This document is also available on our website at www.ons.gov.uk.

Table 4.1 Household expenditure based on COICOP classification, 2001-02 to 2013 at 2013 prices[1]

United Kingdom

		2001-02	2002-03	2003-04	2004-05	2005-06	2006[2]	2006[3]	2007	2008	2009	2010	2011	2012	2013
Weighted number of households (thousands)		24,450	24,350	24,670	24,430	24,800	24,790	25,440	25,350	25,690	25,980	26,320	26,110	26,410	26,840
Total number of households in sample		7,470	6,930	7,050	6,800	6,790	6,650	6,650	6,140	5,850	5,830	5,260	5,690	5,600	5,140
Total number of persons in sample		18,120	16,590	16,970	16,260	16,090	15,850	15,850	14,650	13,830	13,740	12,180	13,430	13,180	12,120
Total number of adults in sample		13,450	12,450	12,620	12,260	12,170	12,000	12,000	11,220	10,640	10,650	9,430	10,330	10,200	9,350
Weighted average number of persons per household		2.4	2.4	2.4	2.4	2.4	2.4	2.3	2.4	2.4	2.3	2.3	2.4	2.3	2.4
Commodity or service		Average weekly household expenditure (£)													
1	Food & non-alcoholic drinks	62.10	63.70	63.60	65.20	65.10	65.80	65.00	64.60	62.40	60.90	60.10	58.70	58.90	58.80
2	Alcoholic drinks, tobacco & narcotics	18.20	17.90	18.10	17.20	16.00	16.10	16.10	15.70	14.60	14.40	14.50	13.50	13.30	12.00
3	Clothing & footwear	15.40	16.10	17.00	18.80	18.90	19.90	19.60	19.50	20.50	21.60	24.30	22.10	23.60	22.60
4	Housing (net)[4], fuel & power	61.70	61.90	64.20	63.70	65.30	65.40	65.40	67.90	64.00	66.30	69.60	69.20	70.70	74.40
5	Household goods & services	36.00	35.80	37.10	37.60	35.80	36.30	35.90	36.20	34.80	31.20	34.10	28.20	28.70	33.10
6	Health	6.30	6.50	6.60	6.40	6.90	7.20	7.20	6.80	5.90	5.90	5.50	7.00	6.50	6.20
7	Transport	88.00	88.60	88.20	83.60	83.10	82.10	80.50	79.20	77.10	70.50	72.20	67.90	64.80	70.40
8	Communication	11.30	11.50	12.10	12.80	13.20	13.10	12.90	13.70	14.10	13.60	14.50	14.20	14.20	14.50
9	Recreation & culture	53.80	55.30	57.10	59.40	58.70	60.20	59.20	59.60	62.80	59.70	58.90	64.70	62.20	63.90
10	Education	14.20	12.50	11.80	14.00	13.40	13.90	13.50	11.50	9.40	9.80	13.40	9.00	7.90	8.80
11	Restaurants & hotels	48.50	49.80	47.60	47.90	47.00	47.40	47.00	45.00	43.90	43.70	43.40	42.00	41.60	40.40
12	Miscellaneous goods & services	41.50	43.70	43.20	43.40	41.30	41.70	41.30	40.00	39.50	38.00	38.00	39.90	38.80	39.10
1-12	All expenditure groups	457.00	463.30	466.80	470.00	464.80	469.10	463.60	459.80	449.00	435.80	448.50	436.30	431.30	444.30
13	Other expenditure items[5]	78.30	75.90	76.80	77.10	80.10	78.30	76.20	71.90	75.30	78.40	72.00	72.60	69.70	73.00
Total expenditure		**535.30**	**539.20**	**543.60**	**547.10**	**544.90**	**547.40**	**539.80**	**531.70**	**524.40**	**514.10**	**520.50**	**508.90**	**501.00**	**517.30**
Average weekly expenditure per person (£)															
Total expenditure		**225.30**	**226.40**	**230.60**	**229.20**	**231.10**	**231.50**	**230.90**	**225.60**	**222.40**	**219.70**	**223.30**	**216.20**	**213.90**	**219.40**
		Average weekly household income (£)													
Gross income (£)		**729**	**728**	**742**	**770**	**773**	**791**	**782**	**794**	**829**	**776**	**772**	**752**	**738**	**739**
Disposable income (£)		**596**	**597**	**603**	**627**	**628**	**642**	**635**	**643**	**676**	**635**	**637**	**618**	**612**	**614**

Note: The commodity and service categories are not comparable to those in publications before 2001-02.
1 Figures have been deflated to 2013 prices using deflators specific to the COICOP category.
2 From 2001-02 to this version of 2006, figures shown are based on weighted data using non-response weights based on the 1991 Census and population figures from the 1991 and 2001 Censuses.
3 From this version of 2006, figures shown are based on weighted data using updated weights, with non-response weights and population figures based on the 2001 Census.
4 Excluding mortgage interest payments, council tax and Northern Ireland rates.
5 An improvement to the imputation of mortgage interest payments has been implemented for 2006 data onwards. This means there is a slight discontinuity between 2006 and earlier years.

ONS, Family Spending 2013,

Table 4.2 Household expenditure as a percentage of total expenditure based on COICOP classification, 2001-02 to 2013 at 2013 prices[1]
United Kingdom

		2001-02	2002-03	2003-04	2004-05	2005-06	2006[2]	2006[3]	2007	2008	2009	2010	2011	2012	2013
Weighted number of households (thousands)		24,450	24,350	24,670	24,430	24,800	24,790	25,440	25,350	25,690	25,980	26,320	26,110	26,410	26,840
Total number of households in sample		7,470	6,930	7,050	6,800	6,790	6,650	6,650	6,140	5,850	5,830	5,260	5,690	5,600	5,140
Total number of persons in sample		18,120	16,590	16,970	16,260	16,090	15,850	15,850	14,650	13,830	13,740	12,180	13,430	13,180	12,120
Total number of adults in sample		13,450	12,450	12,620	12,260	12,170	12,000	12,000	11,220	10,640	10,650	9,430	10,330	10,200	9,350
Weighted average number of persons per household		2.4	2.4	2.4	2.4	2.4	2.4	2.3	2.4	2.4	2.3	2.3	2.4	2.3	2.4
Commodity or service		Average weekly household expenditure (£)													
1	Food & non-alcoholic drinks	*12*	*12*	*12*	*12*	*12*	*12*	*12*	*12*	*12*	*12*	*12*	*12*	*12*	*11*
2	Alcoholic drinks, tobacco & narcotics	*3*	*3*	*3*	*3*	*3*	*3*	*3*	*3*	*3*	*3*	*3*	*3*	*3*	*2*
3	Clothing & footwear	*3*	*3*	*3*	*3*	*3*	*4*	*4*	*4*	*4*	*4*	*5*	*4*	*5*	*4*
4	Housing (net)[4], fuel & power	*12*	*11*	*12*	*12*	*12*	*12*	*12*	*13*	*12*	*13*	*13*	*14*	*14*	*14*
5	Household goods & services	*7*	*7*	*7*	*7*	*7*	*7*	*7*	*7*	*7*	*6*	*7*	*6*	*6*	*6*
6	Health	*1*	*1*	*1*	*1*	*1*	*1*	*1*	*1*	*1*	*1*	*1*	*1*	*1*	*1*
7	Transport	*16*	*16*	*16*	*15*	*15*	*15*	*15*	*15*	*15*	*14*	*14*	*13*	*13*	*14*
8	Communication	*2*	*2*	*2*	*2*	*2*	*2*	*2*	*3*	*3*	*3*	*3*	*3*	*3*	*3*
9	Recreation & culture	*10*	*10*	*10*	*11*	*11*	*11*	*11*	*11*	*12*	*12*	*11*	*13*	*12*	*12*
10	Education	*3*	*2*	*2*	*3*	*2*	*3*	*2*	*2*	*2*	*2*	*3*	*2*	*2*	*2*
11	Restaurants & hotels	*9*	*9*	*9*	*9*	*9*	*9*	*9*	*8*	*8*	*8*	*8*	*8*	*8*	*8*
12	Miscellaneous goods & services	*8*	*8*	*8*	*8*	*8*	*8*	*8*	*8*	*8*	*7*	*7*	*8*	*8*	*8*
1-12	All expenditure groups	*85*	*86*	*86*	*86*	*85*	*86*	*86*	*86*	*86*	*85*	*86*	*86*	*86*	*86*
13	Other expenditure items[5]	*15*	*14*	*14*	*14*	*15*	*14*	*14*	*14*	*14*	*15*	*14*	*14*	*14*	*14*
Total expenditure		*100*	*100*	*100*	*100*	*100*	*100*	*100*	*100*	*100*	*100*	*100*	*100*	*100*	*100*

Note: The commodity and service categories are not comparable to those in publications before 2001-02.
1 Figures have been deflated to 2013 prices using deflators specific to the COICOP category.
2 From 2001-02 to this version of 2006, figures shown are based on weighted data using non-response weights based on the 1991 Census and population figures from the 1991 and 2001 Censuses.
3 From this version of 2006, figures shown are based on weighted data using updated weights, with non-response weights and population figures based on the 2001 Census.
4 Excluding mortgage interest payments, council tax and Northern Ireland rates.
5 An improvement to the imputation of mortgage interest payments has been implemented for 2006 data onwards. This means there is a slight discontinuity between 2006 and earlier years.

Table 4.3 Household expenditure 2001-02 to 2013 COICOP based on current[1] prices

United Kingdom

		2001-02	2002-03	2003-04	2004-05	2005-06	2006[2]	2006[3]	2007	2008	2009	2010	2011	2012	2013
Weighted number of households (thousands)		24,450	24,350	24,670	24,430	24,800	24,790	25,440	25,350	25,690	25,980	26,320	26,110	26,410	26,840
Total number of households in sample		7,470	6,930	7,050	6,800	6,790	6,650	6,650	6,140	5,850	5,830	5,260	5,690	5,600	5,140
Total number of persons in sample		18,120	16,590	16,970	16,260	16,090	15,850	15,850	14,650	13,830	13,740	12,180	13,430	13,180	12,120
Total number of adults in sample		13,450	12,450	12,620	12,260	12,170	12,000	12,000	11,220	10,640	10,650	9,430	10,330	10,200	9,350
Weighted average number of persons per household		2.4	2.4	2.4	2.4	2.4	2.4	2.3	2.4	2.4	2.3	2.3	2.4	2.3	2.4
Commodity or service		Average weekly household expenditure (£)													
1	Food & non-alcoholic drinks	41.80	42.70	43.50	44.70	45.30	46.90	46.30	48.10	50.70	52.20	53.20	54.80	56.80	58.80
2	Alcoholic drinks, tobacco & narcotics	11.40	11.40	11.70	11.30	10.80	11.10	11.10	11.20	10.80	11.20	11.80	12.00	12.60	12.00
3	Clothing & footwear	22.90	22.30	22.70	23.90	22.70	23.20	23.00	22.00	21.60	20.90	23.40	21.70	23.40	22.60
4	Housing (net)[4], fuel & power	35.90	36.90	39.00	40.40	44.20	47.60	47.50	51.80	53.00	57.30	60.40	63.30	68.00	74.40
5	Household goods & services	30.50	30.20	31.30	31.60	30.00	30.30	29.90	30.70	30.10	27.90	31.40	27.30	28.50	33.10
6	Health	4.50	4.80	5.00	4.90	5.50	5.90	5.80	5.70	5.10	5.30	5.00	6.60	6.40	6.20
7	Transport	57.80	59.20	60.70	59.60	61.70	62.00	60.80	61.70	63.40	58.40	64.90	65.70	64.10	70.40
8	Communication	10.40	10.60	11.20	11.70	11.90	11.70	11.60	11.90	12.00	11.70	13.00	13.30	13.80	14.50
9	Recreation & culture	54.10	56.40	57.30	59.00	57.50	58.50	57.60	57.40	60.10	57.90	58.10	63.90	61.50	63.90
10	Education	5.60	5.20	5.20	6.50	6.60	7.20	7.00	6.80	6.20	7.00	10.00	7.00	6.80	8.80
11	Restaurants & hotels	33.40	35.40	34.90	36.10	36.70	37.90	37.60	37.20	37.70	38.40	39.20	39.70	40.50	40.40
12	Miscellaneous goods & services	30.70	33.10	33.60	34.90	34.60	36.00	35.70	35.30	35.60	35.00	35.90	38.60	38.40	39.10
1-12	All expenditure groups	338.80	348.30	356.20	364.70	367.60	378.30	373.80	379.80	386.30	383.10	406.30	413.90	420.70	444.30
13	Other expenditure items[5]	59.50	57.90	61.90	69.70	75.80	77.60	75.10	79.30	84.60	71.80	67.30	69.70	68.30	73.00
Total expenditure		**398.30**	**406.20**	**418.10**	**434.40**	**443.40**	**455.90**	**449.00**	**459.20**	**471.00**	**455.00**	**473.60**	**483.60**	**489.00**	**517.30**
Average weekly expenditure per person (£) **Total expenditure**		**167.60**	**170.50**	**177.40**	**182.00**	**188.00**	**192.80**	**192.00**	**194.80**	**199.80**	**194.40**	**203.10**	**205.40**	**208.70**	**219.40**
		Average weekly household income (£)													
Gross income (£)		**547**	**552**	**570**	**601**	**616**	**642**	**635**	**659**	**713**	**683**	**700**	**713**	**720**	**739**
Disposable income (£)		**447**	**453**	**464**	**489**	**500**	**521**	**515**	**534**	**582**	**558**	**578**	**587**	**597**	**614**

Note: The commodity and service categories are not comparable to those in publications before 2001-02.
1 Data in Table 4.3 have not been deflated to 2013 prices and therefore show the actual expenditure for the year they were collected. Because inflation is not taken into account, comparisons between the years should be made with caution.
2 From 2001-02 to this version of 2006, figures shown are based on weighted data using non-response weights based on the 1991 Census and population figures from the 1991 and 2001 Censuses.
3 From this version of 2006, figures shown are based on weighted data using updated weights, with non-response weights and population figures based on the 2001 Census.
4 Excluding mortgage interest payments, council tax and Northern Ireland rates.
5 An improvement to the imputation of mortgage interest payments has been implemented for 2006 data onwards. This means there is a slight discontinuity between 2006 and earlier years.

Office for
National Statistics

List of tables: Appendix A

Abstract

This appendix provides a range of tables based on the information collected by the Living Costs and Food Survey. The table titles listed here are links that can be used to access the tables: click on the title, and this will bring up the table in Excel.

List of tables: Appendix A

The table titles listed here are links that can be used to access the tables: click on the title, and this will bring up the table in Excel.

Table A10 Household expenditure as a percentage of total expenditure by age of household reference person, 2013 United Kingdom (51 Kb Excel sheet)

Table A11 Detailed household expenditure by age of household reference person, 2013 United Kingdom (255.5 Kb Excel sheet)

Table A12 Household expenditure by gross income quintile group where the household reference person is aged under 30, 2011-2013 United Kingdom (56.5 Kb Excel sheet)

Table A13 Household expenditure by gross income quintile group where the household reference person is aged 30 to 49, 2011-2013 United Kingdom (55.5 Kb Excel sheet)

Table A14 Household expenditure by gross income quintile group where the household reference person is aged 50 to 64, 2011-2013 United Kingdom (52.5 Kb Excel sheet)

Table A15 Household expenditure by gross income quintile group where the household reference person is aged 65 to 74, 2011-2013 United Kingdom (57.5 Kb Excel sheet)

Table A16 Household expenditure by gross income quintile group where the household reference person is aged 75 or over, 2011-2013 United Kingdom (64.5 Kb Excel sheet)

Table A17 Household expenditure by economic activity status of the household reference person, 2013 United Kingdom (69 Kb Excel sheet)

Table A18 Household expenditure by gross income: the household reference person is a full time employee, 2013 United Kingdom (60.5 Kb Excel sheet)

Table A19 Household expenditure by gross income: the household reference person is self-employed, 2011-2013 United Kingdom (47 Kb Excel sheet)

Table A20 Household expenditure by number of persons working, 2013 United Kingdom (47.5 Kb Excel sheet)

Table A21 Household expenditure by age at which the household reference person completed continuous full-time education, 2013 United Kingdom (53 Kb Excel sheet)

Table A22 Household expenditure by socio-economic classification of household reference person, 2013 United Kingdom (111 Kb Excel sheet)

Table A23 Expenditure by household composition, 2013 United Kingdom (109 Kb Excel sheet)

Table A24 Expenditure of one person retired households mainly dependent on state pensions by gross income quintile group, 2011-2013 United Kingdom (95.5 Kb Excel sheet)

Table A25 Expenditure of one person retired households not mainly dependent on state pensions by gross income quintile group, 2011-2013 United Kingdom (181 Kb Excel sheet)

Table A26 Expenditure of one adult non-retired households by gross income quintile group, 2011-2013 United Kingdom (95.5 Kb Excel sheet)

Table A27 Expenditure of one adult households with children by gross income quintile group, 2011-2013 United Kingdom (80.5 Kb Excel sheet)

Table A28 Expenditure of two adult households with children by gross income quintile group, 2011-2013 United Kingdom (95 Kb Excel sheet)

Table A29 Expenditure of two adult non-retired households by gross income quintile group, 2011-2013 United Kingdom (148 Kb Excel sheet)

Table A30 Expenditure of two adult retired households mainly dependent on state pensions by gross income quintile group, 2011-2013 United Kingdom (95 Kb Excel sheet)

Table A31 Expenditure of two adult retired households not mainly dependent on state pensions by gross income quintile group, 2011-2013 United Kingdom (111 Kb Excel sheet)

Table A32 Household expenditure by tenure, 2013 United Kingdom (56.5 Kb Excel sheet)

Table A33 Household expenditure by UK Countries and regions, 2011-2013 (57.5 Kb Excel sheet)

Table A34 Household expenditure as a percentage of total expenditure by UK Countries and regions, 2011-2013 (70.5 Kb Excel sheet)

Table A35 Detailed household expenditure by UK Countries and regions, 2011-2013 (103 Kb Excel sheet)

Table A36 Household expenditure by urban/rural areas (GB), 2011-2013 (51 Kb Excel sheet)

Table A37 Income and source of income by household composition, 2013 United Kingdom (50.5 Kb Excel sheet)

Table A38 Income and source of income by age of household reference person, 2013 United Kingdom (46 Kb Excel sheet)

Table A39 Income and source of income by gross income quintile group, 2013 United Kingdom (45 Kb Excel sheet)

Table A40 Income and source of income by household tenure, 2013 United Kingdom (48 Kb Excel sheet)

Table A41 Income and source of income by UK Countries and regions, 2011-2013 (47 Kb Excel sheet)

Table A42 Income and source of income by GB urban/rural area, 2011-2013 (45 Kb Excel sheet)

Background notes

1. **Symbols and conventions used in Family Spending 2014 edition**

   [ ] Figures should be used with extra caution because they are based on fewer than 20 reporting households.

   .. The data is suppressed if the unweighted sample counts are less than 10 reporting households.

   \- No figures are available because there are no reporting households.

   Rounding: Individual figures have been rounded independently. The sum of component items does not therefore necessarily add to the totals shown.

Averages: These are averages (means) for all households included in the column or row, and unless specified, are not restricted to those households reporting expenditure on a particular item or income of a particular type.

Period covered: Calendar year 2013 (1 January 2013 to 31 December 2013).

2. Contacts

For information about the content of this publication, contact ONS Social Surveys Data Advice and Relations team

Tel +44 (0)1633 455678

Email: socialsurveys@ons.gsi.gov.uk

Other customer enquiries

Other customer enquiries

ONS Customer Contact Centre

Tel: 0845 601 3034

International: +44 (0) 1633 817521

Minicom: +44 (0)1633 815044

Email: info@ons.gsi.gov.uk

Fax: +44 (0)1633 652747

Post: Room D265, Government Buildings,

Cardiff Road, Newport, South Wales NP10 8XG

www.ons.gov.uk

Media enquiries

Tel: +44 (0)845 604 1858

Email: press.office@ons.gsi.gov.uk

Editor:

Giles Horsfield

giles.horsfield@ons.gsi.gov.uk

3. A National Statistics publication

National Statistics are produced to high professional standards set out in the Code of Practice for Official Statistics. They are produced free from political influence.

4. **About us**

The Office for National Statistics

The Office for National Statistics (ONS) is the executive office of the UK Statistics Authority, a non-ministerial department which reports directly to Parliament. ONS is the UK government's single largest statistical producer. It compiles information about the UK's society and economy, and provides the evidence-base for policy and decision-making, the allocation of resources, and public accountability. The Director-General of ONS reports directly to the National Statistician who is the Authority's Chief Executive and the Head of the Government Statistical Service.

The Government Statistical Service

The Government Statistical Service (GSS) is a network of professional statisticians and their staff operating both within the Office for National Statistics and across more than 30 other government departments and agencies.

5. **Copyright and reproduction**

ISSN 2040-1647

6. Details of the policy governing the release of new data are available by visiting www.statisticsauthority.gov.uk/assessment/code-of-practice/index.html or from the Media Relations Office email: media.relations@ons.gsi.gov.uk

These National Statistics are produced to high professional standards and released according to the arrangements approved by the UK Statistics Authority.

Copyright

This document is also available on our website at www.ons.gov.uk.

Table A1
Components of household expenditure, 2013
United Kingdom

	Average weekly expenditure all households (£)	Total weekly expenditure (£ million)	Recording households in sample	Percentage standard error (full method)
Total number of households			**5,140**	
Commodity or service				
1 Food & non-alcoholic drinks	**58.80**	**1,579**	**5,110**	***1.1***
1.1 Food	54.00	1,448	5,110	*1.1*
1.1.1 Bread, rice and cereals	5.60	149	5,020	*1.2*
1.1.1.1 Rice	0.40	11	1,310	*5.8*
1.1.1.2 Bread	2.80	75	4,870	*1.2*
1.1.1.3 Other breads and cereals	2.30	63	4,180	*1.5*
1.1.2 Pasta products	0.40	12	2,060	*2.7*
1.1.3 Buns, cakes, biscuits etc.	3.60	96	4,620	*1.6*
1.1.3.1 Buns, crispbread and biscuits	2.20	58	4,290	*1.7*
1.1.3.2 Cakes and puddings	1.40	38	3,330	*2.2*
1.1.4 Pastry (savoury)	0.80	22	1,950	*2.5*
1.1.5 Beef (fresh, chilled or frozen)	1.90	51	2,170	*3.4*
1.1.6 Pork (fresh, chilled or frozen)	0.70	18	1,210	*3.4*
1.1.7 Lamb (fresh, chilled or frozen)	0.70	18	810	*5.1*
1.1.8 Poultry (fresh, chilled or frozen)	2.40	65	2,720	*2.5*
1.1.9 Bacon and ham	1.00	27	2,270	*2.6*
1.1.10 Other meats and meat preparations	6.30	168	4,550	*1.6*
1.1.10.1 Sausages	0.90	24	2,260	*2.6*
1.1.10.2 Offal, pate etc.	0.10	3	660	*9.5*
1.1.10.3 Other preserved or processed meat and meat preparations	5.20	140	4,410	*1.7*
1.1.10.4 Other fresh, chilled or frozen edible meat	0.00	1	40	*25.0*
1.1.11 Fish and fish products	2.60	71	3,360	*2.4*
1.1.11.1 Fish (fresh, chilled or frozen)	0.80	23	1,260	*4.7*
1.1.11.2 Seafood, dried, smoked or salted fish	0.60	15	1,150	*3.8*
1.1.11.3 Other preserved or processed fish and seafood	1.20	33	2,650	*2.4*
1.1.12 Milk	2.40	65	4,710	*1.5*
1.1.12.1 Whole milk	0.40	11	1,190	*3.7*
1.1.12.2 Low fat milk	1.70	46	4,100	*1.7*
1.1.12.3 Preserved milk	0.30	8	400	*8.1*
1.1.13 Cheese and curd	2.00	54	3,740	*1.9*
1.1.14 Eggs	0.70	20	2,960	*1.9*
1.1.15 Other milk products	2.10	55	3,910	*1.6*
1.1.15.1 Other milk products	1.00	26	3,000	*2.0*
1.1.15.2 Yoghurt	1.10	29	2,820	*2.0*
1.1.16 Butter	0.50	13	1,670	*2.9*
1.1.17 Margarine, other vegetable fats and peanut butter	0.50	14	2,290	*2.1*
1.1.18 Cooking oils and fats	0.30	9	1,170	*4.0*
1.1.18.1 Olive oil	0.20	4	460	*5.9*
1.1.18.2 Edible oils and other edible animal fats	0.20	5	790	*5.2*
1.1.19 Fresh fruit	3.30	89	4,330	*1.8*
1.1.19.1 Citrus fruits (fresh)	0.50	14	2,220	*2.8*
1.1.19.2 Bananas (fresh)	0.50	13	3,250	*1.9*
1.1.19.3 Apples (fresh)	0.60	16	2,340	*2.3*
1.1.19.4 Pears (fresh)	0.20	4	840	*4.5*
1.1.19.5 Stone fruits (fresh)	0.40	12	1,510	*3.4*
1.1.19.6 Berries (fresh)	1.10	29	2,440	*2.6*
1.1.20 Other fresh, chilled or frozen fruits	0.40	10	1,430	*3.7*
1.1.21 Dried fruit and nuts	0.70	20	1,830	*3.8*
1.1.22 Preserved fruit and fruit based products	0.10	4	860	*4.3*
1.1.23 Fresh vegetables	4.30	116	4,630	*1.6*
1.1.23.1 Leaf and stem vegetables (fresh or chilled)	0.90	25	3,210	*2.1*
1.1.23.2 Cabbages (fresh or chilled)	0.40	12	2,340	*2.3*
1.1.23.3 Vegetables grown for their fruit (fresh, chilled or frozen)	1.50	41	3,820	*1.9*
1.1.23.4 Root crops, non-starchy bulbs and mushrooms (fresh, chilled or frozen)	1.50	39	4,130	*2.0*

Note: The commodity and service categories are not comparable with those in publications before 2001-02.
The numbering is sequential, it does not use actual COICOP codes.
Please see background notes for symbols and conventions used in this report.

Table A1
Components of household expenditure, 2013 (cont.)
United Kingdom

Commodity or service	Average weekly expenditure all house-holds (£)	Total weekly expenditure (£ million)	Recording house-holds in sample	Percentage standard error (full method)
1 Food & non-alcoholic drinks (continued)				
1.1.24 Dried vegetables	0.10	2	240	*11.3*
1.1.25 Other preserved or processed vegetables	1.40	38	3,740	*2.0*
1.1.26 Potatoes	1.00	27	3,240	*1.8*
1.1.27 Other tubers and products of tuber vegetables	1.60	43	3,610	*1.7*
1.1.28 Sugar and sugar products	0.50	12	2,060	*3.4*
1.1.28.1 Sugar	0.30	8	1,720	*3.0*
1.1.28.2 Other sugar products	0.20	4	610	*7.3*
1.1.29 Jams, marmalades	0.30	8	1,430	*3.8*
1.1.30 Chocolate	1.80	48	3,350	*2.3*
1.1.31 Confectionery products	0.70	18	2,450	*2.6*
1.1.32 Edible ices and ice cream	0.60	16	1,700	*2.8*
1.1.33 Other food products	2.70	71	4,260	*1.9*
1.1.33.1 Sauces, condiments	1.30	35	3,450	*1.8*
1.1.33.2 Baker's yeast, dessert preparations, soups	1.10	29	2,840	*3.7*
1.1.33.3 Salt, spices, culinary herbs and other food products	0.30	8	1,280	*4.7*
1.2 Non-alcoholic drinks	4.90	130	4,610	*1.5*
1.2.1 Coffee	0.70	20	1,650	*2.7*
1.2.2 Tea	0.50	12	1,680	*2.7*
1.2.3 Cocoa and powdered chocolate	0.10	3	480	*5.7*
1.2.4 Fruit and vegetable juices	1.20	33	2,900	*2.3*
1.2.5 Mineral or spring waters	0.30	8	1,130	*6.0*
1.2.6 Soft drinks (inc. fizzy and ready to drink fruit drinks)	2.00	54	3,310	*2.1*
2 Alcoholic drink, tobacco & narcotics	**12.00**	**323**	**3,220**	***2.3***
2.1 Alcoholic drinks	7.70	207	2,750	*2.8*
2.1.1 Spirits and liqueurs (brought home)	1.60	42	730	*5.2*
2.1.2 Wines, fortified wines (brought home)	4.00	107	1,880	*4.0*
2.1.2.1 Wine from grape or other fruit (brought home)	3.50	93	1,710	*3.9*
2.1.2.2 Fortified wine (brought home)	0.20	4	180	*8.7*
2.1.2.3 Champagne and sparkling wines (brought home)	0.40	10	230	*13.4*
2.1.3 Beer, lager, ciders and perry (brought home)	2.10	56	1,500	*3.4*
2.1.3.1 Beer and lager (brought home)	1.70	45	1,230	*3.9*
2.1.3.2 Ciders and perry (brought home)	0.40	11	520	*5.8*
2.1.4 Alcopops (brought home)	0.00	1	80	*12.7*
2.2 Tobacco and narcotics	4.30	116	1,040	*3.9*
2.2.1 Cigarettes	3.50	94	910	*4.5*
2.2.2 Cigars, other tobacco products and narcotics	0.80	22	360	*7.2*
2.2.2.1 Cigars	[0.00]	[1]	20	*29.1*
2.2.2.2 Other tobacco	0.80	21	340	*7.3*
2.2.2.3 Narcotics	[0.00]	[0]	..	*84.9*
3 Clothing & footwear	**22.60**	**607**	**3,330**	***2.6***
3.1 Clothing	18.30	490	3,150	*2.8*
3.1.1 Men's outer garments	4.70	125	980	*5.6*
3.1.2 Men's under garments	0.40	11	370	*7.4*
3.1.3 Women's outer garments	7.80	209	1,800	*3.6*
3.1.4 Women's under garments	1.10	31	870	*5.3*
3.1.5 Boys' outer garments (5-15)	0.80	22	350	*7.2*
3.1.6 Girls' outer garments (5-15)	0.90	25	400	*7.2*
3.1.7 Infants' outer garments (under 5)	0.80	20	400	*6.8*
3.1.8 Children's under garments (under 16)	0.40	11	420	*6.1*

Note: The commodity and service categories are not comparable with those in publications before 2001-02.
The numbering is sequential, it does not use actual COICOP codes.
Please see background notes for symbols and conventions used in this report.

Table A1
Components of household expenditure, 2013 (cont.)
United Kingdom

Commodity or service	Average weekly expenditure all house-holds (£)	Total weekly expenditure (£ million)	Recording house-holds in sample	Percentage standard error (full method)
3 Clothing & footwear (continued)				
3.1.9 Accessories	0.80	22	740	*7.2*
3.1.9.1 Men's accessories	0.30	8	260	*11.5*
3.1.9.2 Women's accessories	0.40	9	400	*7.6*
3.1.9.3 Children's accessories	0.10	2	160	*10.9*
3.1.9.4 Protective head gear (crash helmets)	[0.10]	[2]	20	*36.5*
3.1.10 Haberdashery, clothing materials and clothing hire	0.20	6	240	*12.0*
3.1.11 Dry cleaners, laundry and dyeing	0.30	7	150	*13.8*
3.1.11.1 Dry cleaners and dyeing	0.20	7	120	*15.4*
3.1.11.2 Laundry, launderettes	0.00	1	30	*22.7*
3.2 Footwear	4.30	117	1,330	*3.8*
3.2.1 Footwear for men	1.50	41	390	*7.0*
3.2.2 Footwear for women	2.00	54	780	*5.2*
3.2.3 Footwear for children (5 to 15 years) and infants (under 5)	0.70	20	360	*7.0*
3.2.4 Repair and hire of footwear	0.00	1	40	*20.1*
4 Housing(net)[1], fuel & power	**74.40**	**1,996**	**5,130**	***1.6***
4.1 Actual rentals for housing	48.10	1,292	1,650	*2.7*
4.1.1 Gross rent	48.00	1,290	1,640	*2.7*
4.1.2 *less* housing benefit, rebates and allowances received	16.10	431	1,050	*4.0*
4.1.3 Net rent[2]	32.00	858	1,350	*3.5*
4.1.4 Second dwelling - rent	[0.10]	[2]	..	*45.4*
4.2 Maintenance and repair of dwelling	7.10	190	2,110	*6.0*
4.2.1 Central heating repairs	1.20	33	1,270	*5.6*
4.2.2 House maintenance etc.	4.00	108	880	*7.3*
4.2.3 Paint, wallpaper, timber	1.30	35	370	*19.3*
4.2.4 Equipment hire, small materials	0.50	15	340	*14.9*
4.3 Water supply and miscellaneous services relating to the dwelling	8.70	233	4,970	*1.3*
4.3.1 Water charges	7.40	198	4,940	*0.8*
4.3.2 Other regular housing payments including service charge for rent	1.30	34	470	*7.9*
4.3.3 Refuse collection, including skip hire	[0.00]	[1]	..	*58.5*
4.4 Electricity, gas and other fuels[3]	26.50	712	5,100	*0.9*
4.4.1 Electricity	12.10	324	5,100	*1.1*
4.4.2 Gas	12.40	334	4,280	*1.3*
4.4.3 Other fuels	2.00	54	350	*8.0*
4.4.3.1 Coal and coke	0.10	3	80	*16.3*
4.4.3.2 Oil for central heating	1.70	46	240	*8.3*
4.4.3.3 Paraffin, wood, peat, hot water etc.	0.20	6	60	*28.2*
5 Household goods & services	**33.10**	**890**	**4,750**	***3.5***
5.1 Furniture and furnishings, carpets and other floor coverings[4]	18.20	488	2,000	*5.6*
5.1.1 Furniture and furnishings	14.80	398	1,750	*6.2*
5.1.1.1 Furniture	13.90	374	1,270	*6.6*
5.1.1.2 Fancy, decorative goods	0.80	20	690	*10.9*
5.1.1.3 Garden furniture	0.20	4	30	*29.5*
5.1.2 Floor coverings	3.40	90	580	*8.3*
5.1.2.1 Soft floor coverings	3.10	83	560	*8.6*
5.1.2.2 Hard floor coverings	0.30	7	40	*27.8*
5.2 Household textiles	1.80	50	910	*6.9*
5.2.1 Bedroom textiles, including duvets and pillows	0.80	22	370	*8.5*
5.2.2 Other household textiles, including cushions, towels, curtains	1.00	28	910	*9.6*

Note: The commodity and service categories are not comparable with those in publications before 2001-02.
The numbering is sequential, it does not use actual COICOP codes.
Please see background notes for symbols and conventions used in this report.
1 Excluding mortgage interest payments, council tax and Northern Ireland rates.
2 The figure included in total expenditure is net rent as opposed to gross rent.
3 Recording of expenditure on gas and electricity via combined payment packages was changed in 2013. Recording of expenditure via slot meters was also changed.
4 Recording of expenditure on furniture was changed in 2013.

Table A1
Components of household expenditure, 2013 (cont.)
United Kingdom

Commodity or service	Average weekly expenditure all house-holds (£)	Total weekly expenditure (£ million)	Recording house-holds in sample	Percentage standard error (full method)
5 Household goods & services (continued)				
5.3 Household appliances	3.10	82	460	*7.6*
5.3.1 Gas cookers	[0.00]	[0]	..	*82.6*
5.3.2 Electric cookers, combined gas/electric cookers	0.10	3	40	*36.2*
5.3.3 Clothes washing machines and drying machines	0.60	15	60	*21.4*
5.3.4 Refrigerators, freezers and fridge-freezers	0.30	8	40	*29.9*
5.3.5 Other major electrical appliances, dishwashers, micro-waves vacuum cleaners, heaters etc.	1.20	33	150	*14.2*
5.3.6 Fire extinguisher, water softener, safes etc	-	-	-	-
5.3.7 Small electric household appliances, excluding hairdryers	0.50	13	180	*11.9*
5.3.8 Repairs to gas and electrical appliances and spare parts	0.40	10	50	*17.7*
5.3.9 Rental/hire of major household appliances	[0.00]	[0]	..	*49.0*
5.4 Glassware, tableware and household utensils	1.60	42	1,470	*5.1*
5.4.1 Glassware, china, pottery, cutlery and silverware	0.50	14	550	*8.5*
5.4.2 Kitchen and domestic utensils	0.60	17	870	*6.0*
5.4.3 Repair of glassware, tableware and household utensils	[0.00]	[0]	..	*135.1*
5.4.4 Storage and other durable household articles	0.40	11	460	*8.2*
5.5 Tools and equipment for house and garden	2.40	63	1,530	*9.9*
5.5.1 Electrical tools	0.30	7	50	*27.9*
5.5.2 Garden tools, equipment and accessories e.g. lawn mowers etc.	0.60	16	250	*32.1*
5.5.3 Small tools	0.30	8	320	*10.7*
5.5.4 Door, electrical and other fittings	0.60	15	350	*11.9*
5.5.5 Electrical consumables	0.60	17	960	*4.9*
5.6 Goods and services for routine household maintenance	6.10	164	4,360	*3.0*
5.6.1 Cleaning materials	2.40	64	3,520	*2.1*
5.6.1.1 Detergents, washing-up liquid, washing powder	1.00	28	2,210	*2.6*
5.6.1.2 Disinfectants, polishes, other cleaning materials etc.	1.30	36	2,890	*2.5*
5.6.2 Household goods and hardware	1.40	38	3,290	*3.2*
5.6.2.1 Kitchen disposables	0.80	22	2,780	*4.1*
5.6.2.2 Household hardware and appliances, matches	0.30	8	650	*7.1*
5.6.2.3 Kitchen gloves, cloths etc.	0.20	4	830	*5.1*
5.6.2.4 Pins, needles, tape measures, nails, nuts and bolts etc.	0.10	4	330	*10.1*
5.6.3 Domestic services, carpet cleaning, hire/repair of furniture/furnishings	2.30	62	760	*6.7*
5.6.3.1 Domestic services, including cleaners, gardeners, au pairs	1.80	48	350	*8.6*
5.6.3.2 Carpet cleaning, ironing service, window cleaner	0.50	13	500	*8.2*
5.6.3.3 Hire/repair of household furniture and furnishings	[0.00]	[1]	..	*42.4*
6 Health	**6.20**	**167**	**2,720**	***5.6***
6.1 Medical products, appliances and equipment	4.00	106	2,560	*7.5*
6.1.1 Medicines, prescriptions and healthcare products	2.30	61	2,400	*9.4*
6.1.1.1 NHS prescription charges and payments	0.20	6	200	*9.3*
6.1.1.2 Medicines and medical goods (not NHS)	1.30	35	2,160	*3.7*
6.1.1.3 Other medical products (e.g. plasters, condoms, hot water bottle etc.)	0.20	5	340	*9.4*
6.1.1.4 Non-optical appliances and equipment (e.g. wheelchairs, batteries for hearing aids, shoe build-up)	0.50	15	40	*37.1*
6.1.2 Spectacles, lenses, accessories and repairs	1.70	46	380	*12.2*
6.1.2.1 Purchase of spectacles, lenses, prescription sunglasses	1.70	45	330	*12.5*
6.1.2.2 Accessories/repairs to spectacles/lenses	0.00	1	60	*20.2*
6.2 Hospital services	2.30	61	410	*8.0*
6.2.1 Out patient services	2.20	59	400	*8.0*
6.2.1.1 NHS medical, optical, dental and medical auxiliary services	0.80	22	220	*9.4*
6.2.1.2 Private medical, optical, dental and medical auxiliary services	1.40	37	200	*11.1*
6.2.1.3 Other services	-	-	-	-
6.2.2 In-patient hospital services	[0.10]	[2]	..	*65.9*

Note: The commodity and service categories are not comparable with those in publications before 2001-02.
The numbering is sequential, it does not use actual COICOP codes.
Please see background notes for symbols and conventions used in this report.

Table A1
Components of household expenditure, 2013 (cont.)
United Kingdom

Commodity or service	Average weekly expenditure all households (£)	Total weekly expenditure (£ million)	Recording households in sample	Percentage standard error (full method)
7 Transport	**70.40**	**1,891**	**4,460**	***2.1***
7.1 Purchase of vehicles	21.10	566	1,080	*5.3*
7.1.1 Purchase of new cars and vans	8.30	223	280	*10.1*
7.1.1.1 Outright purchases	4.90	132	90	*13.5*
7.1.1.2 Loan/Hire Purchase of new car/van	3.40	91	190	*14.3*
7.1.2 Purchase of second hand cars or vans	12.00	322	790	*5.1*
7.1.2.1 Outright purchases	8.00	214	490	*5.8*
7.1.2.2 Loan/Hire Purchase of second hand car/van	4.00	108	340	*9.2*
7.1.3 Purchase of motorcycles	0.80	21	70	*20.7*
7.1.3.1 Outright purchases of new or second hand motorcycles	[0.20]	[6]	20	*27.9*
7.1.3.2 Loan/Hire Purchase of new or second hand motorcycles	[0.20]	[5]	10	*67.4*
7.1.3.3 Purchase of bicycles and other vehicles	0.40	11	40	*25.2*
7.2 Operation of personal transport	34.00	913	3,870	*1.8*
7.2.1 Spares and accessories	2.30	62	370	*10.4*
7.2.1.1 Car/van accessories and fittings	0.10	4	100	*23.1*
7.2.1.2 Car/van spare parts	1.70	46	200	*13.1*
7.2.1.3 Motorcycle accessories and spare parts	[0.20]	[6]	20	*34.0*
7.2.1.4 Bicycle accessories, repairs and other costs	0.20	6	90	*19.7*
7.2.2 Petrol, diesel and other motor oils	23.50	631	3,280	*1.7*
7.2.2.1 Petrol	15.70	422	2,550	*2.2*
7.2.2.2 Diesel oil	7.60	205	1,140	*3.5*
7.2.2.3 Other motor oils	0.20	4	80	*30.4*
7.2.3 Repairs and servicing	5.70	153	2,500	*3.3*
7.2.3.1 Car or van repairs, servicing and other work	5.70	153	2,500	*3.3*
7.2.3.2 Motorcycle repairs and servicing	0.00	1	20	*31.0*
7.2.4 Other motoring costs	2.50	67	1,950	*5.6*
7.2.4.1 Motoring organisation subscription (e.g. AA and RAC)	0.40	10	760	*6.0*
7.2.4.2 Garage rent, other costs (excluding fines), car washing etc.	0.70	20	360	*9.5*
7.2.4.3 Parking fees, tolls, and permits (excluding motoring fines)	0.90	24	1,070	*10.4*
7.2.4.4 Driving lessons	0.30	8	50	*19.0*
7.2.4.5 Anti-freeze, battery water, cleaning materials	0.10	4	260	*12.5*
7.3 Transport services[5]	15.30	412	2,290	*4.3*
7.3.1 Rail and tube fares	3.90	104	750	*6.9*
7.3.1.1 Season tickets	1.90	51	220	*11.0*
7.3.1.2 Other than season tickets	2.00	53	610	*6.6*
7.3.2 Bus and coach fares	1.60	43	820	*6.1*
7.3.2.1 Season tickets	0.60	17	210	*9.6*
7.3.2.2 Other than season tickets	1.00	26	700	*6.2*
7.3.3 Combined fares	0.80	21	110	*14.6*
7.3.3.1 Combined fares other than season tickets	0.20	5	60	*19.5*
7.3.3.2 Combined fares season tickets	0.60	16	60	*18.3*
7.3.4 Other travel and transport	9.10	243	1,480	*6.3*
7.3.4.1 Air fares (within UK)	0.20	6	80	*41.0*
7.3.4.2 Air fares (international)	5.20	139	470	*10.3*
7.3.4.3 School travel	[0.00]	[0]	10	*43.4*
7.3.4.4 Taxis and hired cars with drivers	1.10	30	610	*6.2*
7.3.4.5 Other personal travel and transport services	0.30	8	330	*8.2*
7.3.4.6 Hire of self-drive cars, vans, bicycles	[0.20]	[6]	20	*32.1*
7.3.4.7 Car leasing	1.80	49	170	*9.3*
7.3.4.8 Water travel, ferries and season tickets	0.20	6	60	*29.8*

Note: The commodity and service categories are not comparable with those in publications before 2001-02.
The numbering is sequential, it does not use actual COICOP codes.
Please see background notes for symbols and conventions used in this report.
5 Recording of expenditure on flights was changed in 2013.

Table A1
Components of household expenditure, 2013 (cont.)
United Kingdom

Commodity or service	Average weekly expenditure all house-holds (£)	Total weekly expenditure (£ million)	Recording house-holds in sample	Percentage standard error (full method)
8 Communication	**14.50**	**388**	**4,920**	***1.2***
8.1 Postal services	0.60	16	760	*6.4*
8.2 Telephone and telefax equipment	0.50	14	170	*15.3*
8.2.1 Telephone purchase	0.10	2	30	*25.4*
8.2.2 Mobile phone purchase	0.50	13	150	*16.9*
8.2.3 Answering machine, fax machine, modem purchase	-	-	-	-
8.3 Telephone and telefax services	10.60	284	4,860	*1.2*
8.3.1 Telephone account	3.90	106	4,480	*1.1*
8.3.2 Telephone coin and other payments	0.00	0	20	*29.1*
8.3.3 Mobile phone account	6.00	160	2,970	*1.7*
8.3.4 Mobile phone - other payments	0.60	17	450	*6.2*
8.4 Internet subscription fees	2.80	74	3,840	*1.3*
9 Recreation & culture	**63.90**	**1,716**	**5,090**	***2.6***
9.1 Audio-visual, photographic and information processing equipment	5.10	138	1,220	*8.0*
9.1.1 Audio equipment and accessories, CD players	0.90	25	460	*12.1*
9.1.1.1 Audio equipment, CD players including in car	0.50	12	70	*22.5*
9.1.1.2 Audio accessories e.g. tapes, headphones etc.	0.50	12	410	*6.7*
9.1.2 TV, video and computers	3.90	106	910	*9.8*
9.1.2.1 Purchase of TV and digital decoder	0.60	16	60	*25.5*
9.1.2.2 Satellite dish purchase and installation	[0.00]	[0]	..	*74.9*
9.1.2.3 Cable TV connection	[0.00]	[0]	..	*77.3*
9.1.2.4 Video recorder	[0.00]	[0]	..	*90.7*
9.1.2.5 DVD player/recorder	0.10	3	20	*38.0*
9.1.2.6 Blank, pre-recorded video cassettes, DVDs	0.70	19	530	*6.5*
9.1.2.7 Personal computers, printers and calculators	2.40	63	350	*14.1*
9.1.2.8 Spare parts for TV, video, audio	0.00	1	40	*24.9*
9.1.2.9 Repair of audio-visual, photographic and information processing	0.10	2	20	*35.5*
9.1.3 Photographic, cine and optical equipment	0.30	8	60	*26.9*
9.1.3.1 Photographic and cine equipment	0.30	7	50	*27.2*
9.1.3.2 Camera films	[0.00]	[0]	..	*54.9*
9.1.3.3 Optical instruments, binoculars, telescopes, microscopes	[0.00]	[0]	..	*51.7*
9.2 Other major durables for recreation and culture	2.10	56	110	*20.1*
9.2.1 Purchase of boats, trailers and horses	[0.30]	[8]	10	*29.0*
9.2.2 Purchase of caravans, mobile homes (including decoration)	0.70	18	20	*47.2*
9.2.3 Accessories for boats, horses, caravans and motor caravans	[0.00]	[1]	..	*49.2*
9.2.4 Musical instruments (purchase and hire)	0.20	5	30	*43.3*
9.2.5 Major durables for indoor recreation	[0.00]	[0]	..	*81.0*
9.2.6 Maintenance and repair of other major durables	0.60	15	30	*35.7*
9.2.7 Purchase of motor caravan (new and second-hand) - outright purchase	[0.30]	[8]	..	*42.5*
9.2.8 Purchase of motor caravan (new and second-hand) - loan/HP	[0.00]	[0]	..	*96.9*
9.3 Other recreational items and equipment, gardens and pets	10.40	280	3,470	*3.1*
9.3.1 Games, toys and hobbies	2.30	61	1,230	*4.6*
9.3.2 Computer software and games	0.80	23	240	*12.2*
9.3.2.1 Computer software and game cartridges	0.60	17	230	*9.8*
9.3.2.2 Computer games consoles	0.20	6	20	*31.4*
9.3.3 Equipment for sport, camping and open-air recreation	0.90	24	330	*10.1*
9.3.4 Horticultural goods, garden equipment and plants etc.	2.20	58	1,720	*4.0*
9.3.4.1 BBQ and swings	0.10	2	30	*30.3*
9.3.4.2 Plants, flowers, seeds, fertilisers, insecticides	2.00	54	1,670	*4.0*
9.3.4.3 Garden decorative	0.10	1	40	*30.6*
9.3.4.4 Artificial flowers, pot pourri	0.00	1	50	*21.7*
9.3.5 Pets and pet food	4.30	115	1,980	*5.4*
9.3.5.1 Pet food	2.20	60	1,860	*3.5*
9.3.5.2 Pet purchase and accessories	0.80	22	580	*10.7*
9.3.5.3 Veterinary and other services for pets identified separately	1.20	33	180	*12.0*

Note: The commodity and service categories are not comparable with those in publications before 2001-02.
The numbering is sequential, it does not use actual COICOP codes.
Please see background notes for symbols and conventions used in this report.

Table A1
Components of household expenditure, 2013 (cont.)
United Kingdom

Commodity or service		Average weekly expenditure all house-holds (£)	Total weekly expenditure (£ million)	Recording house-holds in sample	Percentage standard error (full method)
9	**Recreation & culture (continued)**				
9.4	Recreational and cultural services	18.60	499	4,860	*2.0*
9.4.1	Sports admissions, subscriptions, leisure class fees and equipment hire	5.50	149	1,830	*5.0*
9.4.1.1	Spectator sports: admission charges	0.60	16	140	*18.5*
9.4.1.2	Participant sports (excluding subscriptions)	1.00	27	680	*5.8*
9.4.1.3	Subscriptions to sports and social clubs	1.90	51	850	*9.2*
9.4.1.4	Leisure class fees	2.00	53	780	*8.3*
9.4.1.5	Hire of equipment for sport and open air recreation	0.00	1	30	*30.9*
9.4.2	Cinema, theatre and museums etc.	2.30	63	810	*5.4*
9.4.2.1	Cinemas	0.70	18	440	*5.2*
9.4.2.2	Live entertainment: theatre, concerts, shows	1.10	30	270	*8.8*
9.4.2.3	Museums, zoological gardens, theme parks, houses and gardens	0.50	14	200	*11.9*
9.4.3	TV, video, satellite rental, cable subscriptions and TV licences	6.70	179	4,520	*1.3*
9.4.3.1	TV licences	2.30	61	4,270	*0.4*
9.4.3.2	Satellite subscriptions	3.30	88	1,850	*2.4*
9.4.3.3	Rent for TV/Satellite/VCR	0.00	1	20	*24.5*
9.4.3.4	Cable subscriptions	1.00	27	810	*5.1*
9.4.3.5	TV slot meter payments	[0.00]	[0]	..	*64.6*
9.4.3.6	Video, cassette and CD hire	0.10	2	170	*12.6*
9.4.4	Miscellaneous entertainments	1.20	33	1,000	*6.5*
9.4.4.1	Admissions to clubs, dances, discos, bingo	0.50	15	410	*10.2*
9.4.4.2	Social events and gatherings	0.30	7	210	*14.6*
9.4.4.3	Subscriptions for leisure activities and other subscriptions	0.40	11	520	*10.4*
9.4.5	Development of film, deposit for film development, passport photos, holiday and school photos	0.20	6	170	*19.8*
9.4.6	Gambling payments	2.60	70	2,180	*3.8*
9.4.6.1	Football pools stakes	0.00	1	30	*33.3*
9.4.6.2	Bingo stakes excluding admission	0.20	6	90	*21.3*
9.4.6.3	Lottery	1.90	52	1,970	*3.6*
9.4.6.4	Bookmaker, tote, other betting stakes	0.40	12	400	*10.6*
9.5	Newspapers, books and stationery	5.30	141	4,140	*2.2*
9.5.1	Books	1.10	29	980	*5.3*
9.5.2	Stationery, diaries, address books, art materials	0.70	20	1,200	*6.3*
9.5.3	Cards, calendars, posters and other printed matter	1.10	30	2,210	*3.7*
9.5.4	Newspapers	1.60	42	2,420	*2.9*
9.5.5	Magazines and periodicals	0.80	20	1,820	*5.0*
9.6	Package holidays[6]	22.40	602	960	*5.6*
9.6.1	Package holidays - UK	1.40	39	220	*9.2*
9.6.2	Package holidays - abroad	21.00	563	790	*5.9*
10	**Education**	**8.80**	**236**	**310**	***17.9***
10.1	Education fees	8.50	228	210	*18.6*
10.1.1	Nursery and primary education	0.50	14	20	*30.2*
10.1.2	Secondary education	1.70	45	30	*28.6*
10.1.3	Sixth form college/college education	0.30	9	30	*49.9*
10.1.4	University education	5.40	145	70	*26.2*
10.1.5	Other education	0.60	15	60	*29.3*
10.2	Payments for school trips, other ad-hoc expenditure	0.30	9	110	*13.4*
10.2.1	Nursery and primary education	0.10	3	60	*19.4*
10.2.2	Secondary education	0.20	4	40	*19.7*
10.2.3	Sixth form college/college education	[0.00]	[0]	..	*53.1*
10.2.4	University education	[0.00]	[0]	..	*57.4*
10.2.5	Other education	[0.00]	[1]	..	*69.9*

Note: The commodity and service categories are not comparable with those in publications before 2001-02.
The numbering is sequential, it does not use actual COICOP codes.
Please see background notes for symbols and conventions used in this report.
6 Recording of expenditure on package holidays was changed in 2013.

Table A1
Components of household expenditure, 2013 (cont.)
United Kingdom

Commodity or service	Average weekly expenditure all house-holds (£)	Total weekly expenditure (£ million)	Recording house-holds in sample	Percentage standard error (full method)
11 Restaurants & hotels	**40.40**	**1,084**	**4,440**	***1.9***
11.1 Catering services	33.50	900	4,390	*1.8*
11.1.1 Restaurant and café meals	15.90	427	3,540	*2.4*
11.1.2 Alcoholic drinks (away from home)	7.10	192	2,130	*3.2*
11.1.3 Take away meals eaten at home	4.20	113	2,030	*2.8*
11.1.4 Other take-away and snack food	4.40	117	2,750	*2.4*
11.1.4.1 Hot and cold food	3.10	84	2,400	*2.5*
11.1.4.2 Confectionery	0.30	9	1,200	*3.9*
11.1.4.3 Ice cream	0.10	4	400	*7.7*
11.1.4.4 Soft drinks	0.80	21	1,740	*3.2*
11.1.5 Contract catering (food)	0.10	3	20	*28.9*
11.1.6 Canteens	1.80	48	1,280	*4.1*
11.1.6.1 School meals	0.70	18	480	*6.5*
11.1.6.2 Meals bought and eaten at the workplace	1.10	30	970	*5.2*
11.2 Accommodation services	6.80	183	1,240	*5.4*
11.2.1 Holiday in the UK	4.00	109	1,030	*4.6*
11.2.2 Holiday abroad	2.70	73	260	*11.1*
11.2.3 Room hire	[0.10]	[2]	20	*45.6*
12 Miscellaneous goods and services	**39.10**	**1,050**	**5,040**	***2.1***
12.1 Personal care	11.20	300	4,470	*2.1*
12.1.1 Hairdressing, beauty treatment	3.40	93	1,200	*4.1*
12.1.2 Toilet paper	0.80	23	2,230	*2.2*
12.1.3 Toiletries and soap	2.50	66	3,580	*2.2*
12.1.3.1 Toiletries (disposable including tampons, lipsyl, toothpaste etc.)	1.50	41	3,030	*2.8*
12.1.3.2 Bar of soap, liquid soap, shower gel etc.	0.40	11	1,620	*3.5*
12.1.3.3 Toilet requisites (durable including razors, hairbrushes, toothbrushes etc.)	0.50	14	1,140	*4.4*
12.1.4 Baby toiletries and accessories (disposable)	0.60	17	860	*5.7*
12.1.5 Hair products, cosmetics and electrical appliances for personal care	3.80	101	2,750	*3.6*
12.1.5.1 Hair products	0.80	22	1,590	*3.4*
12.1.5.2 Cosmetics and related accessories	2.70	72	2,090	*4.0*
12.1.5.3 Electrical appliances for personal care, including hairdryers, shavers etc.	0.30	7	90	*24.2*
12.2 Personal effects	3.00	81	1,180	*6.5*
12.2.1 Jewellery, clocks and watches and other personal effects	1.60	44	780	*9.6*
12.2.2 Leather and travel goods (excluding baby items)	1.00	26	440	*10.8*
12.2.3 Sunglasses (non-prescription)	0.20	4	70	*27.8*
12.2.4 Baby equipment (excluding prams and pushchairs)	0.10	1	40	*24.4*
12.2.5 Prams, pram accessories and pushchairs	[0.10]	[3]	20	*43.8*
12.2.6 Repairs to personal goods	0.10	2	30	*34.6*
12.3 Social protection	4.10	109	270	*13.5*
12.3.1 Residential homes	[0.40]	[11]	..	*95.1*
12.3.2 Home help	0.60	15	20	*43.8*
12.3.3 Nursery, crèche, playschools	1.10	29	120	*14.8*
12.3.4 Child care payments	2.00	53	160	*13.6*

Note: The commodity and service categories are not comparable with those in publications before 2001-02.
The numbering is sequential, it does not use actual COICOP codes.
Please see background notes for symbols and conventions used in this report.

Table A1
Components of household expenditure, 2013 (cont.)
United Kingdom

Commodity or service	Average weekly expenditure all house-holds (£)	Total weekly expenditure (£ million)	Recording house-holds in sample	Percentage standard error (full method)
12 Miscellaneous goods and services (continued)				
12.4 Insurance	16.80	451	4,590	*2.0*
12.4.1 Household insurances	5.10	136	4,030	*1.9*
12.4.1.1 Structure insurance	2.40	65	3,270	*1.8*
12.4.1.2 Contents insurance	2.40	65	3,930	*1.6*
12.4.1.3 Insurance for household appliances	0.20	6	120	*29.7*
12.4.2 Medical insurance premiums	2.00	54	690	*7.2*
12.4.3 Vehicle insurance including boat insurance	9.50	256	3,870	*2.2*
12.4.3.1 Vehicle insurance	9.50	256	3,870	*2.2*
12.4.3.2 Boat insurance (not home)	[0.00]	[0]	..	*74.1*
12.4.4 Non-package holiday, other travel insurance	0.20	5	30	*48.4*
12.5 Other services	4.10	110	1,720	*6.9*
12.5.1 Moving house	2.10	57	290	*11.4*
12.5.1.1 Moving and storage of furniture	0.30	9	150	*12.3*
12.5.1.2 Property transaction - purchase and sale	0.70	18	60	*19.9*
12.5.1.3 Property transaction - sale only	0.60	16	40	*25.9*
12.5.1.4 Property transaction - purchase only	0.40	10	50	*20.8*
12.5.1.5 Property transaction - other payments	0.20	5	90	*14.9*
12.5.2 Bank, building society, post office, credit card charges	0.50	14	1,040	*5.6*
12.5.2.1 Bank and building society charges	0.40	12	910	*5.0*
12.5.2.2 Bank and Post Office counter charges	[0.00]	[1]	..	*86.4*
12.5.2.3 Annual standing charge for credit cards	0.10	1	170	*13.1*
12.5.2.4 Commission travellers' cheques and currency	-	-	-	-
12.5.3 Other services and professional fees	1.50	40	710	*12.4*
12.5.3.1 Other professional fees including court fines	0.30	7	40	*21.2*
12.5.3.2 Legal fees	0.30	9	20	*36.0*
12.5.3.3 Funeral expenses	[0.10]	[3]	..	*76.3*
12.5.3.4 TU and professional organisations	0.70	18	570	*16.0*
12.5.3.5 Other payments for services e.g. photocopying	0.10	3	80	*28.5*
1-12 All expenditure groups	**444.30**	**11,926**	**5,140**	***1.2***
13 Other expenditure items	**73.00**	**1,960**	**4,880**	***6.4***
13.1 Housing: mortgage interest payments, council tax etc.	44.30	1,190	4,620	*2.2*
13.1.1 Mortgage interest payments	21.40	575	1,600	*3.5*
13.1.2 Mortgage protection premiums	1.00	27	570	*5.3*
13.1.3 Council tax, domestic rates	20.10	541	4,590	*0.9*
13.1.4 Council tax, mortgage (second dwelling)	1.80	48	70	*25.1*
13.2 Licences, fines and transfers	3.80	103	3,750	*5.9*
13.2.1 Stamp duty, licences and fines (excluding motoring fines)	0.70	20	90	*30.0*
13.2.2 Motoring fines	[0.00]	[1]	..	*35.9*
13.2.3 Motor vehicle road taxation payments less refunds	3.10	82	3,730	*1.5*
13.3 Holiday spending	11.80	318	230	*37.1*
13.3.1 Money spent abroad	11.80	318	230	*37.1*
13.3.2 Duty free goods bought in UK	-	-	-	-

Note: The commodity and service categories are not comparable with those in publications before 2001-02.
The numbering is sequential, it does not use actual COICOP codes.
Please see background notes for symbols and conventions used in this report.

Table A1
Components of household expenditure, 2013 (cont.)
United Kingdom

Commodity or service	Average weekly expenditure all house-holds (£)	Total weekly expenditure (£ million)	Recording house-holds in sample	Percentage standard error (full method)
13 Other expenditure items (continued)				
13.4 Money transfers and credit	13.00	349	2,430	*8.4*
13.4.1 Money, cash gifts given to children	0.10	4	100	*17.7*
13.4.1.1 Money given to children for specific purposes	0.10	4	100	*18.0*
13.4.1.2 Cash gifts to children (no specific purpose)	[0.00]	[0]	0	*64.6*
13.4.2 Cash gifts and donations[7]	11.70	314	2,080	*9.2*
13.4.2.1 Money/presents given to those outside the household	3.90	105	780	*7.8*
13.4.2.2 Charitable donations and subscriptions	2.90	78	1,440	*9.4*
13.4.2.3 Money sent abroad	2.90	77	200	*32.1*
13.4.2.4 Maintenance allowance expenditure	2.00	54	150	*11.7*
13.4.3 Club instalment payments (child) and interest on credit cards	1.20	32	600	*7.5*
13.4.3.1 Club instalment payment	-	-	-	-
13.4.3.2 Interest on credit cards	1.20	32	600	*7.5*
Total expenditure	**517.30**	**13,886**	**5,140**	***1.5***
14 Other items recorded				
14.1 Life assurance, contributions to pension funds	19.90	533	2,390	*3.7*
14.1.1 Life assurance premiums e.g. mortgage endowment policies	3.00	81	1,370	*6.1*
14.1.2 Contributions to pension and superannuation funds etc.	12.70	342	1,440	*3.5*
14.1.3 Personal pensions	4.10	110	440	*11.1*
14.2 Other insurance including friendly societies	1.40	37	920	*12.0*
14.3 Income tax, payments less refunds	88.50	2,377	3,960	*2.8*
14.3.1 Income tax paid by employees under PAYE	66.90	1,796	2,480	*3.3*
14.3.2 Income tax paid direct e.g. by retired or unoccupied persons	2.10	55	140	*17.7*
14.3.3 Income tax paid direct by self-employed	4.80	130	200	*15.1*
14.3.4 Income tax deducted at source from income under covenant from investments or from annuities and pensions	12.50	334	2,230	*4.6*
14.3.5 Income tax on bonus earnings	3.30	87	620	*15.5*
14.3.6 Income tax refunds under PAYE	0.20	6	30	*43.8*
14.3.7 Income tax refunds other than PAYE	0.80	21	310	*10.0*
14.4 National insurance contribution	28.30	759	2,480	*1.8*
14.4.1 NI contributions paid by employees	28.20	757	2,460	*1.8*
14.4.2 NI contributions paid by non-employees	0.10	1	30	*24.9*
14.5 Purchase or alteration of dwellings (contracted out), mortgages	48.90	1,312	1,840	*5.9*
14.5.1 Outright purchase of houses, flats etc. including deposits	[3.60]	[96]	10	*46.0*
14.5.2 Capital repayment of mortgage	23.20	624	1,330	*3.4*
14.5.3 Central heating installation	0.90	24	100	*12.6*
14.5.4 DIY improvements: Double glazing, kitchen units, sheds etc.	0.80	21	70	*29.9*
14.5.5 Home improvements - contracted out	15.50	417	640	*9.4*
14.5.6 Bathroom fittings	0.30	9	50	*33.0*
14.5.7 Purchase of materials for Capital Improvements	0.10	4	20	*35.3*
14.5.8 Purchase of second dwelling	4.40	117	40	*35.9*
14.6 Savings and investments	5.70	152	710	*8.3*
14.6.1 Savings, investments (excluding AVCs)	4.80	128	510	*8.8*
14.6.2 Additional Voluntary Contributions	0.60	16	60	*24.4*
14.6.3 Food stamps, other food related expenditure	0.30	7	190	*11.6*
14.7 Pay off loan to clear other debt	2.60	71	280	*7.9*
14.8 Windfall receipts from gambling etc. [8]	1.20	31	470	*12.8*

Note: The commodity and service categories are not comparable with those in publications before 2001-02.
The numbering is sequential, it does not use actual COICOP codes.
Please see background notes for symbols and conventions used in this report.
7 Recording of expenditure on money sent abroad was changed in 2013.
8 Expressed as an income figure as opposed to an expenditure figure.

Table A2
Expenditure on food and non-alcoholic drinks by place of purchase, 2013
United Kingdom

		Large supermarket chains[1]			Other outlets			Internet Expenditure[2]		
		Average weekly expenditure all house-holds (£)	Total weekly expenditure (£ million)	Recording house-holds in sample	Average weekly expenditure all house-holds (£)	Total weekly expenditure (£ million)	Recording house-holds in sample	Average weekly expenditure all house-holds (£)	Total weekly expenditure (£ million)	Recording house-holds in sample
1	**Food and non-alcoholic drinks**	**46.50**	**1,247**	**5,020**	**9.20**	**246**	**4,380**	**3.20**	**85**	**380**
1.1	Food	42.70	1,145	5,020	8.40	226	4,300	2.90	77	370
1.1.1	Bread, rice and cereals	4.50	120	4,830	0.80	21	1,910	0.30	7	290
1.1.2	Pasta products	0.40	10	1,830	0.00	1	200	0.00	1	160
1.1.3	Buns, cakes, biscuits etc.	2.90	79	4,350	0.50	14	1,440	0.20	4	260
1.1.4	Pastry (savoury)	0.70	20	1,820	0.00	1	110	0.10	1	100
1.1.5	Beef (fresh, chilled or frozen)	1.30	35	1,780	0.50	14	420	0.10	2	110
1.1.6	Pork (fresh, chilled or frozen)	0.50	14	1,010	0.10	3	200	0.00	1	40
1.1.7	Lamb (fresh, chilled or frozen)	0.40	11	590	0.20	6	200	0.00	1	30
1.1.8	Poultry (fresh, chilled or frozen)	1.90	50	2,350	0.40	11	420	0.20	4	160
1.1.9	Bacon and ham	0.80	22	1,950	0.20	4	370	0.00	1	110
1.1.10	Other meats and meat preparations	5.10	136	4,270	0.90	23	1,240	0.30	9	260
1.1.11	Fish and fish products	2.10	56	3,050	0.40	11	490	0.10	4	180
1.1.12	Milk	1.70	47	4,230	0.60	15	1,470	0.10	3	250
1.1.13	Cheese and curd	1.70	46	3,470	0.20	4	420	0.10	3	220
1.1.14	Eggs	0.60	15	2,400	0.10	3	600	0.00	1	150
1.1.15	Other milk products	1.80	49	3,720	0.10	3	410	0.10	3	230
1.1.16	Butter	0.40	11	1,490	0.00	1	150	0.00	1	80
1.1.17	Margarine, other vegetable fats and peanut butter	0.50	12	2,090	0.00	1	170	0.00	1	120
1.1.18	Cooking oils and fats	0.30	7	1,020	0.00	1	120	0.00	1	60
1.1.19	Fresh fruit	2.80	75	4,080	0.30	8	820	0.20	5	260
1.1.20	Other fresh, chilled or frozen fruits	0.30	8	1,270	0.00	1	160	0.00	1	70
1.1.21	Dried fruit and nuts	0.50	14	1,570	0.20	4	320	0.00	1	110
1.1.22	Preserved fruit and fruit based products	0.10	3	750	0.00	0	80	0.00	0	50
1.1.23	Fresh vegetables	3.60	96	4,420	0.50	13	1,070	0.30	7	290
1.1.24	Dried vegetables and other preserved and processed vegetables	0.70	18	2,770	0.70	20	2,380	0.10	2	190
1.1.25	Potatoes	0.80	22	2,860	0.10	4	530	0.00	1	170
1.1.26	Other tubers and products of tuber vegetables	1.40	37	3,300	0.20	4	750	0.10	3	210
1.1.27	Sugar and sugar products	0.40	10	1,740	0.10	2	330	0.00	1	110
1.1.28	Jams, marmalades	0.20	6	1,240	0.10	1	180	0.00	0	60
1.1.29	Chocolate	1.30	35	2,910	0.40	11	1,190	0.10	2	120
1.1.30	Confectionery products	0.40	11	1,880	0.30	7	1,030	0.00	0	50
1.1.31	Edible ices and ice cream	0.50	13	1,520	0.10	1	190	0.00	1	90
1.1.32	Other food products	2.10	55	3,920	0.40	11	910	0.20	5	260
1.2	Non-alcoholic drinks	3.80	102	4,320	0.70	20	1,700	0.30	8	300
1.2.1	Coffee	0.60	16	1,400	0.10	3	270	0.00	1	80
1.2.2	Tea	0.40	10	1,400	0.10	2	280	0.00	1	80
1.2.3	Cocoa and powdered chocolate	0.10	3	390	0.00	0	70	0.00	0	30
1.2.4	Fruit and vegetable juices (inc fruit squash)	1.10	29	2,640	0.10	2	340	0.10	3	190
1.2.5	Mineral or spring waters	0.20	6	970	0.00	1	200	0.00	1	60
1.2.6	Soft drinks	1.50	39	2,880	0.40	11	1,190	0.10	3	160

Note: The commodity and service categories are not comparable with those in publications before 2001-02
The numbering is sequential, it does not use actual COICOP codes.
Please see background notes for symbols and conventions used in this report
1 In 2011 the list of large supermarket chains was updated
2 Includes internet expenditure from large supermarket chains

Table A3
Expenditure on clothing and footwear by place of purchase, 2013
United Kingdom

	Large supermarket chains[1]			Clothing chains			Other outlets[2]		
	Average weekly expenditure all households (£)	Total weekly expenditure (£ million)	Recording households in sample	Average weekly expenditure all households (£)	Total weekly expenditure (£ million)	Recording households in sample	Average weekly expenditure all households (£)	Total weekly expenditure (£ million)	Recording households in sample
3 Clothing and footwear	**2.10**	**57**	**1,250**	**7.70**	**207**	**1,640**	**12.40**	**332**	**2,300**
3.1 Clothing	1.90	51	1,170	6.90	185	1,580	9.10	244	2,000
3.1.1 Men's outer garments	0.20	6	160	1.60	44	410	2.80	75	540
3.1.2 Men's under garments	0.10	2	130	0.20	5	140	0.20	4	120
3.1.3 Women's outer garments	0.70	18	420	3.30	89	920	3.80	102	920
3.1.4 Women's under garments	0.20	6	310	0.60	16	420	0.30	8	240
3.1.5 Boys' outer garments	0.10	3	110	0.20	6	100	0.50	13	180
3.1.6 Girls' outer garments	0.10	4	120	0.30	8	140	0.50	13	230
3.1.7 Infants' outer garments	0.20	5	150	0.30	7	140	0.30	8	170
3.1.8 Children's under garments	0.20	4	190	0.10	4	130	0.10	3	140
3.1.9 Accessories	0.10	2	160	0.20	6	210	0.40	11	440
3.1.9.1 Men's accessories	0.00	1	50	0.10	2	70	0.20	5	150
3.1.9.2 Women's accessories	0.00	1	70	0.10	4	140	0.20	5	230
3.1.9.3 Children's accessories	0.00	0	40	0.00	0	30	0.10	1	100
3.1.1 Haberdashery and clothing hire	0.00	0	40	[0.00]	[0]	..	0.20	6	200
3.2 Footwear	0.20	5	220	0.80	22	360	3.30	88	890
3.2.1 Men's	0.00	1	40	0.20	6	80	1.30	34	280
3.2.2 Women's	0.10	3	120	0.50	14	250	1.40	38	480
3.2.3 Children's	0.10	2	70	0.10	2	60	0.60	16	250

Note: The commodity and service categories are not comparable with those in publications before 2001-02.
The numbering system is sequential, it does not use actual COICOP codes.
Please see background notes for symbols and conventions used in this report.
1 In 2011 the list of large supermarket chains was updated.
2 Includes internet expenditure from large supermarket chains.

Table A4
Household expenditure by gross income decile group, 2013
United Kingdom

		Lowest ten per cent	Second decile group	Third decile group	Fourth decile group	Fifth decile group	Sixth decile group	Seventh decile group	Eighth decile group	Ninth decile group	Highest ten per cent	All house-holds
Lower boundary of group (£ per week)			178	265	358	462	574	696	856	1,078	1,442	
Weighted number of households (thousands)		2,690	2,680	2,690	2,690	2,680	2,690	2,680	2,680	2,690	2,680	26,840
Total number of households in sample		500	510	540	550	530	530	510	500	490	480	5,140
Total number of persons in sample		650	860	1,030	1,180	1,190	1,360	1,430	1,450	1,440	1,530	12,120
Total number of adults in sample		570	690	820	920	950	1,020	1,040	1,090	1,120	1,140	9,350
Weighted average number of persons per household		1.3	1.7	1.9	2.1	2.3	2.6	2.7	2.8	3.0	3.2	2.4
Commodity or service		Average weekly household expenditure (£)										
1	Food & non-alcoholic drinks	30.50	37.80	44.50	49.60	54.30	63.30	65.00	71.80	78.70	92.60	58.80
2	Alcoholic drinks, tobacco & narcotics	7.30	6.90	9.30	10.60	11.30	12.90	14.20	14.30	15.30	18.30	12.00
3	Clothing & footwear	6.00	7.40	13.10	13.30	17.40	24.90	26.30	33.20	36.50	47.90	22.60
4	Housing(net)[1], fuel & power	50.10	57.70	67.90	73.70	78.40	81.80	79.10	79.20	81.40	94.50	74.40
5	Household goods & services	13.30	15.30	20.80	22.90	27.60	30.50	41.70	37.10	43.50	78.90	33.10
6	Health	1.70	2.70	3.00	4.90	4.30	7.20	8.20	10.20	10.30	9.80	6.20
7	Transport	15.70	19.30	33.40	41.50	56.70	77.00	76.90	95.70	125.10	163.10	70.40
8	Communication	6.90	8.30	10.40	12.10	13.70	15.70	17.30	18.20	20.30	21.70	14.50
9	Recreation & culture	17.60	21.80	32.00	40.60	57.20	59.40	69.10	84.60	94.60	162.40	63.90
10	Education	[4.30]	[1.70]	[3.40]	[16.70]	6.30	1.50	5.80	13.50	9.60	25.20	8.80
11	Restaurants & hotels	9.30	12.50	20.60	25.90	30.10	40.40	46.80	53.40	69.90	94.80	40.40
12	Miscellaneous goods & services	11.30	15.50	22.90	26.30	32.00	37.80	46.10	49.40	63.60	86.50	39.10
1-12	All expenditure groups	174.10	206.80	281.30	338.00	389.30	452.60	496.60	560.60	648.70	895.60	444.30
13	Other expenditure items	15.80	21.80	33.50	40.00	51.60	62.90	76.90	91.20	113.00	223.80	73.00
Total expenditure		**189.80**	**228.60**	**314.80**	**378.00**	**440.90**	**515.50**	**573.50**	**651.90**	**761.70**	**1119.50**	**517.30**
Average weekly expenditure per person (£)												
Total expenditure		**147.90**	**138.00**	**167.60**	**176.60**	**192.60**	**199.00**	**208.80**	**230.20**	**256.90**	**350.10**	**219.40**

Note: The commodity and service categories are not comparable to those in publications before 2001-02.
Please see background notes for symbols and conventions used in this report.
1 Excluding mortgage interest payments, council tax and Northern Ireland rates.

Table A5
Household expenditure as a percentage of total expenditure by gross income decile group, 2013
United Kingdom

	Lowest ten per cent	Second decile group	Third decile group	Fourth decile group	Fifth decile group	Sixth decile group	Seventh decile group	Eighth decile group	Ninth decile group	Highest ten per cent	All house-holds
Lower boundary of group (£ per week)		178	265	358	462	574	696	856	1,078	1,442	
Weighted number of households (thousands)	2,690	2,680	2,690	2,690	2,680	2,690	2,680	2,680	2,690	2,680	26,840
Total number of households in sample	500	510	540	550	530	530	510	500	490	480	5,140
Total number of persons in sample	650	860	1,030	1,180	1,190	1,360	1,430	1,450	1,440	1,530	12,120
Total number of adults in sample	570	690	820	920	950	1,020	1,040	1,090	1,120	1,140	9,350
Weighted average number of persons per household	1.3	1.7	1.9	2.1	2.3	2.6	2.7	2.8	3.0	3.2	2.4
Commodity or service					Percentage of total expenditure						
1 Food & non-alcoholic drinks	*16*	*17*	*14*	*13*	*12*	*12*	*11*	*11*	*10*	*8*	*11*
2 Alcoholic drinks, tobacco & narcotics	*4*	*3*	*3*	*3*	*3*	*3*	*2*	*2*	*2*	*2*	*2*
3 Clothing & footwear	*3*	*3*	*4*	*4*	*4*	*5*	*5*	*5*	*5*	*4*	*4*
4 Housing(net)[1], fuel & power	*26*	*25*	*22*	*19*	*18*	*16*	*14*	*12*	*11*	*8*	*14*
5 Household goods & services	*7*	*7*	*7*	*6*	*6*	*6*	*7*	*6*	*6*	*7*	*6*
6 Health	*1*	*1*	*1*	*1*	*1*	*1*	*1*	*2*	*1*	*1*	*1*
7 Transport	*8*	*8*	*11*	*11*	*13*	*15*	*13*	*15*	*16*	*15*	*14*
8 Communication	*4*	*4*	*3*	*3*	*3*	*3*	*3*	*3*	*3*	*2*	*3*
9 Recreation & culture	*9*	*10*	*10*	*11*	*13*	*12*	*12*	*13*	*12*	*15*	*12*
10 Education	*[2]*	*[1]*	*[1]*	*[4]*	*1*	*0*	*1*	*2*	*1*	*2*	*2*
11 Restaurants & hotels	*5*	*5*	*7*	*7*	*7*	*8*	*8*	*8*	*9*	*8*	*8*
12 Miscellaneous goods & services	*6*	*7*	*7*	*7*	*7*	*7*	*8*	*8*	*8*	*8*	*8*
1-12 All expenditure groups	*92*	*90*	*89*	*89*	*88*	*88*	*87*	*86*	*85*	*80*	*86*
13 Other expenditure items	*8*	*10*	*11*	*11*	*12*	*12*	*13*	*14*	*15*	*20*	*14*
Total expenditure	***100***	***100***	***100***	***100***	***100***	***100***	***100***	***100***	***100***	***100***	***100***

Note: The commodity and service categories are not comparable to those in publications before 2001-02.
Please see background notes for symbols and conventions used in this report.
1 Excluding mortgage interest payments, council tax and Northern Ireland rates.

Table A6
Detailed household expenditure by gross income decile group, 2013
United Kingdom

	Lowest ten per cent	Second decile group	Third decile group	Fourth decile group	Fifth decile group	Sixth decile group	Seventh decile group	Eighth decile group	Ninth decile group	Highest ten per cent	All house-holds
Lower boundary of group (£ per week)		178	265	358	462	574	696	856	1,078	1,442	
Weighted number of households (thousands)	2,690	2,680	2,690	2,690	2,680	2,690	2,680	2,680	2,690	2,680	26,840
Total number of households in sample	500	510	540	550	530	530	510	500	490	480	5,140
Total number of persons in sample	650	860	1,030	1,180	1,190	1,360	1,430	1,450	1,440	1,530	12,120
Total number of adults in sample	570	690	820	920	950	1,020	1,040	1,090	1,120	1,140	9,350
Weighted average number of persons per household	1.3	1.7	1.9	2.1	2.3	2.6	2.7	2.8	3.0	3.2	2.4
Commodity or service	Average weekly household expenditure (£)										
1 Food & non-alcoholic drinks	**30.50**	**37.80**	**44.50**	**49.60**	**54.30**	**63.30**	**65.00**	**71.80**	**78.70**	**92.60**	**58.80**
1.1 Food	28.20	34.60	41.10	45.30	50.00	58.10	59.40	65.90	71.90	85.00	54.00
1.1.1 Bread, rice and cereals	3.00	3.80	4.20	5.00	5.50	5.80	6.20	6.90	7.30	7.90	5.60
1.1.2 Pasta products	0.20	0.20	0.30	0.30	0.40	0.40	0.50	0.60	0.70	0.80	0.40
1.1.3 Buns, cakes, biscuits etc.	1.80	2.60	2.90	3.20	3.40	4.00	3.90	4.40	4.40	5.20	3.60
1.1.4 Pastry (savoury)	0.40	0.40	0.50	0.60	0.80	0.80	1.10	1.00	1.10	1.50	0.80
1.1.5 Beef (fresh, chilled or frozen)	0.90	0.90	1.50	1.40	1.60	2.10	1.90	2.30	2.80	3.70	1.90
1.1.6 Pork (fresh, chilled or frozen)	0.30	0.60	0.70	0.50	0.70	0.70	0.80	0.80	0.80	0.80	0.70
1.1.7 Lamb (fresh, chilled or frozen)	0.50	0.40	0.60	0.60	0.70	0.50	0.60	0.80	0.80	1.10	0.70
1.1.8 Poultry (fresh, chilled or frozen)	1.00	1.20	1.50	1.90	2.10	2.80	2.60	3.40	3.10	4.50	2.40
1.1.9 Bacon and ham	0.60	0.70	0.80	1.00	0.90	1.10	1.10	1.20	1.30	1.50	1.00
1.1.10 Other meat and meat preparations	3.60	4.40	5.00	5.40	5.60	7.00	6.80	7.70	8.20	9.10	6.30
1.1.11 Fish and fish products	1.30	1.70	2.10	2.10	2.60	2.50	3.00	3.10	3.70	4.40	2.60
1.1.12 Milk	1.50	1.80	2.20	2.30	2.50	2.60	2.60	2.70	2.90	3.20	2.40
1.1.13 Cheese and curd	1.00	1.20	1.40	1.60	1.80	2.20	2.20	2.40	2.70	3.50	2.00
1.1.14 Eggs	0.50	0.50	0.60	0.60	0.70	0.70	0.80	0.80	1.00	1.10	0.70
1.1.15 Other milk products	1.00	1.30	1.60	1.70	1.80	2.40	2.40	2.40	2.50	3.40	2.10
1.1.16 Butter	0.30	0.40	0.30	0.40	0.50	0.50	0.50	0.50	0.70	0.70	0.50
1.1.17 Margarine, other vegetable fats and peanut butter	0.30	0.40	0.40	0.50	0.60	0.50	0.60	0.50	0.60	0.60	0.50
1.1.18 Cooking oils and fats	0.20	0.20	0.30	0.30	0.40	0.30	0.30	0.40	0.40	0.50	0.30
1.1.19 Fresh fruit	1.50	2.10	2.40	2.50	3.00	3.60	3.70	3.70	4.60	5.90	3.30
1.1.20 Other fresh, chilled or frozen fruits	0.20	0.20	0.30	0.30	0.30	0.40	0.40	0.50	0.50	0.80	0.40
1.1.21 Dried fruit and nuts	0.30	0.40	0.50	0.50	0.60	0.80	0.80	0.80	1.20	1.50	0.70
1.1.22 Preserved fruit and fruit based products	0.10	0.10	0.10	0.10	0.10	0.20	0.10	0.20	0.10	0.20	0.10
1.1.23 Fresh vegetables	2.30	2.60	3.10	3.30	3.90	4.50	4.70	5.30	6.10	7.60	4.30
1.1.24 Dried vegetables	[0.00]	[0.00]	[0.00]	0.10	0.10	0.10	0.00	0.10	0.10	0.10	0.10
1.1.25 Other preserved or processed vegetables	0.70	0.80	0.90	1.10	1.20	1.50	1.60	1.80	1.90	2.60	1.40
1.1.26 Potatoes	0.60	0.70	0.90	0.90	1.00	1.10	1.10	1.20	1.20	1.20	1.00
1.1.27 Other tubers and products of tuber vegetables	0.90	1.10	1.20	1.40	1.50	1.80	1.90	2.10	2.10	2.10	1.60
1.1.28 Sugar and sugar products	0.30	0.30	0.40	0.40	0.40	0.60	0.50	0.50	0.60	0.70	0.50
1.1.29 Jams, marmalades	0.20	0.30	0.30	0.20	0.30	0.30	0.30	0.30	0.30	0.30	0.30
1.1.30 Chocolate	0.80	1.00	1.30	1.60	1.40	2.00	1.90	2.40	2.50	2.70	1.80
1.1.31 Confectionery products	0.40	0.60	0.50	0.60	0.60	0.80	0.70	0.90	0.90	0.90	0.70
1.1.32 Edible ices and ice cream	0.20	0.40	0.40	0.60	0.60	0.70	0.70	0.70	0.70	0.90	0.60
1.1.33 Other food products	1.30	1.50	1.90	2.30	2.30	2.90	2.90	3.50	3.90	4.20	2.70
1.2 Non-alcoholic drinks	2.30	3.10	3.40	4.20	4.30	5.30	5.60	6.00	6.90	7.50	4.90
1.2.1 Coffee	0.40	0.60	0.50	0.80	0.60	0.80	0.80	0.80	1.00	1.10	0.70
1.2.2 Tea	0.30	0.40	0.40	0.40	0.50	0.50	0.50	0.50	0.50	0.60	0.50
1.2.3 Cocoa and powdered chocolate	0.10	0.10	0.10	0.10	0.10	0.10	0.10	0.20	0.20	0.20	0.10
1.2.4 Fruit and vegetable juices (inc. fruit squash)	0.50	0.70	0.80	0.90	1.10	1.20	1.60	1.50	1.90	2.40	1.20
1.2.5 Mineral or spring waters	0.10	0.20	0.30	0.20	0.20	0.30	0.30	0.30	0.40	0.60	0.30
1.2.6 Soft drinks (inc. fizzy and ready to drink fruit drinks)	0.90	1.20	1.30	1.80	1.90	2.50	2.30	2.70	2.90	2.60	2.00

Note: The commodity and service categories are not comparable to those in publications before 2001-02
The numbering system is sequential, it does not use actual COICOP codes
Please see background notes for symbols and conventions used in this report

Table A6
Detailed household expenditure by gross income decile group, 2013 (cont.)
United Kingdom

Commodity or service	Lowest ten per cent	Second decile group	Third decile group	Fourth decile group	Fifth decile group	Sixth decile group	Seventh decile group	Eighth decile group	Ninth decile group	Highest ten per cent	All house- holds
	Average weekly household expenditure (£)										
2 Alcoholic drink, tobacco & narcotics	**7.30**	**6.90**	**9.30**	**10.60**	**11.30**	**12.90**	**14.20**	**14.30**	**15.30**	**18.30**	**12.00**
2.1 Alcoholic drinks	3.50	3.40	4.60	5.00	6.40	8.00	9.00	9.80	11.90	15.30	7.70
2.1.1 Spirits and liqueurs (brought home)	1.20	1.10	1.20	1.40	1.30	1.70	1.90	1.70	1.90	2.20	1.60
2.1.2 Wines, fortified wines (brought home)	1.20	1.40	2.00	1.80	3.30	3.80	4.40	5.10	7.00	9.80	4.00
2.1.3 Beer, lager, ciders and perry (brought home)	1.00	0.90	1.40	1.70	1.70	2.40	2.70	2.90	3.00	3.30	2.10
2.1.4 Alcopops (brought home)	[0.10]	[0.00]	[0.00]	[0.00]	[0.00]	[0.00]	[0.00]	[0.10]	[0.00]	[0.10]	0.00
2.2 Tobacco and narcotics	3.70	3.50	4.70	5.60	4.90	4.90	5.20	4.40	3.40	2.90	4.30
2.2.1 Cigarettes	2.50	2.70	4.00	4.70	4.10	3.90	4.20	3.80	2.90	2.30	3.50
2.2.2 Cigars, other tobacco products and narcotics	1.30	0.80	0.70	0.80	0.80	1.10	1.00	0.60	0.50	0.60	0.80
3 Clothing & footwear	**6.00**	**7.40**	**13.10**	**13.30**	**17.40**	**24.90**	**26.30**	**33.20**	**36.50**	**47.90**	**22.60**
3.1 Clothing	4.80	5.90	10.60	10.60	14.10	19.90	21.20	26.20	29.60	39.70	18.30
3.1.1 Men's outer garments	0.70	1.30	2.90	2.20	3.40	5.50	5.30	7.20	7.90	10.10	4.70
3.1.2 Men's under garments	[0.10]	[0.10]	0.40	0.30	0.40	0.50	0.60	0.70	0.60	0.60	0.40
3.1.3 Women's outer garments	2.30	2.30	4.20	4.20	6.60	7.40	9.80	10.50	12.10	18.60	7.80
3.1.4 Women's under garments	0.50	0.60	0.80	0.60	0.80	1.30	1.10	1.40	2.00	2.40	1.10
3.1.5 Boys' outer garments (5-15)	[0.30]	[0.30]	0.50	0.70	1.10	1.10	1.10	1.20	1.00	1.20	0.80
3.1.6 Girls' outer garments (5-15)	[0.20]	0.40	0.40	0.70	0.60	1.10	0.80	1.40	1.70	2.00	0.90
3.1.7 Infants' outer garments (under 5)	[0.10]	0.30	0.50	0.60	0.50	0.80	0.70	1.30	1.60	1.30	0.80
3.1.8 Children's under garments (under 16)	[0.10]	0.20	0.10	0.50	0.20	0.50	0.40	0.60	0.60	0.70	0.40
3.1.9 Accessories	0.30	0.20	0.50	0.50	0.40	1.20	1.00	1.30	1.30	1.60	0.80
3.1.10 Haberdashery and clothing hire	[0.10]	[0.10]	0.20	0.10	0.20	0.30	0.10	0.30	0.40	0.40	0.20
3.1.11 Dry cleaners, laundry and dyeing	[0.20]	[0.10]	[0.10]	[0.20]	[0.10]	[0.20]	[0.20]	0.40	0.40	0.70	0.30
3.2 Footwear	1.20	1.50	2.50	2.70	3.30	5.00	5.20	7.00	6.90	8.30	4.30
4 Housing (net)[1], fuel & power	**50.10**	**57.70**	**67.90**	**73.70**	**78.40**	**81.80**	**79.10**	**79.20**	**81.40**	**94.50**	**74.40**
4.1 Actual rentals for housing	78.10	66.70	60.50	53.70	47.90	43.70	34.50	33.40	30.90	31.70	48.10
4.1.1 Gross rent	78.10	66.70	60.50	53.70	47.90	43.70	34.40	33.20	30.90	31.20	48.00
4.1.2 *less* housing benefit, rebates & allowances rec'd	57.20	42.00	28.60	16.50	9.30	4.00	1.10	0.90	[1.10]	[0.00]	16.10
4.1.3 Net rent[2]	20.90	24.80	32.00	37.20	38.50	39.70	33.30	32.30	29.80	31.20	32.00
4.1.4 Second dwelling rent	-	-	-	-	-	-	[0.10]	[0.20]	-	[0.50]	[0.10]
4.2 Maintenance and repair of dwelling	1.90	2.90	4.70	4.30	5.70	7.60	8.90	8.90	11.40	14.60	7.10
4.3 Water supply and miscellaneous services relating to the dwelling	7.00	7.50	7.90	8.20	8.60	8.50	9.30	9.50	9.40	11.00	8.70
4.4 Electricity, gas and other fuels[3]	20.20	22.50	23.30	24.00	25.60	26.10	27.50	28.30	30.90	37.20	26.50
4.4.1 Electricity	9.50	10.70	11.20	11.10	12.00	11.80	12.40	12.90	13.50	15.80	12.10
4.4.2 Gas	9.20	9.90	11.30	11.80	12.20	12.50	12.90	13.40	13.80	17.10	12.40
4.4.3 Other fuels	[1.40]	1.90	0.80	1.10	1.40	1.80	2.20	2.00	3.50	4.20	2.00

Note: The commodity and service categories are not comparable to those in publications before 2001-02
The numbering system is sequential, it does not use actual COICOP codes
Please see background notes for symbols and conventions used in this report
1 Excluding mortgage interest payments, council tax and Northern Ireland rates
2 The figure included in total expenditure is net rent as opposed to gross rent
3 Recording of expenditure on gas and electricity via combined payment packages was changed in 2013. Recording of expenditure via slot meters was also changed

Table A6
Detailed household expenditure by gross income decile group, 2013 (cont.)
United Kingdom

	Commodity or service	Lowest ten per cent	Second decile group	Third decile group	Fourth decile group	Fifth decile group	Sixth decile group	Seventh decile group	Eighth decile group	Ninth decile group	Highest ten per cent	All house-holds
		Average weekly household expenditure (£)										
5	**Household goods & services**	**13.30**	**15.30**	**20.80**	**22.90**	**27.60**	**30.50**	**41.70**	**37.10**	**43.50**	**78.90**	**33.10**
5.1	Furniture and furnishings, carpets and other floor coverings[4]	6.90	7.70	9.60	11.10	13.30	16.40	23.20	20.00	23.50	50.20	18.20
5.1.1	Furniture and furnishings	5.80	5.70	8.00	8.20	10.10	12.90	19.20	16.40	19.70	42.30	14.80
5.1.2	Floor coverings	1.10	2.00	1.60	2.80	3.20	3.50	4.00	3.60	3.80	7.90	3.40
5.2	Household textiles	0.80	0.70	0.90	1.10	2.60	1.60	2.70	2.20	2.80	3.00	1.80
5.3	Household appliances	1.80	1.70	2.60	2.90	3.00	3.30	4.20	3.60	3.10	4.30	3.10
5.4	Glassware, tableware and household utensils	0.50	0.50	0.80	1.10	1.10	1.50	1.40	2.00	2.30	4.30	1.60
5.5	Tools and equipment for house and garden	0.70	0.70	1.30	1.50	1.90	1.90	4.40	3.00	4.60	3.60	2.40
5.6	Goods and services for routine household maintenance	2.60	4.00	5.50	5.20	5.60	5.80	5.60	6.30	7.10	13.50	6.10
5.6.1	Cleaning materials	1.30	1.60	1.80	1.90	2.30	2.30	2.60	2.90	3.10	4.00	2.40
5.6.2	Household goods and hardware	0.70	0.90	1.00	1.20	1.30	1.50	1.60	1.70	1.80	2.60	1.40
5.6.3	Domestic services, carpet cleaning, hire/repair of furniture/furnishings	0.60	1.50	2.70	2.10	2.00	2.00	1.40	1.60	2.30	6.90	2.30
6	**Health**	**1.70**	**2.70**	**3.00**	**4.90**	**4.30**	**7.20**	**8.20**	**10.20**	**10.30**	**9.80**	**6.20**
6.1	Medical products, appliances and equipment	1.10	2.00	1.90	2.50	3.10	5.10	4.80	7.20	6.00	6.10	4.00
6.1.1	Medicines, prescriptions, healthcare products etc.	0.90	1.40	1.00	1.60	1.70	3.00	2.40	4.10	4.00	2.50	2.30
6.1.2	Spectacles, lenses, accessories and repairs	[0.20]	[0.60]	0.80	0.90	1.30	2.10	2.40	3.10	2.10	3.50	1.70
6.2	Hospital services	[0.60]	0.70	1.10	2.40	1.30	2.10	3.40	3.00	4.20	3.80	2.30
7	**Transport**	**15.70**	**19.30**	**33.40**	**41.50**	**56.70**	**77.00**	**76.90**	**95.70**	**125.10**	**163.10**	**70.40**
7.1	Purchase of vehicles	4.10	3.90	7.20	10.90	15.40	26.00	22.10	27.00	42.70	51.80	21.10
7.1.1	Purchase of new cars and vans	[2.20]	[1.00]	[2.90]	[3.50]	[6.40]	10.20	8.10	6.60	18.00	24.10	8.30
7.1.2	Purchase of second hand cars or vans	1.90	2.80	4.30	7.20	8.70	15.00	12.80	18.90	22.20	26.10	12.00
7.1.3	Purchase of motorcycles and other vehicles	[0.10]	[0.00]	[0.00]	[0.10]	[0.30]	[0.80]	[1.10]	[1.40]	[2.50]	[1.60]	0.80
7.2	Operation of personal transport	6.90	10.60	17.50	22.00	31.50	37.40	41.10	48.30	57.50	67.30	34.00
7.2.1	Spares and accessories	[0.50]	[0.40]	1.00	0.30	2.90	2.20	3.20	2.80	3.20	6.30	2.30
7.2.2	Petrol, diesel and other motor oils	4.90	7.50	12.70	15.50	20.50	26.50	28.70	34.90	40.40	43.60	23.50
7.2.3	Repairs and servicing	1.10	2.20	2.60	3.90	5.80	6.30	6.40	7.30	9.70	11.90	5.70
7.2.4	Other motoring costs	0.40	0.50	1.20	2.30	2.30	2.30	2.70	3.30	4.20	5.50	2.50
7.3	Transport services[5]	4.70	4.80	8.60	8.60	9.80	13.70	13.80	20.50	24.90	44.00	15.30
7.3.1	Rail and tube fares	1.00	0.50	1.20	1.70	1.90	2.40	3.10	4.80	7.90	14.10	3.90
7.3.2	Bus and coach fares	1.20	1.10	1.20	1.60	1.80	2.30	1.80	1.90	1.90	1.40	1.60
7.3.3	Combined fares	[0.00]	[0.00]	[0.60]	[0.50]	[0.50]	[0.90]	[0.20]	[1.20]	[1.70]	2.30	0.80
7.3.4	Other travel and transport	2.40	3.20	5.60	4.80	5.60	8.10	8.80	12.60	13.40	26.20	9.10
8	**Communication**	**6.90**	**8.30**	**10.40**	**12.10**	**13.70**	**15.70**	**17.30**	**18.20**	**20.30**	**21.70**	**14.50**
8.1	Postal services	0.30	0.30	0.30	0.60	0.50	0.70	0.40	0.80	1.00	1.10	0.60
8.2	Telephone and telefax equipment	[0.10]	[0.10]	[0.60]	[0.40]	[0.20]	0.80	0.80	[0.50]	1.10	0.60	0.50
8.3	Telephone and telefax services	5.10	6.40	7.50	8.60	10.10	11.00	12.80	13.50	14.70	15.90	10.60
8.4	Internet subscription fees	1.40	1.40	2.00	2.50	2.80	3.30	3.20	3.40	3.40	4.10	2.80

Note: The commodity and service categories are not comparable to those in publications before 2001-02
The numbering system is sequential, it does not use actual COICOP codes
Please see background notes for symbols and conventions used in this report
4 Recording of expenditure on furniture was changed in 2013
5 Recording of expenditure on flights was changed in 2013

Table A6
Detailed household expenditure by gross income decile group, 2013 (cont.)
United Kingdom

Commodity or service	Lowest ten per cent	Second decile group	Third decile group	Fourth decile group	Fifth decile group	Sixth decile group	Seventh decile group	Eighth decile group	Ninth decile group	Highest ten per cent	All house-holds
	Average weekly household expenditure (£)										
9 Recreation & culture	**17.60**	**21.80**	**32.00**	**40.60**	**57.20**	**59.40**	**69.10**	**84.60**	**94.60**	**162.40**	**63.90**
9.1 Audio-visual, photographic and information processing equipment	[2.10]	1.10	2.30	3.70	4.00	4.10	5.50	8.40	7.20	13.00	5.10
9.1.1 Audio equipment and accessories, CD players	0.20	0.10	0.20	0.40	0.70	0.80	1.40	1.80	1.40	2.10	0.90
9.1.2 TV, video and computers	1.80	1.00	1.90	3.20	2.80	3.10	3.90	6.40	4.80	10.50	3.90
9.1.3 Photographic, cine and optical equipment	[0.00]	[0.00]	[0.30]	[0.10]	[0.50]	[0.20]	[0.10]	[0.20]	[0.90]	[0.50]	0.30
9.2 Other major durables for recreation and culture	[0.30]	[1.20]	[0.40]	[1.00]	[0.50]	[0.10]	[3.00]	[0.90]	[5.70]	7.80	2.10
9.3 Other recreational items and equipment, gardens and pets	3.80	4.30	6.60	7.70	8.90	10.30	12.30	15.30	15.80	19.70	10.40
9.3.1 Games, toys and hobbies	0.60	0.90	1.10	1.30	1.70	2.40	2.30	3.60	3.90	5.10	2.30
9.3.2 Computer software and games	[0.20]	[0.20]	[0.40]	0.60	[0.80]	1.00	1.30	0.70	1.40	1.70	0.80
9.3.3 Equipment for sport, camping and open-air recreation	[0.20]	[0.10]	0.50	0.50	0.70	1.00	1.20	1.80	1.60	1.10	0.90
9.3.4 Horticultural goods, garden equipment and plants	0.80	1.00	1.60	2.00	2.30	2.00	2.30	2.50	2.90	4.10	2.20
9.3.5 Pets and pet food	1.90	2.10	3.00	3.30	3.30	3.90	5.20	6.70	5.90	7.60	4.30
9.4 Recreational and cultural services	6.50	8.00	11.60	13.10	15.40	19.00	21.20	26.30	27.40	37.40	18.60
9.4.1 Sports admissions, subscriptions, leisure class fees and equipment hire	0.90	1.00	1.90	3.00	3.50	5.80	6.00	8.60	8.80	16.00	5.50
9.4.2 Cinema, theatre and museums etc.	[0.30]	0.40	1.10	1.10	2.00	2.20	2.50	3.40	4.60	5.70	2.30
9.4.3 TV, video, satellite rental, cable subscriptions and TV licences	3.60	4.00	4.90	6.00	6.80	6.70	7.70	8.60	8.70	9.50	6.70
9.4.4 Miscellaneous entertainments	0.30	0.50	0.40	0.60	0.80	1.40	1.50	1.90	1.90	2.90	1.20
9.4.5 Development of film, deposit for film development, passport photos, holiday and school photos	[0.00]	[0.10]	[0.20]	[0.10]	[0.20]	[0.10]	0.30	0.60	0.30	0.40	0.20
9.4.6 Gambling payments	1.50	2.00	3.10	2.20	2.00	3.00	3.20	3.20	3.10	2.90	2.60
9.5 Newspapers, books and stationery	2.20	3.20	4.00	4.00	4.90	5.80	5.90	6.70	6.90	9.10	5.30
9.5.1 Books	0.30	0.40	0.70	0.80	1.00	1.10	0.90	1.70	1.60	2.50	1.10
9.5.2 Diaries, address books, cards etc.	0.60	0.80	1.10	1.20	1.50	1.90	2.10	2.40	3.00	4.00	1.90
9.5.3 Newspapers	0.90	1.50	1.70	1.50	1.70	1.80	1.80	1.90	1.40	1.50	1.60
9.5.4 Magazines and periodicals	0.40	0.50	0.50	0.50	0.70	1.10	1.00	0.80	0.90	1.10	0.80
9.6 Package holidays[6]	2.90	4.10	7.10	11.20	23.50	20.10	21.30	27.10	31.60	75.40	22.40
9.6.1 Package holidays - UK	[0.50]	1.10	0.90	2.00	1.70	1.30	0.90	1.60	2.10	2.40	1.40
9.6.2 Package holidays - abroad	2.30	3.00	6.20	9.20	21.80	18.80	20.40	25.50	29.50	73.10	21.00
10 Education	**[4.30]**	**[1.70]**	**[3.40]**	**[16.70]**	**6.30**	**1.50**	**5.80**	**13.50**	**9.60**	**25.20**	**8.80**
10.1 Education fees	[4.30]	[1.60]	[3.20]	[16.50]	[5.80]	[1.30]	5.30	13.10	8.90	24.70	8.50
10.2 Payments for school trips, other ad-hoc expenditure	[0.00]	[0.10]	[0.20]	[0.20]	[0.40]	[0.20]	0.40	[0.40]	[0.70]	[0.50]	0.30
11 Restaurants & hotels	**9.30**	**12.50**	**20.60**	**25.90**	**30.10**	**40.40**	**46.80**	**53.40**	**69.90**	**94.80**	**40.40**
11.1 Catering services	8.20	10.90	17.50	22.60	24.80	33.90	40.40	45.60	58.70	72.90	33.50
11.1.1 Restaurant and café meals	3.90	5.30	8.60	11.00	11.50	16.50	18.20	20.10	27.70	36.10	15.90
11.1.2 Alcoholic drinks (away from home)	1.80	1.80	3.30	4.70	5.40	6.40	8.90	10.30	12.90	15.90	7.10
11.1.3 Take away meals eaten at home	1.40	1.60	2.80	3.10	3.30	4.70	5.40	6.00	6.90	6.80	4.20
11.1.4 Other take-away and snack food	1.00	1.60	1.90	2.80	3.10	4.20	5.40	6.40	7.60	9.70	4.40
11.1.5 Contract catering (food) and canteens	0.20	0.60	0.90	1.10	1.50	2.10	2.50	2.80	3.40	4.30	1.90
11.2 Accommodation services	1.10	1.50	3.10	3.40	5.30	6.50	6.40	7.80	11.30	21.80	6.80
11.2.1 Holiday in the UK	0.90	0.90	2.60	2.30	4.30	4.30	4.30	4.50	7.20	9.40	4.00
11.2.2 Holiday abroad	[0.20]	[0.60]	[0.60]	[1.10]	[1.00]	2.20	2.10	3.30	3.80	12.30	2.70
11.2.3 Room hire	[0.00]	[0.00]	[0.00]	-	[0.00]	[0.00]	[0.00]	[0.00]	[0.30]	[0.20]	[0.10]

Note: The commodity and service categories are not comparable to those in publications before 2001-02
The numbering system is sequential, it does not use actual COICOP codes
Please see background notes for symbols and conventions used in this report
6 Recording of expenditure on package holidays was changed in 2013

Table A6
Detailed household expenditure by gross income decile group, 2013 (cont.)
United Kingdom

Commodity or service	Lowest ten per cent	Second decile group	Third decile group	Fourth decile group	Fifth decile group	Sixth decile group	Seventh decile group	Eighth decile group	Ninth decile group	Highest ten per cent	All house-holds
	Average weekly household expenditure (£)										
12 Miscellaneous goods & services	**11.30**	**15.50**	**22.90**	**26.30**	**32.00**	**37.80**	**46.10**	**49.40**	**63.60**	**86.50**	**39.10**
12.1 Personal care	4.10	5.00	8.10	7.90	8.50	11.10	13.80	14.20	16.70	22.30	11.20
12.1.1 Hairdressing, beauty treatment	1.20	1.40	3.00	2.40	2.40	3.20	3.90	4.80	5.00	7.20	3.40
12.1.2 Toilet paper	0.50	0.60	0.60	0.70	0.80	0.90	1.10	1.00	1.00	1.30	0.80
12.1.3 Toiletries and soap	1.10	1.30	1.70	2.00	1.90	2.50	2.90	3.30	3.60	4.50	2.50
12.1.4 Baby toiletries and accessories (disposable)	0.20	0.30	0.40	0.40	0.60	0.80	0.80	0.70	0.80	1.10	0.60
12.1.5 Hair products, cosmetics and related electrical appliances	1.10	1.40	2.40	2.40	2.80	3.80	5.20	4.40	6.30	8.10	3.80
12.2 Personal effects	0.50	1.10	1.30	1.70	2.30	2.30	4.30	4.50	4.40	7.60	3.00
12.3 Social protection	[0.40]	[1.10]	[1.00]	[0.90]	[3.20]	2.30	3.80	5.80	10.90	11.20	4.10
12.4 Insurance	5.00	7.30	9.80	13.30	14.90	18.00	20.20	20.40	25.70	33.10	16.80
12.4.1 Household insurances - structural, contents and appliances	1.90	3.60	3.70	3.90	4.70	5.30	5.70	6.20	6.60	9.10	5.10
12.4.2 Medical insurance premiums	[0.20]	[0.20]	0.50	0.60	1.30	2.10	2.50	2.10	2.90	7.80	2.00
12.4.3 Vehicle insurance including boat insurance	2.70	3.60	5.60	8.50	8.90	10.60	11.90	12.10	15.20	16.00	9.50
12.4.4 Non-package holiday, other travel insurance	[0.20]	-	[0.00]	[0.30]	[0.00]	[0.00]	[0.10]	[0.00]	[1.00]	[0.20]	0.20
12.5 Other services	1.30	1.00	2.70	2.50	3.00	4.20	3.90	4.40	5.80	12.40	4.10
12.5.1 Moving house	[1.00]	[0.70]	[0.40]	1.60	[1.40]	2.20	2.00	2.10	3.00	6.90	2.10
12.5.2 Bank, building society, post office, credit card charges	0.20	0.20	0.30	0.30	0.50	0.70	0.40	0.70	0.60	1.10	0.50
12.5.3 Other services and professional fees	[0.10]	[0.10]	2.00	0.60	1.00	1.30	1.50	1.50	2.20	4.30	1.50
1-12 All expenditure groups	**174.10**	**206.80**	**281.30**	**338.00**	**389.30**	**452.60**	**496.60**	**560.60**	**648.70**	**895.60**	**444.30**
13 Other expenditure items	**15.80**	**21.80**	**33.50**	**40.00**	**51.60**	**62.90**	**76.90**	**91.20**	**113.00**	**223.80**	**73.00**
13.1 Housing: mortgage interest payments, council tax etc.	9.80	13.20	20.30	25.80	32.30	40.60	54.30	59.10	72.70	115.50	44.30
13.2 Licences, fines and transfers	1.00	1.40	2.10	2.50	3.00	4.60	4.30	4.70	7.80	6.70	3.80
13.3 Holiday spending	[1.50]	[1.90]	[4.50]	[2.20]	5.10	[4.10]	6.30	8.30	10.70	74.00	11.80
13.4 Money transfers and credit	3.40	5.20	6.60	9.50	11.20	13.60	12.00	19.10	21.90	27.60	13.00
13.4.1 Money, cash gifts given to children	[0.00]	[0.00]	[0.00]	[0.00]	[0.20]	[0.30]	[0.10]	[0.20]	0.30	[0.20]	0.10
13.4.2 Cash gifts and donations [7]	3.00	5.00	6.10	8.70	9.70	12.20	10.20	16.70	20.10	25.20	11.70
13.4.3 Club instalment payments (child) and interest on credit cards	0.40	0.20	0.50	0.80	1.20	1.10	1.70	2.30	1.50	2.20	1.20
Total expenditure	**189.80**	**228.60**	**314.80**	**378.00**	**440.90**	**515.50**	**573.50**	**651.90**	**761.70**	**1119.50**	**517.30**
14 Other items recorded											
14.1 Life assurance and contributions to pension funds	1.20	1.60	2.70	4.50	6.70	11.50	17.70	28.50	41.60	82.50	19.90
14.2 Other insurance inc. friendly societies	0.20	0.20	0.50	0.70	1.00	3.10	1.40	1.50	2.00	3.30	1.40
14.3 Income tax, payments *less* refunds	0.40	3.40	13.20	23.00	37.30	52.80	74.20	106.30	163.60	411.50	88.50
14.4 National insurance contributions	[0.30]	0.50	2.60	7.10	13.80	20.80	32.40	45.50	65.30	94.30	28.30
14.5 Purchase or alteration of dwellings, mortgages	14.10	8.50	10.80	14.70	38.50	35.50	63.10	58.70	75.90	169.20	48.90
14.6 Savings and investments	[0.60]	0.50	1.10	1.40	3.40	3.10	4.50	6.60	11.90	23.50	5.70
14.7 Pay off loan to clear other debt	[0.10]	[0.30]	1.10	1.10	2.50	2.60	4.20	4.60	5.10	4.90	2.60
14.8 Windfall receipts from gambling etc [8]	0.80	0.60	1.20	0.90	0.60	1.20	1.20	1.90	1.10	2.00	1.20

Note: The commodity and service categories are not comparable to those in publications before 2001-02
The numbering system is sequential, it does not use actual COICOP codes
Please see background notes for symbols and conventions used in this report
7 Recording of expenditure on money sent abroad was changed in 2013.
8 Expressed as an income figure as opposed to an expenditure figure

Table A7
Household expenditure by disposable income decile group, 2013
United Kingdom

	Lowest ten per cent	Second decile group	Third decile group	Fourth decile group	Fifth decile group	Sixth decile group	Seventh decile group	Eighth decile group	Ninth decile group	Highest ten per cent	All house-holds
Lower boundary of group (£ per week)		174	256	333	417	504	600	720	882	1,150	
Weighted number of households (thousands)	2,690	2,690	2,680	2,680	2,690	2,680	2,690	2,680	2,690	2,680	26,840
Total number of households in sample	500	510	550	530	530	540	520	500	500	480	5,140
Total number of persons in sample	660	830	970	1,130	1,250	1,340	1,490	1,420	1,490	1,540	12,120
Total number of adults in sample	570	670	790	890	960	1,020	1,060	1,080	1,150	1,170	9,350
Weighted average number of persons per household	1.3	1.6	1.7	2.1	2.3	2.5	2.9	2.8	3.0	3.2	2.4
Commodity or service	Average weekly household expenditure (£)										
1 Food & non-alcoholic drinks	30.70	38.50	41.70	47.90	55.80	61.00	66.40	72.90	79.90	93.20	58.80
2 Alcoholic drinks, tobacco & narcotics	7.10	6.90	9.60	10.50	10.70	12.20	15.50	13.50	15.30	18.90	12.00
3 Clothing & footwear	6.70	7.10	10.10	15.80	17.10	24.20	28.40	31.30	37.10	48.20	22.60
4 Housing(net)[1], fuel & power	51.00	57.40	66.00	75.40	81.20	77.60	78.10	80.70	81.90	94.50	74.40
5 Household goods & services	13.80	15.30	20.40	23.90	26.00	36.20	34.20	38.70	43.30	80.00	33.10
6 Health	1.90	2.60	3.10	4.40	4.20	7.60	7.80	11.30	8.90	10.40	6.20
7 Transport	16.30	19.10	33.30	41.70	60.00	72.80	79.00	96.80	117.60	167.80	70.40
8 Communication	7.10	8.10	10.60	11.80	13.70	16.10	16.50	18.30	20.30	22.00	14.50
9 Recreation & culture	18.30	22.20	32.30	39.30	53.20	62.80	70.10	81.10	99.80	160.40	63.90
10 Education	[4.30]	[1.80]	[3.90]	[14.40]	7.20	1.90	3.20	6.50	21.40	23.40	8.80
11 Restaurants & hotels	10.60	12.00	19.40	26.50	30.00	38.80	47.10	54.40	71.40	93.60	40.40
12 Miscellaneous goods & services	12.00	15.20	23.10	24.60	32.90	37.50	46.70	52.70	58.20	88.30	39.10
1-12 All expenditure groups	179.90	206.10	273.60	336.10	391.80	448.80	493.10	558.40	655.20	900.80	444.30
13 Other expenditure items	16.40	23.20	35.00	40.30	50.80	65.60	79.00	84.60	117.20	218.30	73.00
Total expenditure	**196.30**	**229.30**	**308.60**	**376.40**	**442.70**	**514.40**	**572.10**	**643.00**	**772.40**	**1119.10**	**517.30**
Average weekly expenditure per person (£) Total expenditure	**150.30**	**143.10**	**176.40**	**177.60**	**188.70**	**205.30**	**198.40**	**229.10**	**256.00**	**344.80**	**219.40**

Note: The commodity and service categories are not comparable to those in publications before 2001-02.
Please see background notes for symbols and conventions used in this report.
1 Excluding mortgage interest payments, council tax and Northern Ireland rates.

Table A8
Household expenditure as a percentage of total expenditure by disposable income decile group, 2013
United Kingdom

		Lowest ten per cent	Second decile group	Third decile group	Fourth decile group	Fifth decile group	Sixth decile group	Seventh decile group	Eighth decile group	Ninth decile group	Highest ten per cent	All house-holds
Lower boundary of group (£ per week)			174	256	333	417	504	600	720	882	1,150	
Weighted number of households (thousands)		2,690	2,690	2,680	2,680	2,690	2,680	2,690	2,680	2,690	2,680	26,840
Total number of households in sample		500	510	550	530	530	540	520	500	500	480	5,140
Total number of persons in sample		660	830	970	1,130	1,250	1,340	1,490	1,420	1,490	1,540	12,120
Total number of adults in sample		570	670	790	890	960	1,020	1,060	1,080	1,150	1,170	9,350
Weighted average number of persons per household		1.3	1.6	1.7	2.1	2.3	2.5	2.9	2.8	3.0	3.2	2.4
Commodity or service						Percentage of total expenditure						
1	Food & non-alcoholic drinks	*16*	*17*	*14*	*13*	*13*	*12*	*12*	*11*	*10*	*8*	*11*
2	Alcoholic drinks, tobacco & narcotics	*4*	*3*	*3*	*3*	*2*	*2*	*3*	*2*	*2*	*2*	*2*
3	Clothing & footwear	*3*	*3*	*3*	*4*	*4*	*5*	*5*	*5*	*5*	*4*	*4*
4	Housing(net)[1], fuel & power	*26*	*25*	*21*	*20*	*18*	*15*	*14*	*13*	*11*	*8*	*14*
5	Household goods & services	*7*	*7*	*7*	*6*	*6*	*7*	*6*	*6*	*6*	*7*	*6*
6	Health	*1*	*1*	*1*	*1*	*1*	*1*	*1*	*2*	*1*	*1*	*1*
7	Transport	*8*	*8*	*11*	*11*	*14*	*14*	*14*	*15*	*15*	*15*	*14*
8	Communication	*4*	*4*	*3*	*3*	*3*	*3*	*3*	*3*	*3*	*2*	*3*
9	Recreation & culture	*9*	*10*	*10*	*10*	*12*	*12*	*12*	*13*	*13*	*14*	*12*
10	Education	*[2]*	*[1]*	*[1]*	*[4]*	*2*	*0*	*1*	*1*	*3*	*2*	*2*
11	Restaurants & hotels	*5*	*5*	*6*	*7*	*7*	*8*	*8*	*8*	*9*	*8*	*8*
12	Miscellaneous goods & services	*6*	*7*	*7*	*7*	*7*	*7*	*8*	*8*	*8*	*8*	*8*
1-12	All expenditure groups	*92*	*90*	*89*	*89*	*89*	*87*	*86*	*87*	*85*	*80*	*86*
13	Other expenditure items	*8*	*10*	*11*	*11*	*11*	*13*	*14*	*13*	*15*	*20*	*14*
Total expenditure		***100***	***100***	***100***	***100***	***100***	***100***	***100***	***100***	***100***	***100***	***100***

Note: The commodity and service categories are not comparable to those in publications before 2001-02.
Please see background notes for symbols and conventions used in this report.
1 Excluding mortgage interest payments, council tax and Northern Ireland rates.

Table A9
Household expenditure by age of household reference person, 2013
United Kingdom

	Less than 30	30 to 49	50 to 64	65 to 74	75 or over	All house-holds
Weighted number of households (thousands)	2,610	9,640	7,100	3,850	3,640	26,840
Total number of households in sample	380	1,770	1,420	910	670	5,140
Total number of persons in sample	980	5,430	3,120	1,600	980	12,120
Total number of adults in sample	690	3,310	2,800	1,580	980	9,350
Weighted average number of persons per household	2.5	3.0	2.3	1.8	1.4	2.4
Commodity or service	Average weekly household expenditure (£)					
1 Food & non-alcoholic drinks	44.30	65.00	65.10	56.80	42.50	58.80
2 Alcoholic drinks, tobacco & narcotics	8.90	12.50	15.50	11.60	6.60	12.00
3 Clothing & footwear	21.40	28.10	25.40	18.50	7.90	22.60
4 Housing (net)[1], fuel & power	120.50	85.00	63.60	60.30	49.20	74.40
5 Household goods & services	25.00	34.80	39.60	33.40	21.80	33.10
6 Health	3.20	5.10	8.00	8.20	5.80	6.20
7 Transport	50.90	86.20	82.90	62.50	26.90	70.40
8 Communication	14.90	17.30	15.50	11.30	8.00	14.50
9 Recreation & culture	36.40	72.10	74.30	71.30	34.10	63.90
10 Education	23.20	13.10	4.90	[2.00]	[2.00]	8.80
11 Restaurants & hotels	38.60	48.40	45.10	35.60	16.30	40.40
12 Miscellaneous goods & services	30.70	48.30	40.00	32.40	26.30	39.10
1-12 All expenditure groups	417.90	515.90	479.70	403.80	247.40	444.30
13 Other expenditure items	44.00	93.90	85.40	48.70	40.20	73.00
Total expenditure	**462.00**	**609.80**	**565.10**	**452.50**	**287.60**	**517.30**
Average weekly expenditure per person (£)						
Total expenditure	**187.50**	**205.70**	**247.90**	**251.00**	**203.00**	**219.40**

Note: The commodity and service categories are not comparable to those in publications before 2001-02.
Please see background notes for symbols and conventions used in this report.
1 Excluding mortgage interest payments, council tax and Northern Ireland rates.

Table A10
Household expenditure as a percentage of total expenditure by age of household reference person, 2013
United Kingdom

		Less than 30	30 to 49	50 to 64	65 to 74	75 or over	All house-holds
Weighted number of households (thousands)		2,610	9,640	7,100	3,850	3,640	26,840
Total number of households in sample		380	1,770	1,420	910	670	5,140
Total number of persons in sample		980	5,430	3,120	1,600	980	12,120
Total number of adults in sample		690	3,310	2,800	1,580	980	9,350
Weighted average number of persons per household		2.5	3.0	2.3	1.8	1.4	2.4
Commodity or service		Percentage of total expenditure					
1	Food & non-alcoholic drinks	*10*	*11*	*12*	*13*	*15*	*11*
2	Alcoholic drinks, tobacco & narcotics	*2*	*2*	*3*	*3*	*2*	*2*
3	Clothing & footwear	*5*	*5*	*4*	*4*	*3*	*4*
4	Housing(net)[1], fuel & power	*26*	*14*	*11*	*13*	*17*	*14*
5	Household goods & services	*5*	*6*	*7*	*7*	*8*	*6*
6	Health	*1*	*1*	*1*	*2*	*2*	*1*
7	Transport	*11*	*14*	*15*	*14*	*9*	*14*
8	Communication	*3*	*3*	*3*	*2*	*3*	*3*
9	Recreation & culture	*8*	*12*	*13*	*16*	*12*	*12*
10	Education	*5*	*2*	*1*	*[0]*	*[1]*	*2*
11	Restaurants & hotels	*8*	*8*	*8*	*8*	*6*	*8*
12	Miscellaneous goods & services	*7*	*8*	*7*	*7*	*9*	*8*
1-12	All expenditure groups	*90*	*85*	*85*	*89*	*86*	*86*
13	Other expenditure items	*10*	*15*	*15*	*11*	*14*	*14*
Total expenditure		***100***	***100***	***100***	***100***	***100***	***100***

Note: The commodity and service categories are not comparable to those in publications before 2001-02.
Please see background notes for symbols and conventions used in this report.
1 Excluding mortgage interest payments, council tax and Northern Ireland rates.

Table A11
Detailed household expenditure by age of household reference person, 2013
United Kingdom

		Less than 30	30 to 49	50 to 64	65 to 74	75 or over	All house-holds
Weighted number of households (thousands)		2,610	9,640	7,100	3,850	3,640	26,840
Total number of households in sample		380	1,770	1,420	910	670	5,140
Total number of persons in sample		980	5,430	3,120	1,600	980	12,120
Total number of adults in sample		690	3,310	2,800	1,580	980	9,350
Weighted average number of persons per household		2.5	3.0	2.3	1.8	1.4	2.4
Commodity or service		Average weekly household expenditure (£)					
1	**Food & non-alcoholic drinks**	**44.30**	**65.00**	**65.10**	**56.80**	**42.50**	**58.80**
1.1	Food	40.20	59.30	59.80	52.60	39.80	54.00
1.1.1	Bread, rice and cereals	4.90	6.60	5.90	4.80	3.60	5.60
1.1.2	Pasta products	0.50	0.60	0.40	0.20	0.10	0.40
1.1.3	Buns, cakes, biscuits etc.	2.30	3.90	3.90	3.50	3.10	3.60
1.1.4	Pastry (savoury)	0.90	1.10	0.80	0.50	0.30	0.80
1.1.5	Beef (fresh, chilled or frozen)	1.20	1.90	2.50	2.00	1.30	1.90
1.1.6	Pork (fresh, chilled or frozen)	0.40	0.60	0.80	0.70	0.70	0.70
1.1.7	Lamb (fresh, chilled or frozen)	0.30	0.50	0.80	0.90	0.70	0.70
1.1.8	Poultry (fresh, chilled or frozen)	2.00	2.90	2.70	1.90	1.40	2.40
1.1.9	Bacon and ham	0.60	1.00	1.20	1.20	0.90	1.00
1.1.10	Other meat and meat preparations	4.60	6.60	7.30	6.00	4.90	6.30
1.1.11	Fish and fish products	1.50	2.30	3.20	3.10	2.60	2.60
1.1.12	Milk	2.10	2.70	2.40	2.40	2.00	2.40
1.1.13	Cheese and curd	1.40	2.40	2.20	1.90	1.30	2.00
1.1.14	Eggs	0.60	0.80	0.80	0.80	0.60	0.70
1.1.15	Other milk products	1.40	2.30	2.10	2.10	1.60	2.10
1.1.16	Butter	0.30	0.40	0.60	0.60	0.50	0.50
1.1.17	Margarine, other vegetable fats and peanut butter	0.30	0.50	0.60	0.60	0.40	0.50
1.1.18	Cooking oils and fats	0.20	0.40	0.40	0.40	0.20	0.30
1.1.19	Fresh fruit	2.10	3.60	3.40	3.60	2.80	3.30
1.1.20	Other fresh, chilled or frozen fruits	0.20	0.40	0.50	0.40	0.30	0.40
1.1.21	Dried fruit and nuts	0.40	0.70	0.90	0.90	0.60	0.70
1.1.22	Preserved fruit and fruit based products	0.10	0.10	0.10	0.20	0.20	0.10
1.1.23	Fresh vegetables	3.00	4.70	4.90	4.40	3.10	4.30
1.1.24	Dried vegetables	[0.00]	0.10	0.10	0.00	[0.00]	0.10
1.1.25	Other preserved or processed vegetables	1.20	1.70	1.60	1.10	0.70	1.40
1.1.26	Potatoes	0.50	0.90	1.10	1.20	0.90	1.00
1.1.27	Other tubers and products of tuber vegetables	1.50	2.00	1.70	1.20	0.80	1.60
1.1.28	Sugar and sugar products	0.50	0.50	0.50	0.40	0.30	0.50
1.1.29	Jams, marmalades	0.20	0.20	0.30	0.40	0.40	0.30
1.1.30	Chocolate	1.30	2.00	2.00	1.70	1.10	1.80
1.1.31	Confectionery products	0.60	0.90	0.60	0.60	0.50	0.70
1.1.32	Edible ices and ice cream	0.40	0.70	0.60	0.50	0.40	0.60
1.1.33	Other food products	2.70	3.20	2.70	2.30	1.50	2.70
1.2	Non-alcoholic drinks	4.10	5.80	5.30	4.20	2.80	4.90
1.2.1	Coffee	0.30	0.70	0.90	0.90	0.60	0.70
1.2.2	Tea	0.20	0.40	0.50	0.60	0.60	0.50
1.2.3	Cocoa and powdered chocolate	0.00	0.10	0.10	0.20	0.10	0.10
1.2.4	Fruit and vegetable juices (inc. fruit squash)	1.10	1.60	1.30	1.00	0.60	1.20
1.2.5	Mineral or spring waters	0.30	0.40	0.30	0.20	0.10	0.30
1.2.6	Soft drinks (inc. fizzy and ready to drink fruit drinks)	2.20	2.60	2.10	1.30	0.70	2.00

Note: The commodity and service categories are not comparable to those in publications before 2001-02.
The numbering system is sequential, it does not use actual COICOP codes.
Please see background notes for symbols and conventions used in this report.

Table A11
Detailed household expenditure by age of household reference person, 2013 (cont.)
United Kingdom

		Less than 30	30 to 49	50 to 64	65 to 74	75 or over	All households
Commodity or service		Average weekly household expenditure (£)					
2	**Alcoholic drink, tobacco & narcotics**	**8.90**	**12.50**	**15.50**	**11.60**	**6.60**	**12.00**
2.1	Alcoholic drinks	4.80	7.60	10.00	8.10	5.10	7.70
2.1.1	Spirits and liqueurs (brought home)	1.40	1.10	2.10	1.90	1.40	1.60
2.1.2	Wines, fortified wines (brought home)	1.70	3.90	5.10	4.70	2.80	4.00
2.1.3	Beer, lager, ciders and perry (brought home)	1.70	2.50	2.70	1.40	0.80	2.10
2.1.4	Alcopops (brought home)	[0.10]	0.10	[0.00]	[0.00]	[0.00]	0.00
2.2	Tobacco and narcotics	4.00	5.00	5.50	3.50	1.50	4.30
2.2.1	Cigarettes	3.20	3.90	4.70	2.70	1.30	3.50
2.2.2	Cigars, other tobacco products and narcotics	0.90	1.10	0.80	0.80	[0.20]	0.80
3	**Clothing & footwear**	**21.40**	**28.10**	**25.40**	**18.50**	**7.90**	**22.60**
3.1	Clothing	17.20	22.50	20.30	15.70	6.30	18.30
3.1.1	Men's outer garments	6.30	5.20	5.60	3.60	1.20	4.70
3.1.2	Men's under garments	0.50	0.40	0.50	0.40	0.30	0.40
3.1.3	Women's outer garments	6.30	8.70	9.40	7.70	3.30	7.80
3.1.4	Women's under garments	0.90	1.10	1.40	1.20	0.80	1.10
3.1.5	Boys' outer garments (5-15)	[0.20]	1.70	0.60	0.30	[0.00]	0.80
3.1.6	Girls' outer garments (5-15)	0.30	1.80	0.60	0.50	[0.00]	0.90
3.1.7	Infants' outer garments (under 5)	1.10	1.20	0.60	0.40	[0.10]	0.80
3.1.8	Children's under garments (under 16)	0.40	0.80	0.20	0.20	[0.00]	0.40
3.1.9	Accessories	0.70	1.10	0.80	0.70	0.30	0.80
3.1.10	Haberdashery, clothing materials and clothing hire	[0.20]	0.20	0.20	0.50	0.10	0.20
3.1.11	Dry cleaners, laundry and dyeing	[0.30]	0.30	0.30	0.30	[0.20]	0.30
3.2	Footwear	4.20	5.50	5.00	2.80	1.60	4.30
4	**Housing (net)[1], fuel & power**	**120.50**	**85.00**	**63.60**	**60.30**	**49.20**	**74.40**
4.1	Actual rentals for housing	117.60	59.00	30.40	28.30	24.90	48.10
4.1.1	Gross rent	117.50	58.90	30.30	28.30	24.90	48.00
4.1.2	*less* housing benefit, rebates & allowances rec'd	29.10	16.70	11.80	15.20	14.30	16.10
4.1.3	Net rent[2]	88.40	42.20	18.50	13.10	10.60	32.00
4.1.4	Second dwelling rent	[0.10]	[0.10]	[0.10]	-	-	[0.10]
4.2	Maintenance and repair of dwelling	3.20	6.50	7.50	11.50	6.10	7.10
4.3	Water supply and miscellaneous services relating to the dwelling	8.40	9.30	8.30	8.30	8.50	8.70
4.4	Electricity, gas and other fuels[3]	20.40	26.90	29.10	27.40	24.10	26.50
4.4.1	Electricity	10.70	12.70	12.80	11.60	10.50	12.10
4.4.2	Gas	9.30	13.00	13.60	12.00	11.60	12.40
4.4.3	Other fuels	[0.40]	1.20	2.80	3.90	2.00	2.00

Note: The commodity and service categories are not comparable to those in publications before 2001-02.

The numbering system is sequential, it does not use actual COICOP codes.

Please see background notes for symbols and conventions used in this report.

1 Excluding mortgage interest payments, council tax and Northern Ireland rates.

2 The figure included in total expenditure is net rent as opposed to gross rent.

3 Recording of expenditure on gas and electricity via combined payment packages was changed in 2013. Recording of expenditure via slot meters was also changed.

Table A11
Detailed household expenditure by age of household reference person, 2013 (cont.)
United Kingdom

Commodity or service		Less than 30	30 to 49	50 to 64	65 to 74	75 or over	All house-holds
		Average weekly household expenditure (£)					
5	**Household goods & services**	**25.00**	**34.80**	**39.60**	**33.40**	**21.80**	**33.10**
5.1	Furniture and furnishings and floor coverings[4]	17.30	21.30	21.00	15.40	7.90	18.20
5.1.1	Furniture and furnishings	15.30	17.70	17.40	11.10	6.00	14.80
5.1.2	Floor coverings	1.90	3.70	3.70	4.30	2.00	3.40
5.2	Household textiles	0.90	1.80	2.50	2.10	1.20	1.80
5.3	Household appliances	1.50	2.60	4.00	3.40	3.10	3.10
5.4	Glassware, tableware and household utensils	0.80	1.80	1.90	1.50	0.70	1.60
5.5	Tools and equipment for house and garden	1.50	1.70	3.30	3.80	1.40	2.40
5.6	Goods and services for routine household maintenance	2.90	5.50	6.90	7.10	7.40	6.10
5.6.1	Cleaning materials	1.50	2.60	2.60	2.30	1.80	2.40
5.6.2	Household goods and hardware	1.00	1.50	1.60	1.50	1.10	1.40
5.6.3	Domestic services, carpet cleaning, hire of furniture/furnishings	0.40	1.40	2.70	3.20	4.50	2.30
6	**Health**	**3.20**	**5.10**	**8.00**	**8.20**	**5.80**	**6.20**
6.1	Medical products, appliances and equipment	2.90	3.10	5.50	4.80	3.00	4.00
6.1.1	Medicines, prescriptions and healthcare products	2.50	2.30	2.40	1.90	2.20	2.30
6.1.2	Spectacles, lenses, accessories and repairs	0.50	0.90	3.20	2.90	[0.80]	1.70
6.2	Hospital services	[0.30]	2.00	2.40	3.40	2.80	2.30
7	**Transport**	**50.90**	**86.20**	**82.90**	**62.50**	**26.90**	**70.40**
7.1	Purchase of vehicles	12.70	25.70	24.70	21.30	7.50	21.10
7.1.1	Purchase of new cars and vans	[2.50]	7.30	11.30	12.20	[5.10]	8.30
7.1.2	Purchase of second hand cars or vans	9.60	17.00	12.70	8.90	2.50	12.00
7.1.3	Purchase of motorcycles and other vehicles	[0.60]	1.40	[0.80]	[0.20]	-	0.80
7.2	Operation of personal transport	21.80	40.60	41.10	30.90	14.70	34.00
7.2.1	Spares and accessories	0.60	3.10	2.40	1.80	1.70	2.30
7.2.2	Petrol, diesel and other motor oils	16.00	28.00	29.20	20.90	8.60	23.50
7.2.3	Repairs and servicing	3.50	6.50	6.80	5.70	3.10	5.70
7.2.4	Other motoring costs	1.70	2.90	2.80	2.40	1.30	2.50
7.3	Transport services[5]	16.40	19.90	17.00	10.20	4.60	15.30
7.3.1	Rail and tube fares	4.80	6.20	3.50	1.10	0.60	3.90
7.3.2	Bus and coach fares	2.50	2.00	2.20	0.40	0.20	1.60
7.3.4	Combined fares	[1.40]	1.10	0.80	[0.20]	-	0.80
7.3.5	Other travel and transport	7.70	10.60	10.50	8.50	3.90	9.10
8	**Communication**	**14.90**	**17.30**	**15.50**	**11.30**	**8.00**	**14.50**
8.1	Postal services	0.30	0.60	0.60	0.80	0.60	0.60
8.2	Telephone and telefax equipment	[0.30]	0.50	0.90	[0.20]	[0.30]	0.50
8.3	Telephone and telefax services	11.70	13.20	10.70	7.60	5.60	10.60
8.4	Internet subscription fees	2.60	3.10	3.10	2.60	1.50	2.80

Note: The commodity and service categories are not comparable to those in publications before 2001-02.

The numbering system is sequential, it does not use actual COICOP codes.

Please see background notes for symbols and conventions used in this report.

4 Recording of expenditure on furniture was changed in 2013.

5 Recording of expenditure on flights was changed in 2013.

Table A11
Detailed household expenditure by age of household reference person, 2013 (cont.)
United Kingdom

Commodity or service		Less than 30	30 to 49	50 to 64	65 to 74	75 or over	All households
		Average weekly household expenditure (£)					
9	**Recreation & culture**	**36.40**	**72.10**	**74.30**	**71.30**	**34.10**	**63.90**
9.1	Audio-visual, photographic and information processing equipment	2.00	7.60	5.10	3.40	2.60	5.10
9.1.1	Audio equipment and accessories, CD players	0.70	1.60	0.90	0.30	[0.10]	0.90
9.1.2	TV, video and computers	1.30	5.80	3.90	2.70	2.20	3.90
9.1.3	Photographic, cine and optical equipment	[0.00]	0.30	[0.30]	[0.30]	[0.30]	0.30
9.2	Other major durables for recreation and culture	[0.30]	3.00	1.70	3.50	[0.30]	2.10
9.3	Other recreational items and equipment, gardens and pets	6.00	12.40	11.80	10.70	5.50	10.40
9.3.1	Games, toys and hobbies	1.60	3.30	2.20	2.00	0.50	2.30
9.3.2	Computer software and games	[1.10]	1.30	0.60	0.50	[0.30]	0.80
9.3.3	Equipment for sport, camping and open-air recreation	[0.40]	1.30	1.00	0.60	[0.20]	0.90
9.3.4	Horticultural goods, garden equipment and plants	1.20	1.70	2.60	3.00	2.10	2.20
9.3.5	Pets and pet food	1.70	4.80	5.40	4.70	2.20	4.30
9.4	Recreational and cultural services	14.00	22.30	21.40	17.50	7.70	18.60
9.4.1	Sports admissions, subscriptions, leisure class fees and equipment hire	4.20	7.70	6.40	3.50	1.40	5.50
9.4.2	Cinema, theatre and museums etc.	1.70	2.80	2.70	2.10	0.90	2.30
9.4.3	TV, video, satellite rental, cable subscriptions and TV licences	6.00	7.90	7.60	6.50	2.20	6.70
9.4.4	Miscellaneous entertainments	0.90	1.50	1.30	1.00	0.80	1.20
9.4.5	Development of film, deposit for film development, passport photos, holiday and school photos	[0.10]	0.30	0.20	0.40	[0.10]	0.20
9.4.6	Gambling payments	1.20	2.00	3.30	4.10	2.40	2.60
9.5	Newspapers, books and stationery	3.00	4.50	5.60	7.50	5.90	5.30
9.5.1	Books	0.80	1.20	1.20	1.20	0.70	1.10
9.5.2	Diaries, address books, cards etc.	1.30	2.10	2.00	2.00	1.30	1.90
9.5.3	Newspapers	0.10	0.60	1.60	3.40	3.10	1.60
9.5.4	Magazines and periodicals	0.70	0.60	0.80	1.00	0.70	0.80
9.6	Package holidays[6]	11.00	22.30	28.70	28.70	12.10	22.40
9.6.1	Package holidays - UK	[0.50]	1.30	0.90	2.20	2.50	1.40
9.6.2	Package holidays - abroad	10.50	20.90	27.80	26.40	9.60	21.00
10	**Education**	**23.20**	**13.10**	**4.90**	**[2.00]**	**[2.00]**	**8.80**
10.1	Education fees	23.00	12.30	4.70	[2.00]	[2.00]	8.50
10.2	Payments for school trips, other ad-hoc expenditure	[0.10]	0.70	[0.20]	[0.00]	-	0.30
11	**Restaurants & hotels**	**38.60**	**48.40**	**45.10**	**35.60**	**16.30**	**40.40**
11.1	Catering services	35.00	40.80	36.90	27.60	12.90	33.50
11.1.1	Restaurant and café meals	13.70	17.10	17.90	16.90	9.20	15.90
11.1.2	Alcoholic drinks (away from home)	8.50	7.80	8.90	6.20	2.10	7.10
11.1.3	Take away meals eaten at home	5.80	5.80	4.10	2.40	0.90	4.20
11.1.4	Other take-away and snack food	5.00	6.70	4.40	1.70	0.60	4.40
11.1.5	Contract catering (food) and canteens	2.00	3.40	1.70	0.40	[0.00]	1.90
11.2	Accommodation services	3.60	7.60	8.10	8.00	3.40	6.80
11.2.1	Holiday in the UK	1.60	4.50	4.40	4.90	2.80	4.00
11.2.2	Holiday abroad	[1.90]	2.90	3.70	3.00	[0.60]	2.70
11.2.3	Room hire	[0.00]	[0.10]	[0.00]	[0.10]	-	[0.10]

Note: The commodity and service categories are not comparable to those in publications before 2001-02.
The numbering system is sequential, it does not use actual COICOP codes.
Please see background notes for symbols and conventions used in this report.
6 Recording of expenditure on package holidays was changed in 2013.

Table A11
Detailed household expenditure by age of household reference person, 2013 (cont.)
United Kingdom

Commodity or service	Less than 30	30 to 49	50 to 64	65 to 74	75 or over	All house-holds
	Average weekly household expenditure (£)					
12 Miscellaneous goods & services	**30.70**	**48.30**	**40.00**	**32.40**	**26.30**	**39.10**
12.1 Personal care	9.70	12.90	12.20	9.80	7.10	11.20
12.1.1 Hairdressing, beauty treatment	2.30	3.50	3.80	3.40	3.60	3.40
12.1.2 Toilet paper	0.60	1.00	0.90	0.70	0.60	0.80
12.1.3 Toiletries and soap	2.10	2.80	2.80	2.20	1.40	2.50
12.1.4 Baby toiletries and accessories (disposable)	1.40	1.10	0.30	0.20	0.10	0.60
12.1.5 Hair products, cosmetics and related electrical appliances	3.30	4.50	4.40	3.30	1.50	3.80
12.2 Personal effects	1.70	3.80	3.70	2.70	0.70	3.00
12.3 Social protection	3.90	8.20	[0.60]	[0.40]	[3.80]	4.10
12.4 Insurance	11.50	18.20	19.20	16.70	12.30	16.80
12.4.1 Household insurances - structural, contents and appliances	1.90	4.90	5.80	5.80	5.50	5.10
12.4.2 Medical insurance premiums	[0.30]	1.50	2.50	3.70	1.80	2.00
12.4.3 Vehicle insurance including boat insurance	9.20	11.60	10.90	6.70	4.70	9.50
12.4.4 Non-package holiday, other travel insurance	[0.10]	[0.10]	[0.00]	[0.60]	[0.20]	0.20
12.5 Other services	3.90	5.20	4.40	2.70	2.30	4.10
12.5.1 Moving house	2.20	2.80	2.00	1.50	[1.10]	2.10
12.5.2 Bank, building society, post office, credit card charges	0.50	0.60	0.60	0.30	0.20	0.50
12.5.3 Other services and professional fees	1.20	1.80	1.80	0.80	[1.00]	1.50
1-12 All expenditure groups	**417.90**	**515.90**	**479.70**	**403.80**	**247.40**	**444.30**
13 Other expenditure items	**44.00**	**93.90**	**85.40**	**48.70**	**40.20**	**73.00**
13.1 Housing: mortgage interest payments, council tax etc.	31.30	65.40	43.70	24.70	20.00	44.30
13.2 Licences, fines and transfers	2.60	4.10	4.30	4.80	1.90	3.80
13.3 Holiday spending	[6.00]	8.90	25.20	7.50	[2.20]	11.80
13.4 Money transfers and credit	4.10	15.40	12.10	11.70	16.20	13.00
13.4.1 Money, cash gifts given to children	[0.10]	0.30	[0.10]	[0.00]	[0.00]	0.10
13.4.2 Cash gifts and donations[7]	3.20	13.20	10.90	11.20	16.00	11.70
13.4.3 Club instalment payments (child) and interest on credit cards	0.90	1.90	1.10	0.50	0.20	1.20
Total expenditure	**462.00**	**609.80**	**565.10**	**452.50**	**287.60**	**517.30**
14 Other items recorded						
14.1 Life assurance & contributions to pension funds	10.00	29.30	26.10	8.90	1.30	19.90
14.2 Other insurance inc. friendly societies	0.40	1.50	1.50	1.00	2.00	1.40
14.3 Income tax, payments *less* refunds	51.70	126.60	101.10	50.80	29.60	88.50
14.4 National insurance contributions	27.90	45.10	33.30	3.20	[0.80]	28.30
14.5 Purchase or alteration of dwellings, mortgages	14.90	68.70	61.00	29.50	17.50	48.90
14.6 Savings and investments	4.10	7.10	7.00	5.10	0.90	5.70
14.7 Pay off loan to clear other debt	1.70	4.70	2.20	[1.20]	[0.40]	2.60
14.8 Windfall receipts from gambling etc[8]	2.60	1.00	0.80	1.40	0.90	1.20

Note: The commodity and service categories are not comparable to those in publications before 2001-02.
The numbering system is sequential, it does not use actual COICOP codes.
Please see background notes for symbols and conventions used in this report.
7 Recording of expenditure on money sent abroad was changed in 2013.
8 Expressed as an income figure as opposed to an expenditure figure.

Table A12
Household expenditure by gross income quintile group where the household reference person is aged under 30, 2011-2013
United Kingdom

		Lowest twenty per cent	Second quintile group	Third quintile group	Fourth quintile group	Highest twenty per cent	All house-holds
Lower boundary of group (£ per week)[1]			265	462	696	1,078	
Average weighted number of households (thousands)		620	540	670	610	330	2,770
Total number of households in sample (over 3 years)		330	280	320	270	140	1,350
Total number of persons in sample (over 3 years)		690	740	890	730	340	3,370
Total number of adults in sample (over 3 years)		410	450	620	600	310	2,390
Weighted average number of persons per household		2.0	2.5	2.7	2.6	2.4	2.4
Commodity or service		Average weekly household expenditure (£)					
1	Food & non-alcoholic drinks	31.60	40.50	47.40	49.40	50.20	43.40
2	Alcoholic drinks, tobacco & narcotics	7.00	8.90	9.20	10.70	13.40	9.50
3	Clothing & footwear	12.20	17.20	20.40	26.50	36.90	21.30
4	Housing(net)[2], fuel & power	68.90	110.30	117.40	128.40	135.30	110.10
5	Household goods & services	11.40	16.90	30.20	26.90	35.00	23.20
6	Health	0.60	1.90	2.40	5.30	4.70	2.80
7	Transport	12.50	39.80	53.90	77.00	122.60	55.20
8	Communication	7.80	13.20	15.60	18.10	20.80	14.60
9	Recreation & culture	19.40	29.30	38.30	58.30	94.50	43.60
10	Education	10.80	9.80	[10.60]	28.80	[17.60]	15.60
11	Restaurants & hotels	16.20	26.10	35.60	54.10	86.20	39.90
12	Miscellaneous goods & services	10.30	25.50	34.10	46.70	52.60	32.10
1-12	All expenditure groups	208.70	339.40	415.00	530.30	669.70	411.20
13	Other expenditure items	7.10	25.70	48.40	67.30	127.70	48.50
Total expenditure		**215.90**	**365.00**	**463.40**	**597.60**	**797.40**	**459.70**
Average weekly expenditure per person (£)							
Total expenditure		**110.30**	**144.30**	**172.80**	**227.70**	**339.10**	**188.60**

Note: The commodity and service categories are not comparable to those in publications before 2001-02.
Please see background notes for symbols and conventions used in this report.
This table is based on a three year average.
1 Lower boundary of 2013 gross income quintile groups (£ per week).
2 Excluding mortgage interest payments, council tax and Northern Ireland rates.

Table A13
Household expenditure by gross income quintile group where the household reference person is aged 30 to 49, 2011-2013
United Kingdom

		Lowest twenty per cent	Second quintile group	Third quintile group	Fourth quintile group	Highest twenty per cent	All house-holds
Lower boundary of group (£ per week)[1]			265	462	696	1,078	
Average weighted number of households (thousands)		1,060	1,390	1,900	2,350	2,790	9,490
Total number of households in sample (over 3 years)		640	870	1,180	1,460	1,650	5,800
Total number of persons in sample (over 3 years)		1,240	2,490	3,600	4,760	5,510	17,600
Total number of adults in sample (over 3 years)		810	1,390	2,120	2,960	3,510	10,800
Weighted average number of persons per household		1.9	2.8	3.0	3.2	3.3	3.0
Commodity or service		Average weekly household expenditure (£)					
1	Food & non-alcoholic drinks	34.60	47.80	58.20	67.60	79.70	62.70
2	Alcoholic drinks, tobacco & narcotics	9.50	10.70	11.30	14.40	15.20	12.90
3	Clothing & footwear	8.60	17.80	23.00	29.60	42.70	28.00
4	Housing(net)[2], fuel & power	58.20	77.00	80.40	73.20	87.50	77.70
5	Household goods & services	13.40	16.30	25.50	32.50	52.30	32.40
6	Health	1.40	2.60	3.10	5.50	9.00	5.10
7	Transport	23.10	43.30	60.70	87.50	130.30	81.00
8	Communication	8.60	13.30	15.70	18.20	20.40	16.50
9	Recreation & culture	20.80	34.20	52.40	70.90	123.10	71.50
10	Education	5.20	11.90	2.30	5.60	21.10	10.40
11	Restaurants & hotels	14.10	24.80	36.00	47.30	81.40	48.00
12	Miscellaneous goods & services	13.50	23.70	34.80	47.10	78.00	46.50
1-12	All expenditure groups	211.00	323.30	403.20	499.40	740.60	492.70
13	Other expenditure items	22.60	43.10	68.90	97.70	169.10	96.50
Total expenditure		**233.50**	**366.30**	**472.20**	**597.10**	**909.70**	**589.20**
Average weekly expenditure per person (£)							
Total expenditure		**123.60**	**132.20**	**159.20**	**188.60**	**279.30**	**199.60**

Note: The commodity and service categories are not comparable to those in publications before 2001-02.
Please see background notes for symbols and conventions used in this report.
This table is based on a three year average.
1 Lower boundary of 2013 gross income quintile groups (£ per week).
2 Excluding mortgage interest payments, council tax and Northern Ireland rates.

Table A14
Household expenditure by gross income quintile group where the household reference person is aged 50 to 64, 2011-2013
United Kingdom

		Lowest twenty per cent	Second quintile group	Third quintile group	Fourth quintile group	Highest twenty per cent	All house-holds
Lower boundary of group (£ per week)[1]			265	462	696	1,078	
Weighted number of households (thousands)		1,260	1,110	1,290	1,540	1,760	6,960
Total number of households in sample (over 3 years)		820	720	800	950	1,270	4,560
Total number of persons in sample (over 3 years)		1,120	1,280	1,720	2,300	3,610	10,030
Total number of adults in sample (over 3 years)		1,060	1,180	1,560	2,050	3,190	9,040
Weighted average number of persons per household		1.4	1.8	2.2	2.6	3.0	2.3
Commodity or service		Average weekly household expenditure (£)					
1	Food & non-alcoholic drinks	33.60	47.10	58.60	70.60	88.90	62.50
2	Alcoholic drinks, tobacco & narcotics	10.40	12.40	16.10	17.20	20.80	15.90
3	Clothing & footwear	8.00	15.10	18.50	29.50	47.10	25.70
4	Housing(net)[2], fuel & power	46.90	58.50	59.20	62.40	66.90	59.50
5	Household goods & services	15.80	25.30	27.10	38.90	54.40	34.30
6	Health	2.30	4.10	6.50	9.70	12.50	7.60
7	Transport	21.70	42.90	65.90	87.90	146.70	79.50
8	Communication	7.70	11.30	13.40	16.30	21.20	14.60
9	Recreation & culture	21.50	43.20	61.70	84.10	127.80	73.10
10	Education	[1.20]	[1.10]	3.10	4.60	16.70	6.20
11	Restaurants & hotels	13.80	23.80	34.70	49.90	84.60	45.10
12	Miscellaneous goods & services	15.20	24.10	32.40	44.70	67.50	39.50
1-12	All expenditure groups	198.20	308.80	397.10	515.70	755.30	463.60
13	Other expenditure items	23.80	38.70	55.60	74.20	148.30	74.70
Total expenditure		**222.00**	**347.60**	**452.70**	**590.00**	**903.60**	**538.30**
Average weekly expenditure per person (£)							
Total expenditure		**161.80**	**190.30**	**208.00**	**230.20**	**300.40**	**237.10**

Note: The commodity and service categories are not comparable to those in publications before 2001-02.
Please see background notes for symbols and conventions used in this report.
This table is based on a three year average.
1 Lower boundary of 2013 gross income quintile groups (£ per week).
2 Excluding mortgage interest payments, council tax and Northern Ireland rates.

Table A15
Household expenditure by gross income quintile group where the household reference person is aged 65 to 74, 2011-2013
United Kingdom

		Lowest twenty per cent	Second quintile group	Third quintile group	Fourth quintile group	Highest twenty per cent	All house-holds
Lower boundary of group (£ per week)[1]			265	462	696	1,078	
Average weighted number of households (thousands)		930	1,090	840	540	310	3,710
Total number of households in sample (over 3 years)		640	820	630	380	210	2,680
Total number of persons in sample (over 3 years)		750	1,410	1,220	830	490	4,710
Total number of adults in sample (over 3 years)		750	1,400	1,210	830	480	4,650
Weighted average number of persons per household		1.2	1.7	1.9	2.3	2.6	1.8
Commodity or service		Average weekly household expenditure (£)					
1	Food & non-alcoholic drinks	35.10	49.70	61.90	70.70	93.20	55.60
2	Alcoholic drinks, tobacco & narcotics	6.90	9.30	12.80	14.50	19.00	11.10
3	Clothing & footwear	7.50	11.90	21.40	24.80	41.00	17.30
4	Housing(net)[2], fuel & power	40.20	49.70	52.90	66.10	86.10	53.60
5	Household goods & services	10.60	23.60	33.30	39.00	60.10	27.90
6	Health	3.10	5.80	8.60	13.10	12.60	7.50
7	Transport	15.50	40.40	66.40	86.40	143.00	55.50
8	Communication	6.80	9.70	11.20	14.10	17.80	10.70
9	Recreation & culture	28.30	48.10	87.50	93.00	140.90	66.50
10	Education	-	[0.30]	[0.30]	[3.00]	11.90	1.60
11	Restaurants & hotels	11.70	23.90	38.60	49.20	80.40	32.80
12	Miscellaneous goods & services	15.60	23.00	33.90	45.30	100.60	33.10
1-12	All expenditure groups	181.20	295.30	428.70	519.20	806.80	372.90
13	Other expenditure items	16.50	33.20	55.10	62.10	113.10	45.30
Total expenditure		**197.70**	**328.50**	**483.80**	**581.30**	**920.00**	**418.20**
Average weekly expenditure per person (£) Total expenditure		**167.10**	**194.20**	**249.00**	**256.90**	**350.30**	**234.60**

Note: The commodity and service categories are not comparable to those in publications before 2001-02.
Please see background notes for symbols and conventions used in this report.
This table is based on a three year average.
1 Lower boundary of 2013 gross income quintile groups (£ per week).
2 Excluding mortgage interest payments, council tax and Northern Ireland rates.

Table A16
Household expenditure by gross income quintile group where the household reference person is aged 75 or over, 2011-2013
United Kingdom

		Lowest twenty per cent	Second quintile group	Third quintile group	Fourth quintile group	Highest twenty per cent	All house-holds
Lower boundary of group (£ per week)[1]			265	462	696	1,078	
Average weighted number of households (thousands)		1,420	1,160	590	250	110	3,530
Total number of households in sample (over 3 years)		750	700	370	160	70	2,040
Total number of persons in sample (over 3 years)		860	1,060	660	320	140	3,020
Total number of adults in sample (over 3 years)		860	1,060	650	310	130	3,010
Weighted average number of persons per household		1.1	1.5	1.8	2.0	2.0	1.4
Commodity or service		Average weekly household expenditure (£)					
1	Food & non-alcoholic drinks	30.10	41.40	53.10	63.50	75.10	41.50
2	Alcoholic drinks, tobacco & narcotics	3.50	6.10	7.20	11.70	22.60	6.20
3	Clothing & footwear	5.10	7.40	12.40	14.00	23.50	8.30
4	Housing (net)[2], fuel & power	38.60	44.80	52.80	54.60	60.90	44.90
5	Household goods & services	10.40	20.90	26.90	31.70	64.90	19.90
6	Health	3.30	5.80	12.40	17.40	98.90	9.30
7	Transport	8.80	20.10	38.40	51.00	133.00	24.10
8	Communication	6.10	7.60	9.30	10.60	14.50	7.70
9	Recreation & culture	15.70	32.20	48.50	64.60	87.10	32.30
10	Education	[0.00]	[2.50]	[4.70]	[5.30]	[22.40]	2.70
11	Restaurants & hotels	7.90	16.00	26.40	37.30	56.00	17.20
12	Miscellaneous goods & services	18.90	25.60	36.00	46.20	57.30	27.20
1-12	All expenditure groups	148.40	230.60	328.20	408.00	716.20	241.30
13	Other expenditure items	16.50	31.50	49.70	79.90	107.50	34.60
Total expenditure		**164.90**	**262.10**	**378.00**	**487.90**	**823.70**	**275.90**
Average weekly expenditure per person (£)							
Total expenditure		**147.90**	**178.90**	**213.70**	**245.90**	**407.00**	**193.00**

Note: The commodity and service categories are not comparable to those in publications before 2001-02.
Please see background notes for symbols and conventions used in this report.
This table is based on a three year average.
1 Lower boundary of 2013 gross income quintile groups (£ per week).
2 Excluding mortgage interest payments, council tax and Northern Ireland rates.

Table A17
Household expenditure by economic activity status of the household reference person, 2013
United Kingdom

	Employees			Self-employed	All in employment[1]	Unemployed	All economically active[1]	Economically inactive			All households
	Full-time	Part-time	All					Retired	Other	All	
Weighted number of households (thousands)	11,180	2,700	13,880	2,210	16,180	850	17,020	7,120	2,700	9,820	26,840
Total number of households in sample	2,030	540	2,570	410	2,990	150	3,140	1,480	530	2,000	5,140
Total number of persons in sample	5,680	1,350	7,030	1,100	8,160	340	8,490	2,370	1,260	3,630	12,120
Total number of adults in sample	4,070	960	5,040	820	5,880	230	6,100	2,340	910	3,250	9,350
Weighted average number of persons per household	2.8	2.6	2.7	2.7	2.7	2.1	2.7	1.6	2.4	1.8	2.4
Commodity or service	Average weekly household expenditure (£)										
1 Food & non-alcoholic drinks	66.20	59.40	64.90	70.90	65.50	36.10	64.00	48.50	53.00	49.70	58.80
2 Alcoholic drinks, tobacco & narcotics	13.60	12.10	13.30	13.70	13.30	10.60	13.20	9.10	12.40	10.00	12.00
3 Clothing & footwear	29.80	24.90	28.80	30.10	28.90	7.60	27.80	12.00	17.90	13.60	22.60
4 Housing (net)[2], fuel & power	85.50	84.10	85.20	91.10	86.00	74.80	85.40	53.00	61.00	55.20	74.40
5 Household goods & services	38.40	35.30	37.80	41.30	38.20	18.00	37.20	26.60	25.00	26.20	33.10
6 Health	6.40	8.10	6.70	6.10	6.60	2.00	6.40	6.50	4.40	6.00	6.20
7 Transport	96.60	59.80	89.40	101.80	90.70	29.70	87.70	38.10	46.70	40.50	70.40
8 Communication	17.90	14.60	17.30	18.30	17.30	10.60	17.00	9.30	12.00	10.10	14.50
9 Recreation & culture	78.80	64.60	76.00	74.10	75.40	17.80	72.60	49.10	48.50	49.00	63.90
10 Education	7.60	14.30	8.90	17.60	10.10	[9.70]	10.10	[1.30]	20.70	6.60	8.80
11 Restaurants & hotels	53.00	38.20	50.10	54.30	50.50	19.20	48.90	23.40	31.30	25.60	40.40
12 Miscellaneous goods & services	50.00	38.00	47.60	47.70	47.40	14.70	45.80	27.60	27.30	27.50	39.10
1-12 All expenditure groups	543.70	453.30	526.10	566.90	530.00	250.70	516.10	304.50	360.30	319.90	444.30
13 Other expenditure items	96.90	53.60	88.40	97.00	89.20	23.00	85.90	40.10	78.50	50.60	73.00
Total expenditure	**640.60**	**506.80**	**614.50**	**664.00**	**619.20**	**273.70**	**602.00**	**344.60**	**438.80**	**370.50**	**517.30**
Average weekly expenditure per person (£)											
Total expenditure	**232.70**	**196.10**	**225.90**	**248.00**	**228.50**	**127.50**	**224.50**	**218.50**	**184.70**	**206.20**	**219.40**

Note: The commodity and service categories are not comparable to those in publications before 2001-02.
Please see background notes for symbols and conventions used in this report.
1 Includes households where household reference person was on a Government supported training scheme.
2 Excluding mortgage interest payments, council tax and Northern Ireland rates.

Table A18

Household expenditure by gross income: the household reference person is a full-time employee, 2013

United Kingdom

		Lowest twenty per cent	Second quintile group	Third quintile group	Fourth quintile group	Highest twenty per cent	All house-holds
Lower boundary of group (£ per week)[1]			265	462	696	1,078	
Weighted number of households (thousands)		130	1,170	2,360	3,440	4,080	11,180
Total number of households in sample		30	210	440	640	720	2,030
Total number of persons in sample		50	420	1,080	1,860	2,270	5,680
Total number of adults in sample		40	310	760	1,290	1,660	4,070
Weighted average number of persons per household		2.1	1.9	2.4	2.8	3.1	2.8
Commodity or service		Average weekly household expenditure (£)					
1	Food & non-alcoholic drinks	30.40	39.90	54.50	65.70	82.00	66.20
2	Alcoholic drinks, tobacco & narcotics	[4.70]	11.50	11.80	13.90	15.30	13.60
3	Clothing & footwear	[4.00]	11.20	17.90	30.40	42.20	29.80
4	Housing (net)[2], fuel & power	91.90	91.50	90.60	79.80	85.40	85.50
5	Household goods & services	[38.70]	13.50	24.10	37.00	55.00	38.40
6	Health	[0.80]	3.00	3.40	7.10	8.70	6.40
7	Transport	[64.50]	39.50	63.00	85.90	142.30	96.60
8	Communication	12.90	12.70	15.30	18.40	20.60	17.90
9	Recreation & culture	41.20	34.40	44.50	72.10	118.10	78.80
10	Education	[16.90]	[2.60]	2.00	3.50	15.60	7.60
11	Restaurants & hotels	15.90	25.00	31.40	49.10	77.90	53.00
12	Miscellaneous goods & services	16.90	22.30	31.00	44.90	74.10	50.00
1-12	All expenditure groups	338.90	307.00	389.50	507.70	737.20	543.70
13	Other expenditure items	51.20	45.30	58.00	85.10	145.40	96.90
Total expenditure		**390.10**	**352.30**	**447.50**	**592.80**	**882.60**	**640.60**
Average weekly expenditure per person (£)							
Total expenditure		**181.50**	**182.10**	**182.70**	**209.70**	**283.00**	**232.70**

Note: The commodity and service categories are not comparable to those in publications before 2001-02.
Please see background notes for symbols and conventions used in this report.

1 Lower boundary of 2013 gross income quintile groups (£ per week).

2 Excluding mortgage interest payments, council tax and Northern Ireland rates.

Table A19
Household expenditure by gross income: the household reference person is self-employed, 2011-2013
United Kingdom

		Lowest twenty per cent	Second quintile group	Third quintile group	Fourth quintile group	Highest twenty per cent	All house-holds
Lower boundary of group (£ per week) [1]			265	462	696	1,078	
Average weighted number of households (thousands)		250	390	530	490	510	2,160
Total number of households in sample (over 3 years)		150	240	340	300	310	1,330
Total number of persons in sample (over 3 years)		270	570	940	890	980	3,650
Total number of adults in sample (over 3 years)		210	400	660	680	720	2,680
Weighted average number of persons per household		1.8	2.4	2.8	3.0	3.2	2.7
Commodity or service		Average weekly household expenditure (£)					
1	Food & non-alcoholic drinks	39.20	53.10	65.90	75.00	92.10	68.70
2	Alcoholic drinks, tobacco & narcotics	10.00	10.20	13.00	17.30	19.60	14.60
3	Clothing & footwear	12.40	20.10	25.60	31.60	52.50	30.80
4	Housing(net)[2], fuel & power	69.20	83.00	80.90	80.10	88.60	81.40
5	Household goods & services	18.20	22.50	33.00	32.90	59.50	35.50
6	Health	2.00	2.40	5.60	6.70	9.10	5.70
7	Transport	41.70	69.30	70.00	96.50	164.00	94.20
8	Communication	10.50	15.00	15.90	19.30	25.00	18.00
9	Recreation & culture	26.00	39.90	62.30	77.40	129.10	72.90
10	Education	[2.00]	[9.10]	3.70	16.90	33.30	14.30
11	Restaurants & hotels	22.40	30.80	41.20	54.70	98.30	53.20
12	Miscellaneous goods & services	22.80	29.50	39.10	51.70	80.90	48.10
1-12	All expenditure groups	276.40	384.90	456.30	560.00	852.00	537.40
13	Other expenditure items	46.10	57.80	79.70	88.90	179.90	97.40
Total expenditure		**322.50**	**442.70**	**536.00**	**648.90**	**1031.80**	**634.80**
Average weekly expenditure per person (£) Total expenditure		**180.80**	**187.00**	**191.30**	**217.20**	**322.30**	**231.50**

Note: The commodity and service categories are not comparable to those in publications before 2001-02.
Please see background notes for symbols and conventions used in this report.
This table is based on a three year average.
1 Lower boundary of 2013 gross income quintile groups (£ per week).
2 Excluding mortgage interest payments, council tax and Northern Ireland rates.

Table A20
Household expenditure by number of persons working, 2013
United Kingdom

	Number of persons working: None	One	Two	Three	Four or more	All house-holds
Weighted number of households (thousands)	9,140	7,670	8,190	1,430	400	26,840
Total number of households in sample	1,880	1,470	1,490	240	60	5,140
Total number of persons in sample	3,120	3,360	4,470	890	290	12,120
Total number of adults in sample	2,790	2,390	3,190	740	250	9,350
Weighted average number of persons per household	1.6	2.2	3.0	3.7	4.7	2.4
Weighted average age of head of household	67	47	43	49	52	53
Employment status of the household reference person[1]:						
- % working full-time or self-employed	*0*	*62*	*86*	*83*	*90*	*48*
- % working part-time	*0*	*22*	*12*	*13*	*10*	*10*
- % not working	*100*	*16*	*2*	*3*	*0*	*42*
Commodity or service	Average weekly household expenditure (£)					
1 Food & non-alcoholic drinks	43.90	52.90	72.60	92.90	107.50	58.80
2 Alcoholic drinks, tobacco & narcotics	9.30	11.10	14.00	19.30	24.70	12.00
3 Clothing & footwear	10.60	20.60	31.70	47.00	63.20	22.60
4 Housing(net)[2], fuel & power	53.10	87.00	83.70	89.40	75.80	74.40
5 Household goods & services	24.20	31.60	42.30	45.70	36.30	33.10
6 Health	5.30	5.40	6.80	13.00	8.00	6.20
7 Transport	32.30	62.20	104.10	130.20	195.90	70.40
8 Communication	8.90	13.70	18.80	25.50	27.00	14.50
9 Recreation & culture	40.60	55.30	87.00	103.00	149.10	63.90
10 Education	6.70	8.30	12.20	7.30	[3.10]	8.80
11 Restaurants & hotels	21.30	34.60	58.20	77.30	90.10	40.40
12 Miscellaneous goods & services	24.10	32.10	56.40	63.20	76.70	39.10
1-12 All expenditure groups	280.30	414.80	587.70	713.60	857.40	444.30
13 Other expenditure items	34.00	62.50	118.60	95.50	154.10	73.00
Total expenditure	**314.20**	**477.30**	**706.30**	**809.10**	**1011.50**	**517.30**
Average weekly expenditure per person (£)						
Total expenditure	**195.80**	**213.10**	**238.20**	**220.20**	**215.40**	**219.40**

Note: The commodity and service categories are not comparable to those in publications before 2001-02.
Please see background notes for symbols and conventions used in this report.
1 Excludes households where the household reference person was on a Government-supported training scheme.
2 Excluding mortgage interest payments, council tax and Northern Ireland rates.

Table A21
Household expenditure by age at which the household reference person completed continuous full-time education, 2013
United Kingdom

		Aged 14 and under	Aged 15	Aged 16	Aged 17 and under 19	Aged 19 and under 22	Aged 22 or over
Weighted number of households (thousands)		290	2,850	6,900	4,400	3,130	3,440
Total number of households in sample		60	610	1,330	840	570	600
Total number of persons in sample		140	1,260	3,580	2,190	1,450	1,620
Total number of adults in sample		100	1,100	2,590	1,560	1,050	1,140
Weighted average number of persons per household		2.3	2.1	2.7	2.6	2.5	2.6
Weighted average age of head of household		53	58	47	45	44	42
Commodity or service		Average weekly household expenditure (£)					
1	Food & non-alcoholic drinks	56.30	55.20	61.60	62.00	65.40	68.80
2	Alcoholic drinks, tobacco & narcotics	14.10	14.10	14.80	12.50	11.60	11.50
3	Clothing & footwear	13.80	17.40	25.20	26.10	31.80	29.80
4	Housing(net)[1], fuel & power	71.30	59.20	69.80	75.70	80.90	108.50
5	Household goods & services	15.90	30.00	31.50	35.10	44.70	43.60
6	Health	2.40	3.90	5.30	7.30	6.40	8.60
7	Transport	35.10	52.00	73.80	81.70	94.60	105.30
8	Communication	9.50	12.40	16.10	16.00	16.10	18.10
9	Recreation & culture	36.80	54.80	61.60	74.80	77.50	86.30
10	Education	[15.60]	[0.50]	2.10	3.10	8.70	20.60
11	Restaurants & hotels	21.40	30.50	41.10	46.60	53.20	57.70
12	Miscellaneous goods & services	19.30	28.10	36.90	44.00	48.30	59.60
1-12	All expenditure groups	311.70	358.00	440.00	485.00	539.20	618.40
13	Other expenditure items	25.60	37.80	63.10	79.60	97.10	151.80
Total expenditure		**337.30**	**395.80**	**503.10**	**564.60**	**636.30**	**770.20**
Average weekly expenditure per person (£)							
Total expenditure		**145.00**	**185.80**	**187.00**	**216.60**	**253.40**	**291.80**

Note: The commodity and service categories are not comparable to those in publications before 2001-02.
Please see background notes for symbols and conventions used in this report.
This table does not include households where the HRP is aged 70 or over, or is still in continuous full-time education.
1 Excluding mortgage interest payments, council tax and Northern Ireland rates.

Table A22
Household expenditure by socio-economic classification of household reference person, 2013
United Kingdom

	Large employers & higher managerial	Higher professional	Lower managerial & professional	Intermediate	Small employers	Lower supervisory	Semi-routine	Routine	Long-term unemployed[1]	Students	Occupation not stated[2]	All households
Weighted number of households (thousands)	880	2,710	5,000	1,950	1,740	1,340	2,210	1,960	540	540	7,970	26,840
Total number of households in sample	170	490	930	370	320	250	420	380	100	80	1,640	5,140
Total number of persons in sample	490	1,370	2,440	910	860	700	1,080	1,050	250	210	2,760	12,120
Total number of adults in sample	360	970	1,810	650	630	500	750	720	160	180	2,630	9,350
Weighted average number of persons per household	2.9	2.7	2.6	2.5	2.7	2.8	2.6	2.8	2.3	2.6	1.7	2.4
Commodity or service					Average weekly household expenditure (£)							
1 Food & non-alcoholic drinks	75.60	73.90	68.50	58.20	66.20	60.20	54.50	54.00	43.60	41.20	48.70	58.80
2 Alcoholic drinks, tobacco & narcotics	12.70	12.10	13.90	12.90	14.00	15.00	13.70	12.80	7.20	9.30	9.50	12.00
3 Clothing & footwear	30.90	37.60	30.90	21.70	25.20	26.10	21.00	19.50	14.20	19.40	12.40	22.60
4 Housing (net)[3], fuel & power	76.90	89.10	80.00	81.60	82.40	79.60	82.90	80.70	56.10	158.00	52.70	74.40
5 Household goods & services	78.10	40.50	46.60	31.80	33.50	26.00	23.00	23.40	18.10	18.40	25.90	33.10
6 Health	11.80	8.80	8.30	4.50	4.60	4.20	4.20	4.90	0.60	2.80	6.10	6.20
7 Transport	134.40	123.60	101.60	66.50	84.60	70.50	47.90	53.40	31.10	46.20	38.40	70.40
8 Communication	19.10	18.00	18.30	16.00	17.10	16.20	14.90	13.40	11.00	15.20	9.40	14.50
9 Recreation & culture	136.00	91.30	81.60	68.20	61.10	58.10	48.10	42.90	19.60	43.40	50.10	63.90
10 Education	12.60	22.30	4.70	2.00	9.50	[3.20]	3.50	[1.30]	[1.20]	164.50	2.10	8.80
11 Restaurants & hotels	80.80	63.70	56.00	39.20	43.10	38.00	31.80	31.00	15.50	46.70	24.20	40.40
12 Miscellaneous goods & services	67.30	65.50	53.30	36.60	39.20	38.10	26.40	28.90	14.20	28.10	27.40	39.10
1-12 All expenditure groups	736.20	646.30	563.90	439.30	480.40	435.00	372.10	366.20	232.30	593.20	306.80	444.30
13 Other expenditure items	143.80	140.20	98.20	64.20	68.90	63.80	41.80	45.00	13.70	28.10	53.90	73.00
Total expenditure	**880.00**	**786.50**	**662.10**	**503.40**	**549.40**	**498.80**	**413.90**	**411.10**	**246.00**	**621.20**	**360.60**	**517.30**
Average weekly expenditure per person (£)												
Total expenditure	**307.20**	**290.50**	**253.50**	**204.40**	**206.90**	**175.00**	**159.50**	**149.00**	**105.10**	**239.20**	**215.80**	**219.40**

Note: Changes to categories of socio-economic classification were made in 2011. See Appendix B for details.
The commodity and service categories are not comparable to those in publications before 2001-02.
Please see background notes for symbols and conventions used in this report.
1 Includes those who have never worked.
2 Includes those who are economically inactive.
3 Excludes mortgage interest payments, council tax and Northern Ireland rates.

Table A23
Expenditure by household composition, 2013
United Kingdom

	Retired households				Non-retired		Retired and non-retired households						
	State pension[1]		Other retired				One adult		Two adults			Three or more adults	
	One person	Two adults	One person	Two adults	One person	Two adults	with one child	with two or more children	with one child	with two children	with three or more children	without children	with children
Weighted number of households (thousands)	870	450	2,830	2,510	4,090	5,720	710	650	2,200	2,290	900	2,490	1,120
Total number of households in sample	150	110	550	590	740	1,080	150	150	400	460	190	390	200
Total number of persons in sample	150	230	550	1,180	740	2,150	290	480	1,200	1,820	1,020	1,340	970
Total number of adults in sample	150	230	550	1,180	740	2,150	150	150	800	910	380	1,340	640
Weighted average number of persons per household	1.0	2.0	1.0	2.0	1.0	2.0	2.0	3.2	3.0	4.0	5.3	3.5	4.9
Commodity or service	Average weekly household expenditure (£)												
1 Food & non-alcoholic drinks	28.90	57.90	32.30	62.30	29.50	58.90	40.90	57.80	68.90	82.90	89.50	86.70	104.20
2 Alcoholic drinks, tobacco & narcotics	2.60	7.90	6.70	12.20	9.40	14.30	7.50	12.40	13.20	12.00	11.50	17.80	20.50
3 Clothing & footwear	4.00	8.70	7.90	16.90	13.40	24.30	15.00	19.20	28.70	34.30	31.40	37.50	48.00
4 Housing(net)[2], fuel & power	43.80	46.80	49.60	57.20	70.30	85.20	75.10	73.90	88.80	79.30	86.60	91.80	83.10
5 Household goods & services	11.40	22.10	22.10	35.90	22.60	40.80	15.30	27.00	32.70	39.00	32.20	47.70	47.70
6 Health	2.10	5.60	4.80	9.60	2.80	8.20	1.20	2.50	4.90	8.00	2.70	9.40	8.00
7 Transport	8.40	36.80	22.90	57.30	37.40	93.40	29.80	39.30	85.00	102.20	83.80	114.20	127.60
8 Communication	6.90	8.60	8.00	10.40	10.00	16.10	11.30	13.80	18.10	18.10	19.10	21.90	23.80
9 Recreation & culture	17.30	46.70	29.60	77.80	32.60	76.60	34.60	44.00	62.30	95.50	76.90	98.20	94.90
10 Education	-	[0.20]	[0.00]	[3.50]	[2.80]	5.70	[6.00]	[2.10]	15.70	13.50	14.60	35.10	10.30
11 Restaurants & hotels	7.60	23.20	13.10	36.70	23.50	52.10	17.40	28.60	45.70	51.90	45.70	69.00	71.20
12 Miscellaneous goods & services	14.60	26.90	22.50	35.80	21.20	42.20	21.10	35.10	50.90	61.60	56.20	52.40	63.90
1-12 All expenditure groups	147.70	291.50	219.60	415.50	275.40	517.70	275.10	355.70	515.00	598.40	550.20	681.50	703.20
13 Other expenditure items	15.80	31.90	39.20	47.40	48.40	78.70	35.00	37.30	94.90	118.20	109.40	127.80	96.70
Total expenditure	**163.50**	**323.40**	**258.90**	**462.90**	**323.80**	**596.30**	**310.10**	**393.10**	**609.90**	**716.60**	**659.60**	**809.30**	**799.90**
Average weekly expenditure per person (£) Total expenditure	**163.50**	**161.70**	**258.90**	**231.50**	**323.80**	**298.20**	**155.10**	**121.30**	**203.30**	**179.10**	**125.20**	**234.50**	**163.20**

Note: The commodity and service categories are not comparable to those in publications before 2001-02.
Please see background notes for symbols and conventions used in this report.
1 Mainly dependent on state pensions and not economically active - see definitions in Appendix B.
2 Excluding mortgage interest payments, council tax and Northern Ireland rates.

Table A24

Expenditure of one person retired households mainly dependent on state pensions[1] by gross income quintile group, 2011-2013

United Kingdom

		Lowest twenty per cent	Second quintile group	Third quintile group	Fourth quintile group	Highest twenty per cent	All house-holds
Lower boundary of group (£ per week)[2]			265	462	696	1,078	
Average weighted number of households (thousands)		690	80	0	0	0	760
Total number of households in sample (over 3 years)		390	40	0	0	0	430
Total number of persons in sample (over 3 years)		390	40	0	0	0	430
Total number of adults in sample (over 3 years)		390	40	0	0	0	430
Weighted average number of persons per household		1.0	1.0	0	0	0	1.0
Commodity or service		Average weekly household expenditure (£)					
1	Food & non-alcoholic drinks	28.70	29.60	-	-	-	28.80
2	Alcoholic drinks, tobacco & narcotics	3.20	[4.10]	-	-	-	3.30
3	Clothing & footwear	4.70	[3.70]	-	-	-	4.60
4	Housing(net)[3], fuel & power	37.30	47.30	-	-	-	38.30
5	Household goods & services	9.30	17.30	-	-	-	10.10
6	Health	3.50	[1.30]	-	-	-	3.30
7	Transport	9.90	[10.60]	-	-	-	10.00
8	Communication	6.50	6.70	-	-	-	6.60
9	Recreation & culture	17.50	25.20	-	-	-	18.30
10	Education	[0.10]	-	-	-	-	[0.10]
11	Restaurants & hotels	7.90	9.90	-	-	-	8.10
12	Miscellaneous goods & services	19.10	14.00	-	-	-	18.50
1-12	All expenditure groups	147.70	169.70	-	-	-	149.90
13	Other expenditure items	17.80	16.70	-	-	-	17.70
Total expenditure		**165.50**	**186.40**	-	**-**	**-**	**167.60**
Average weekly expenditure per person (£)							
Total expenditure		**165.50**	**186.40**	**-**	**-**	**-**	**167.60**

Note: The commodity and service categories are not comparable to those in publications before 2001-02.
Please see background notes for symbols and conventions used in this report.
This table is based on a three year average.
1 Mainly dependent on state pensions and not economically active - see definitions in Appendix B.
2 Lower boundary of 2013 gross income quintile groups (£ per week).
3 Excluding mortgage interest payments, council tax and Northern Ireland rates.

Table A25
Expenditure of one person retired households not mainly dependent on state pension by gross income quintile group, 2011-2013
United Kingdom

		Lowest twenty per cent	Second quintile group	Third quintile group	Fourth quintile group	Highest twenty per cent	All house-holds
Lower boundary of group (£ per week)[1]			265	462	696	1,078	
Average weighted number of households (thousands)		1,440	960	310	90	40	2,840
Total number of households in sample (over 3 years)		850	580	190	60	30	1,700
Total number of persons in sample (over 3 years)		850	580	190	60	30	1,700
Total number of adults in sample (over 3 years)		850	580	190	60	30	1,700
Weighted average number of persons per household		1.0	1.0	1.0	1.0	1.0	1.0
Commodity or service		Average weekly household expenditure (£)					
1	Food & non-alcoholic drinks	29.10	33.00	36.20	35.70	42.20	31.60
2	Alcoholic drinks, tobacco & narcotics	5.10	6.60	6.60	6.50	[16.10]	6.00
3	Clothing & footwear	6.30	8.60	10.10	[7.60]	[26.10]	7.80
4	Housing(net)[2] fuel & power	39.30	43.90	58.30	56.30	61.00	43.80
5	Household goods & services	10.50	20.20	33.80	19.50	91.60	18.00
6	Health	2.80	6.40	6.00	18.80	[10.30]	5.00
7	Transport	9.80	21.00	32.10	54.70	154.50	19.70
8	Communication	6.20	8.60	9.60	9.60	13.70	7.60
9	Recreation & culture	20.80	33.30	49.00	61.80	72.90	30.20
10	Education	-	[1.50]	[7.80]	[7.60]	[1.10]	[1.50]
11	Restaurants & hotels	8.10	16.50	26.00	30.10	35.00	13.90
12	Miscellaneous goods & services	15.20	23.30	37.40	61.60	122.20	23.30
1-12	All expenditure groups	153.20	223.10	313.10	369.80	646.80	208.50
13	Other expenditure items	15.20	33.10	60.60	139.60	132.90	31.70
Total expenditure		**168.40**	**256.20**	**373.70**	**509.40**	**779.70**	**240.10**
Average weekly expenditure per person (£) **Total expenditure**		**168.40**	**256.20**	**373.70**	**509.40**	**779.70**	**240.10**

Note: The commodity and service categories are not comparable to those in publications before 2001-02.
Please see background notes for symbols and conventions used in this report.
This table is based on a three year average.
1 Lower boundary of 2013 gross income quintile groups (£ per week).
2 Excluding mortgage interest payments, council tax and Northern Ireland rates.

Table A26
Expenditure of one adult non-retired households by gross income quintile group, 2011-2013
United Kingdom

		Lowest twenty per cent	Second quintile group	Third quintile group	Fourth quintile group	Highest twenty per cent	All house-holds
Lower boundary of group (£ per week)[1]			265	462	696	1,078	
Average weighted number of households (thousands)		1,570	930	790	450	230	3,960
Total number of households in sample (over 3 years)		920	560	470	260	130	2,340
Total number of persons in sample (over 3 years)		920	560	470	260	130	2,340
Total number of adults in sample (over 3 years)		920	560	470	260	130	2,340
Weighted average number of persons per household		1.0	1.0	1.0	1.0	1.0	1.0
Commodity or service		Average weekly household expenditure (£)					
1	Food & non-alcoholic drinks	24.00	28.70	32.10	32.20	36.10	28.40
2	Alcoholic drinks, tobacco & narcotics	8.10	9.20	10.40	7.90	11.70	9.00
3	Clothing & footwear	5.60	11.60	14.30	22.50	28.80	12.10
4	Housing(net)[2], fuel & power	50.00	69.40	70.70	76.30	75.20	63.10
5	Household goods & services	12.60	14.90	24.30	32.50	40.10	19.40
6	Health	1.10	3.80	3.60	9.40	7.00	3.50
7	Transport	15.60	37.00	49.10	60.60	98.70	37.20
8	Communication	6.70	9.90	11.70	12.30	17.90	9.70
9	Recreation & culture	16.80	28.40	38.10	59.90	97.40	33.40
10	Education	3.90	[1.50]	[0.50]	[1.40]	[10.50]	2.80
11	Restaurants & hotels	11.70	20.00	30.20	39.10	69.10	23.70
12	Miscellaneous goods & services	10.60	19.50	25.80	31.90	43.00	20.00
1-12	All expenditure groups	166.70	253.90	310.70	386.00	535.50	262.40
13	Other expenditure items	18.20	41.90	68.20	90.20	172.60	50.80
Total expenditure		**184.90**	**295.80**	**378.90**	**476.20**	**708.20**	**313.30**
Average weekly expenditure per person (£)							
Total expenditure		**184.90**	**295.80**	**378.90**	**476.20**	**708.20**	**313.30**

Note: The commodity and service categories are not comparable to those in publications before 2001-02.
Please see background notes for symbols and conventions used in this report.
This table is based on a three year average.
1 Lower boundary of 2013 gross income quintile groups (£ per week).
2 Excluding mortgage interest payments, council tax and Northern Ireland rates.

Table A27
Expenditure of one adult households with children by gross income quintile group, 2011-2013
United Kingdom

	Lowest twenty per cent	Second quintile group	Third quintile group	Fourth quintile group	Highest twenty per cent	All house-holds
Lower boundary of group (£ per week)[1]		265	462	696	1,078	
Average weighted number of households (thousands)	510	450	250	110	30	1,350
Total number of households in sample (over 3 years)	370	350	190	80	20	990
Total number of persons in sample (over 3 years)	890	990	530	190	60	2,660
Total number of adults in sample (over 3 years)	370	350	190	80	20	990
Weighted average number of persons per household	2.4	2.8	2.8	2.5	2.8	2.6
Commodity or service	Average weekly household expenditure (£)					
1 Food & non-alcoholic drinks	38.40	47.20	56.80	46.00	67.80	45.90
2 Alcoholic drinks, tobacco & narcotics	8.40	8.10	11.30	9.30	[20.70]	9.10
3 Clothing & footwear	13.10	21.40	21.60	26.70	[35.20]	18.90
4 Housing(net)[2], fuel & power	53.80	73.00	72.40	68.50	101.10	65.90
5 Household goods & services	13.20	18.60	18.00	26.70	65.80	18.10
6 Health	1.60	1.70	2.70	2.80	[15.40]	2.20
7 Transport	14.10	32.80	47.90	81.40	115.50	34.00
8 Communication	8.00	12.00	13.90	16.90	22.10	11.50
9 Recreation & culture	18.80	37.40	50.10	77.60	116.90	37.30
10 Education	1.80	3.40	4.50	[14.40]	[46.60]	4.80
11 Restaurants & hotels	12.40	22.00	33.80	45.80	40.60	22.70
12 Miscellaneous goods & services	13.70	27.50	43.00	51.90	77.50	28.10
1-12 All expenditure groups	197.40	305.10	376.10	468.10	725.20	298.40
13 Other expenditure items	11.40	30.00	55.50	90.30	146.40	34.90
Total expenditure	**208.70**	**335.10**	**431.60**	**558.30**	**871.70**	**333.30**
Average weekly expenditure per person (£) Total expenditure	**87.40**	**121.10**	**153.60**	**219.10**	**[316.40]**	**127.50**

Note: The commodity and service categories are not comparable to those in publications before 2001-02.
Please see background notes for symbols and conventions used in this report.
This table is based on a three year average.
1 Lower boundary of 2013 gross income quintile groups (£ per week).
2 Excluding mortgage interest payments, council tax and Northern Ireland rates.

Table A28
Expenditure of two adult households with children by gross income quintile group, 2011-2013
United Kingdom

		Lowest twenty per cent	Second quintile group	Third quintile group	Fourth quintile group	Highest twenty per cent	All house-holds
Lower boundary of group (£ per week)[1]			265	462	696	1,078	
Average weighted number of households (thousands)		230	650	1,200	1,490	1,710	5,270
Total number of households in sample (over 3 years)		140	400	750	980	1,110	3,370
Total number of persons in sample (over 3 years)		490	1,550	2,910	3,780	4,250	12,990
Total number of adults in sample (over 3 years)		270	790	1,500	1,960	2,220	6,750
Weighted average number of persons per household		3.6	3.9	3.8	3.8	3.8	3.8
Commodity or service		Average weekly household expenditure (£)					
1	Food & non-alcoholic drinks	54.40	60.80	67.90	77.10	92.50	77.00
2	Alcoholic drinks, tobacco & narcotics	12.70	12.50	10.90	13.00	15.60	13.30
3	Clothing & footwear	15.80	22.40	26.90	31.50	44.70	33.00
4	Housing(net)[2], fuel & power	63.20	84.30	84.60	70.50	80.00	78.10
5	Household goods & services	18.50	17.50	28.30	31.60	55.10	36.20
6	Health	0.70	1.80	3.30	6.10	7.90	5.30
7	Transport	34.40	44.80	66.30	91.60	131.60	90.50
8	Communication	9.90	14.80	17.20	18.20	20.00	17.80
9	Recreation & culture	30.10	34.40	55.70	74.60	125.20	79.60
10	Education	[1.00]	6.50	2.90	7.10	32.90	14.10
11	Restaurants & hotels	17.50	26.60	37.30	44.10	77.10	49.90
12	Miscellaneous goods & services	20.30	27.30	37.30	54.50	88.10	56.70
1-12	All expenditure groups	278.60	353.70	438.50	519.90	770.60	551.40
13	Other expenditure items	22.20	40.70	69.50	102.60	177.90	108.20
Total expenditure		**300.80**	**394.40**	**508.00**	**622.50**	**948.40**	**659.60**
Average weekly expenditure per person (£)							
Total expenditure		**84.20**	**102.30**	**132.60**	**164.30**	**250.10**	**173.60**

Note: The commodity and service categories are not comparable to those in publications before 2001-02.
Please see background notes for symbols and conventions used in this report.
This table is based on a three year average.
1 Lower boundary of 2013 gross income quintile groups (£ per week).
2 Excluding mortgage interest payments, council tax and Northern Ireland rates.

Table A29
Expenditure of two adult non-retired households by gross income quintile group, 2011-2013
United Kingdom

		Lowest twenty per cent	Second quintile group	Third quintile group	Fourth quintile group	Highest twenty per cent	All house-holds
Lower boundary of group (£ per week)[1]			265	462	696	1,078	
Average weighted number of households (thousands)		420	750	1,280	1,660	1,700	5,810
Total number of households in sample (over 3 years)		260	480	820	1,010	1,020	3,600
Total number of persons in sample (over 3 years)		520	960	1,650	2,030	2,050	7,190
Total number of adults in sample (over 3 years)		520	960	1,650	2,030	2,050	7,190
Weighted average number of persons per household		2.0	2.0	2.0	2.0	2.0	2.0
Commodity or service		Average weekly household expenditure (£)					
1	Food & non-alcoholic drinks	42.70	48.70	54.80	57.90	63.50	56.60
2	Alcoholic drinks, tobacco & narcotics	12.50	13.10	13.70	15.60	16.10	14.70
3	Clothing & footwear	8.80	14.10	18.20	23.80	37.60	24.30
4	Housing(net)[2], fuel & power	58.50	74.20	74.10	77.50	89.00	78.20
5	Household goods & services	17.20	26.60	29.60	34.80	48.30	35.30
6	Health	3.50	3.60	5.80	7.00	11.90	7.50
7	Transport	35.00	53.00	61.20	85.70	133.50	86.40
8	Communication	10.00	12.70	13.60	15.70	18.10	15.10
9	Recreation & culture	27.10	49.80	58.50	74.10	120.10	77.50
10	Education	[10.00]	[4.50]	3.00	3.60	5.40	4.50
11	Restaurants & hotels	21.80	27.60	33.50	49.00	85.00	51.40
12	Miscellaneous goods & services	19.60	26.10	30.90	41.10	62.10	41.50
1-12	All expenditure groups	266.80	354.00	396.90	485.70	690.60	493.10
13	Other expenditure items	34.20	41.70	52.70	75.90	139.40	81.90
Total expenditure		**300.90**	**395.70**	**449.70**	**561.60**	**830.00**	**575.00**
Average weekly expenditure per person (£) **Total expenditure**		**150.50**	**197.80**	**224.80**	**280.80**	**415.00**	**287.50**

Note: The commodity and service categories are not comparable to those in publications before 2001-02.
Please see background notes for symbols and conventions used in this report.
This table is based on a three year average.
1 Lower boundary of 2013 gross income quintile groups (£ per week).
2 Excluding mortgage interest payments, council tax and Northern Ireland rates.

Table A30

Expenditure of two adult retired households mainly dependent on state pensions[1] by gross income quintile group, 2011-2013

United Kingdom

		Lowest twenty per cent	Second quintile group	Third quintile group	Fourth quintile group	Highest twenty per cent	All house-holds
Lower boundary of group (£ per week)[2]			265	462	696	1,078	
Average weighted number of households (thousands)		150	260	20	..	0	420
Total number of households in sample (over 3 years)		110	190	10	..	0	320
Total number of persons in sample (over 3 years)		220	380	30	..	0	630
Total number of adults in sample (over 3 years)		220	380	30	..	0	630
Weighted average number of persons per household		2.0	2.0	2.0	2.0	0	2.0
Commodity or service		Average weekly household expenditure (£)					
1	Food & non-alcoholic drinks	50.80	56.00	[48.90]	[15.70]	-	53.80
2	Alcoholic drinks, tobacco & narcotics	8.60	7.60	[8.80]	[9.00]	-	8.00
3	Clothing & footwear	8.50	9.00	[17.00]	[0.40]	-	9.20
4	Housing(net)[3], fuel & power	43.80	45.10	[60.10]	[9.90]	-	45.30
5	Household goods & services	14.40	24.50	[7.60]	[0.90]	-	20.20
6	Health	6.70	6.60	[2.60]	-	-	6.40
7	Transport	24.80	33.10	[34.20]	[17.80]	-	30.20
8	Communication	7.40	8.20	[7.50]	[1.60]	-	7.90
9	Recreation & culture	39.00	47.20	[46.80]	[11.50]	-	44.40
10	Education	-	[0.10]	-	-	-	[0.10]
11	Restaurants & hotels	16.70	21.20	[31.00]	[8.60]	-	19.90
12	Miscellaneous goods & services	17.70	34.30	[23.10]	[4.10]	-	27.30
1-12	All expenditure groups	238.50	292.80	[287.40]	[79.60]	-	272.50
13	Other expenditure items	25.50	34.50	[23.00]	[7.60]	-	31.20
Total expenditure		**264.00**	**327.30**	**[310.40]**	**[87.20]**	-	**303.70**
Average weekly expenditure per person (£)							
Total expenditure		**132.00**	**163.60**	**[155.20]**	**[43.60]**	-	**151.90**

Note: The commodity and service categories are not comparable to those in publications before 2001-02.
Please see background notes for symbols and conventions used in this report.
This table is based on a three year average.
1 Mainly dependent on the state pensions and not economically active - see definitions in Appendix B.
2 Lower boundary of 2013 gross income quintile groups (£ per week).
3 Excluding mortgage interest payments, council tax and Northern Ireland rates.

Table A31
Expenditure of two adult retired households not mainly dependent on state pensions by gross income quintile group, 2011-2013
United Kingdom

		Lowest twenty per cent	Second quintile group	Third quintile group	Fourth quintile group	Highest twenty per cent	All house-holds
Lower boundary of group (£ per week)[1]			265	462	696	1,078	
Average weighted number of households (thousands)		190	870	870	410	160	2,490
Total number of households in sample (over 3 years)		110	650	650	300	120	1,820
Total number of persons in sample (over 3 years)		230	1,290	1,290	600	230	3,640
Total number of adults in sample (over 3 years)		230	1,290	1,290	600	230	3,640
Weighted average number of persons per household		2.0	2.0	2.0	2.0	2.0	2.0
Commodity or service		Average weekly household expenditure (£)					
1	Food & non-alcoholic drinks	53.30	55.40	61.70	67.90	83.30	61.20
2	Alcoholic drinks, tobacco & narcotics	8.60	9.20	10.90	14.70	20.70	11.40
3	Clothing & footwear	8.80	11.60	16.70	21.00	41.10	16.50
4	Housing(net)[2], fuel & power	48.00	49.40	49.50	61.50	80.30	53.30
5	Household goods & services	17.10	26.50	29.70	44.60	65.30	32.30
6	Health	3.10	5.90	12.20	19.10	73.30	14.20
7	Transport	21.70	38.00	62.30	75.50	93.70	54.60
8	Communication	9.10	8.60	10.60	11.50	15.20	10.20
9	Recreation & culture	24.60	46.30	82.50	96.90	150.40	71.90
10	Education	-	[2.00]	[0.80]	[2.10]	[10.80]	2.00
11	Restaurants & hotels	17.90	23.20	35.80	46.60	82.80	34.70
12	Miscellaneous goods & services	30.10	23.80	34.10	44.90	78.50	34.60
1-12	All expenditure groups	242.30	300.00	406.90	506.40	795.40	396.90
13	Other expenditure items	19.90	30.60	50.50	62.50	106.90	46.80
Total expenditure		**262.20**	**330.60**	**457.50**	**568.90**	**902.30**	**443.70**
Average weekly expenditure per person (£) Total expenditure		**131.10**	**165.30**	**228.70**	**284.40**	**451.20**	**221.80**

Note: The commodity and service categories are not comparable to those in publications before 2001-02.
Please see background notes for symbols and conventions used in this report.
This table is based on a three year average.
1 Lower boundary of 2013 gross income quintile groups (£ per week).
2 Excluding mortgage interest payments, council tax and Northern Ireland rates.

Table A32
Household expenditure by tenure, 2013
United Kingdom

	Owners			Social rented from			Private rented[4]				All
	Owned outright	**Buying with a mortgage[1]**	**All**	**Council[2]**	**Registered Social Landlord[3]**	**All**	**Rent free**	**Rent paid, unfurn-ished[5]**	**Rent paid, furnished**	**All**	**tenures**
Weighted number of households (thousands)	8,890	8,480	17,370	2,420	2,330	4,750	270	3,550	910	4,720	26,840
Total number of households in sample	1,860	1,600	3,470	460	450	900	50	610	120	780	5,140
Total number of persons in sample	3,570	4,650	8,210	1,000	1,010	2,010	120	1,500	290	1,900	12,120
Total number of adults in sample	3,340	3,210	6,550	740	700	1,430	90	1,040	250	1,370	9,350
Weighted average number of persons per household	1.9	2.9	2.4	2.2	2.3	2.2	2.2	2.4	2.2	2.4	2.4
Commodity or service	Average weekly household expenditure (£)										
1 Food & non-alcoholic drinks	57.80	71.80	64.60	43.30	48.10	45.60	54.60	52.10	43.30	50.60	58.80
2 Alcoholic drinks, tobacco & narcotics	10.70	14.10	12.40	12.20	12.30	12.20	13.30	11.20	7.60	10.60	12.00
3 Clothing & footwear	20.90	31.00	25.80	11.10	12.80	11.90	26.10	20.60	23.90	21.60	22.60
4 Housing(net)[6], fuel & power	48.30	49.40	48.80	71.30	85.60	78.30	31.90	167.40	192.10	164.40	74.40
5 Household goods & services	37.90	43.70	40.70	17.80	18.30	18.10	17.20	22.90	11.80	20.40	33.10
6 Health	9.60	6.90	8.30	2.20	2.10	2.10	[8.10]	2.60	2.00	2.80	6.20
7 Transport	68.10	101.00	84.10	28.20	31.90	30.00	61.40	63.70	48.70	60.70	70.40
8 Communication	12.10	18.40	15.20	11.00	12.00	11.50	13.00	15.20	14.10	14.80	14.50
9 Recreation & culture	70.70	92.20	81.20	28.60	27.80	28.20	42.80	38.30	26.60	36.30	63.90
10 Education	4.50	8.30	6.40	[0.80]	4.80	2.70	[7.80]	16.40	[57.80]	23.90	8.80
11 Restaurants & hotels	40.40	55.30	47.70	16.10	17.90	17.00	37.30	34.40	47.40	37.00	40.40
12 Miscellaneous goods & services	38.60	56.90	47.60	14.50	19.00	16.70	31.20	32.60	22.60	30.60	39.10
1-12 All expenditure groups	419.60	548.80	482.70	257.00	292.50	274.40	344.60	477.50	497.90	473.80	444.30
13 Other expenditure items	55.20	141.20	97.20	16.50	18.40	17.40	38.10	42.40	31.30	40.00	73.00
Total expenditure	**474.80**	**690.00**	**579.90**	**273.50**	**310.80**	**291.80**	**382.80**	**519.90**	**529.30**	**513.90**	**517.30**
Average weekly expenditure per person (£)											
Total expenditure	**246.40**	**240.30**	**242.80**	**126.90**	**135.70**	**131.30**	**175.70**	**213.40**	**236.40**	**215.60**	**219.40**

Note: The commodity and service categories are not comparable to those in publications before 2001-02.
Please see background notes for symbols and conventions used in this report.
1 Including shared owners (who own part of the equity and pay mortgage, part rent).
2 "Council" includes local authorities, New Towns and Scottish Homes, but see note 3 below.
3 Formerly Housing Associations.
4 All tenants whose accommodation goes with the job of someone in the household are allocated to "rented privately", even if the landlord is a local authority or housing association or Housing Action Trust, or if the accommodation is rent free. Squatters are also included in this category.
5 "Unfurnished" includes the answers: "partly furnished".
6 Excluding mortgage interest payments, council tax and Northern Ireland rates.

Table A33
Household expenditure by UK countries and regions, 2011-2013

		North East	North West	Yorks & the Humber	East Midlands	West Midlands	East	London	South East	South West	England	Wales	Scotland	Northern Ireland	United Kingdom
Average weighted number of households (thousands)		1,130	2,970	2,310	1,950	2,330	2,500	3,190	3,540	2,200	22,130	1,250	2,330	740	26,450
Total number of households in sample (over 3 years)		800	1,860	1,500	1,300	1,570	1,600	1,510	2,230	1,430	13,790	760	1,400	480	16,430
Total number of persons in sample (over 3 years)		1,820	4,340	3,490	3,000	3,770	3,820	3,770	5,300	3,330	32,640	1,800	3,100	1,200	38,740
Total number of adults in sample (over 3 years)		1,430	3,320	2,690	2,360	2,910	2,940	2,770	4,070	2,610	25,090	1,410	2,460	920	29,880
Weighted average number of persons per household		2.2	2.3	2.3	2.3	2.4	2.3	2.5	2.4	2.4	2.4	2.4	2.2	2.4	2.4
Commodity or service		Average weekly household expenditure (£)													
1	Food & non-alcoholic drinks	48.60	53.00	49.80	55.40	53.90	60.10	60.30	63.20	59.80	56.90	55.30	54.80	62.60	56.80
2	Alcoholic drinks, tobacco & narcotics	12.00	12.50	12.30	12.00	11.90	11.60	10.60	12.60	11.30	11.90	10.60	14.90	15.30	12.20
3	Clothing & footwear	22.40	21.70	19.80	19.70	19.70	20.40	25.30	24.60	23.20	22.10	22.20	23.00	35.00	22.60
4	Housing(net)[1], fuel & power	58.70	63.30	61.30	60.80	61.20	69.00	103.20	74.80	65.30	70.80	56.70	56.90	56.50	68.50
5	Household goods & services	28.80	30.80	26.00	28.20	27.50	30.50	31.00	35.50	32.00	30.50	23.40	26.50	25.20	29.60
6	Health	3.30	4.20	5.30	6.60	5.30	6.90	6.50	10.70	8.20	6.70	4.80	4.80	6.30	6.40
7	Transport	52.20	58.00	57.90	66.10	63.60	75.20	62.50	84.50	73.10	67.30	60.70	65.80	65.40	66.80
8	Communication	12.20	12.70	12.50	13.80	13.30	14.50	16.20	14.80	14.00	14.00	13.30	12.60	14.40	13.80
9	Recreation & culture	57.70	60.10	56.40	63.20	59.60	70.70	60.50	75.60	67.80	64.30	61.50	54.30	57.70	63.10
10	Education	5.30	5.60	4.80	9.30	7.70	5.10	13.10	7.80	10.30	7.90	11.70	3.50	2.90	7.50
11	Restaurants & hotels	35.30	37.10	36.80	34.00	36.90	39.80	50.10	46.10	41.60	40.70	32.70	36.80	47.10	40.20
12	Miscellaneous goods & services	31.00	37.80	34.80	38.40	35.80	42.30	41.40	47.90	38.80	39.70	31.80	32.50	40.70	38.70
1-12	All expenditure groups	367.60	396.80	377.60	407.40	396.20	446.20	480.60	498.00	445.50	432.80	384.60	386.50	429.10	426.30
13	Other expenditure items	57.00	61.90	53.50	59.30	59.30	77.20	99.00	87.40	72.70	72.60	54.20	62.40	55.50	70.30
Total expenditure		**424.60**	**458.70**	**431.10**	**466.70**	**455.50**	**523.40**	**579.60**	**585.40**	**518.20**	**505.40**	**438.80**	**449.00**	**484.70**	**496.70**
Average weekly expenditure per person (£) Total expenditure		**190.50**	**197.10**	**189.00**	**204.40**	**192.30**	**224.50**	**231.00**	**244.20**	**218.40**	**214.10**	**182.80**	**202.10**	**200.70**	**211.20**

Note: The commodity and service categories are not comparable to those in publications before 2001-02.
Please see background notes for symbols and conventions used in this report.
This table is based on a three year average.
1 Excluding mortgage interest payments, council tax and Northern Ireland rates.

Table A34
Household expenditure as a percentage of total expenditure by UK countries and regions, 2011-2013

	North East	North West	Yorks & the Humber	East Midlands	West Midlands	East	London	South East	South West	England	Wales	Scotland	Northern Ireland	United Kingdom
Average weighted number of households (thousands)	1,130	2,970	2,310	1,950	2,330	2,500	3,190	3,540	2,200	22,130	1,250	2,330	740	26,450
Total number of households in sample (over 3 years)	800	1,860	1,500	1,300	1,570	1,600	1,510	2,230	1,430	13,790	760	1,400	480	16,430
Total number of persons in sample (over 3 years)	1,820	4,340	3,490	3,000	3,770	3,820	3,770	5,300	3,330	32,640	1,800	3,100	1,200	38,740
Total number of adults in sample (over 3 years)	1,430	3,320	2,690	2,360	2,910	2,940	2,770	4,070	2,610	25,090	1,410	2,460	920	29,880
Weighted average number of persons per household	2.2	2.3	2.3	2.3	2.4	2.3	2.5	2.4	2.4	2.4	2.4	2.2	2.4	2.4
Commodity or service					Percentage of total expenditure									
1 Food & non-alcoholic drinks	*11*	*12*	*12*	*12*	*12*	*11*	*10*	*11*	*12*	*11*	*13*	*12*	*13*	*11*
2 Alcoholic drinks, tobacco & narcotics	*3*	*3*	*3*	*3*	*3*	*2*	*2*	*2*	*2*	*2*	*2*	*3*	*3*	*2*
3 Clothing & footwear	*5*	*5*	*5*	*4*	*4*	*4*	*4*	*4*	*4*	*4*	*5*	*5*	*7*	*5*
4 Housing(net)[1], fuel & power	*14*	*14*	*14*	*13*	*13*	*13*	*18*	*13*	*13*	*14*	*13*	*13*	*12*	*14*
5 Household goods & services	*7*	*7*	*6*	*6*	*6*	*6*	*5*	*6*	*6*	*6*	*5*	*6*	*5*	*6*
6 Health	*1*	*1*	*1*	*1*	*1*	*1*	*1*	*2*	*2*	*1*	*1*	*1*	*1*	*1*
7 Transport	*12*	*13*	*13*	*14*	*14*	*14*	*11*	*14*	*14*	*13*	*14*	*15*	*13*	*13*
8 Communication	*3*	*3*	*3*	*3*	*3*	*3*	*3*	*3*	*3*	*3*	*3*	*3*	*3*	*3*
9 Recreation & culture	*14*	*13*	*13*	*14*	*13*	*14*	*10*	*13*	*13*	*13*	*14*	*12*	*12*	*13*
10 Education	*1*	*1*	*1*	*2*	*2*	*1*	*2*	*1*	*2*	*2*	*3*	*1*	*1*	*2*
11 Restaurants & hotels	*8*	*8*	*9*	*7*	*8*	*8*	*9*	*8*	*8*	*8*	*7*	*8*	*10*	*8*
12 Miscellaneous goods & services	*7*	*8*	*8*	*8*	*8*	*8*	*7*	*8*	*7*	*8*	*7*	*7*	*8*	*8*
1-12 All expenditure groups	*87*	*87*	*88*	*87*	*87*	*85*	*83*	*85*	*86*	*86*	*88*	*86*	*89*	*86*
13 Other expenditure items	*13*	*13*	*12*	*13*	*13*	*15*	*17*	*15*	*14*	*14*	*12*	*14*	*11*	*14*
Total expenditure	***100***	***100***	***100***	***100***	***100***	***100***	***100***	***100***	***100***	***100***	***100***	***100***	***100***	***100***

Note: The commodity and service categories are not comparable to those in publications before 2001-02.
Please see background notes for symbols and conventions used in this report.
This table is based on a three year average.
1 Excluding mortgage interest payments, council tax and Northern Ireland rates.

Table A35
Detailed household expenditure by UK countries and regions, 2011-2013

	North East	North West	Yorks & the Humber	East Midlands	West Midlands	East	London	South East	South West	England	Wales	Scotland	Northern Ireland	United Kingdom
Average weighted number of households (thousands)	1,130	2,970	2,310	1,950	2,330	2,500	3,190	3,540	2,200	22,130	1,250	2,330	740	26,450
Total number of households in sample (over 3 years)	800	1,860	1,500	1,300	1,570	1,600	1,510	2,230	1,430	13,790	760	1,400	480	16,430
Total number of persons in sample (over 3 years)	1,820	4,340	3,490	3,000	3,770	3,820	3,770	5,300	3,330	32,640	1,800	3,100	1,200	38,740
Total number of adults in sample (over 3 years)	1,430	3,320	2,690	2,360	2,910	2,940	2,770	4,070	2,610	25,090	1,410	2,460	920	29,880
Weighted average number of persons per household	2.2	2.3	2.3	2.3	2.4	2.3	2.5	2.4	2.4	2.4	2.4	2.2	2.4	2.4
Commodity or service	Average weekly household expenditure (£)													
1 Food & non-alcoholic drinks	**48.60**	**53.00**	**49.80**	**55.40**	**53.90**	**60.10**	**60.30**	**63.20**	**59.80**	**56.90**	**55.30**	**54.80**	**62.60**	**56.80**
1.1 Food	44.60	48.50	45.70	51.00	49.30	55.20	55.30	58.10	55.00	52.20	50.70	49.70	57.30	52.10
1.1.1 Bread, rice and cereals	4.80	5.20	4.80	5.30	5.30	5.50	5.60	5.50	5.50	5.30	5.20	5.30	6.10	5.30
1.1.2 Pasta products	0.40	0.40	0.40	0.40	0.40	0.50	0.60	0.50	0.40	0.40	0.40	0.40	0.40	0.40
1.1.3 Buns, cakes, biscuits etc.	3.10	3.20	3.10	3.50	3.40	3.80	3.50	3.80	4.00	3.50	3.30	3.30	4.30	3.50
1.1.4 Pastry (savoury)	0.80	0.80	0.80	0.70	0.70	0.80	0.70	0.80	0.80	0.80	0.60	0.80	0.60	0.80
1.1.5 Beef (fresh, chilled or frozen)	1.70	1.60	1.60	1.80	1.70	1.90	1.60	1.90	1.70	1.70	1.70	2.00	3.20	1.80
1.1.6 Pork (fresh, chilled or frozen)	0.70	0.60	0.60	0.70	0.70	0.80	0.70	0.70	0.80	0.70	0.80	0.50	0.80	0.70
1.1.7 Lamb (fresh, chilled or frozen)	0.40	0.60	0.50	0.50	0.70	0.70	1.20	0.80	0.60	0.70	0.70	0.30	0.40	0.70
1.1.8 Poultry (fresh, chilled or frozen)	1.80	2.20	1.90	2.30	2.20	2.50	2.70	2.50	2.20	2.30	2.20	2.10	2.80	2.30
1.1.9 Bacon and ham	0.90	1.10	0.90	1.00	1.00	1.00	0.70	1.10	1.10	1.00	1.10	1.20	1.50	1.00
1.1.10 Other meat and meat preparations	5.90	6.00	5.50	5.60	5.70	6.10	5.50	6.30	6.10	5.90	6.50	6.70	7.00	6.00
1.1.11 Fish and fish products	2.00	2.20	2.20	2.20	2.30	2.80	3.30	2.90	2.50	2.60	2.20	2.20	2.10	2.50
1.1.12 Milk	2.20	2.50	2.40	2.70	2.40	2.50	2.40	2.50	2.70	2.50	2.60	2.20	2.70	2.50
1.1.13 Cheese and curd	1.40	1.70	1.70	2.00	1.80	2.20	2.00	2.30	2.20	2.00	1.70	1.70	1.70	1.90
1.1.14 Eggs	0.60	0.70	0.60	0.70	0.60	0.70	0.80	0.80	0.70	0.70	0.60	0.60	0.70	0.70
1.1.15 Other milk products	1.60	1.80	1.70	2.00	1.80	2.20	2.10	2.40	2.30	2.00	1.80	1.80	2.00	2.00
1.1.16 Butter	0.50	0.50	0.40	0.50	0.40	0.50	0.40	0.50	0.50	0.50	0.40	0.60	0.50	0.50
1.1.17 Margarine, other vegetable fats and peanut butter	0.40	0.50	0.50	0.60	0.60	0.60	0.40	0.60	0.60	0.50	0.60	0.50	0.40	0.50
1.1.18 Cooking oils and fats	0.30	0.30	0.30	0.30	0.30	0.30	0.50	0.30	0.30	0.30	0.30	0.20	0.30	0.30
1.1.19 Fresh fruit	2.20	2.70	2.70	3.00	2.80	3.50	3.90	4.00	3.60	3.30	2.80	2.80	3.30	3.20
1.1.20 Other fresh, chilled or frozen fruits	0.30	0.30	0.30	0.30	0.30	0.40	0.50	0.50	0.40	0.40	0.30	0.30	0.50	0.40
1.1.21 Dried fruit and nuts	0.40	0.50	0.50	0.60	0.50	0.70	0.90	0.90	0.70	0.70	0.50	0.50	0.60	0.60
1.1.22 Preserved fruit and fruit based products	0.10	0.10	0.10	0.10	0.10	0.20	0.10	0.10	0.20	0.10	0.10	0.10	0.10	0.10
1.1.23 Fresh vegetables	3.10	3.50	3.40	4.10	3.80	4.60	5.20	5.30	4.60	4.30	3.80	3.20	3.60	4.20
1.1.24 Dried vegetables	0.00	0.00	0.00	0.10	0.00	0.00	0.10	0.10	0.00	0.10	0.00	0.10	0.00	0.10
1.1.25 Other preserved or processed vegetables	1.20	1.20	1.10	1.30	1.30	1.50	1.70	1.50	1.40	1.40	1.30	1.20	1.30	1.40
1.1.26 Potatoes	0.80	0.90	0.80	0.90	0.90	0.90	0.80	1.00	0.90	0.90	1.00	0.80	1.40	0.90
1.1.27 Other tubers and products of tuber vegetables	1.50	1.50	1.40	1.50	1.60	1.60	1.20	1.50	1.50	1.50	1.60	1.80	1.90	1.50
1.1.28 Sugar and sugar products	0.30	0.40	0.30	0.50	0.40	0.50	0.40	0.50	0.50	0.40	0.50	0.30	0.40	0.40
1.1.29 Jams, marmalades	0.20	0.20	0.20	0.30	0.20	0.30	0.40	0.30	0.30	0.30	0.30	0.30	0.40	0.30
1.1.30 Chocolate	1.70	1.70	1.50	1.70	1.70	1.80	1.50	1.90	1.90	1.70	1.90	1.80	2.10	1.70
1.1.31 Confectionery products	0.70	0.70	0.70	0.70	0.70	0.70	0.50	0.70	0.60	0.60	0.70	0.80	0.90	0.70
1.1.32 Edible ices and ice cream	0.50	0.50	0.50	0.50	0.50	0.60	0.60	0.70	0.60	0.60	0.50	0.60	0.60	0.60
1.1.33 Other food products	2.30	2.40	2.20	2.60	2.30	2.80	2.70	2.90	2.60	2.60	2.40	2.50	2.70	2.60
1.2 Non-alcoholic drinks	4.00	4.50	4.10	4.40	4.60	4.90	5.10	5.10	4.70	4.70	4.60	5.10	5.30	4.70
1.2.1 Coffee	0.60	0.70	0.70	0.70	0.70	0.70	0.60	0.80	0.80	0.70	0.80	0.70	0.70	0.70
1.2.2 Tea	0.40	0.50	0.40	0.50	0.50	0.50	0.50	0.50	0.60	0.50	0.50	0.40	0.60	0.50
1.2.3 Cocoa and powdered chocolate	0.10	0.10	0.10	0.10	0.10	0.10	0.10	0.20	0.10	0.10	0.10	0.10	0.10	0.10
1.2.4 Fruit and vegetable juices (inc. fruit squash)	0.90	1.10	1.00	1.10	1.20	1.40	1.40	1.50	1.30	1.20	1.10	1.20	1.10	1.20
1.2.5 Mineral or spring waters	0.20	0.20	0.20	0.20	0.20	0.20	0.50	0.30	0.20	0.30	0.20	0.30	0.40	0.30
1.2.6 Soft drinks (inc. fizzy and ready to drink fruit drinks)	1.90	1.80	1.70	1.80	1.90	1.90	2.00	1.90	1.60	1.80	1.90	2.50	2.50	1.90

Note: The commodity and service categories are not comparable to those in publications before 2001-02.
The numbering system is sequential, it does not use actual COICOP codes.
Please see background notes for symbols and conventions used in this report.
This table is based on a three year average.

Table A35
Detailed household expenditure by UK countries and regions, 2011-2013 (cont.)

	Commodity or service	North East	North West	Yorks & the Humber	East Midlands	West Midlands	East	London	South East	South West	England	Wales	Scotland	Northern Ireland	United Kingdom
		Average weekly household expenditure (£)													
2	**Alcoholic drink, tobacco & narcot**	**12.00**	**12.50**	**12.30**	**12.00**	**11.90**	**11.60**	**10.60**	**12.60**	**11.30**	**11.90**	**10.60**	**14.90**	**15.30**	**12.20**
2.1	Alcoholic drinks	7.00	7.50	7.50	7.80	7.30	7.80	6.90	8.40	7.70	7.60	6.40	8.10	7.90	7.60
2.1.1	Spirits and liqueurs (brought home)	1.70	1.50	1.60	1.60	1.70	1.40	1.40	1.40	1.40	1.50	1.00	2.20	2.10	1.50
2.1.2	Wines, fortified wines (brought home)	2.80	3.70	3.30	3.90	3.30	4.50	4.10	5.10	4.40	4.00	3.10	4.10	3.40	4.00
2.1.3	Beer, lager, ciders and perry (brought home)	2.50	2.20	2.60	2.30	2.20	1.90	1.40	2.00	1.90	2.00	2.20	1.70	2.20	2.00
2.1.4	Alcopops (brought home)	[0.00]	0.10	0.00	0.10	0.10	0.10	[0.00]	0.10	0.00	0.00	[0.10]	0.10	[0.20]	0.10
2.2	Tobacco and narcotics	5.10	5.00	4.80	4.20	4.70	3.90	3.70	4.20	3.70	4.30	4.30	6.80	7.50	4.60
2.2.1	Cigarettes	4.40	4.30	4.10	3.50	3.80	3.00	3.30	3.40	2.40	3.50	3.30	6.00	6.60	3.80
2.2.2	Cigars, other tobacco products and narcotics	0.70	0.70	0.80	0.70	0.90	0.90	0.40	0.80	1.30	0.80	1.00	0.80	0.90	0.80
3	**Clothing & footwear**	**22.40**	**21.70**	**19.80**	**19.70**	**19.70**	**20.40**	**25.30**	**24.60**	**23.20**	**22.10**	**22.20**	**23.00**	**35.00**	**22.60**
3.1	Clothing	18.20	17.70	15.90	15.60	16.10	16.70	20.60	19.30	18.80	17.80	17.90	18.90	27.50	18.20
3.1.1	Men's outer garments	4.40	4.20	4.40	3.80	4.20	3.90	5.90	4.70	4.30	4.50	3.50	5.00	9.00	4.60
3.1.2	Men's under garments	0.50	0.40	0.30	0.40	0.40	0.40	0.50	0.50	0.40	0.40	0.50	0.40	0.60	0.40
3.1.3	Women's outer garments	8.30	7.70	6.70	7.10	6.50	7.60	8.40	8.20	8.90	7.70	7.90	8.00	10.90	7.90
3.1.4	Women's under garments	1.00	1.00	0.90	1.00	1.00	1.10	1.00	1.40	1.30	1.10	1.10	1.00	1.60	1.10
3.1.5	Boys' outer garments (5-15)	0.80	0.80	0.70	0.60	0.80	0.70	0.70	0.70	0.60	0.70	1.20	0.80	1.20	0.80
3.1.6	Girls' outer garments (5-15)	0.90	1.20	0.90	0.70	0.90	0.90	1.10	1.00	0.80	0.90	1.40	1.10	1.40	1.00
3.1.7	Infants' outer garments (under 5)	0.70	0.80	0.70	0.70	0.60	0.60	0.90	0.70	0.70	0.70	1.00	1.00	1.00	0.80
3.1.8	Children's under garments (under 16)	0.40	0.40	0.30	0.20	0.40	0.40	0.40	0.50	0.30	0.40	0.50	0.40	0.40	0.40
3.1.9	Accessories	0.90	0.70	0.40	0.60	0.70	0.60	0.90	0.90	0.90	0.80	0.60	0.80	0.90	0.80
3.1.10	Haberdashery, clothing materials and clothing hire	0.10	0.20	0.30	0.30	0.30	0.20	0.10	0.40	0.30	0.20	0.20	0.20	[0.10]	0.20
3.1.11	Dry cleaners, laundry and dyeing	[0.20]	0.20	0.10	0.10	0.10	0.30	0.60	0.40	0.10	0.30	[0.20]	0.10	[0.30]	0.20
3.2	Footwear	4.30	4.00	3.80	4.00	3.60	3.80	4.70	5.30	4.40	4.30	4.30	4.20	7.60	4.40
4	**Housing (net)[1], fuel & power**	**58.70**	**63.30**	**61.30**	**60.80**	**61.20**	**69.00**	**103.20**	**74.80**	**65.30**	**70.80**	**56.70**	**56.90**	**56.50**	**68.50**
4.1	Actual rentals for housing	45.10	42.10	39.90	34.00	37.60	39.70	93.80	44.90	34.80	47.70	32.40	31.80	27.10	45.00
4.1.1	Gross rent	44.90	42.10	39.80	33.70	37.60	39.60	93.80	44.90	34.50	47.60	32.40	31.60	27.10	44.90
4.1.2	*less* housing benefit, rebates & allowances rec'd	20.80	17.20	15.50	12.30	15.00	11.40	31.30	13.30	10.80	16.70	13.70	13.80	10.90	16.10
4.1.3	Net rent[2]	24.00	24.90	24.30	21.40	22.60	28.30	62.50	31.50	23.70	31.00	18.70	17.80	16.20	28.80
4.1.4	Second dwelling rent	[0.20]	[0.00]	[0.10]	[0.30]	[0.00]	[0.10]	[0.00]	[0.00]	[0.30]	0.10	[0.00]	[0.20]	-	0.10
4.2	Maintenance and repair of dwelling	5.00	7.10	6.30	7.40	6.10	7.80	7.30	9.80	8.10	7.50	5.20	6.70	5.40	7.20
4.3	Water supply and miscellaneous services relating to the dwelling	7.50	8.60	7.80	7.80	8.30	8.60	10.60	8.90	10.10	8.80	8.60	7.30	0.50	8.40
4.4	Electricity, gas and other fuels[3]	22.00	22.70	22.90	23.90	24.20	24.20	22.70	24.50	23.10	23.50	24.10	25.00	34.40	23.90
4.4.1	Electricity	10.10	10.70	10.30	10.70	11.20	11.50	10.30	11.60	11.50	10.90	11.20	11.80	12.10	11.10
4.4.2	Gas	10.90	11.40	11.40	11.00	11.60	10.20	12.40	11.50	8.70	11.10	10.70	11.40	3.00	10.90
4.4.3	Other fuels	1.00	0.60	1.10	2.20	1.30	2.50	0.10	1.40	2.90	1.40	2.20	1.80	19.30	2.00

Note: The commodity and service categories are not comparable to those in publications before 2001-02.
The numbering system is sequential, it does not use actual COICOP codes.
Please see background notes for symbols and conventions used in this report.
This table is based on a three year average.
1 Excluding mortgage interest payments, council tax and Northern Ireland rates.
2 The figure included in total expenditure is net rent as opposed to gross rent.
3 Recording of expenditure on gas and electricity via combined payment packages was changed in 2013. Recording of expenditure via slot meters was also changed.

Table A35
Detailed household expenditure by UK countries and regions, 2011-2013 (cont.)

	Commodity or service	North East	North West	Yorks & the Humber	East Midlands	West Midlands	East	London	South East	South West	England	Wales	Scotland	Northern Ireland	United Kingdom
		Average weekly household expenditure (£)													
5	**Household goods & services**	**28.80**	**30.80**	**26.00**	**28.20**	**27.50**	**30.50**	**31.00**	**35.50**	**32.00**	**30.50**	**23.40**	**26.50**	**25.20**	**29.60**
5.1	Furniture and furnishings, carpets and other floor coverings[4]	16.00	17.20	12.70	13.90	13.50	15.50	17.10	18.50	16.40	15.90	11.80	13.90	12.10	15.40
5.1.1	Furniture and furnishings	11.80	13.40	10.80	10.40	10.80	12.70	14.00	14.00	13.00	12.60	8.80	11.60	8.90	12.20
5.1.2	Floor coverings	4.20	3.80	1.90	3.50	2.80	2.70	3.10	4.50	3.40	3.30	3.10	2.30	3.10	3.20
5.2	Household textiles	1.80	1.70	1.60	1.50	1.60	1.60	1.50	1.50	2.20	1.60	1.40	1.60	1.90	1.60
5.3	Household appliances	2.60	4.10	2.90	3.70	3.10	2.60	2.60	3.80	3.30	3.30	2.00	3.10	1.80	3.10
5.4	Glassware, tableware and household utensils	1.60	1.30	1.20	1.30	1.30	1.70	1.60	2.00	1.70	1.60	1.20	1.40	1.60	1.50
5.5	Tools and equipment for house and garden	2.50	1.70	2.20	2.50	2.20	2.40	1.90	2.40	2.20	2.20	1.90	1.70	2.00	2.10
5.6	Goods and services for routine household maintenance	4.30	4.70	5.30	5.40	5.70	6.70	6.30	7.40	6.20	5.90	5.00	4.80	5.80	5.80
5.6.1	Cleaning materials	1.80	2.10	2.10	2.20	2.30	2.60	2.30	2.70	2.30	2.30	2.30	2.10	2.20	2.30
5.6.2	Household goods and hardware	1.00	1.10	1.10	1.20	1.30	1.50	1.60	1.80	1.50	1.40	1.20	1.20	1.40	1.40
5.6.3	Domestic services, carpet cleaning and hire/repair of furniture/furnishings	1.50	1.60	2.20	1.90	2.00	2.60	2.40	2.90	2.40	2.20	1.50	1.50	2.20	2.10
6	**Health**	**3.30**	**4.20**	**5.30**	**6.60**	**5.30**	**6.90**	**6.50**	**10.70**	**8.20**	**6.70**	**4.80**	**4.80**	**6.30**	**6.40**
6.1	Medical products, appliances and equipment	2.20	2.40	3.50	4.00	3.60	4.10	3.60	4.20	5.20	3.70	2.80	2.50	2.70	3.50
6.1.1	Medicines, prescriptions, healthcare products and equipment	1.10	1.50	2.10	2.10	2.40	2.60	2.10	2.30	2.80	2.20	1.30	1.50	1.60	2.00
6.1.2	Spectacles, lenses, accessories and repairs	1.10	0.90	1.50	1.90	1.20	1.50	1.50	1.90	2.50	1.60	1.40	1.10	[1.10]	1.50
6.2	Hospital services	1.10	1.80	1.70	2.60	1.70	2.90	2.90	6.50	3.00	3.00	2.00	2.30	3.50	2.90
7	**Transport**	**52.20**	**58.00**	**57.90**	**66.10**	**63.60**	**75.20**	**62.50**	**84.50**	**73.10**	**67.30**	**60.70**	**65.80**	**65.40**	**66.80**
7.1	Purchase of vehicles	15.20	17.70	18.20	20.30	18.80	21.10	14.60	25.30	20.30	19.40	18.10	21.00	8.00	19.10
7.1.1	Purchase of new cars and vans	4.20	5.90	5.80	6.20	7.00	6.60	3.60	9.00	4.40	6.00	5.50	8.70	[4.40]	6.20
7.1.2	Purchase of second hand cars or vans	10.60	11.40	11.80	13.10	11.40	13.90	10.30	15.30	15.10	12.60	12.10	11.80	3.50	12.30
7.1.3	Purchase of motorcycles and other vehicles	[0.50]	[0.30]	0.60	[1.10]	[0.50]	[0.60]	0.80	1.10	0.90	0.70	[0.60]	[0.50]	[0.00]	0.70
7.2	Operation of personal transport	29.00	30.70	31.50	37.50	35.40	41.00	25.30	44.20	43.50	35.60	36.40	32.30	45.30	35.60
7.2.1	Spares and accessories	2.20	1.60	1.40	2.60	2.60	3.00	1.20	3.10	3.90	2.40	2.20	1.90	2.30	2.30
7.2.2	Petrol, diesel and other motor oils	21.00	22.40	22.70	25.10	24.70	26.90	16.30	28.60	27.50	24.00	27.60	23.20	35.10	24.40
7.2.3	Repairs and servicing	4.00	4.80	5.40	7.30	5.60	8.40	5.80	9.10	8.80	6.80	4.50	5.50	5.90	6.50
7.2.4	Other motoring costs	1.90	1.90	2.00	2.50	2.60	2.80	2.00	3.40	3.30	2.50	2.10	1.70	1.90	2.40
7.3	Transport services[5]	7.90	9.60	8.30	8.30	9.30	13.10	22.60	14.90	9.30	12.30	6.20	12.40	12.10	12.00
7.3.1	Rail and tube fares	1.90	2.00	1.80	1.70	1.70	5.80	7.10	6.20	1.60	3.70	1.00	2.20	0.80	3.40
7.3.2	Bus and coach fares	1.90	1.90	1.60	1.70	2.00	0.90	1.70	1.40	1.30	1.60	0.70	2.10	1.10	1.60
7.3.3	Combined fares	[0.20]	[0.10]	[0.10]	[0.10]	[0.10]	0.40	5.20	0.40	[0.00]	0.90	[0.00]	[0.00]	[0.10]	0.80
7.3.4	Other travel and transport	4.00	5.50	4.80	4.90	5.50	6.00	8.60	6.90	6.40	6.10	4.50	8.10	10.20	6.30
8	**Communication**	**12.20**	**12.70**	**12.50**	**13.80**	**13.30**	**14.50**	**16.20**	**14.80**	**14.00**	**14.00**	**13.30**	**12.60**	**14.40**	**13.80**
8.1	Postal services	0.50	0.50	0.60	0.70	0.40	0.60	0.70	0.60	0.80	0.60	0.40	0.60	0.70	0.60
8.2	Telephone and telefax equipment	0.40	0.40	0.50	0.50	0.60	0.50	0.60	0.50	0.60	0.50	1.20	0.20	[0.70]	0.50
8.3	Telephone and telefax services	9.00	9.50	9.20	10.10	10.00	10.50	12.10	10.90	9.90	10.30	9.30	9.30	10.40	10.20
8.4	Internet subscription fees	2.30	2.30	2.20	2.50	2.40	2.90	2.80	2.90	2.70	2.60	2.40	2.50	2.60	2.60

Note: The commodity and service categories are not comparable to those in publications before 2001-02.

The numbering system is sequential, it does not use actual COICOP codes.

Please see background notes for symbols and conventions used in this report.

This table is based on a three year average.

4 Recording of expenditure on furniture was changed in 2013.

5 Recording of expenditure on flights was changed in 2013.

ONS, Family Spending 2013,

Table A35
Detailed household expenditure by UK countries and regions, 2011-2013 (cont.)

Commodity or service	North East	North West	Yorks & the Humber	East Midlands	West Midlands	East	London	South East	South West	England	Wales	Scotland	Northern Ireland	United Kingdom
	Average weekly household expenditure (£)													
9 Recreation & culture	**57.70**	**60.10**	**56.40**	**63.20**	**59.60**	**70.70**	**60.50**	**75.60**	**67.80**	**64.30**	**61.50**	**54.30**	**57.70**	**63.10**
9.1 Audio-visual, photographic and information processing equipment	5.40	4.30	5.50	6.70	5.10	7.80	5.70	6.10	4.90	5.70	5.20	4.30	5.90	5.60
9.1.1 Audio equipment and accessories, CD players	0.70	0.80	1.10	1.20	0.90	1.40	0.70	1.00	1.20	1.00	1.00	0.90	0.80	1.00
9.1.2 TV, video and computers	4.40	3.00	4.30	5.10	3.80	5.20	4.70	4.60	3.40	4.30	4.20	2.90	4.70	4.10
9.1.3 Photographic, cine and optical equipment	[0.30]	0.40	0.20	[0.30]	[0.30]	[1.20]	0.40	0.60	0.30	0.50	[0.10]	[0.50]	[0.40]	0.40
9.2 Other major durables for recreation and culture	[0.50]	2.40	1.50	3.10	2.80	2.20	0.80	1.50	2.60	1.90	[1.80]	1.30	[0.30]	1.80
9.3 Other recreational items and equipment, gardens and pets	8.80	10.30	9.60	11.20	10.60	12.30	8.20	14.10	13.60	11.10	10.90	9.80	10.10	11.00
9.3.1 Games, toys and hobbies	2.50	2.40	2.20	2.20	1.90	2.10	1.90	2.70	2.70	2.30	2.40	2.20	1.80	2.30
9.3.2 Computer software and games	1.20	1.10	0.80	0.80	1.00	1.00	1.40	1.70	1.10	1.20	0.90	0.70	0.70	1.10
9.3.3 Equipment for sport, camping and open-air recreation	0.90	1.00	0.80	1.20	0.80	1.10	1.00	1.00	1.00	1.00	0.70	0.80	1.00	0.90
9.3.4 Horticultural goods, garden equipment and plants	1.90	2.30	1.90	2.50	2.20	2.80	1.60	3.10	2.70	2.40	2.20	2.20	2.80	2.30
9.3.5 Pets and pet food	2.30	3.50	3.90	4.50	4.80	5.30	2.30	5.50	6.20	4.30	4.60	4.00	3.80	4.30
9.4 Recreational and cultural services	17.70	19.10	16.50	17.50	17.30	19.30	20.80	24.60	19.70	19.60	17.40	18.10	18.90	19.40
9.4.1 Sports admissions, subscriptions, leisure class fees and equipment hire	4.50	5.60	4.20	5.00	4.90	5.80	8.40	9.30	6.10	6.30	3.90	4.60	4.70	6.00
9.4.2 Cinema, theatre and museums etc.	1.90	2.20	1.90	2.00	2.00	2.30	2.80	4.10	2.30	2.50	2.10	2.00	1.80	2.40
9.4.3 TV, video, satellite rental, cable subscriptions and TV licences	6.60	6.90	6.10	6.40	6.60	6.70	6.20	6.80	6.30	6.50	7.40	7.00	6.60	6.60
9.4.4 Miscellaneous entertainments	0.90	0.90	1.20	1.10	0.90	1.20	1.10	1.50	1.80	1.20	0.90	1.20	1.10	1.20
9.4.5 Development of film, deposit for film development, passport photos, holiday and school photos	[0.10]	0.20	0.10	0.40	0.30	0.50	0.40	0.30	0.40	0.30	0.20	0.20	[0.40]	0.30
9.4.6 Gambling payments	3.70	3.30	2.90	2.50	2.60	2.80	2.00	2.70	2.90	2.80	2.90	3.10	4.40	2.80
9.5 Newspapers, books and stationery	4.80	4.90	4.90	5.20	5.00	5.80	5.60	6.60	6.50	5.60	5.20	5.70	5.50	5.60
9.5.1 Books	0.80	1.10	1.00	0.90	0.90	1.30	1.70	1.40	1.50	1.20	1.10	1.10	0.90	1.20
9.5.2 Diaries, address books, cards etc.	1.70	1.70	1.60	1.90	1.70	2.10	1.80	2.40	2.20	1.90	1.80	1.70	1.50	1.90
9.5.3 Newspapers	1.70	1.40	1.50	1.60	1.50	1.60	1.40	1.90	1.70	1.60	1.60	2.20	2.30	1.70
9.5.4 Magazines and periodicals	0.60	0.70	0.80	0.70	0.90	0.90	0.70	0.90	1.10	0.80	0.70	0.70	0.80	0.80
9.6 Package holidays[6]	20.50	19.20	18.50	19.60	18.70	23.30	19.30	22.60	20.50	20.30	20.90	14.90	17.00	19.80
9.6.1 Package holidays - UK	1.20	1.40	1.50	2.00	1.70	2.10	1.00	2.00	1.30	1.60	2.10	1.00	[0.90]	1.50
9.6.2 Package holidays - abroad	19.30	17.80	17.00	17.60	17.00	21.20	18.30	20.70	19.20	18.70	18.80	14.00	16.10	18.30
10 Education	**5.30**	**5.60**	**4.80**	**9.30**	**7.70**	**5.10**	**13.10**	**7.80**	**10.30**	**7.90**	**11.70**	**3.50**	**2.90**	**7.50**
10.1 Education fees	[5.10]	5.10	4.50	8.90	7.30	4.50	12.50	7.40	9.80	7.40	11.40	3.40	2.60	7.10
10.2 Payments for school trips, other ad-hoc expenditure	[0.20]	0.50	0.30	0.40	0.40	0.60	0.60	0.40	0.50	0.50	[0.30]	[0.10]	[0.20]	0.40
11 Restaurants & hotels	**35.30**	**37.10**	**36.80**	**34.00**	**36.90**	**39.80**	**50.10**	**46.10**	**41.60**	**40.70**	**32.70**	**36.80**	**47.10**	**40.20**
11.1 Catering services	30.50	30.00	30.20	29.10	29.60	32.50	41.80	36.90	33.00	33.30	28.90	30.60	43.80	33.10
11.1.1 Restaurant and café meals	11.70	12.90	12.70	13.50	13.30	15.90	19.20	18.80	16.20	15.40	13.60	13.70	18.20	15.30
11.1.2 Alcoholic drinks (away from home)	7.50	7.20	7.10	6.50	7.20	6.40	9.10	7.50	7.80	7.40	5.40	6.40	10.00	7.30
11.1.3 Take away meals eaten at home	4.00	3.90	4.00	3.70	4.10	4.20	4.90	3.80	3.30	4.00	4.10	4.60	7.20	4.20
11.1.4 Other take-away and snack food	4.00	4.00	4.00	3.50	3.40	4.20	6.50	4.20	3.90	4.30	3.80	4.20	5.50	4.30
11.1.5 Contract catering (food) and canteens	3.30	2.10	2.40	2.00	1.50	1.90	2.20	2.50	1.80	2.20	2.00	1.60	2.90	2.10
11.2 Accommodation services	4.80	7.10	6.60	4.80	7.40	7.30	8.30	9.20	8.60	7.40	3.70	6.30	3.20	7.00
11.2.1 Holiday in the UK	3.30	4.20	4.30	3.90	4.70	4.90	2.70	5.00	5.50	4.30	3.00	4.40	1.50	4.20
11.2.2 Holiday abroad	1.50	2.80	2.30	0.90	2.60	2.30	5.60	4.10	2.40	3.00	0.60	1.80	1.70	2.80
11.2.3 Room hire	[0.00]	[0.00]	[0.00]	[0.00]	[0.10]	[0.10]	[0.00]	[0.00]	[0.70]	0.10	[0.00]	[0.00]	[0.10]	0.10

Note: The commodity and service categories are not comparable to those in publications before 2001-02.

The numbering system is sequential, it does not use actual COICOP codes.

Please see background notes for symbols and conventions used in this report.

This table is based on a three year average.

6 Recording of expenditure on package holidays was changed in 2013.

Table A35
Detailed household expenditure by UK countries and regions, 2011-2013 (cont.)

Commodity or service	North East	North West	Yorks & the Humber	East Midlands	West Midlands	East	London	South East	South West	England	Wales	Scotland	Northern Ireland	United Kingdom
	Average weekly household expenditure (£)													
12 Miscellaneous goods & services	**31.00**	**37.80**	**34.80**	**38.40**	**35.80**	**42.30**	**41.40**	**47.90**	**38.80**	**39.70**	**31.80**	**32.50**	**40.70**	**38.70**
12.1 Personal care	8.70	10.30	9.50	10.60	11.10	11.40	12.30	12.40	10.40	11.00	8.80	10.80	15.30	11.00
12.1.1 Hairdressing, beauty treatment	2.30	3.10	3.30	3.30	3.70	3.70	3.40	4.20	3.20	3.50	2.30	3.20	4.90	3.40
12.1.2 Toilet paper	0.70	0.80	0.80	0.90	0.90	0.90	0.90	0.90	0.80	0.80	0.80	0.80	0.90	0.80
12.1.3 Toiletries and soap	1.90	2.20	2.00	2.30	2.40	2.40	2.70	2.60	2.30	2.30	2.10	2.30	3.20	2.40
12.1.4 Baby toiletries and accessories (disposable)	0.50	0.70	0.50	0.70	0.60	0.70	0.90	0.70	0.60	0.70	0.70	0.60	0.50	0.70
12.1.5 Hair products, cosmetics and electrical personal appliances	3.30	3.60	3.00	3.40	3.60	3.70	4.50	4.00	3.50	3.70	2.90	4.00	5.60	3.70
12.2 Personal effects	4.30	2.90	2.20	4.10	2.30	3.10	3.70	4.50	3.20	3.40	1.90	3.10	2.70	3.20
12.3 Social protection	1.80	3.60	3.60	3.60	2.70	5.10	3.80	4.30	3.10	3.70	2.60	3.20	4.70	3.60
12.4 Insurance	12.20	16.90	16.10	16.10	16.50	17.90	17.50	20.80	17.10	17.30	15.20	12.40	15.50	16.70
12.4.1 Household insurances - structural, contents and appliances	4.00	4.80	4.80	5.10	4.70	5.40	5.00	6.00	5.50	5.10	5.00	4.60	4.30	5.10
12.4.2 Medical insurance premiums	0.60	1.30	1.40	1.50	1.30	2.20	2.80	3.80	1.90	2.10	1.00	1.10	1.20	1.90
12.4.3 Vehicle insurance including boat insurance	7.60	10.80	9.80	9.50	10.40	10.10	9.30	10.70	9.60	9.90	9.20	6.60	9.90	9.60
12.4.4 Non-package holiday, other travel insurance	[0.00]	[0.00]	[0.10]	[0.10]	[0.10]	[0.10]	[0.30]	0.20	[0.10]	0.10	[0.00]	[0.10]	[0.00]	0.10
12.5 Other services	4.00	4.00	3.30	4.00	3.20	4.70	4.20	6.00	5.00	4.40	3.20	3.00	2.60	4.10
12.5.1 Moving house	1.30	1.30	1.30	1.90	1.40	2.40	2.50	2.80	2.30	2.00	[0.40]	1.20	[0.30]	1.80
12.5.2 Bank, building society, post office, credit card charges	0.30	0.40	0.40	0.50	0.50	0.50	0.70	0.60	0.70	0.50	0.30	0.50	0.20	0.50
12.5.3 Other services and professional fees	2.40	2.30	1.60	1.60	1.20	1.80	1.00	2.70	2.00	1.80	2.50	1.30	2.10	1.80
1-12 All expenditure groups	**367.60**	**396.80**	**377.60**	**407.40**	**396.20**	**446.20**	**480.60**	**498.00**	**445.50**	**432.80**	**384.60**	**386.50**	**429.10**	**426.30**
13 Other expenditure items	**57.00**	**61.90**	**53.50**	**59.30**	**59.30**	**77.20**	**99.00**	**87.40**	**72.70**	**72.60**	**54.20**	**62.40**	**55.50**	**70.30**
13.1 Housing: mortgage interest payments council tax etc.	35.10	40.50	36.30	42.40	39.70	51.40	55.10	58.50	51.10	47.10	36.20	42.60	28.00	45.70
13.2 Licences, fines and transfers	2.50	3.30	2.80	3.60	3.70	4.20	3.80	4.20	4.20	3.70	3.10	2.80	3.80	3.60
13.3 Holiday spending	10.00	8.50	6.20	3.70	6.70	7.80	22.40	9.70	5.30	9.60	8.00	5.80	6.20	9.10
13.4 Money transfers and credit	9.40	9.60	8.20	9.60	9.20	13.80	17.80	15.10	12.00	12.20	6.90	11.20	17.50	12.00
13.4.1 Money, cash gifts given to children	[0.10]	0.20	0.10	0.10	0.10	0.10	[0.10]	0.20	0.10	0.10	0.20	0.10	[0.20]	0.10
13.4.2 Cash gifts and donations[7]	8.30	8.10	6.80	7.90	8.00	11.90	16.00	13.00	9.80	10.50	6.00	9.80	16.30	10.40
13.4.3 Club instalment payments (child) and interest on credit cards	0.90	1.30	1.20	1.50	1.20	1.80	1.70	1.90	2.10	1.60	0.70	1.30	1.10	1.50
Total expenditure	**424.60**	**458.70**	**431.10**	**466.70**	**455.50**	**523.40**	**579.60**	**585.40**	**518.20**	**505.40**	**438.80**	**449.00**	**484.70**	**496.70**
14 Other items recorded														
14.1 Life assurance, contributions to pension funds	13.70	17.40	15.90	16.50	17.50	19.50	24.30	25.60	20.80	19.90	14.70	19.60	15.00	19.50
14.2 Other insurance inc. friendly societies	0.70	1.00	1.30	1.30	1.00	1.60	1.50	1.80	1.80	1.40	0.70	0.90	0.80	1.30
14.3 Income tax, payments less refunds	59.90	73.80	67.50	70.80	71.00	102.10	138.30	119.60	84.90	92.80	59.90	78.80	63.00	89.20
14.4 National insurance contributions	22.50	26.40	24.00	24.20	25.20	31.50	36.90	32.50	25.30	28.60	21.80	25.80	26.70	28.00
14.5 Purchase or alteration of dwellings, mortgages	30.60	42.40	35.10	42.20	36.30	49.90	51.60	60.20	61.50	47.30	30.30	40.80	28.00	45.40
14.6 Savings and investments	4.00	4.10	4.30	5.10	3.90	6.60	6.50	6.80	7.70	5.60	4.80	4.70	6.50	5.50
14.7 Pay off loan to clear other debt	3.30	2.80	3.20	2.60	2.80	2.90	2.20	4.60	3.90	3.20	1.30	2.20	[0.30]	2.90
14.8 Windfall receipts from gambling etc[8]	4.30	1.50	0.90	1.10	0.90	1.20	0.70	1.10	1.40	1.30	0.90	1.80	1.70	1.30

Note: The commodity and service categories are not comparable to those in publications before 2001-02.

The numbering system is sequential, it does not use actual COICOP codes.

Please see background notes for symbols and conventions used in this report.

This table is based on a three year average.

7 Recording of expenditure on money sent abroad was changed in 2013.

8 Expressed as an income figure as opposed to an expenditure figure.

Table A36
Household expenditure by urban/rural areas (GB)[1], 2011-2013

		Urban	Rural
Average number of weighted households (thousands)		19,940	5,770
Total number of households in sample (over 3 years)		12,170	3,780
Total number of persons in sample (over 3 years)		28,780	8,760
Total number of adults in sample (over 3 years)		22,000	6,960
Weighted average number of persons per household		2.4	2.3
Commodity or service		Average weekly household expenditure (£)	
1	Food & non-alcoholic drinks	55.00	62.30
2	Alcoholic drinks, tobacco & narcotics	11.70	13.40
3	Clothing & footwear	21.80	23.60
4	Housing (net)[2] fuel & power	69.70	66.50
5	Household goods & services	28.30	35.00
6	Health	5.70	8.70
7	Transport	61.40	85.50
8	Communication	13.80	14.00
9	Recreation & culture	60.30	73.70
10	Education	7.70	7.70
11	Restaurants & hotels	39.30	42.50
12	Miscellaneous goods & services	37.40	43.00
1-12	All expenditure groups	412.10	475.90
13	Other expenditure items	69.70	74.60
Total expenditure		**481.70**	**550.50**
Average weekly expenditure per person (£)			
Total expenditure		**204.50**	**236.50**

Note: The commodity and service categories are not comparable to those in publications before 2001-02.
Please see background notes for symbols and conventions used in this report.
This table is based on a three year average.
1 Combined urban/rural classification for England & Wales and Scotland - see definitions in Appendix B.
2 Excludes mortgage interest payments, council tax.

Table A37
Income and source of income by household composition, 2013
United Kingdom

	Weighted number of households	Number of households in the sample	Weekly household income: Disposable	Weekly household income: Gross	Source of income: Wages and salaries	Self employment	Investments	Annuities and pensions[1]	Social security benefits[2]	Other sources
Composition of household	(000s)	Number	£	£	Percentage of gross weekly household income					
All households	**26,840**	**5,140**	**614**	**739**	***65***	***7***	***3***	***9***	***14***	***1***
Composition of household										
One adult	7,790	1,430	319	373	*45*	*5*	*5*	*18*	*26*	*1*
Retired households mainly dependent on state pensions[3]	870	150	188	189	-	-	*1*	*6*	*93*	*[0]*
Other retired households	2,830	550	308	335	-	-	*10*	*42*	*48*	*[0]*
Non-retired households	4,090	740	355	439	*73*	*8*	*3*	*6*	*9*	*1*
One adult, one child	710	150	307	341	*53*	*[6]*	*0*	*[2]*	*35*	*4*
One adult, two or more children	650	150	402	440	*43*	*[3]*	*2*	*[2]*	*42*	*9*
One man and one woman	7,930	1,660	671	802	*58*	*7*	*5*	*16*	*15*	*0*
Retired households mainly dependent on state pensions[3]	450	110	302	305	-	-	*1*	*8*	*91*	-
Other retired households	2,390	570	531	582	*4*	*[1]*	*7*	*46*	*41*	*[0]*
Non-retired households	5,090	980	769	949	*75*	*8*	*4*	*7*	*5*	*0*
Two men or two women	760	120	599	715	*73*	*[6]*	*3*	*4*	*11*	*[2]*
Two men or two women with children	160	40	514	564	*56*	*[2]*	*[4]*	*[0]*	*35*	*[4]*
One man one woman, one child	2,100	380	744	922	*83*	*10*	*1*	*[1]*	*5*	*1*
One man one woman, two children	2,250	450	890	1,130	*85*	*6*	*3*	*[0]*	*6*	*0*
One man one woman, three children	690	140	776	942	*68*	*15*	*1*	*[0]*	*14*	*1*
Two adults, four or more children	200	50	638	735	*62*	*[3]*	*[2]*	-	*32*	*[1]*
Three adults	1,580	260	880	1,063	*70*	*10*	*2*	*7*	*8*	*3*
Three adults, one or more children	860	160	897	1,089	*72*	*11*	*2*	*[1]*	*11*	*3*
Four or more adults	910	130	1,079	1,273	*73*	*7*	*3*	*4*	*7*	*5*
Four or more adults, One or more children	260	40	1,131	1,399	*72*	*[8]*	*[2]*	*[6]*	*10*	*[2]*

Please see background notes for symbols and conventions used in this report.

1 Other than social security benefits.

2 Excluding housing benefit and council tax benefit (rates rebate in Northern Ireland) - see definitions in Appendix B.

3 Mainly dependent on state pension and not economically active - see definitions in Appendix B.

Table A38
Income and source of income by age of household reference person, 2013
United Kingdom

	Weighted number of house-holds	Number of house-holds in the sample	Weekly household income		Source of income					
			Dispo-sable	Gross	Wages and salaries	Self employ-ment	Invest-ments	Annuities and pensions[1]	Social security benefits[2]	Other sources
Age of head of household	(000s)	Number	£	£	Percentage of gross weekly household income					
Less than 30	2,610	380	505	590	*78*	*4*	*1*	*[0]*	*11*	*7*
30 to 49	9,640	1,770	735	921	*82*	*7*	*2*	*0*	*7*	*1*
50 to 64	7,100	1,420	669	811	*69*	*9*	*4*	*9*	*8*	*1*
65 to 74	3,850	910	509	565	*17*	*7*	*6*	*33*	*37*	*0*
75 or over	3,640	670	377	407	*4*	*[2]*	*9*	*36*	*49*	*[0]*

Please see background notes for symbols and conventions used in this report.
1 Other than social security benefits.
2 Excluding housing benefit and council tax benefit (rates rebate in Northern Ireland) - see definitions in Appendix B.

Table A39
Income and source of income by gross income quintile group, 2013
United Kingdom

	Weighted number of house-holds	Number of house-holds in the sample	Weekly household income		Source of income					
			Dispo-sable	Gross	Wages and salaries	Self employ-ment	Invest-ments	Annuities and pensions[1]	Social security benefits[2]	Other sources
Gross income quintile group	(000s)	Number	£	£	Percentage of gross weekly household income					
Lowest twenty per cent	5,370	1,010	166	168	*10*	*4*	*2*	*9*	*74*	*1*
Second quintile group	5,380	1,090	337	362	*32*	*5*	*2*	*17*	*42*	*2*
Third quintile group	5,360	1,060	506	573	*53*	*6*	*2*	*16*	*21*	*2*
Fourth quintile group	5,370	1,020	728	866	*71*	*7*	*2*	*9*	*9*	*2*
Highest twenty per cent	5,370	970	1,335	1,725	*78*	*8*	*5*	*5*	*2*	*1*

Please see background notes for symbols and conventions used in this report.
1 Other than social security benefits.
2 Excluding housing benefit and council tax benefit (rates rebate in Northern Ireland) - see definitions in Appendix B.

Table A40
Income and source of income by household tenure, 2013
United Kingdom

	Weighted number of households	Number of households in the sample	Weekly household income		Source of income					
			Disposable	Gross	Wages and salaries	Self employment	Investments	Annuities and pensions[1]	Social security benefits[2]	Other sources
Tenure of dwelling	(000s)	Number	£	£	Percentage of gross weekly household income					
Owners										
Owned outright	8,890	1,860	580	676	39	7	7	25	22	0
Buying with a mortgage[3]	8,480	1,600	850	1,071	83	8	2	2	4	1
All	17,370	3,470	712	869	65	8	4	11	11	1
Social rented from										
Council[4]	2420	460	325	352	45	5	0	4	43	2
Registered social landlord[5]	2,330	450	335	370	51	5	0	3	39	2
All	4,750	900	330	361	48	5	0	3	41	2
Private rented[6]										
Rent free	270	50	466	552	70	[7]	1	[5]	16	[0]
Rent paid, unfurnished[7]	3,550	610	550	657	75	7	2	2	12	1
Rent paid, furnished	910	120	518	609	73	[6]	1	[0]	3	16
All	4,720	780	539	642	75	7	2	2	11	4

Please see background notes for symbols and conventions used in this report.

1 Other than social security benefits.

2 Excluding housing benefit and council tax benefit (rates rebate in Northern Ireland) - see definitions in Appendix B.

3 Including shared owners (who own part of the equity and pay mortgage, part rent).

4 "Council" includes local authorities, new towns, and Scottish homes, but see note 5 below.

5 Formerly housing association.

6 All tenants whose accommodation goes with the job of someone in the household are allocated to "rented privately", even if the landlord is a local authority, housing association, or housing action trust, or if the accommodation is rent free. Squatters are also included in this category.

7 'Unfurnished' includes the answers: 'partly furnished'.

Table A41
Income and source of income by UK Countries and regions, 2011-2013

Regions	Weighted number of of house-holds (000s)	Total number of house-holds Number	Weekly household income: Dispo-sable £	Weekly household income: Gross £	Source of income: Wages and salaries	Self employ-ment	Invest-ments	Annuities and pensions[1]	Social security benefits[2]	Other sources
					Percentage of gross weekly household income					
United Kingdom	26,450	16,430	599	724	*65*	*8*	*3*	*9*	*14*	*1*
North East	1,130	800	488	574	*65*	*3*	*1*	*10*	*18*	*3*
North West	2,970	1,860	549	656	*66*	*6*	*2*	*8*	*16*	*2*
Yorkshire and the Humber	2,310	1,500	536	634	*64*	*7*	*3*	*8*	*16*	*2*
East Midlands	1,950	1,300	553	657	*65*	*6*	*3*	*9*	*15*	*2*
West Midlands	2,330	1,570	550	653	*64*	*7*	*2*	*9*	*16*	*2*
East	2,500	1,600	635	776	*68*	*7*	*2*	*8*	*13*	*1*
London	3,190	1,510	713	898	*70*	*10*	*3*	*6*	*10*	*1*
South East	3,540	2,230	705	868	*65*	*9*	*4*	*10*	*11*	*1*
South West	2,200	1,430	613	731	*60*	*9*	*4*	*11*	*14*	*2*
England	22,130	13,790	610	739	*66*	*8*	*3*	*9*	*14*	*1*
Wales	1,250	760	529	618	*62*	*7*	*2*	*10*	*18*	*1*
Scotland	2,330	1,400	564	674	*64*	*7*	*2*	*10*	*16*	*1*
Northern Ireland	740	480	516	610	*66*	*5*	*1*	*10*	*17*	*1*

Please see background notes for symbols and conventions used in this report.
This table is based on a three year average.
1 Other than social security benefits.
2 Excluding housing benefit and council tax benefit (rates rebate in Northern Ireland) - see definitions in Appendix B.

ONS, Family Spending 2013,

Table A42
Income and source of income by GB urban/rural area, 2011-2013

GB urban rural areas	Weighted number of house-holds (000s)	Total number of house-holds Number	Weekly household income: Dispo-sable £	Weekly household income: Gross £	Source of income: Wages and salaries	Self employ-ment	Invest-ments	Annuities and pensions[1]	Social security benefits[2]	Other sources
					Percentage of gross weekly household income					
Urban	19,940	12,170	583	703	*67*	*7*	*2*	*8*	*14*	*2*
Rural	5,770	3,780	668	813	*61*	*10*	*4*	*11*	*13*	*1*

Please see background notes for symbols and conventions used in this report.
This table is based on a three year average.
1 Other than social security benefits.
2 Excluding housing benefit and council tax benefit (rates rebate in Northern Ireland) - see definitions in Appendix B.

ONS, Family Spending 2013,

Table A43
Income and source of income by socio-economic classification, 2013
United Kingdom

NS-SEC Group[3]	Weighted number of house-holds	Number of house-holds in the sample	Weekly household income: Dispo-sable	Weekly household income: Gross	Source of income: Wages and salaries	Self employ-ment	Invest-ments	Annuities and pensions[1]	Social security benefits[2]	Other sources
	(000s)	Number	£	£	Percentage of gross weekly household income					
Large employers/higher managerial	880	170	1,245	1,681	*85*	*5*	*5*	*3*	*2*	*0*
Higher professional	2,710	490	1,059	1,369	*78*	*12*	*4*	*4*	*2*	*0*
Lower managerial and professional	5,000	930	812	1,014	*84*	*4*	*3*	*4*	*4*	*1*
Intermediate	1,950	370	595	720	*83*	*1*	*2*	*4*	*9*	*1*
Small employers	1,740	320	591	645	*24*	*52*	*4*	*6*	*13*	*1*
Lower supervisory	1,340	250	607	730	*86*	*[1]*	*1*	*3*	*9*	*1*
Semi-routine	2,210	420	440	503	*78*	*1*	*1*	*3*	*16*	*1*
Routine	1,960	380	482	557	*77*	*2*	*1*	*3*	*16*	*1*
Long-term unemployed[4]	540	100	243	262	*[37]*	*[2]*	*[2]*	*[2]*	*57*	*[1]*
Students	540	80	459	514	*51*	*[3]*	*2*	*[1]*	*5*	*39*
Occupation not stated[5]	7,970	1,640	396	432	*10*	*1*	*7*	*35*	*47*	*0*

Note: Changes to categories of socio-economic classification were made in 2011. Please see Appendix B for details
Please see background notes for symbols and conventions used in this report.
1 Other than social security benefits.
2 Excluding housing benefit and council tax benefit (rates rebate in Northern Ireland) - see definitions in Appendix B.
3 National Statistics Socio-economic classification (NS-SEC) - see definitions in Appendix B.
4 Includes those who have never worked.
5 Includes those who are economically inactive - see definitions in Appendix B.

Table A44
Income and source of income, 1970 to 2013
United Kingdom

	Weighted number of households	Number of households in the sample	Weekly household income[1]				Source of income					
			Current prices		Constant prices[2]							
			Disposable	Gross	Disposable	Gross	Wages and salaries	Self employment	Investments	Annuities and pensions[3]	Social security benefits[4]	Other sources
	(000s)	Number	£	£	£	£	Percentage of gross weekly household income					
1970		6,390	28	34	290	349	*77*	*7*	*4*	*3*	*9*	*1*
1980		6,940	115	140	345	423	*75*	*6*	*3*	*3*	*13*	*1*
1990		7,050	258	317	455	559	*67*	*10*	*6*	*5*	*11*	*1*
1995-96		6,800	307	381	447	555	*64*	*9*	*5*	*7*	*14*	*2*
1996-97		6,420	325	397	463	565	*65*	*9*	*4*	*7*	*14*	*1*
1997-98		6,410	343	421	480	590	*67*	*8*	*4*	*7*	*13*	*1*
1998-99[5]	24,660	6,630	371	457	512	630	*68*	*8*	*4*	*7*	*12*	*1*
1999-2000	25,340	7,100	391	480	533	654	*66*	*10*	*5*	*7*	*12*	*1*
2000-01	25,030	6,640	409	503	553	680	*67*	*9*	*4*	*7*	*12*	*1*
2001-02[6]	24,450	7,470	447	547	596	729	*68*	*8*	*4*	*7*	*12*	*1*
2002-03	24,350	6,930	453	552	597	728	*68*	*8*	*3*	*7*	*12*	*1*
2003-04	24,670	7,050	464	570	603	742	*67*	*9*	*3*	*7*	*13*	*1*
2004-05	24,430	6,800	489	601	627	770	*68*	*8*	*3*	*7*	*13*	*1*
2005-06	24,800	6,790	500	616	628	773	*67*	*8*	*3*	*7*	*13*	*1*
2006[7]	24,790	6,650	521	642	642	791	*67*	*9*	*3*	*7*	*12*	*1*
2006[8]	25,440	6,650	515	635	635	782	*67*	*9*	*3*	*7*	*13*	*1*
2007	25,350	6,140	534	659	643	794	*67*	*8*	*4*	*7*	*13*	*1*
2008	25,690	5,850	582	713	676	829	*67*	*9*	*4*	*7*	*12*	*1*
2009	25,980	5,830	558	683	635	776	*66*	*8*	*3*	*8*	*14*	*1*
2010	26,320	5,260	578	700	637	772	*65*	*10*	*2*	*8*	*14*	*1*
2011	26,110	5,690	587	713	618	752	*66*	*7*	*2*	*9*	*14*	*1*
2012	26,410	5,600	597	720	612	738	*65*	*8*	*3*	*9*	*14*	*1*
2013	26,840	5,140	614	739	614	739	*65*	*7*	*3*	*9*	*14*	*1*

Please see background notes for symbols and conventions used in this report.

1 Does not include imputed income from owner-occupied and rent-free households.

2 Constant prices have been deflated using the CPI All Items Index for years from 1998. Before 1988, the index is based on modelled or indicative data

3 Other than social security benefits.

4 Excluding housing benefit and council tax benefit (rates rebate in Northern Ireland) and their predecessors in earlier years - see Appendix B.

5 Based on weighted data from 1998-99 onwards.

6 From 2001-02 onwards, weighting is based on the population estimates from the 2001 Census.

7 From 1998-99 to this version of 2006, figures shown are based on weighted data using non-response weights based on the 1991 Census and population figures from the 1991 and 2001 Censuses.

8 From this version of 2006, figures shown are based on weighted data using updated weights, with non-response weights and population figures based on the 2001 Census.

Table A45
Percentage of households with durable goods 1970 to 2013
United Kingdom

	Car/ van	Central heating[1]	Washing machine	Tumble dryer	Dish-washer	Micro-wave	Tele-phone	Mobile phone	DVD Player	Home computer	Internet connection
1970	52	30	65	--	--	--	35	--	--	--	--
1975	57	47	72	--	--	--	52	--	--	--	--
1980	60	59	79	--	--	--	72	--	--	--	--
1985	63	69	83	--	--	--	81	--	--	13	--
1990	67	79	86	--	--	--	87	--	--	17	--
1994-95	69	84	89	50	18	67	91	--	--	--	--
1995-96	70	85	91	50	20	70	92	--	--	--	--
1996-97	69	87	91	51	20	75	93	16	--	27	--
1997-98	70	89	91	51	22	77	94	20	--	29	--
1998-99	72	89	92	51	24	80	95	26	--	32	9
1998-99[2]	72	89	92	51	23	79	95	27	--	33	10
1999-2000	71	90	91	52	23	80	95	44	--	38	19
2000-01	72	91	93	53	25	84	93	47	--	44	32
2001-02[3]	74	92	93	54	27	86	94	64	--	49	39
2002-03	74	93	94	56	29	87	94	70	31	55	45
2003-04	75	94	94	57	31	89	92	76	50	58	49
2004-05	75	95	95	58	33	90	93	78	67	62	53
2005-06	74	94	95	58	35	91	92	79	79	65	55
2006[4]	76	95	96	59	38	91	91	80	83	67	59
2006[5]	74	95	96	59	37	91	91	79	83	67	58
2007	75	95	96	57	37	91	89	78	86	70	61
2008	74	95	96	59	37	92	90	79	88	72	66
2009	76	95	96	58	39	93	88	81	90	75	71
2010	75	96	96	57	40	92	87	80	88	77	73
2011	75	96	97	56	41	92	88	87	88	79	77
2012	75	96	97	56	42	93	88	87	87	81	79
2013	76	96	97	56	42	92	89	92	85	83	82

Please see background notes for symbols and conventions used in this report.

-- Data not available.

1 Full or partial.

2 From this version of 1998-99, figures shown are based on weighted data and including children's expenditure.

3 From 2001-02 onwards, weighting is based on the population figures from the 2001 census.

4 From 1998-99 to this version of 2006, figures shown are based on weighted data using non-response weights based on the 1991 Census and population figures from the 1991 and 2001 Census.

5 From this version of 2006, figures shown are based on weighted data using updated weights, with non-response weights and population figures based on the 2001 Census.

Table A46

Percentage[1] of households with durable goods by income group and household composition, 2013

United Kingdom

	Central heating[2]	Washing machine	Tumble dryer	Micro-wave	Dish-washer	Home computer	Internet connection	Tele-phone	Mobile phone	DVD Player
All households	**96**	**97**	**56**	**92**	**42**	**83**	**82**	**89**	**92**	**85**
Gross income decile group										
Lowest ten per cent	93	90	32	89	13	55	51	67	82	66
Second decile group	95	93	41	91	17	54	51	85	78	77
Third decile group	95	96	50	94	28	70	69	87	86	80
Fourth decile group	96	98	54	94	31	81	81	88	92	83
Fifth decile group	95	98	58	93	38	87	86	90	95	87
Sixth decile group	96	99	61	95	43	94	92	91	96	87
Seventh decile group	97	99	61	90	49	96	95	93	97	88
Eighth decile group	96	100	63	92	54	98	97	93	98	89
Ninth decile group	97	100	64	93	66	99	98	96	98	94
Highest ten per cent	99	100	72	94	80	100	100	98	99	95
Household composition										
One adult, retired mainly dependent on state pensions[3]	95	88	31	88	19	27	21	96	53	70
One adult, other retired	95	90	41	92	24	48	45	93	71	74
One adult, non-retired	94	95	39	91	25	79	77	74	93	77
One adult, one child	94	99	48	89	27	81	84	74	97	83
One adult, two or more children	99	100	60	92	32	89	90	77	100	86
Two adults, retired mainly dependent on state pensions[3]	95	97	55	93	33	66	62	99	83	89
Two adults, other retired	97	99	66	95	51	80	78	97	90	91
Two adults, non-retired	95	99	59	92	47	94	93	90	97	89
Two adults, one child	97	99	63	91	49	94	93	89	98	85
Two adults, two children	98	100	69	92	58	98	98	94	99	91
Two adults, three children	98	100	65	96	54	97	97	94	99	85
Two adults, four or more children	99	100	63	91	[27]	97	97	99	99	83
Three adults	97	99	69	95	54	97	95	89	98	89
Three adults, one or more children	97	100	68	98	55	98	98	95	100	91
All other households without children	96	100	63	96	55	98	98	89	99	89
All other households with children	97	100	61	100	59	95	95	90	96	87

Please see background notes for symbols and conventions used in this report.

1 See table A47 for number of recording households.

2 Full or partial.

3 Mainly dependent on state pensions and not economically active - see Appendix B.

Table A47
Percentage of households with cars by income group, tenure and household composition, 2013
United Kingdom

	One car/van	Two cars/vans	Three or more cars/vans	All with cars/vans	Weighted number of house-holds (000s)	House-holds in the sample (number)
All households	**46**	**24**	**6**	**76**	**26,840**	**5,140**
Gross income decile group						
Lowest ten per cent	30	[3]	[0]	33	2,690	500
Second decile group	42	4	[0]	47	2,680	510
Third decile group	55	7	[1]	63	2,690	540
Fourth decile group	61	12	[1]	75	2,690	550
Fifth decile group	61	19	[3]	83	2,680	530
Sixth decile group	56	28	4	88	2,690	530
Seventh decile group	50	34	6	89	2,680	510
Eighth decile group	39	42	11	93	2,680	500
Ninth decile group	34	46	15	95	2,690	490
Highest ten per cent	27	43	24	94	2,680	480
Tenure of dwelling[1]						
Owners						
Owned outright	50	23	7	81	8,890	1,860
Buying with a mortgage	44	39	10	93	8,480	1,600
All	47	31	9	87	17,370	3,470
Social rented from						
Council	36	7	[1]	44	2,420	460
Registered social landlord [2]	43	8	[1]	51	2,330	450
All	39	7	[1]	47	4,750	900
Private rented						
Rent free	54	[19]	[6]	79	270	50
Rent paid, unfurnished	49	16	[3]	67	3,550	610
Rent paid, furnished	33	[10]	-	43	910	120
All	46	15	[2]	63	4,720	780
Household composition						
One adult, retired mainly dependent on state pensions[3]	30	-	-	30	870	150
One adult, other retired	47	[1]	[0]	49	2,830	550
One adult, non-retired	58	4	[0]	61	4,090	740
One adult, one child	49	[3]	-	52	710	150
One adult, two or more children	60	[1]	-	61	650	150
Two adults, retired mainly dependent on state pensions[3]	71	[12]	[2]	85	450	110
Two adults, other retired	59	25	[3]	86	2,510	590
Two adults, non-retired	42	38	6	86	5,720	1080
Two adults, one child	44	39	5	88	2,200	400
Two adults, two children	39	49	[2]	90	2,290	460
Two adults, three children	48	40	[3]	91	700	140
Two adults, four or more children	46	[27]	[3]	76	200	50
Three adults	30	29	28	87	1,580	260
Three adults, one or more children	33	31	23	87	860	160
All other households without children	27	23	37	88	910	130
All other households with children	[17]	[33]	[35]	86	260	40

Please see background notes for symbols and conventions used in this report.
1 See footnotes in Table A32.
2 Formerly housing association.
3 Mainly dependent on state pensions and not economically active - see Appendix B.

Table A48
Percentage of households with durable goods by UK Countries and regions, 2011-2013

	North East	North West	Yorks and the Humber	East Midlands	West Midlands	East	London	South East	South West	England	Wales	Scotland	Northern Ireland	United Kingdom
Average weighted number of households (thousands)	1,130	2,970	2,310	1,950	2,330	2,500	3,190	3,540	2,200	22,130	1,250	2,330	740	26,450
Total number of households in sample (over 3 years)	800	1,860	1,500	1,300	1,570	1,600	1,510	2,230	1,430	13,790	760	1,400	480	16,430
Percentage of households by region and Country														
Car/van	*65*	*74*	*72*	*79*	*75*	*82*	*61*	*84*	*84*	*76*	*80*	*71*	*75*	*75*
One	*42*	*44*	*44*	*45*	*43*	*44*	*46*	*45*	*45*	*44*	*49*	*44*	*39*	*44*
Two	*19*	*25*	*24*	*27*	*25*	*30*	*13*	*32*	*31*	*25*	*25*	*22*	*28*	*25*
Three or more	*4*	*5*	*4*	*6*	*7*	*8*	*3*	*8*	*8*	*6*	*6*	*5*	*8*	*6*
Central heating full or partial	*98*	*96*	*95*	*95*	*95*	*96*	*96*	*96*	*95*	*96*	*93*	*96*	*99*	*96*
Fridge-freezer or deep freezer	*96*	*97*	*97*	*97*	*97*	*98*	*96*	*98*	*98*	*97*	*98*	*98*	*98*	*97*
Washing machine	*98*	*96*	*97*	*97*	*97*	*98*	*97*	*98*	*98*	*97*	*99*	*98*	*98*	*97*
Tumble dryer	*55*	*58*	*57*	*58*	*59*	*58*	*42*	*58*	*60*	*56*	*61*	*56*	*49*	*56*
Dishwasher	*32*	*35*	*36*	*40*	*37*	*49*	*39*	*52*	*46*	*42*	*38*	*40*	*51*	*42*
Microwave	*95*	*93*	*94*	*93*	*95*	*92*	*89*	*92*	*91*	*92*	*96*	*94*	*95*	*93*
Telephone	*86*	*85*	*84*	*87*	*87*	*91*	*88*	*92*	*92*	*88*	*90*	*88*	*85*	*88*
Mobile phone	*89*	*90*	*91*	*91*	*89*	*89*	*92*	*92*	*87*	*90*	*78*	*88*	*67*	*89*
DVD player	*87*	*88*	*87*	*88*	*86*	*88*	*79*	*89*	*88*	*86*	*89*	*89*	*73*	*86*
Home computer	*76*	*79*	*77*	*81*	*79*	*84*	*85*	*86*	*84*	*82*	*80*	*77*	*72*	*81*
Internet connection	*74*	*78*	*75*	*80*	*77*	*82*	*84*	*85*	*82*	*80*	*78*	*75*	*69*	*79*

Please see background notes for symbols and conventions used in this report.
This table is based on a three year average.

Table A49

Percentage of households by size, composition and age in each gross income decile group, 2013

United Kingdom

	Lowest ten per cent	Second decile group	Third decile group	Fourth decile group	Fifth decile group	Sixth decile group	Seventh decile group	Eighth decile group	Ninth decile group	Highest ten per cent	All house-holds
Lower boundary of group (£ per week)		178	265	358	462	574	696	856	1,078	1,442	
Weighted number of households (thousands)	2,690	2,680	2,690	2,690	2,680	2,690	2,680	2,680	2,690	2,680	26,840
Number of households in the sample	500	510	540	550	530	530	510	500	490	480	5,140
Size of household											
One person	79	57	46	32	24	21	12	10	5	[4]	29
Two persons	16	28	35	41	46	38	40	36	39	32	35
Three persons	4	9	10	14	16	18	21	25	23	21	16
Four persons	[1]	4	5	9	8	13	18	20	25	30	13
Five persons	[1]	[1]	[3]	3	[4]	7	6	6	6	11	5
Six or more persons	-	[0]	[1]	[1]	[2]	4	3	[2]	[2]	[3]	2
All sizes	100	100	100	100	100	100	100	100	100	100	100
Household composition											
One adult, retired mainly dependent on state pensions[1]	15	14	[2]	[0]	-	-	-	-	-	-	3
One adult, other retired	22	28	23	14	8	6	[1]	[2]	[1]	[1]	11
One adult, non-retired	41	15	21	18	16	15	11	8	4	[3]	15
One adult, one child	7	5	4	4	[2]	[1]	[1]	[1]	[0]	[0]	3
One adult, two or more children	[2]	6	4	5	[3]	[1]	[2]	[1]	[0]	[1]	2
Two adults, retired mainly dependent on state pensions[1]	-	6	8	[2]	[1]	[0]	-	[0]	-	-	2
Two adults, other retired	[1]	8	13	18	17	15	11	5	4	[2]	9
Two adults, non-retired	8	8	9	17	26	22	28	30	35	29	21
Two adults, one child	[1]	[4]	6	6	8	12	11	12	11	11	8
Two adults, two children	[0]	[3]	4	5	6	9	15	13	14	17	9
Two adults, three children	[1]	[1]	[2]	[2]	[3]	4	[3]	4	[2]	5	3
Two adults, four or more children	-	-	[0]	[1]	[1]	[2]	[2]	[1]	[0]	[0]	1
Three adults	[1]	-	[1]	[4]	5	5	8	12	12	10	6
Three adults, one or more children	-	[1]	[1]	[2]	[2]	[3]	[4]	5	7	6	3
All other households without children	[0]	[0]	[1]	[2]	[1]	[3]	[3]	[4]	7	12	3
All other households with children	-	-	[0]	-	[0]	[2]	[1]	[2]	[2]	[3]	1
All compositions	100	100	100	100	100	100	100	100	100	100	100
Age of household reference person											
15 and under 20 years	[1]	[0]	-	[0]	[0]	-	[0]	[0]	-	-	[0]
20 and under 25 years	7	[4]	[2]	[4]	[5]	[3]	[3]	[2]	[1]	[0]	3
25 and under 30 years	[4]	5	7	6	6	8	9	9	[4]	[3]	6
30 and under 35 years	4	[3]	4	8	8	7	10	10	10	12	8
35 and under 40 years	[3]	[4]	5	7	8	10	9	11	12	12	8
40 and under 45 years	6	6	6	8	7	11	11	13	15	15	10
45 and under 50 years	11	5	8	8	10	9	13	12	13	16	10
50 and under 55 years	9	5	6	8	5	8	13	16	16	14	10
55 and under 60 years	7	4	7	5	11	8	7	8	12	11	8
60 and under 65 years	13	8	7	11	10	8	9	5	8	6	9
65 and under 70 years	7	11	13	10	11	10	7	6	5	4	8
70 and under 75 years	8	9	9	9	7	5	4	[3]	[3]	[2]	6
75 and under 80 years	7	13	11	8	6	5	[2]	[3]	[1]	[0]	6
80 and under 85 years	5	12	9	4	[4]	[3]	[2]	[1]	[1]	[1]	4
85 and under 90 years	[5]	7	[4]	[4]	[2]	[2]	[1]	[0]	-	[1]	3
90 years or more	[2]	[3]	[1]	[1]	[1]	[2]	[0]	-	-	-	1
All ages	100	100	100	100	100	100	100	100	100	100	100

Please see background notes for symbols and conventions used in this report.

1 Mainly dependent on state pensions and not economically active - see Appendix B.

Table A50

Percentage of households by economic activity, tenure and socio-economic classification in each gross income decile group, 2013

United Kingdom

	Lowest ten per cent	Second decile group	Third decile group	Fourth decile group	Fifth decile group	Sixth decile group	Seventh decile group	Eighth decile group	Ninth decile group	Highest ten per cent	All households
Lower boundary of group (£ per week)		178	265	358	462	574	696	856	1,078	1,442	
Weighted number of households (thousands)	2,690	2,680	2,690	2,690	2,680	2,690	2,680	2,680	2,690	2,680	26,840
Number of households in the sample	500	510	540	550	530	530	510	500	490	480	5,140
Number of economically active persons in household											
No person	67	68	54	40	29	21	12	8	5	4	31
One person	29	27	37	41	38	35	31	21	13	15	29
Two persons	[3]	5	8	16	30	39	48	57	58	57	32
Three persons	[1]	-	[1]	[2]	[2]	[4]	7	12	18	14	6
Four or more persons	-	-	[0]	[0]	[0]	[1]	[1]	[3]	6	11	2
All economically active persons	100	100	100	100	100	100	100	100	100	100	100
Tenure of dwelling[1]											
Owners											
Owned outright	26	39	43	41	40	36	29	26	25	26	33
Buying with a mortgage	6	6	11	17	24	35	47	52	57	62	32
All	32	45	53	58	64	70	76	79	82	88	65
Social rented from											
Council	25	19	14	12	8	4	[3]	[3]	[2]	[1]	9
Registered social landlord [2]	22	19	12	10	9	5	4	[3]	[3]	-	9
All	47	38	26	22	17	9	7	6	[5]	[1]	18
Private rented											
Rent free	[2]	[1]	[2]	[1]	[1]	[1]	[1]	[1]	[1]	[1]	1
Rent paid, unfurnished	15	13	15	16	16	15	12	11	9	9	13
Rent paid, furnished	[4]	[3]	[4]	[3]	[3]	[5]	[3]	[4]	[3]	[1]	3
All	21	17	21	20	19	21	16	16	13	11	18
All tenures	100	100	100	100	100	100	100	100	100	100	100
Socio-economic classification											
Higher managerial and professional											
Large employers/higher managerial	[1]	-	[1]	[0]	[1]	[2]	[3]	5	6	15	3
Higher professional	[1]	[1]	[2]	[2]	5	10	9	16	24	31	10
Lower managerial and professional	5	[3]	7	11	14	18	29	30	38	31	19
Intermediate	[3]	[3]	6	9	11	10	8	11	6	5	7
Small employers	6	6	8	6	9	8	8	6	5	[4]	6
Lower supervisory	[2]	[1]	[4]	7	5	8	7	7	5	[3]	5
Semi-routine	9	10	10	12	15	8	8	6	[3]	[1]	8
Routine	9	8	8	8	8	9	10	6	5	[1]	7
Long-term unemployed[3]	11	4	[1]	[1]	[1]	[0]	[0]	[1]	[1]	-	2
Students	[5]	[2]	[1]	[3]	[2]	[2]	[2]	[2]	[1]	[1]	2
Occupation not stated[4]	47	62	52	41	30	25	16	10	7	7	30
All occupational groups	100	100	100	100	100	100	100	100	100	100	100

Note: Changes to categories of socio-economic classification were made in 2011. Please see Appendix B for details.

Please see background notes for symbols and conventions used in this report.

1 See footnotes in Table A32.

2 Formerly housing association.

3 Includes those who have never worked.

4 Includes those who are economically inactive - see definitions in Appendix B.

Table A51
Average weekly household expenditure by Output Area Classification (OAC) supergroup, 2013
United Kingdom

	Blue collar Communities	City living	Countryside	Prospering suburbs	Constrained by circumstances	Typical traits	Multicultural	
	OAC Super-group 1	**OAC Super-group 2**	**OAC Super-group 3**	**OAC Super-group 4**	**OAC Super-group 5**	**OAC Super-group 6**	**OAC Super-group 7**	**All house-holds**
Weighted number of households (thousands)	4,380	1,750	3,580	5,950	3,060	5,180	2,930	26,840
Total number of households in sample	860	280	740	1,220	590	1,000	450	5,140
Total number of persons in sample	2,050	580	1,770	2,980	1,260	2,270	1,220	12,120
Total number of adults in sample	1,520	500	1,430	2,320	960	1,780	850	9,350
Weighted average number of persons per household	2.4	2.1	2.4	2.5	2.1	2.3	2.6	2.4
Commodity or service	Average weekly household expenditure (£)							
1 Food & non-alcoholic drinks	52.30	52.80	71.40	67.70	45.90	55.90	57.30	58.80
2 Alcoholic drinks, tobacco & narcotics	12.60	10.40	14.10	11.90	12.30	11.70	10.10	12.00
3 Clothing & footwear	18.70	20.50	27.80	27.70	13.90	23.20	21.00	22.60
4 Housing (net)[1], fuel & power	65.70	125.50	75.00	60.00	64.70	73.00	97.80	74.40
5 Household goods & services	22.10	40.10	47.20	42.70	22.60	30.90	23.80	33.10
6 Health	4.20	6.70	9.50	9.00	3.40	5.80	3.10	6.20
7 Transport	50.90	68.00	91.30	94.70	41.20	72.90	52.40	70.40
8 Communication	13.70	15.90	15.30	15.10	11.40	14.80	15.00	14.50
9 Recreation & culture	51.00	54.30	81.20	89.50	43.00	61.00	43.00	63.90
10 Education	2.10	29.00	10.00	6.20	1.60	9.40	17.00	8.80
11 Restaurants & hotels	28.30	56.10	47.50	50.10	23.60	42.10	35.00	40.40
12 Miscellaneous goods & services	26.10	42.90	49.20	52.50	22.60	40.00	32.60	39.10
1-12 All expenditure groups	347.80	522.10	539.30	527.20	306.10	440.60	408.10	444.30
13 Other expenditure items	45.20	92.40	82.60	86.70	34.50	73.50	103.00	73.00
Total expenditure	**393.00**	**614.50**	**621.90**	**613.90**	**340.60**	**514.10**	**511.20**	**517.30**
Average weekly expenditure per person (£) Total expenditure	**163.60**	**293.40**	**256.90**	**249.70**	**163.50**	**227.10**	**194.90**	**219.40**

Please see background notes for symbols and conventions used in this report.

1 Excluding mortgage interest payments, council tax and Northern Ireland rates.

Table A52
Average weekly household expenditure by Output Area Classification (OAC) group, 2013
United Kingdom

	Terraced blue collar	Younger blue collar	Older blue collar	Transient communities	Settled in the city	Village life	Agricultural	Accessible countryside	Propsering younger families	Prospering older families	Prospering semis	Thriving suburbs	Senior communities	Older workers	Public housing	Settled households	Least divergent	Young families in terraced homes	Aspiring households	Asian communities	Afro-Caribbean communities	
	OAC group 1A	OAC group 1B	OAC group 1C	OAC group 2A	OAC group 2B	OAC group 3A	OAC group 3B	OAC group 3C	OAC group 4A	OAC group 4B	OAC group 4C	OAC group 4D	OAC group 5A	OAC group 5B	OAC group 5C	OAC group 6A	OAC group 6B	OAC group 6C	OAC group 6D	OAC group 7A	OAC group 7B	All households
Weighted number of households (thousands)	1,110	1,730	1,540	630	1,120	1,530	970	1,080	1,230	1,700	1,790	1,230	470	1,920	670	1,450	1,380	1,230	1,120	1,760	1,160	26,840
Total number of households in sample	210	340	310	90	190	310	200	230	250	370	370	240	90	370	130	280	270	230	210	290	170	5,140
Total number of persons in sample	500	860	690	200	390	730	510	520	660	880	880	560	150	800	300	670	590	520	490	800	420	12,120
Total number of adults in sample	380	580	550	170	330	580	420	440	480	710	690	440	130	610	210	530	470	400	380	560	290	9,350
Weighted average number of persons per household	2.4	2.5	2.2	2.2	2.1	2.3	2.6	2.3	2.7	2.4	2.4	2.4	1.6	2.1	2.3	2.4	2.2	2.2	2.3	2.7	2.5	2.4
Commodity or service											Average weekly household expenditure (£)											
1 Food & non-alcoholic drinks	55.50	50.10	52.60	51.80	53.30	66.20	76.50	74.10	74.50	68.50	60.20	71.00	37.50	47.60	46.80	56.50	55.10	49.30	63.40	60.80	52.10	58.80
2 Alcoholic drinks, tobacco & narcotics	13.80	11.10	13.40	9.90	10.70	13.80	14.30	14.40	12.90	11.70	11.40	12.10	12.20	12.10	12.60	11.60	12.50	11.40	11.40	10.40	9.70	12.00
3 Clothing & footwear	17.50	19.60	18.50	23.40	18.80	26.50	29.10	28.50	33.50	32.00	23.70	21.60	11.00	14.50	14.10	26.20	23.30	16.40	27.00	21.00	21.10	22.60
4 Housing (net)[1], fuel & power	63.10	69.10	63.80	155.30	108.70	67.90	88.40	73.00	57.10	60.70	53.90	70.80	58.50	66.10	65.30	63.90	70.90	72.10	88.40	87.40	113.50	74.40
5 Household goods & services	25.00	19.90	22.50	30.90	45.30	45.30	56.40	41.60	36.60	49.30	39.70	44.30	13.00	24.10	25.00	28.70	27.40	23.20	46.80	25.10	21.90	33.10
6 Health	5.50	3.20	4.40	3.70	8.30	8.80	9.90	10.10	5.30	12.10	8.10	9.90	3.10	3.10	4.30	8.70	3.90	3.60	6.80	4.00	1.80	6.20
7 Transport	52.50	46.00	55.40	48.90	78.70	86.20	102.00	89.00	109.40	105.00	74.40	95.40	26.70	46.50	36.30	84.20	58.60	56.70	93.70	54.10	49.90	70.40
8 Communication	12.60	13.30	14.90	13.80	17.00	15.00	15.60	15.50	16.50	15.40	14.10	14.80	8.40	12.00	11.70	15.30	14.10	13.50	16.40	14.30	16.10	14.50
9 Recreation & culture	46.40	49.90	55.60	49.50	57.00	72.10	83.10	92.20	81.50	104.80	72.30	101.50	40.90	45.50	37.60	60.50	54.50	55.70	75.50	49.90	32.60	63.90
10 Education	[2.70]	[0.90]	[3.10]	[37.60]	[24.10]	[5.00]	[12.90]	[14.60]	3.40	6.90	[0.80]	15.90	[0.10]	[1.90]	[1.80]	[0.70]	[0.90]	[33.20]	4.90	21.40	[10.40]	8.80
11 Restaurants & hotels	26.30	26.50	31.80	52.30	58.30	45.10	53.90	45.20	50.20	57.10	42.20	52.00	16.40	25.40	23.50	46.50	39.00	35.30	47.50	35.80	33.70	40.40
12 Miscellaneous goods & services	26.10	24.00	28.30	38.80	45.20	42.70	61.00	47.80	69.50	54.80	35.30	57.60	18.70	24.50	19.80	39.00	40.90	31.90	48.90	35.30	28.60	39.10
1-12 All expenditure groups	347.00	333.80	364.30	516.10	525.50	494.50	603.10	545.90	550.30	578.20	436.00	566.80	246.50	323.30	298.80	441.80	401.00	402.30	530.50	419.40	391.20	444.30
13 Other expenditure items	47.50	38.80	50.60	66.00	107.30	82.20	68.30	95.90	102.30	94.10	64.70	93.10	25.80	38.30	29.80	71.10	59.00	51.50	118.90	131.40	60.10	73.00
Total expenditure	**394.60**	**372.60**	**414.90**	**582.10**	**632.80**	**576.60**	**671.40**	**641.70**	**652.60**	**672.30**	**500.70**	**659.90**	**272.30**	**361.60**	**328.60**	**512.90**	**460.00**	**453.80**	**649.40**	**550.70**	**451.20**	**517.30**
Average weekly expenditure per person (£)																						
Total expenditure	**162.40**	**147.30**	**185.30**	**269.00**	**307.90**	**245.70**	**255.70**	**274.10**	**242.10**	**276.50**	**213.00**	**273.30**	**167.60**	**170.00**	**144.20**	**216.20**	**212.30**	**203.00**	**285.70**	**201.90**	**183.10**	**219.40**

Please see background notes for symbols and conventions used in this report.
1 Excluding mortgage interest payments, council tax and Northern Ireland rates.

ONS, Family Spending 2013,

Table A53
Average gross normal weekly household income by Output Area Classification (OAC) supergroup, 2013
United Kingdom

	Blue collar Communities	City living	Countryside	Prospering suburbs	Constrained by circumstances	Typical traits	Multicultural	
	OAC Super-group 1	**OAC Super-group 2**	**OAC Super-group 3**	**OAC Super-group 4**	**OAC Super-group 5**	**OAC Super-group 6**	**OAC Super-group 7**	**All house-holds**
Weighted number of households (thousands)	4,380	1,750	3,580	5,950	3,060	5,180	2,930	26,840
Total number of households in sample	860	280	740	1,220	590	1,000	450	5,140
Total number of persons in sample	2,050	580	1,770	2,980	1,260	2,270	1,220	12,120
Total number of adults in sample	1,520	500	1,430	2,320	960	1,780	850	9,350
Weighted average number of persons per household	2.4	2.1	2.4	2.5	2.1	2.3	2.6	2.4
Gross normal weekly household income (£)	**526.40**	**975.20**	**902.80**	**893.90**	**443.00**	**749.00**	**689.70**	**738.80**

Please see background notes for symbols and conventions used in this report.

Office for National Statistics

Survey methodology: Appendix B

Abstract

Appendix B provides further detailed information regarding the methodology of the Living Costs and Food survey, used to produce the estimates presented in Family Spending.

Description of the survey

A household expenditure survey has been conducted each year in the UK since 1957. From 1957 to March 2001 the Family Expenditure Survey (FES) and National Food Survey (NFS) provided information on household expenditure patterns and food consumption. In April 2001 these surveys were combined to form the Expenditure and Food Survey (EFS).

In 2008 selected Government household surveys, on which the Office for National Statistics (ONS) leads, were combined into one Integrated Household Survey (IHS). In anticipation of this, the EFS moved to a calendar-year basis in January 2006. The EFS questionnaire became known as the Living Costs and Food (LCF) module of the IHS in 2008, to accommodate the insertion of a core set of IHS questions.

More information about the IHS can be found on the ONS website. In summary, the survey design allows for the collection of common core data across the pooled samples of the constituent surveys, achieving the biggest pool of UK social data after the Census. The large sample allows a detailed level of analysis to be conducted, and allows results to be reported for smaller geographic areas. The IHS has become the key vehicle for high-profile national data collection initiatives including questions on subjective well-being, and on sexual identity.

The LCF is a voluntary sample survey of private households. The basic unit of the survey is the household. A household comprises one person living alone or a group of people (not necessarily related living at the same address) who share cooking facilities AND share a living room or sitting room or dining area (See 'Definitions').

Each individual aged 16 and over in the household visited is asked to keep diary records of daily expenditure for two weeks. Information about regular expenditure, such as rent and mortgage payments, is obtained from a household interview along with retrospective information on certain large, infrequent expenditures such as those on vehicles. Children aged 7 to 15 are asked to keep a simplified version of the diary.

Detailed questions are asked about the income of each adult member of the household. In addition, personal information such as age, sex and marital status is recorded for each household member. A copy of the LCF questionnaire is available from the UK Data Service.

The survey is continuous, interviews being spread evenly over the year to ensure that seasonal effects are covered. The questionnaire content is reviewed thoroughly to ensure that it is up-to-date and captures information efficiently. Some changes reflect new forms of expenditure or new sources of income, especially benefits. Others are the result of new requirements by the survey's users. (See the section on 'Survey Improvements' for more information.)

The sample design

The LCF sample for Great Britain is a multi-stage stratified random sample with clustering. It is drawn from the Small Users file of the Postcode Address File (PAF) – the Post Office's list of addresses. All Scottish offshore islands and the Isles of Scilly are excluded from the sample because of excessive interview travel costs. Postal sectors are the primary sample unit. 638 postal sectors are randomly selected after being arranged in strata defined by Regions (sub-divided into metropolitan and non-metropolitan areas) and two 2001 Census variables: socio-economic group of the head of household and ownership of cars. These census variables were new stratifiers originally introduced for the 1996/97 survey, and updated following the results of the 2001 Census. The results of the 2011 Census will be used in due course. The Northern Ireland sample is drawn as a random sample of addresses from the Land and Property Services Agency list.

Uses of the survey

LCF expenditure data

Retail Prices Index – The main reason, historically, for instituting a regular survey on expenditure by households has been to provide information on spending patterns for the Retail Prices Index (RPI) and the Consumer Prices Index (CPI). From April 2011 the CPI rather than the RPI is used as basis for indexation of benefits, tax credit and state and public service pensions. The RPI and CPI measure the change in the cost of a selection of goods and services (the 'basket of goods') representative of the expenditure of the vast majority of households. The pattern of expenditure gradually changes from one year to the next, and the composition of the basket of goods needs to be kept up-to-date. Accordingly, regular information is required on spending patterns and much of this is supplied by the LCF. The expenditure weights for the general RPI and CPI need to relate to people within given income limits, for which the LCF is the only source of information.

Household expenditure and Gross Domestic Product (GDP) – LCF data on spending are an important source used in compiling national estimates of household final consumption expenditure which are published regularly in United Kingdom National Accounts (ONS Blue Book). Household final consumption expenditure estimates feed into the National Accounts and estimates of GDP. They will also provide the weights for Purchasing Power Parities (PPPs) for international price comparisons. LCF data are also used in the estimation of taxes on expenditure, in particular VAT.

Regional accounts – LCF expenditure information is one of the sources used by ONS to derive regional estimates of consumption expenditure. It is also used in compiling some of the other estimates for the regional accounts.

The statistical office of the European Union (Eurostat) collates information from family budget surveys conducted by the member states. The LCF is the UK's contribution to this important EU initiative to collect data on household expenditure from member countries.

Other government uses – The Department of Energy and Climate Change and the Department for Transport both use LCF expenditure data in their own fields relating to, for example, energy, housing, cars and transport. The Department for Transport uses LCF data to monitor and forecast levels of car ownership and use, and in studies on the effects of motoring taxes.

Non-government uses – There are also numerous users outside central government, including academic researchers and business and market researchers. One example is an academic study that has used LCF data, as part of a wider study, to obtain a clear picture of utility expenditure patterns across the European Union.

LCF income data

Redistribution of income – LCF information on income and expenditure is used to study how government taxes and benefits affect household income. The Government's interdepartmental tax benefit model is based on the LCF and enables the economic effects of policy measures to be analysed across households. This model is used by HM Treasury and HM Revenue and Customs to estimate the impact on different households of possible changes in taxes and benefits.

Non-government users – As with the expenditure data, LCF income data are also studied extensively outside government. In particular, academic researchers in the economic and social science areas of many universities use the LCF. For example the Institute for Fiscal Studies uses LCF data in research it carries out both for government and on its own account to inform public debate.

Family Spending and Defra reporting

The Department for Environment, Food and Rural Affairs (Defra) publishes separate reports using LCF data on food expenditure to estimate consumption and nutrient intake.

It should be noted that Defra's reporting, in Family Food, on food consumption and nutrient uptake is at person level. Family Spending reports expenditure at household level, meaning that the figures cannot be directly compared to those presented in Family Food. The different approaches reflect the different analytical purposes of the two publications, with person-level being appropriate to nutritional analysis.

Notes

1. Great care is taken to ensure complete confidentiality of information and to protect the identity of LCF households. Only anonymised data are supplied to users.

Response to the survey

Great Britain

A total of 11,484 households were selected in 2013 for the LCF in Great Britain. However, it is not possible to get full response. A small number of households cannot be contacted at all, and in other households one or more members decline to co-operate. 4,993 households in Great Britain co-operated fully in the survey in 2013; that is, they answered the household questionnaire and all adults in the household answered the full income questionnaire and kept the expenditure diary. A further 232 households provided sufficient information to be included as valid responses. The overall response rate for the 2013 LCF was 48% in Great Britain, a decrease from 52% in 2012.

Details of response are shown in Response table 1.

Response table 1: Response in 2013 – Great Britain

	Number of households or addresses	Percentage of set sample	Percentage of effective sample
Sampled addresses	11,484	100	-
Ineligible	1,133	10	-
Extra households (multi-households)	3	0	-
Total eligible	**10,354**		**100**
Co-operating households (includes 232 partials)	4,993		48
Refusals	3,555		34
Non-contact	731		7
Unknown eligibility	622		6
Other non-response	453		4

Table source: Office for National Statistics

Download table

XLS XLS format
(27.5 Kb)

Northern Ireland

In the Northern Ireland survey, the eligible sample was 251 households. The number of co-operating households who provided usable data was 152, giving a response rate of 61%. This represents a decrease of 6 percentage points from the 2012 survey year[1].

Northern Ireland was over-sampled in the years 1997/98 to 2009 in order to provide a large enough sample for some separate analysis. This boost to the Northern Ireland sample was discontinued in 2010.

Partial response

Three types of partial response are accepted on the LCF:

- All adults complete the full income section of the interview, but one or more adults in the household refuse to keep the diary.
- All adults in the household keep the diary, but one or more adults provides only partial income information.
- One or more adults refuse to keep the diary and one or more adults provide only partial income information.

All partial responses must contain a diary from the Main Diary Keeper (MDK), who is the person who does most of the shopping in the household. If the MDK refuses to complete the diary the household is classified as a refusal.

In 2013 partial responses accounted for 5% (232 households) of all co-operating households. Of these partials, the majority (97%) occurred because one or more adults in the household refused to keep the diary. Partial income information was provided in 3% of cases.

Response table 2: Type of partial response in 2013 – Great Britain

Type of partial response		Number of households	Percentage of partials
1.	One or more adults refuse to keep the diary[1]	225	97
2.	One or more adults provide only partial income information	7	3
All		232	100

Table source: Office for National Statistics

Table notes:

1. Diary is present for the main diary keeper.

Download table

XLS XLS format
(33 Kb)

LCF Response rates over time

Response rates to household surveys have generally been declining in recent years. In 2013 the LCF's response rate for Great Britain was 48% (see 'Response to the survey' for a detailed breakdown), compared with around 59% in 2000/01. Response in 2013 was lower than in 2012, when 52% was achieved. It should be noted that the LCF requires satisfactory completion of both the household questionnaire and diary. For more information see the 'Living Costs and Food Survey Technical Report (529.7 Kb Pdf)'.

The Fieldwork

The fieldwork is conducted by the Office for National Statistics (ONS) in Great Britain and by the Northern Ireland Statistics and Research Agency (NISRA) of the Department of Finance and Personnel in Northern Ireland using almost identical questionnaires. Households at the selected addresses are visited and asked to co-operate in the survey. In order to maximise response, interviewers make at least four separate calls, and sometimes many more, at different times of day on households which are difficult to contact. Interviews are conducted by Computer Assisted Personal Interviewing (CAPI) using laptop computers.

During the interview information is collected about the household; certain regular payments such as rent, gas, electricity and telephone accounts; expenditure on certain large items (for example vehicle purchases over the previous 12 months); and income. Each individual aged 16 and over in the household is asked to keep a detailed record of expenditure every day for two weeks.

Children aged between 7 and 15 are also asked to keep a simplified diary of daily expenditure. In 2013 a total of 1,318 children aged between 7 and 15 in responding households in the UK were asked to complete expenditure diaries; 249, or 19%, did not do so. This number includes both refusals and children who had no expenditure during the two weeks. Information provided by all members of the household is kept strictly confidential. Each person aged 16 and over in the household who keeps a diary (and whose income information is collected) is subsequently sent a £10 voucher as a token of appreciation. Children who keep a diary are given a £5 voucher.

Some survey cases are reissued if a response is not obtained, that is, the cases are reallocated to field interviewers at a later date to attempt to achieve a response. In 2013 859 addresses were reissued, of which 25 were converted into responding households. This increased the overall response by 0.2 percentage points.

Eligible response

Under LCF rules, a refusal by just one person to respond to the income section of the questionnaire invalidates the response of the whole household. Similarly, a refusal by the household's main shopper to complete the two-week expenditure diary also results in an invalid response.

Proxy response

Questions about general household affairs are put to all household members or to the household representative person (HRP), and questions about work and income are put to the individual members of the household. Where a member of the household is not present during the household interview, another member of the household (for example a spouse) may be able to provide information about the absent person. The individual's interview is then identified as a proxy interview. Under LCF rules, the expenditure diary cannot be completed by proxy; if a household member is not present during the diary period they are classified as an absent spender.

In 2013 the percentage of fully responding households with a proxy interview in Great Britain was 26%. Analysis of the 2013 data revealed that the inclusion of proxy interviews increased response from above average income households. For the 2013 survey, the average gross normal weekly household income was 21% higher than it would have been if proxy interviews had not been accepted.

Similar findings were obtained with respect to expenditure: total spending was 15% higher than if proxy interviews had not been included. Use of proxies enhances the sample size and hence the precision of the figures obtained. It also enables the survey to capture the income and expenditure from (on average) higher-earning households and hence ensures that these households are represented fully in the survey. This must be weighed against the risk that the proxy interviews may not provide exactly the same information as direct interviews, but the available evidence suggests that including proxies provides higher data quality overall.

Reliability

Great care is taken in collecting information from households, and comprehensive checks are applied during processing so that errors in recording and processing are minimised. The main factors that affect the reliability of the survey results are sampling variability, non-response bias and some incorrect reporting of certain items of expenditure and income. Measures of sampling variability are given alongside some results in this report and are discussed in detail in 'Standard errors and estimates of precision'.

The households which decline to respond to the survey tend to differ in some respects from those that co-operate; it is therefore possible that their patterns of expenditure and income also differ. Currently, non responders are accounted for in the weighting process for LCF data, which compensates for non responders recognised from analysis of the 2001 Census (see 'Weighting' for more information). At present, the LCF is contributing towards the 2011 Census non-response linkage project, which will enable non-response weights to be updated.

Checks are included in the computer assisted personal interviewing (CAPI) program, which are applied to the responses given during the interview. Other procedures are also in place to ensure that users are provided with high quality data. For example, quality control is carried out to ensure that any unusual values (outliers) are genuine, and checks are made on any unusual changes in average spending compared with the previous year.

Income and expenditure balancing

The LCF is designed primarily as a survey of household expenditure on goods and services. It also gathers information about the income of household members, and is an important and detailed source of income data. However, it is not possible to draw up a balance sheet of income and expenditure either for individual households or groups of households.

The majority of expenditure information collected relates to the two-week period immediately following the interview, whereas income components can refer to a much longer period (the most recent 12 months). LCF income does not include withdrawal of savings; loans and money received in payment of loans; receipts from maturing insurance policies; proceeds from the sale of assets (such as a car); and winnings from betting or windfalls, such as legacies. Despite this, recorded expenditure might reflect these items, as well as the effects of living off savings, using capital, borrowing money or income – either recent or from a previous period.

Hence, there is no reason why income and expenditure should balance. In fact measured expenditure exceeds measured income at the bottom end of the income distribution. However, this difference cannot be regarded as a reliable measure of savings or dis-saving.

For further information of what is included in income on the LCF see 'Income headings'.

Imputation of missing information

Although LCF response is generally based on complete households responding, there are areas in the survey for which missing information is imputed (inferred, sometimes in conjunction with other sources). This falls into two broad categories: item imputation and diary imputation. Using a combination of reliable imputation procedures ensures that the LCF data provide a comprehensive picture of the spending patterns and income sources for each household. For more information see the 'Living Costs and Food Survey Technical Report (529.7 Kb Pdf)'.

Notes

1. In 2012, the eligible Northern Ireland sample was 256 households. The number of co-operating households who provided usable data was 171 households, giving a response rate of 67%.

Weighting

Since 1998/99 the survey has been weighted to reduce the effect of non-response bias and produce population totals and means. The weights are produced in two stages. First, the data are weighted to compensate for non-response (sample-based weighting). Second, the sample distribution is weighted so that it matches the population distribution in terms of region, age group and sex (population-based weighting).

Sample based weighting using the Census

Weighting for non-response involves giving each respondent a weight so that they represent the non-respondents that are similar to them in terms of the survey characteristics. Non responders are accounted for in the weighting process for LCF data using results from the 2001 Census linked study of non responders.

The 2001 LCF Census-linked study matched census addresses with the sampled addresses of EFS. In this way it was possible to match the address details of the respondents as well as the non-respondents with corresponding information gathered from the Census for the same address. The information collected during 2001 Census/EFS matching work was then used to identify the types of households that were being under-represented in the survey. Further details of how the weighting classes were produced can be seen in the 'Weighting' section of the 'Living Costs and Food Survey Technical Report (529.7 Kb Pdf)'.

The results of the 2011 Census-linked studies will be used to further update non-response weighting in due course.

Population-based weighting

The second stage of the weighting adjusts the non-response weights so that weighted totals match population totals. As the LCF sample is based on private households, the population totals used in the weighting need to relate to people living in private households. For 2013 data the population totals used were population projections based on estimates rolled forward from the 2011 Census, adjusted to harmonise with the LCF definition of a private household. These estimates used exclude residents of institutions not covered by the LCF, such as those living in bed-and-breakfast accommodation, hostels, residential homes and other institutions.

The non-response weights were calibrated[1] so that weighted totals matched population totals for males and females in different age groups and for regions. An important feature of the population-based weighting is that it is done by adjusting the factors for households not individuals.

The weighting is carried out separately for each quarter of the survey. The main reason is that sample sizes vary more from quarter to quarter than in the past. This is due to reissuing addresses after an interval of a few months where there had previously been no contact or a refusal to a new interviewer. This results in more interviews in the later quarters of the year than in the first quarter. Quarterly weighting, therefore, counteracts any potential bias from the uneven spread of interviews through the year. Quarterly weighting also results in small sample numbers in some of the age/sex categories that were used in previous years. The categories have therefore been widened slightly to avoid this.

Effects of weighting on the data

Table B1 shows the effects of the weighting by comparing unweighted and weighted data from 2013.

Table B1: The effect of weighting on expenditure, 2013

United Kingdom

	Average weekly household expenditure (£)			
Commodity or service	**Unweighted**	**Weighted as published**	**Absolute difference**	**Percentage difference**
All expenditure groups	**441.50**	**444.30**	**2.79**	**0.6**
Food and non-alcoholic drinks	59.30	58.80	-0.53	-0.9
Alcoholic drink, tobacco & narcotics	12.10	12.00	-0.10	-0.8
Clothing and footwear	22.40	22.60	0.18	0.8
Housing, fuel and power	70.00	74.40	4.36	6.2
Household goods and services	33.80	33.10	-0.68	-2.0
Health	6.60	6.20	-0.39	-5.8
Transport	70.80	70.40	-0.31	-0.4
Communication	14.20	14.50	0.27	1.9
Recreation and culture	66.40	63.90	-2.46	-3.7
Education	6.80	8.80	1.96	28.6
Restaurants and hotels	39.80	40.40	0.59	1.5
Miscellaneous	39.20	39.10	-0.10	-0.2
Weekly household income:				
Disposable	608	614	7	1.1
Gross	727	739	12	1.6

Table source: Office for National Statistics

Download table

XLS XLS format
(34.5 Kb)

The weighting decreased the estimate of total average expenditure by £2.79 a week. It had the largest impact on average weekly expenditure on education, increasing the estimate by 28.6%. It also increased the estimate of spending on housing, fuel and power by 6.2%, and reduced the estimate of spending on recreation and culture by 3.7% and the estimate for household goods and services by 2.0%. Weighting also increased the estimates of average income, by £7 a week for disposable household income and by £12 a week (1.6%) for gross household income, which is the income used in most tables in the report.

Re-weighting also has an effect on the variance of estimates. In an analysis on the 1999/2000 data, weighting increased variance slightly for some items and reduced it for others. Overall the effect was to reduce variance slightly.

Notes

1. Implemented by the CALMAR software package before 2007 and GES for 2006–08 (updated weights).

Standard errors and estimates of precision

The Living Costs and Food Survey (LCF) is a sample of households and not a census of the whole population. Therefore, the results are liable to differ to some degree from those that would have been obtained if every single household had been covered. Some of the differences will be systematic, in that lower proportions of certain types of household respond than of others. That aspect is discussed in 'Response to the survey' and 'Weighting'. This section discusses the effect of sampling variability; in other words, the effect of differences in expenditure and income between the households in the sample and in the whole population that arise from random chance.

The degree of variability will depend on the sample size and how widely particular categories of expenditure (or income) vary between households. The sampling variability is smallest for the average expenditure of large groups of households on items purchased frequently and when the level of spending does not vary greatly between households. Conversely, it is largest for small groups of households, and for items purchased infrequently or for which expenditure varies considerably between households. A numerical measure of the likely magnitude of such differences (between the sample estimate and the value of the entire population) is provided by the quantity known as the standard error.

The calculation of standard errors takes into account the fact that the LCF sample is drawn in two stages: first a sample of areas (primary sampling units), then a sample of addresses within each of these areas. The main features of the sample design are described in 'Description of the survey'.

The calculation also takes account of the effect of weighting. The two-stage sample increases sampling variability slightly, but the weighting reduces it for some items.

Standard errors for detailed expenditure items are presented in relative terms in table A1 (153.5 Kb Excel sheet) (standard error as a percentage of the average to which it refers). As the calculation of full standard errors is complex, this is the only table where they are shown. Tables B2 and B3 in this section show the design factor (DEFT), a measure of the efficiency of the survey's sample design. The DEFT is calculated by dividing the full standard error by the standard error that would have applied if the survey had used a simple random sample.

Further standard errors are calculated for the figures and tables in the trends chapter. Figures have been deflated to 2013 prices using the Consumer Prices Index (CPI), using indices specific to each major COICOP category. This is with the exception of specific items to which the CPI is not applicable: for mortgage interest payment and council tax payments the Retail Prices Index (RPI) was used. For the deflated figures using the CPI, standard errors have been calculated.

For more information of the calculation of standard errors see the 'Living Costs and Food Survey Technical Report (529.7 Kb Pdf)'.

Table B2: Percentage standard errors of expenditure of households and number of recording households, 2013

United Kingdom

		Percentage standard error		Percentage standard error	Households recording expenditure	
Commodity or service	**Weighted average weekly household expenditure (£)**	**Simple method**	**Design factor (DEFT)**	**Full method**	**Recording households in sample**	**Percentage of all households**
All expenditure groups	**444.30**	**1.0**	**1.1**	**1.2**	**5,144**	100
Food and non-alcoholic drinks	58.80	0.9	1.1	1.1	5,114	99
Alcoholic drink, tobacco & narcotics	12.00	2.3	1.0	2.3	3,217	63
Clothing and footwear	22.60	2.4	1.1	2.6	3,326	65
Housing, fuel and power	74.40	1.3	1.2	1.6	5,133	100
Household goods and services	33.10	3.4	1.0	3.5	4,749	92
Health	6.20	6.2	0.9	5.6	2,724	53
Transport	70.40	2.0	1.0	2.1	4,455	87
Communication	14.50	1.1	1.1	1.2	4,920	96
Recreation and culture	63.90	2.4	1.1	2.6	5,092	99

		Percentage standard error		Percentage standard error	Households recording expenditure	
Commodity or service	Weighted average weekly household expenditure (£)	Simple method	Design factor (DEFT)	Full method	Recording households in sample	Percentage of all households
Education	8.80	12.2	1.5	17.9	313	6
Restaurants and hotels	40.40	1.8	1.1	1.9	4,435	86
Miscellaneous goods and services	39.10	2.1	1.0	2.1	5,035	98

Table source: Office for National Statistics

Download table

XLS XLS format
(36.5 Kb)

Table B3: Percentage standard errors of income of households and number of recording households, 2013

United Kingdom

		Percentage standard error		Percentage standard error	Households recording income	
Source of income	**Weighted average weekly household income (£)**	**Simple method**	**Design factor (DEFT)**	**Full method**	**Recording households in sample**	**Percentage of all households**
Gross household income	**739**	**1.3**	**1.1**	**1.3**	**5,130**	**100**
Wages and salaries	481	1.9	1.0	1.9	2,980	58
Self-employment	54	6.4	0.9	5.9	648	13
Investments	25	8.0	1.1	8.7	2,325	45
Annuities and pensions (other than social security benefits)	67	3.7	0.8	3.0	1,770	35
Social security benefits	102	1.6	0.7	1.1	3,684	72
Other sources	9	7.7	1.1	8.4	638	12

Table source: Office for National Statistics

Download table

XLS XLS format
(36 Kb)

Using the standard errors – calculating confidence intervals

A common use of standard errors is in calculating confidence intervals. Confidence intervals can be used to estimate a range within which the true population value should lie in. The 95% interval can be taken to mean that there is only a 5% chance that the true population value lies outside the 95% confidence interval (or that 95 times out of 100 the true population value will fall within the interval).

The following formulae are used to calculate a 95% confidence interval:

Lower limit: mean - 1.96 × (percentage standard error ÷ 100) × mean

Upper limit: mean + 1.96 × (percentage standard error ÷ 100) × mean

For example, using the expenditure on food and non-alcoholic drinks to illustrate this calculation; the average expenditure is £58.80 and the corresponding percentage standard error (full method) is 1.1% (rounded to one decimal place). The limits for a 95% confidence interval are then:

Lower limit: 58.80 - 1.96 × (1.1 ÷ 100) ×58.80 = £57.60

Upper limit: 58.80 + 1.96 × (1.1 ÷ 100) ×58.80 = £60.00

Similar calculations can be carried out for other estimates of expenditure and income. The 95% confidence intervals for main expenditure categories are given in table B4.

Table B4: 95 per cent confidence intervals for average household expenditure, 2013

United Kingdom

Commodity or service	Weighted average weekly household expenditure (£)	Lower limit	Upper limit
All expenditure groups	**444.30**	**434.00**	**454.60**
Food and non-alcoholic drinks	58.80	57.60	60.00
Alcoholic drink, tobacco & narcotics	12.00	11.50	12.60
Clothing and footwear	22.60	21.50	23.70
Housing, fuel and power	74.40	72.10	76.70
Household goods and services	33.10	30.90	35.40
Health	6.20	5.50	6.90
Transport	70.40	67.50	73.30
Communication	14.50	14.10	14.80
Recreation and culture	63.90	60.70	67.20
Education	8.80	5.70	11.90
Restaurants and hotels	40.40	38.80	41.90
Miscellaneous goods and services	39.10	37.50	40.80

Table source: Office for National Statistics

Download table

XLS XLS format
(53.5 Kb)

Using the standard errors – statistical significance testing

Statistical significance testing indicates the probability with which we are confident that the difference between the estimates under examination did not occur by chance. Significance testing carried out in the trends chapter is at the 95% level unless otherwise stated. This means the probability that the difference happened by chance is low (1 in 20). For more information of the method used for significance testing see the 'Living Costs and Food Survey Technical Report (529.7 Kb Pdf)'.

Survey improvements

Questionnaire review

In order to ensure the LCF questionnaire is up-to-date it is important that questions are regularly reviewed so that relevant changes can be made. Reviewing the questionnaire is a process of continuous improvement. For example, a pilot survey was carried out in 2012 to evaluate further questionnaire improvements. The changes tested in the pilot have been implemented for the 2013 survey year. Questionnaire changes included: the addition of a new breakdown of spending on different types of furniture and package holidays; collection of flight expenditure in the questionnaire rather than the diary; the addition of a section designed to capture expenditure on combined utility packages; and the addition of new questions about mobile phone ownership.

Comparison with another source

A useful comparison for LCF estimates is with Household Final Consumption Expenditure (HHFCE) figures published in Consumer Trends and used in the UK National Accounts.

This section compares estimates from the LCF with the estimates used in the UK National Accounts. The Household Final Consumption Expenditure estimates use a number of administrative and survey sources, of which the LCF survey is one. As a result differences occur in the estimates published, because of sources and concepts.

For example, conceptual differences can be found for housing expenditure. As explained in Chapter 2: Housing expenditure, Family Spending only includes rental costs in the housing, fuel and power category, whilst mortgage costs are included in the other expenditure items category. In contrast, National Accounts housing data in the housing, fuel and power category includes a value for rentals paid by owner occupiers in order to maintain international comparability. This is a theoretical cost that home owners would have to pay to rent their own home. By international convention, mortgage costs are excluded from National Accounts Household Final Consumption Data.

According to Family Spending data, housing, water, electricity, gas and other fuels was the category where the value of spending increased most over the period 2006 to 2013 (without adjusting for inflation, an increase of 36%). Despite the conceptual differences between the two outputs, National

Accounts household expenditure estimates for the same category also show a large increase (54%) in spending.

Both National Accounts and Chapter 4 of Family Spending provide estimates over time to remove the effects of inflation and to enable figures for different years to be compared on a like-for-like basis. The National Accounts figures adjusted for inflation are known as "volume measures". The volume measures of National Accounts show that housing expenditure has increased 7%, while the prices of goods and services in this category, measured as an implied deflator, have increased by 44% between 2006 and 2013. Adjusted for inflation, Family Spending shows an increase in housing expenditure of 12% over the same period (from £65.40 to £74.40).

A similar pattern can be seen in the food and non-alcoholic drinks category in National Accounts data, showing a reduction in volume (3%) and an increase in the monetary value of spending by around 35% since 2006. Family Spending reported a 21% increase in spending on food since 2006 (from £46.30 to 58.80, not adjusted for inflation). These figures indicate relatively little scope or willingness to cut back on these items, despite significant price rises in some goods and services and the recession of 2008/2009.

Family Spending shows that transport spending at 2013 prices fell from £80.50 in 2006 to £70.40 in 2013, a decrease of 14%. The National Accounts household expenditure on transport shows that spending adjusted for inflation fell by 2%. Prices in this category, again measured as an implied deflator, increased by 40% over the period which suggests that, as with food and non-alcoholic beverages, the rise in prices influenced households' decisions to reduce their purchases.

Definitions

Household

A household comprises of one person living alone or a group of people (not necessarily related) living at the same address who:

- share cooking facilities
- and share a living room or sitting room or dining area

Resident domestic servants are included. The members of a household are not necessarily related by blood or marriage. As the survey covers only private households, people living in hostels, hotels, boarding houses or institutions are excluded. Households are included if some or all members are not British subjects, however, information is not collected from households containing members of the diplomatic service of another country or members of the United States armed forces.

Retired households

Retired households are those where the household reference person is retired. The household reference person is defined as retired if they have reached state pension age and are economically inactive. Since May 2010 the state pension age for women has been increasing gradually to be in line with the male pension age of 65 by 2018. Therefore, if for example a male household reference person is aged over 65 years of age, but working part-time or waiting to take up a part-time job, this household would not be classified as a retired household. For analysis purposes two categories are used in this report:

- ‘A retired household mainly dependent upon state pensions’ is one in which at least three-quarters of the total income of the household is derived from national insurance retirement and similar pensions, including housing and other benefits paid in supplement to or instead of such pensions. The term ‘national insurance retirement and similar pensions’ includes national insurance disablement and war disability pensions, and income support in conjunction with these disability payments.
- ‘Other retired households’ are retired households which do not fulfil the income conditions of 'retired household mainly dependent upon state pensions’ because more than a quarter of the households income derives from other sources. For example, occupational retirement pensions and/or income from investments, or annuities.

Household reference person (HRP)

From 2001/02 the concept of household reference person (HRP) was adopted on all government-sponsored surveys in place of head of household. The household reference person is the householder who:

- owns the household accommodation, or
- is legally responsible for the rent of the accommodation, or
- has the household accommodation as an emolument or perquisite, or
- has the household accommodation by virtue of some relationship to the owner who is not a member of the household.

If there are joint householders the household reference person will be the one with the higher income. If the income is the same, then the eldest householder is taken.

Members of household

In most cases the members of co-operating households are easily identified as the people who satisfy the conditions in the definition of a household (see above), and are present during the record-keeping period. However, difficulties of definition arise where people are temporarily away from the household or else spend their time between two residences. The following rules apply in deciding whether or not such persons are members of the household:

- Married people living and working away from home for any period are included as members, provided they consider the sampled address to be their main residence. In general, other people (such as relatives, friends and boarders) who are either temporarily absent or who spend their time between the sampled address and another address, are included as members if they consider the sampled address to be their main residence. However, there are exceptions which override the subjective main residence rule:
- Children under 16 years of age away at school are included as members.
- Older people receiving education away from home, including children aged 16 and 17, are excluded unless they are at home for all or most of the record-keeping period.

- Visitors staying temporarily with the household, and others who have been in the household for only a short time are treated as members, provided they will be staying with the household for at least one month from the start of record-keeping.

Household composition

A consequence of these definitions is that household compositions quoted in this report include some households where certain members are temporarily absent, for example, a 'two-adult and children' household where one parent is temporarily away from home.

Adult

In the report, people who have reached the age of 18 are classed as adults. In addition, those aged 16 to 18 who are not in full-time education, or who are married, are classed as adults.

Children

In the report, people who are under 18 years of age, in full-time education and have never been married are classed as children.

However, in the definition of clothing, clothing for people aged 16 years and over is classified as clothing for men and women; clothing for those aged 5 to 15 as clothing for boys and girls; and clothing for those under five as babies clothing.

Main Diary Keeper (MDK) (or main shopper)

The MDK is the person in the household who is normally responsible for most of the food shopping. This includes people who organise and pay for the shopping although they do not physically do the shopping themselves.

Rules for identifying the main diary keeper when the household cannot identify this for themselves:

Rule 1: Establish who in the household has the highest income.

Rule 2: If each household member has the same income then find out who is the oldest.

If a paid domestic servant normally performs these tasks then the MDK is the person responsible for seeing that the domestic servant does the shopping.

No address may be coded as a full or partial interview if the diary of the MDK is missing or incomplete.

Spenders

Household members aged 16 and over, excluding those who for special reasons are not capable of keeping diary record-books, are described as spenders. It is unimportant whether or not the individual earns or spends money. If a spender is absent for less than 7 days from the interviewers' initial contact, the interviewer can proceed with the interview.

Absent spenders

If a spender is absent for longer than 7 days they are defined as an 'absent spender'. Absent spenders do not keep a diary and consequently are not eligible for the voucher that is paid to diary keepers.

Non-spenders

If a household member is completely incapable of contributing to the survey by answering questions or keeping a diary, then they are defined as a 'non-spender'. However, incapable people living on their own cannot be designated as non-spenders as they comprise the whole expenditure unit. If this is the case, the interviewer should enlist the help of the person outside of the household who looks after their interests. If there is no-one able or willing to help, the address is coded as incapable.

Economically active

These are people aged 16 and over who fall into the following categories:

- Employees at work – those who at the time of interview were working full-time or part-time as employees or were away from work on holiday. Part-time work is defined as normally working 30 hours a week or less (excluding meal breaks) including regularly worked overtime.
- Employees temporarily away from work – those who, at the time of interview, had a job but were temporarily absent due to, for example, illness, temporary lay-off, or strike.
- Government supported training schemes – those participating in government programmes and schemes who, in the course of their participation, receive training such as Employment Training, and including those who are also employees in employment.
- Self-employed – those who, at the time of interview, said they were self-employed.
- Unemployed – those who, at the time of interview, were out of employment and have sought work within the last four weeks and were available to start work within two weeks, or were waiting to start a job already obtained.
- Unpaid family workers – those working unpaid for their own or a relative's business. In this report, unpaid family workers are included under economically inactive in analyses by economic status (tables A17 (69 Kb Excel sheet) and B5 (70.5 Kb Excel sheet)) because insufficient information is available to assign them to an economic status group.

Economically inactive

- Retired – people who have reached national insurance retirement age and are not economically active. Since May 2010 the female state pension age has been gradually increasing to align with the male pension age of 65 by 2018.
- Unoccupied – people under national insurance retirement age who are not working, nor actively seeking work. This category includes certain self-employed people such as mail order agents and baby-sitters who are not classified as economically active.

National Statistics Socio-economic Classification (NS-SEC)

From 2001 the National Statistics Socio-economic Classification (NS-SEC) was adopted for all official surveys, in place of Social Class based on Occupation (SC) and Socio-economic Groups (SEG). NS-SEC is itself based on the Standard Occupational Classification 2010 (SOC2010) and details of employment status. Although NS-SEC is an occupation-based classification, there are procedures for classifying those not in work.

The main categories used for analysis in Family Spending are:

1 Higher managerial and professional occupations, sub-divided into:

1.1 Large employers and higher managerial occupations

1.2 Higher professional occupations

2 Lower managerial and professional occupations

3 Intermediate occupations

4 Small employers and own account workers

5 Lower supervisory and technical occupations

6 Semi-routine occupations

7 Routine occupations

8 Never worked and long-term unemployed

9 Students

10 Occupation not stated

11 Not classifiable for other reasons

The long-term unemployed are defined as those unemployed and seeking work for 12 months or more. Members of the armed forces, who were assigned to a separate category in social class, are included within the NS-SEC classification. Individuals that have retired within the last 12 months are classified according to their employment. Other retired individuals are assigned to the 'Not classifiable for other reasons' category.

Socio-economic Classification (SE-SEC) regions

These are the same areas as UK regions and countries.

Urban and rural areas

This classification introduced in 2005/06 replaces the previous Department for Transport, Local Government and the Regions (DTLR) 1991 Census-based urban and rural classification, which was used in previous editions of Family Spending. The new classification is applied across Great Britain and is an amalgamation of the Rural and Urban Classification 2004 for England and Wales and the Scottish Executive Urban Rural Classification. These classifications are based on 2001 Census data and have been endorsed as the standard National Statistics Classifications for identifying urban and rural areas across GB. In broad terms, an area is defined as urban or rural depending on whether the population falls inside a settlement of 10,000 or more. For further details concerning these classifications please refer to the Rural/Urban Definition and LA Classification on the Office for National Statistics (ONS) website.

Expenditure

Any definition of expenditure is to some extent arbitrary, and the inclusion of certain types of payment is a matter of convenience or convention depending on the purpose for which the information is to be used. In the tables in this report, total expenditure represents current expenditure on goods and services. Total expenditure, defined in this way, excludes those recorded payments that are really savings or investments: for example, purchases of national savings certificates, life assurance premiums, and contributions to pension funds. Similarly, income tax payments, national insurance contributions, mortgage capital repayments and other payments for major additions to dwellings are excluded. Expenditure data are collected in the diary record-book and in the household schedule. Informants are asked to record in the diary any payments made during the 14 days of record-keeping, whether or not the goods or services paid for have been received. Certain types of expenditure which are usually regular though infrequent, such as insurance, licences and season tickets, and the periods to which they relate, are recorded in the household schedule as well as regular payments such as utility bills.

The cash purchase of motor vehicles is also entered in the household schedule. In addition, expenditure on some items purchased infrequently (thereby being subject to high sampling errors) has been recorded in the household schedule using a retrospective recall period of either 3 or 12 months. These items include carpets, furniture, holidays and some housing costs. In order to avoid duplication, all payments shown in the diary record-book which relate to items listed in the household or income schedules are omitted in the analysis of the data, irrespective of whether there is a corresponding entry on the latter schedules. Amounts paid in respect of periods longer than a week are converted to weekly values.

Expenditure tables in this report show the 12 main commodity groups of spending and these are broken down into items which are numbered hierarchically (see 'Changes to definitions, 1991 to 2013' can be found in the the 'Living Costs and Food Survey Technical Report (529.7 Kb Pdf)' which details a major change to the coding frame used from 2001/02). Table A1 (153.5 Kb Excel sheet) shows a further breakdown in the items themselves into components which can be separately identified. The items are numbered as in the main expenditure tables, and the average weekly household expenditure and percentage standard error is shown against each item or component.

Qualifications which apply to this concept of expenditure are described in the following paragraphs:

- **Goods supplied from a household's own shop or farm**

  Spenders are asked to record and give the value of goods obtained from their own shop or farm, even if the goods are withdrawn from stock for personal use without payment. The value is included as expenditure.

- **Hire purchase and credit sales agreements, and transactions financed by loans repaid by instalments**

Expenditure on transactions under hire purchase or credit sales agreements, or financed by loans repaid by instalments, consists of all instalments that are still being paid at the date of interview, together with down payments on commodities acquired within the preceding three months. These two components (divided by the periods covered) provide the weekly averages which are included in the expenditure on the separate items given in the tables in this report.

- **Club payments and budget account payments, instalments through mail order firms and similar forms of credit transaction**

  When goods are purchased by forms of credit other than hire purchase and credit sales agreement, the expenditure on them may be estimated either from the amount of the instalment which is paid or from the value of the goods which are acquired. Since the particular commodities to which the instalment relates may not be known, details of goods ordered through, for example, clubs or mail order firms, during the month prior to the date of interview, are recorded in the household schedule. The weekly equivalent of the value of the goods is included in the expenditure on the separate items given in the tables in this report. This procedure has the advantage of enabling club transactions to be related to specific articles. Although payments into clubs, etc. are shown in the diary record-book, these entries are excluded from expenditure estimates.

- **Credit card transactions**

  From 1988 purchases made by credit card or charge card have been recorded in the survey on an acquisition basis rather than the formerly used payment basis. Thus, if a spender acquired an item (by use of credit/charge card) during the two week survey period, the value of the item would be included as part of expenditure in that period whether or not any payment was made in this period to the credit card account. Payments made to the card account are ignored. However any payment of credit/charge card interest is included in expenditure if made in the two week period.

- **Income tax**

  Amounts of income tax deducted under the Pay As You Earn (PAYE) scheme or paid directly by those who are employers or self-employed are recorded (together with information about tax refunds). For employers and the self-employed the amounts comprise the actual payments made in the previous 12 months and may not correspond to the tax due on the income arising in that period, for example if no tax has been paid but is due or if tax payments cover more than one financial year. However, the amounts of tax deducted at source from some of the items which appear in the Income Schedule are not directly available. Estimates of the tax paid on bank and building society interest and amounts deducted from dividends on stocks and shares are therefore made by applying the appropriate rates of tax. In the case of income tax paid at source on pensions and annuities, similar adjustments are made. These estimates mainly affect the relatively few households with high incomes from interest and dividends, and households including someone receiving a pension from previous employment.

- **Rented dwellings**

  Expenditure on rented dwellings is taken as the sum of expenditure on a number of items such as rent, council tax, and water rates. For local authority tenants the expenditure is gross rent less any rebate (including rebate received in the form of housing benefit), and for other tenants it is gross rent less any rent allowance received under statutory schemes including the Housing Benefit Scheme. Rebate on council tax or rates (Northern Ireland) is deducted from expenditure on council tax or rates. Receipts from sub-letting part of the dwelling are not deducted from housing costs but appear (net of the expenses of the sub-letting) as investment income.

- **Rent-free dwellings**

  Rent-free dwellings are those owned by someone outside the household and where either no rent is charged or the rent is paid by someone outside the household. Households whose rent is paid directly to the landlord by the DWP do not live rent-free. Payments for council tax for example are regarded as the cost of housing. Rebate on rates (Northern Ireland)/council tax/ water rates (Scotland) (including rebate received in the form of housing benefit), is deducted from expenditure on rates/council tax/water rates. Receipts from sub-letting part of the dwelling are not deducted from housing costs but appear (net of the expenses of the sub-letting) as investment income.
- **Owner-occupied dwellings**
  In the LCF, payments for water rates, ground rent, fuel, maintenance and repair of the dwelling, among other items, are regarded as the cost of housing. Receipts from letting part of the dwelling are not deducted from housing costs but appear (net of the expenses of the letting) as investment income. Mortgage capital repayments and amounts paid for the outright purchase of the dwelling or for major structural alterations are not included as housing expenditure, but are entered under 'other items recorded', as are council tax, rates (Northern Ireland) and mortgage interest payments. Structural insurance is included in 'miscellaneous goods and services'.
- **Second-hand goods and part-exchange transactions**
  The survey expenditure data are based on information about actual payments and therefore include payments for second-hand goods and part-exchange transactions. New payments only are included for part-exchange transactions, that is the costs of the goods obtained less the amounts allowed for the goods which are traded in. Receipts for goods sold or traded in are not included in income.
- **Business expenses**
  The survey covers only private households and is concerned with payments made by members of households as private individuals. Spenders are asked to state whether expenditure that has been recorded on the schedules includes amounts that will be refunded as expenses from a business or organisation or that will be entered as business expenses for income tax purposes, for example rent, telephone charges, travelling expenses and meals out. Any such amounts are deducted from the recorded expenditure.

Income

The standard concept of income in the survey is, as far as possible, that of gross weekly cash income current at the time of interview, that is before the deduction of income tax actually paid, national insurance contributions and other deductions at source. However, for a few tables a concept of disposable income is used, defined as gross weekly cash income less the statutory deductions and payments of income tax (taking refunds into account) and national insurance contributions. Analysis in Chapter 3 of this report and some other analyses of LCF data use 'equivalisation' of incomes: in other words adjustment of household income to allow for the different size and composition of each household. For more information see Chapter 3. The cash levels of certain items of income (and expenditure) recorded in the survey by households receiving supplementary benefit were affected by the Housing Benefit Scheme introduced in stages from November 1982.

From 1984 housing expenditure is given on a strictly net basis and all rent/council tax rebates and allowances and housing benefit are excluded from gross income.

Although information about most types of income is obtained on a current basis, some data, principally income from investment and from self-employment, are estimated over a 12-month period.

For the annual publication of the results in the LCF Family Spending report, the following are excluded from the assessment of income:

- Money received by one member of the household from another (for example housekeeping money, dress allowance, children's pocket money) other than wages paid to resident domestic servants.
- Withdrawals of savings, receipts from maturing insurance policies, proceeds from sale of financial and other assets (such as houses, cars, and furniture), winnings from betting, lump-sum gratuities and windfalls such as legacies.
- The value of educational grants and scholarships not paid in cash.
- The value of income in kind, including the value of goods received free and the abatement in cost of goods received at reduced prices, and of bills paid by someone who is not a member of the household.
- Loans and money received in repayment of loans.

Details are obtained of the income of each member of the household. The income of the household is taken to be the sum of the incomes of all its members. The information does not relate to a common or a fixed time period. Items recorded for periods greater than a week are converted to a weekly value.

Particular points relating to some components of income are as follows:

- **Wages and salaries of employees**
  The normal gross wages or salaries of employees are taken to be their earnings. These are calculated by adding to the normal 'take home' pay amounts deducted at source, such as income tax payments, national insurance contributions and other deductions (for example payments into firm social clubs, superannuation schemes, works transport, and benevolent funds). Employees are asked to give the earnings actually received including bonuses and commission the last time payment was made and, if different, the amount usually received. It is the amount usually received that is regarded as the normal take-home pay. Additions are made so as to include in normal earnings the value of occasional payments, such as bonuses or commissions received quarterly or annually. One of the principal objects in obtaining data on income is to enable expenditure to be classified in ranges of normal income. Average household expenditure is likely to be based on the long-term expectations of the various members of the household as to their incomes rather than be altered by short-term changes affecting individuals. Hence, if employees have been away from work without pay for 13 weeks or less, they are regarded as continuing to receive their normal earnings instead of social security benefits, such as unemployment or sickness benefit, that they may be receiving. Otherwise, normal earnings are disregarded and current short-term social security benefits taken instead. Wages and salaries include any earnings from subsidiary employment as an employee and the earnings of HM Forces.

- **Income from self-employment**

  Income from self-employment covers any personal income from employment other than as an employee: for example, as a sole trader, professional or other person working on his own account or in partnership, including subsidiary work on his own account by a person whose main job is as an employee. It is measured from estimates of income or trading profits, after deduction of business expenses but before deduction of tax, over the most recent 12-month period for which figures can be given. Should either a loss have been made or no profit, income would be taken as the amounts drawn from the business for own use or as any other income received from the job or business. People working as mail order agents or baby-sitters, with no other employment, have been classified as unoccupied rather than as self-employed, and the earnings involved have been classified as earnings from 'other sources' rather than self-employment income.
- **Income from investment**

  Income from investments or from property, other than that in which the household is residing, is the amount received during the 12 months immediately prior to the date of the initial interview. It includes receipts from sub-letting part of the dwelling (net of the expenses of the sub-letting). If income tax has been deducted at source the gross amount is estimated by applying a conversion factor during processing.]
- **Social security benefits**

  Income from social security benefits does not include the short-term payments such as unemployment or sickness benefit, received by an employee who has been away from work for 13 weeks or less, and who is therefore regarded as continuing to receive his normal earnings as described within section labeled 'Definitions'.

Quantiles

The quantiles of a distribution divide it into a number of equal parts; each of which contains the same number of households. In Family Spending, quantiles are applied to both household expenditure and income distributions.

For example, the median of a distribution divides it into two equal parts, so that half the households in a distribution of household income will have income more than the median, and the other half will have income less than the median. Similarly, quartiles, quintiles and deciles divide the distribution into four, five and ten equal parts respectively.

Most of the analysis in Family Spending is done in terms of quintile groups and decile groups.

In the calculation of quantiles for this report, zero values are counted as part of the distribution.

Changes in definitions

Changes in definitions from 1991 to 2013 can be found in the the 'Living Costs and Food Survey Technical Report (529.7 Kb Pdf)'. Changes to definitions made prior to 1991 can be found in earlier editions of Family Spending.

Headings used for identifying 2013 income information

Source of income

References in tables	Components separately identified	Explanatory notes
a. Wages and salaries	Normal 'take-home' pay from main employment 'Take-home' pay from subsidiary employment	(i) In the calculation of household income in this report, where an employee has been away from work without pay for 13 weeks or less his normal wage or salary has been used in estimating his total income instead of social security benefits, such as unemployment or sickness benefits that he may have received. Otherwise such benefits are used in estimating total income (see notes at reference e).
	Employees' income tax deduction Employees' National Insurance contribution	(ii) Normal income from wages and salaries is estimated by adding to the normal 'take-home' pay deductions made at source last time paid, together with the weekly value of occasional additions to wages and salaries (see Income in 'Definitions').
	Superannuation contributions deducted from pay Other deductions	(iii) The components of wages and salaries, for which figures are separately available, amount in total to the normal earnings of employees, regardless of the operation of the 13 week rule in note (i) above. Thus the sum of the components listed here does not in general equal the wages

		and salaries figure in tables of this report.
b. Self-employment	Income from business or profession, including subsidiary self-employment	The earnings or profits of a trade or profession, after deduction of business expenses but before deduction of tax.
c. Investments	Interest on building society shares and deposits Interest on bank deposits and savings accounts, including National Savings Bank Interest on ISAs Interest on Gilt-edged stock and War Loans Interest and dividends from stocks, shares, bonds, trusts, debentures and other securities Rent or income from property, after deducting expenses but inclusive of income tax (including receipts from letting or sub-letting part of own residence, net of the expenses of the letting or sub-letting) Other unearned Income	
d. Annuities and pensions, other than social security	Annuities and income from trust or covenant Pensions from previous employers Personal pensions	
e. Benefits	Child benefit	(i) The calculation of household income in this report takes account of the 13 week rule described at reference a, note (i).

Guardian's allowance

Carer's allowance (formerly Invalid care allowance)

Retirement pension (National Insurance) or old person's pension credit

(ii) The components of social security benefits, for which figures are separately available, amount in total to the benefits received in the week before interview. That is to say, they include amounts that are discounted from the total by the operation of the 13 week rule in note (i). Thus the sum of the components listed here differs from the total of social security benefits used in the income tables of this report.

Widow's pension/bereavement allowance or widowed parent's allowance

(iii) Housing Benefit is treated as a reduction in housing costs and not as income.

War disablement pension or war widow/widower's pension

Severe disablement allowance

Care component of disability living allowance

Mobility component of disability living allowance

Attendance allowance

Job seekers allowance

Winter fuel allowance

Cold Weather Payment

Income support

Working tax credit

Child tax credit

Incapacity benefit

Statutory sick pay (from employer)

Industrial injury disablement benefit

Maternity allowance

Statutory maternity pay

Statutory paternity pay

	Statutory adoption pay Health in pregnancy grant Any other benefit including lump sums and grants Social security benefits excluded from Income calculation by 13 week rule
f. Other sources	Married person's allowance from husband/wife temporarily away from home Alimony or separation allowances; allowances for foster children, allowances from members of the Armed Forces or Merchant Navy, or any other money from friends or relatives, other than husbands outside the household Benefits from trade unions, friendly societies etc. other than pensions Value of meal vouchers Earnings from intermittent or casual work over 12 months, not included in a or b above Student loans and money scholarships received by persons aged 16 and over and aged under 16 Other income for children under 16 e.g. from spare time jobs or income from Trusts or investments

Table source: Office for National Statistics

Download table

XLS XLS format
(44.5 Kb)

Household characteristics and index to tables

Table B5 (70.5 Kb Excel sheet) and Table B6 (87 Kb Excel sheet) show characteristics of households and persons.

Table B7 (55.5 Kb Excel sheet) provides an index to tables in this report and previous editions of Family Spending.

Background notes

1. **Symbols and conventions used in Family Spending 2014 edition**

   [ ] Figures should be used with extra caution because they are based on fewer than 20 reporting households.

   .. The data is suppressed if the unweighted sample counts are less than 10 reporting households.

   \- No figures are available because there are no reporting households.

   Rounding: Individual figures have been rounded independently. The sum of component items does not therefore necessarily add to the totals shown.

   Averages: These are averages (means) for all households included in the column or row, and unless specified, are not restricted to those households reporting expenditure on a particular item or income of a particular type.

   Period covered: Calendar year 2013 (1 January 2013 to 31 December 2013).

2. **Contacts**

   For information about the content of this publication, contact ONS Social Surveys Data Advice and Relations Team.

   Tel +44 (0)1633 455678

   Email: socialsurveys@ons.gsi.gov.uk

   Other customer enquiries

   ONS Customer Contact Centre

   Tel: 0845 601 3034

   International: +44 (0) 1633 817521

   Minicom: +44 (0)1633 815044

   Email: info@ons.gsi.gov.uk

Fax: +44 (0)1633 652747

Post: Room D265, Government Buildings,

Cardiff Road, Newport, South Wales NP10 8XG

www.ons.gov.uk

Media enquiries

Tel: +44 (0)845 604 1858

Email: press.office@ons.gsi.gov.uk

Editor

Giles Horsfield

giles.horsfield@ons.gsi.gov.uk

3. **A National Statistics publication**

National Statistics are produced to high professional standards set out in the Code of Practice for Official Statistics. They are produced free from political influence.

4. **About us**

The Office for National Statistics

The Office for National Statistics (ONS) is the executive office of the UK Statistics Authority, a non-ministerial department which reports directly to Parliament. ONS is the UK government's single largest statistical producer. It compiles information about the UK's society and economy, and provides the evidence-base for policy and decision-making, the allocation of resources, and public accountability. The Director-General of ONS reports directly to the National Statistician who is the Authority's Chief Executive and the Head of the Government Statistical Service.

The Government Statistical Service

The Government Statistical Service (GSS) is a network of professional statisticians and their staff operating both within the Office for National Statistics and across more than 30 other government departments and agencies.

5. **Copyright and reproduction**

For further information, contact the Office of Public Sector Information, Crown Copyright Licensing and Public Sector Information, Kew, Richmond, Surrey, TW9 4DU.

Tel: +44 (0)20 8876 3444

Email: psi@nationalarchives.gsi.gov.uk

ISSN 2040-1647

6. Details of the policy governing the release of new data are available by visiting www.statisticsauthority.gov.uk/assessment/code-of-practice/index.html or from the Media Relations Office email: media.relations@ons.gsi.gov.uk

   These National Statistics are produced to high professional standards and released according to the arrangements approved by the UK Statistics Authority.

Copyright

This document is also available on our website at www.ons.gov.uk.

Table B5
Characteristics of households, 2013, United Kingdom

	Percentage[1] of all house-holds	Weighted number of house-holds (000s)	House-holds in sample (number)
Total number of households	100	26,840	5,140
Size of household			
One person	29	7,790	1,430
Two persons	35	9,400	1,930
Three persons	16	4,300	780
Four persons	13	3,600	670
Five persons	5	1,280	240
Six persons	1	340	70
Seven persons	0	110	30
Eight persons	[0]	10	..
Nine or more persons	[0]	10	..
Composition of household			
One adult	29	7,790	1,430
Retired households mainly dependent on state pensions[2]	3	870	150
Other retired households	11	2,830	550
Non-retired households	15	4,090	740
One man	13	3,490	630
Aged under 65	9	2,300	370
Aged 65 and over	4	1,190	260
One woman	16	4,300	810
Aged under 60	5	1,380	270
Aged 60 and over	11	2,930	540
One adult, one child	3	710	150
One man, one child	0	130	20
One woman, one child	2	590	130
One adult, two or more children	2	650	150
One man, two or more children	[0]	90	20
One woman, two or more children	2	560	130
One man, one woman	30	7,930	1,660
Retired households mainly dependent on state pensions[2]	2	450	110
Other retired households	9	2,390	570
Non-retired households	19	5,090	980
Two men or two women	3	760	120
Two adults with children	20	5,390	1,050
One man one woman, one child	8	2,100	380
Two men or two women, one child	0	100	20
One man one woman, two children	8	2,250	450
Two men or two women, two children	[0]	50	..
One man one woman, three children	3	690	140
Two men or two women, three children	[0]	10	..
Two adults, four children	1	150	40
Two adults, five children	[0]	40	10
Two adults, six or more children	[0]	0	..
Three adults	6	1,580	260
Three adults with children	3	860	160
Three adults, one child	2	460	80
Three adults, two children	1	290	50
Three adults, three children	[0]	90	20
Three adults, four or more children	[0]	30	..

	Percentage[1] of all house-holds	Weighted number of house-holds (000s)	House-holds in sample (number)
Composition of household (cont)			
Four adults	3	740	110
Four adults, one child	1	150	20
Four adults, two or more children	[0]	60	10
Five adults	[0]	120	10
Five adults, one or more children	[0]	40	..
All other households without children	[0]	50	..
All other households with children	[0]	10	..
Number of economically active persons in household			
No person	31	8,220	1,720
One person	29	7,740	1,480
More than one person	41	10,890	1,940
Two persons	32	8,640	1,580
Three persons	6	1,660	280
Four persons	2	520	80
Five persons	[0]	60	..
Six or more persons	[0]	10	..
Households with married women	46	12,470	2,540
Households with married women economically active	26	7,090	1,360
With no dependent children	13	3,490	670
With dependent children	13	3,590	690
One child	5	1,460	260
Two children	6	1,700	340
Three children	1	370	80
Four or more children	[0]	70	10
Households with married women not economically active	20	5,380	1,190
With no dependent children	15	4,100	940
With dependent children	5	1,280	250
One child	2	440	80
Two children	2	470	90
Three children	1	260	50
Four or more children	[0]	120	30
Economic status of household reference person			
Economically active	63	17,020	3,140
Employee at work	52	13,880	2,570
Full-time	42	11,180	2,030
Part-time	10	2,700	540
Government-supported training	[0]	80	10
Unemployed	3	850	150
Self-employed	8	2,210	410
Economically inactive	37	9,820	2,000

Note: Changes to categories of socio economic classification were made in 2011. Please see changes in definitions.
Please see background notes for symbols and conventions used in this report.
1 Based on weighted number of households.
2 Mainly dependent on state pensions and not economically active - see definitions

Table B5
Characteristics of households, 2013, United Kingdom (cont.)

	Percentage[1] of all house-holds	Weighted number of house-holds (000s)	House-holds in sample (number)
Age of household reference person			
15 and under 20 years	*[0]*	70	10
20 and under 25 years	*3*	860	130
25 and under 30 years	*6*	1,680	240
30 and under 35 years	*8*	2,050	360
35 and under 40 years	*8*	2,180	390
40 and under 45 years	*10*	2,620	480
45 and under 50 years	*10*	2,800	540
50 and under 55 years	*10*	2,650	500
55 and under 60 years	*8*	2,160	440
60 and under 65 years	*9*	2,290	480
65 and under 70 years	*8*	2,270	540
70 and under 75 years	*6*	1,580	370
75 and under 80 years	*6*	1,500	300
80 and under 85 years	*4*	1,150	210
85 and under 90 years	*3*	680	110
90 years or more	*1*	300	50
Regions and Countries 2011-2013 (3-year average)			
United Kingdom	*100*	26,450	5,480
North East	*4*	1,130	270
North West	*11*	2,970	620
Yorkshire and the Humber	*9*	2,310	500
East Midlands	*7*	1,950	430
West Midlands	*9*	2,330	520
East of England	*9*	2,500	530
London	*12*	3,190	500
South East	*13*	3,540	740
South West	*8*	2,200	480
England	*84*	22,130	4,600
Wales	*5*	1,250	250
Scotland	*9*	2,330	470
Northern Ireland	*3*	740	160
Socio-economic classification of household reference person			
Higher managerial and professional	*13*	3,590	660
Large employers/higher managerial	*3*	880	170
Higher professional	*10*	2,710	490
Lower managerial and professional	*19*	5,000	930
Intermediate	*7*	1,950	370
Small employers	*6*	1,740	320
Lower supervisory	*5*	1,340	250
Semi-routine	*8*	2,210	420
Routine	*7*	1,960	380
Long-term unemployed[3]	*2*	540	100
Students	*2*	540	80
Occupation not stated[4]	*30*	7,970	1,640

	Percentage[1] of all house-holds	Weighted number of house-holds (000s)	House-holds in sample (number)
GB urban/rural areas 2011-2013 (over 3 years)			
GB Urban	*78*	19,940	4,060
GB rural	*22*	5,770	1,260
Tenure of dwelling[5]			
Owners			
Owned outright	*33*	8,890	1,860
Buying with a mortgage	*32*	8,480	1,600
All	*65*	17,370	3,470
Social rented from			
Council	*9*	2,420	460
Registered social landlord	*9*	2,330	450
All	*18*	4,750	900
Private rented			
Rent free	*1*	270	50
Rent paid, unfurnished	*13*	3,550	610
Rent paid, furnished	*3*	910	120
All	*18*	4,720	780
Households with durable goods			
Car/van	*76*	20,350	4,030
One	*46*	12,230	2,430
Two	*24*	6,410	1,280
Three or more	*6*	1,710	320
Central heating, full or partial	*96*	25,740	4,950
Fridge-freezer or deep freezer	*98*	26,290	5,040
Washing machine	*97*	26,100	5,010
Tumble dryer	*56*	14,950	2,960
Dishwasher	*42*	11,230	2,230
Microwave oven	*92*	24,830	4,780
Telephone	*89*	23,820	4,620
Mobile phone	*92*	24,690	4,750
DVD player	*85*	22,710	4,410
Home computer	*83*	22,380	4,290
Internet connection	*82*	22,040	4,230

Note: Changes to categories of socio-economic classification were made in 2011. Please see changes in definitions.
Please see background notes for symbols and conventions used in this report.
1 Based on weighted number of households.
2 Mainly dependent on state pensions and not economically active - see definitions.
3 Includes those who have never worked.
4 Includes those who are economically inactive - see definitions.
5 See footnotes on Table A32.

Table B6
Characteristics of persons, 2013, United Kingdom

	Males				Females				All persons		
	Percentage[1] of		Weighted number of persons (000s)	Persons in the sample (number)	Percentage[1] of		Weighted number of persons (000s)	Persons in the sample (number)	Percentage[1] of	Weighted number of persons (000s)	Persons in the sample (number)
	all males	all persons			all females	all persons			all persons		
All persons	**100**	**49**	**31,080**	**5,830**	**100**	**51**	**32,210**	**6,290**	**100**	**63,290**	**12,120**
Adults	**77**	**38**	**24,070**	**4,420**	**79**	**40**	**25,510**	**4,940**	**78**	**49,590**	**9,350**
Persons aged under 60	56	27	17,370	2,900	55	28	17,850	3,320	56	35,220	6,220
Persons aged 60 or under 65	6	3	1,810	380	6	3	1,830	410	6	3,640	790
Persons aged 65 or under 70	6	3	1,790	440	5	3	1,740	420	6	3,540	860
Persons aged 70 or over	10	5	3,090	700	13	6	4,090	790	11	7,190	1,490
Children	**23**	**11**	**7,010**	**1,420**	**21**	**11**	**6,700**	**1,350**	**22**	**13,700**	**2,770**
Children under 2 years of age	2	1	700	140	3	1	850	170	2	1,550	310
Children aged 2 or under 5	4	2	1,300	280	4	2	1,150	240	4	2,450	520
Children aged 5 or under 16	13	6	4,090	830	12	6	3,890	790	13	7,980	1,620
Children aged 16 or under 18	3	1	930	170	2	1	800	150	3	1,720	320
Economic activity											
Persons active (aged 16 or over)	55	27	17,180	2,980	47	24	15,260	2,850	51	32,440	5,830
Persons not active	45	22	13,900	2,850	53	27	16,950	3,440	49	30,850	6,300
Men 65 or over and Women 60 or over	14	7	4,220	980	20	10	6,330	1,330	17	10,550	2,310
Others (including children under 16)	31	15	9,680	1,870	33	17	10,620	2,120	32	20,300	3,990

Please see background notes for symbols and conventions used in this report.

1 Based on weighted number of households.

Table B7

Index to tables in reports on the Living Costs and Food Survey 2002/03 to 2013

2013 tables		Table numbers in reports for										
		2012	2011	2010	2009	2008	2007	2006	2005/06	2004/05	2003/04	2002/03
Detailed expenditure and place of purchase												
A1	Detailed expenditure with full-method standard errors	A1	A1	A1	A1	A1	A1	A1	A1	A1	A1	7.1
..	Expenditure on alcoholic drink by type of premises	..	..	..	A2	A2	A2	A2	A2	A2	A2	7.2
A2	Expenditure on food by place of purchase	A2	A2	A2	A3	A3	A3	A3	A3	A3	A3	7.3
..	Expenditure on selected items by place of purchase	..	..	..	A4	A4	A4	A4	A4	A4	A4	7.4
A3	Expenditure on clothing and footwear by place of purchase	A3	A3	A3	A5	A5	A5	A5	A5	A5	A5	7.5
Expenditure by income												
A4	Main items by gross income decile	A4	A4	A4	A6	A6	A6	A6	A6	A6	A6	1.1
A5	Percentage on main items by gross income decile	A5	A5	A5	A7	A7	A7	A7	A7	A7	A7	1.2
A6	Detailed expenditure by gross income decile	A6	A6	A6	A8	A8	A8	A8	A8	A8	A8	1.3
A7	Main items by disposable income decile	A7	A7	A7	A9	A9	A9	A9	A9	A9	A9	1.4
A8	Percentage on main items by disposable income decile	A8	A8	A8	A10	A10	A10	A10	A10	A10	A10	1.5
Expenditure by age and income												
A9	Main items by age of HRP	A9	A9	A9	A11	A11	A11	A11	A11	A11	A11	2.1
A10	Main items as a percentage by age of HRP	A10	A10	A10	A12	A12	A12	A12	A12	A12	A12	2.2
A11	Detailed expenditure by age of HRP	A11	A11	A11	A13	A13	A13	A13	A13	A13	A13	2.3
A12	Aged under 30 by income	A12	A12	A12	A14	A14	A14	A14	A14	A14	A14	2.4
A13	Aged 30 and under 50 by income	A13	A13	A13	A15	A15	A15	A15	A15	A15	A15	2.5
A14	Aged 50 and under 65 by income	A14	A14	A14	A16	A16	A16	A16	A16	A16	A16	2.6
A15	Aged 65 and under 75 by income	A15	A15	A15	A17	A17	A17	A17	A17	A17	A17	2.7
A16	Aged 75 or over by income	A16	A16	A16	A18	A18	A18	A18	A18	A18	A18	2.8
Expenditure by socio-economic characteristics												
A17	By economic activity status of HRP	A17	A17	A17	A19	A19	A19	A19	A19	A19	A19	3.1
A18	HRP is a full-time employee by income	A18	A18	A18	A20	A20	A20	A20	A20	A20	A20	3.2
A19	HRP is self-employed by income	A19	A19	A19	A21	A21	A21	A21	A21	A21	A21	3.3
A20	By number of persons working	A20	A20	A20	A22	A22	A22	A22	A22	A22	A22	3.4
A21	By age HRP completed continuous full-time education	A21	A21	A21	A23	A23	A23	A23	A23	A23	A23	3.5
A22	By socio-economic class of HRP	A22	A22	A22	A24	A24	A24	A24	A24	A24	A24	3.6
Expenditure by composition, income and tenure												
A23	Expenditure by household composition	A23	A23	A23	A25	A25	A25	A25	A25	A25	A25	4.1
A24	One adult retired households mainly dependent on state pensions	A24	A24	A24	A26	A26	A26	A26	A26	A26	A26	4.2
A25	One adult retired households not mainly dependent on state pensions	A25	A25	A25	A27	A27	A27	A27	A27	A27	A27	4.3
A26	One adult non-retired	A26	A26	A26	A28	A28	A28	A28	A28	A28	A28	4.4
A27	One adult with children	A27	A27	A27	A29	A29	A29	A29	A29	A29	A29	4.5
A28	Two adults with children	A28	A28	A28	A30	A30	A30	A30	A30	A30	A30	4.6
A29	Two adults non-retired	A29	A29	A29	A31	A31	A31	A31	A31	A31	A31	4.7
A30	Two adults retired mainly dependent on state pensions	A30	A30	A30	A32	A32	A32	A32	A32	A32	A32	4.8
A31	Two adults retired not mainly dependent on state pensions	A31	A31	A31	A33	A33	A33	A33	A33	A33	A33	4.9
A32	Household expenditure by tenure	A32	A32	A32	A34	A34	A34	A34	A34	A34	A34	4.10
Expenditure by region												
A33	Main items of expenditure by region	A33	A33	A33	A35	A35	A35	A35	A35	A35	A35	5.1
A34	Main items as a percentage of expenditure by region	A34	A34	A34	A36	A36	A36	A36	A36	A36	A36	5.2
A35	Detailed expenditure by region	A35	A35	A35	A37	A37	A37	A37	A37	A37	A37	5.3
A36	Expenditure by urban/rural areas (GB only)	A36	A36	A36	A38	A38	A38	A38	A38	A38	A38	5.4

Notes

.. Tables do not appear in these publications.

Table B7

Index to tables in reports on the Living Costs and Food Survey 2002/03 to 2013

2013 tables	Table numbers in reports for										
	2012	2011	2010	2009	2008	2007	2006	2005/06	2004/05	2003/04	2002/03
Household income											
A37 Income by household composition	A37	A37	A37	A40	A40	A40	A40	A40	A40	A40	8.1
A38 Income by age of HRP	A38	A38	A38	A41	A41	A41	A41	A41	A41	A41	8.2
A39 Income by income group	A39	A39	A39	A42	A42	A42	A42	A42	A42	A42	8.3
A40 Income by household tenure	A40	A40	A40	A43	A43	A43	A43	A43	A43	A43	8.4
A41 Income by regions	A41	A41	A41	A44	A44	A44	A44	A44	A44	A44	8.5
A42 Income by GB urban/rural areas	A42	A42	A42	A45	A45	A45	A45	A45	A45	A45	8.6
A43 Income by socio-economic class	A43	A43	A43	A46	A46	A46	A46	A46	A46	A46	8.7
A44 Income 1970 to 2013	A44	A44	A44	A47	A47	A47	A47	A47	A47	A47	8.8
Households characteristics and ownership of durable goods											
A45 Percentage with durable goods 1970 to 2013	A45	A45	A45	A50	A50	A50	A50	A50	A50	A50	9.3
A46 Percentage with durable goods by income group & household composition	A46	A46	A46	A51	A51	A51	A51	A51	A51	A51	9.4
A47 Percentage with cars	A47	A47	A47	A52	A52	A52	A52	A52	A52	A52	9.5
A48 Percentage with durable goods by UK Countries and regions	A48	A48	A48	A53	A53	A53	A53	A53	A53	A53	9.6
A49 Percentage by size, composition, age, in each income group	A49	A49	A49	A54	A54	A54	A54	A54	A54	A54	9.7
A50 Percentage by economic activity, tenure and socio-economic class in each income group	A50	A50	A50	A55	A55	A55	A55	A55	A55	A55	9.8
Output Area Classification											
A51 Expenditure by OAC supergroup	A51	A51	A51	5.4	A56	5.3	..	..	..	..	..
A52 Expenditure by OAC group	A52	A52	A52	5.5	A57	5.4	..	..	..	..	..
A53 Average gross weekly household income by OAC supergroup	A53	A53	A53	5.6	A58	5.4	..	..	..	..	..
Methodology											
B5 Household characteristics	B5	B5	B5	A48	A48	A48	A48	A48	A48	A48	9.1
B6 Person characteristics	B6	B6	B6	A49	A49	A49	A49	A49	A49	A49	9.2
Trends in household expenditure (moved to Chapter 4)											
4.1 COICOP main items 2001/02 to 2013	4.3	4.3	4.3	4.3	4.3	4.3	4.3	4.3	..	..	..
4.2 COICOP as a percentage of total expenditure 2001/02 to 2013	4.4	4.4	4.4	4.4	4.4	4.4	4.4	4.4	..	..	..
4.3 Household expenditure 2001/02 to 2013 COICOP based on current prices	4.5	4.5	4.5	4.5	4.5	..	..	..	..	..	..
.. FES main items 1995/96 - 2011	4.1	4.1	4.1	4.1	4.1	4.1	4.1	4.1	4.1	4.1	6.1
.. FES as a percentage of total expenditure 1995/96 - 2011	4.2	4.2	4.2	4.2	4.2	4.2	4.2	4.2	4.2	4.2	6.2

Notes

.. Tables do not appear in these publications.